The Hero and the Victim

The Hero and the Victim

NARRATIVES OF CRIMINALITY IN IRAQ WAR FICTION

Gregory Brazeal

LEVER
PRESS

Lever Press (leverpress.org) is a publisher of pathbreaking scholarship. Supported by a consortium of higher education institutions focused on, and renowned for, excellence in both research and teaching, our press is grounded on three essential commitments: to be a digitally native press, to be a peer-reviewed, open access press that charges no fees to either authors or their institutions, and to be a press aligned with the liberal arts ethos.

The complete manuscript of this work was subjected to a fully closed ("double-blind") review process. For more information, please see our Peer Review Commitments and Guidelines at https://www.leverpress.org/peerreview

DOI: https://doi.org/10.3998/mpub.14432099
Print ISBN: 978-1-64315-066-6
Open access ISBN: 978-1-64315-067-3

Library of Congress Control Number: 2024932679

Published in the United States of America by Lever Press, in partnership with Michigan Publishing.

For Taly, Dvora, and Tova

Contents

Member Institution Acknowledgments

Lever Press is a joint venture. This work was made possible by the generous support of Lever Press member libraries from the following institutions:

Amherst College
Atlanta University Center Consortium
Berea College
Bowdoin College
Carleton College
Central Washington University
Claremont Colleges
Claremont Graduate University
Claremont McKenna College
Clark Atlanta University
College of Saint Benedict & Saint John's University
The College of Wooster
Davidson College
Denison University
DePauw University
Grinnell College
Hamilton College
Hampshire College
Harvey Mudd College
Hollins University
Iowa State University
Keck Graduate Institute
Knox College
Lafayette College
Macalester College
Middlebury College
Morehouse College
Morehouse School of Medicine
Norwich University
Occidental College
Penn State University
Pitzer College
Pomona College
Randolph-Macon College

Rollins College
Santa Clara University
Scripps College
Skidmore College
Smith College
Spelman College
Susquehanna University
Swarthmore College
Trinity University
UCLA Library
Union College
University of Idaho
University of Northern Colorado
University of Puget Sound
University of Rhode Island
University of San Francisco
University of Vermont
Vassar College
Washington and Lee University
Whitman College
Whittier College
Willamette University
Williams College

CHAPTER ONE

INTRODUCTION

What might a monument for the American veterans of the war in Iraq look like?

More than 4,000 American troops died in the conflict between the invasion in 2003 and the initial formal withdrawal of troops in 2011, alongside the hundreds of thousands of Iraqi dead. We would expect a U.S. veterans' memorial to make some sense of what happened, to give some meaning to the sacrifices of those Americans who served. Yet today, more than twenty years after the invasion of Iraq, it is difficult to see what that meaning might be. What would a monument for the American veterans of the Iraq War celebrate? Or how would it mourn? What did the casualties of the Iraq War, both the dead and the injured, and their families, and those who served beside them, make their sacrifices for? If there was no purpose, if the war had no meaning, then how are we to make sense of the losses?

We know what kind of monument the Iraq War was supposed to produce. The war had its roots, in part, in the advocacy of a group of foreign policy entrepreneurs who had been pushing for an armed intervention in Iraq since the late 1990s, less than a decade after the Gulf War ended with Saddam Hussein still in power. These "neoconservatives" argued that overthrowing Hussein through the use of American military force would not only liberate Iraq's people, but "would revolutionize the strategic situation in the Middle East...and all to the benefit of American interests." Writers such as Bill Kristol and Robert Kagan conceived of "regime change" in Iraq as the first step toward the creation of a free and democratic Middle East. David Frum and Richard Perle envisioned the dawning of an even broader peace "brought into being by American armed might and defended by American might."[1]

As early as December 2001, Norman Podhoretz suggested that an American invasion of Iraq might help "bring about the long-delayed reform and modernization of Islam" and "set off a benevolent domino effect throughout the entire region." Indeed, Podhoretz considered the possibility that after invading Iraq, "we may...find ourselves forced...to topple five or six or seven more tyrannies in the Islamic world" as part of an "imperial mission" that might also include "the establishment of some kind of American protectorate over the oil fields of Saudi Arabia." Through such imperial military policing, Americans could achieve not only "revenge" for the September 11 attacks, but also an "incandescent moral clarity," a "lovely condition of the spirit" reflecting "'a new birth' of the confidence we used to have in ourselves and in 'America the Beautiful.'"[2]

The memorial for the veterans of this imagined war in Iraq might have been a simple celebration of heroes. It might have honored those brave, selfless Americans who fought and faced death to liberate an oppressed people from a tyrant, and who, in doing so, helped to bring freedom and democracy to the greater Middle East. The memorial might have tried to convey how the warriors' sacrifices opened the way, in fact, to an unprecedented global peace guaranteed by America's overwhelming military superiority, a fulfillment of America's exceptional destiny as a benevolent imperial power, a confirmation of its role as the hegemonic overseer of the pacific and prosperous end of history. Like Podhoretz in his allusion to revenge, the memorial might also have implied, without too much detail, that the war was somehow a just retaliation for the September 11 attacks.[3]

The actual Iraq War that the Bush administration carried out was, of course, nothing like the one imagined by its neoconservative advocates. In the dominant contemporary view, it was a nearly unmitigated disaster for Iraq, the United States, and the world—with the possible exception of

Iran and its allies. Rather than creating a beacon of democratic liberty and prosperity in the Middle East, the war destroyed Iraq's economy, empowered violent extremists, and encouraged sectarian conflict that, over time, led to the displacement of a significant portion of Iraq's population and contributed to the deaths of so many Iraqis that it has proven impossible to arrive at a reliable count, with estimates of civilian deaths ranging into the hundreds of thousands.[4]

With regard to the security interests of the United States, the war diverted attention from those responsible for the September 11 terrorist attacks, and instead served as a recruiting tool and training ground for a new generation of Islamist terrorists. Rather than protecting the United States from foreign threats, as the Bush administration suggested when it falsely claimed that Iraq possessed weapons of mass destruction that threatened the United States, the war instead strengthened one of America's most significant adversaries, the terrorism-exporting, anti-American theocracy in Iran. Even the official U.S. Army history of the Iraq War, released in 2019, concludes that "an emboldened and expansionist Iran appears to be the only victor" of the Iraq War.[5] The war also, eventually, led to the creation of the Islamic State, a terrorist organization that went on to conquer significant portions of Iraq and Syria and to carry out new horrors there.[6]

In general, rather than confirming American hegemony over a unipolar world order, the war divided the United States from many of its allies; undermined America's credibility by showing that its claims, even factual statements offered to the United Nations, could not be trusted; damaged America's reputation among people throughout the world; and displayed the limits of America's military power and the weakness and incompetence of its leadership.[7] All of this the war achieved at a cost that may be as high as three trillion dollars, or even higher—resources that could have been dedicated to America's actual needs, including defense against actual threats to the nation's security.[8]

How might the United States approach a memorial to the veterans of a war like this? What are we to say about American veterans' participation in such a war?

The difficulty of imagining such a memorial can be understood as one instance of a larger problem. Most Americans continue to lack a satisfactory story for what American servicemembers did and experienced in Iraq.[9] This lack pervades and powerfully shapes American literary fiction about the experiences of members of the U.S. military in the Iraq War, the subject of this book.[10] Our general inability to make narrative sense of the role of American servicemembers in the Iraq War is a matter not only of literary interest, but also of political concern, and perhaps even of personal and psychological concern for veterans who struggle to make sense of their service in Iraq.

Of course, there is a sense in which we already have readily available narratives of the Iraq War as a whole. The two primary templates have already been indicated. On the one hand, defenders of the war may attempt to echo its intellectual architects. They may present the war as somehow part of a larger struggle against terrorism, or argue that it was worth all that followed to remove Saddam Hussein from power, or suggest that history may yet vindicate the war as the first, troubled step toward the democratization of the Middle East. In these accounts, the Iraq War remains a story of good triumphing over evil through military force—or at least, a story in which good would have triumphed over evil if only the weak, indecisive, even cowardly president after Bush had not ignored the needs of his generals and seized defeat from the jaws of victory.

On the other hand, critics of the war may echo the Iraqi novelist Sinan Antoon's reflections on the fifteenth anniversary of the invasion, in a *New York Times* Op-Ed. entitled "Fifteen Years Ago, America Destroyed My Country": "The invasion of Iraq is often spoken of in the United States as a 'blunder,' or even a 'colossal mistake.' It was a crime. Those who perpetrated it are still at large." Antoon points specifically at President Bush as a perpetrator of a crime who has escaped justice: "A year ago, I watched Mr. Bush on 'The Ellen DeGeneres Show,' dancing and talking about his paintings." The novelist gestures more generally toward "[t]he pundits and 'experts' who sold us the war," and who "still go on doing what they do."[11]

But what about the American soldiers, sailors, airmen,[12] and marines who fought the war? Were they criminals? If not, what were they? Heroes? Victims? Both?

CRIMINALITY AND AMERICAN WAR CULTURE

Opponents of the Vietnam War sometimes treated returning veterans as though they were wrongdoers, or even complicit in crimes. Although the frequency of Vietnam veterans being spat upon or called "baby killer" is disputed, the stories were not entirely invented. For example, Karl Marlantes, a writer who served in Vietnam as a First Lieutenant in the Marine Corps, has described being spat upon after boarding a train in uniform. "I passed a nice-looking woman who looked up at me and quickly looked away...About five minutes later I saw her get up and come down the aisle. She was looking right at me, lips pressed tight. She stood in front of me and spit on me." Although the number of these "spitting incidents," Marlantes suspects, was "very small," he also notes that after returning from Vietnam, he "couldn't get a date with any girl born north of the Mason-Dixon line," and that he was once followed down the street by anti-war protestors waving "the flags of North Vietnam and the Viet Cong."[13] The philosopher Nancy Sherman, who has spent over two decades working with veterans, quotes a Vietnam veteran who, after stepping off his homecoming flight, encountered protesters at the airport "'jeering and booing, paint thrown on you, spitting water.'" Sherman adds: "[f]rom my conversations with many Vietnam veterans and dissidents of my generation, this homecoming was not atypical."[14]

By contrast, during the years of the Iraq War, it was virtually unthinkable that an American civilian would criticize a soldier in uniform in a public place, much less spit on one. Returning veterans from the Iraq War may have faced a stigma based on rumors and news stories about the prevalence of PTSD.[15] But there were certainly no widespread claims that the returning veterans were criminals, or returned under a cloud of criminality.[16] Indeed, even the suggestion that service in the Iraq War might somehow be associated with criminal guilt would have been taboo, beyond the pale of socially respectable opinion. By far the most common phrase spoken by civilians to veterans was, simply, "thank you for your service."[17]

The disparity between the receptions of American veterans of the Vietnam and Iraq Wars cannot be explained simply based on historical differences between the behavior of soldiers in the two wars. If the Vietnam War had its most heavily publicized atrocity in My Lai, the Iraq War had the similarly publicized Abu Ghraib scandal. Both wars, like all wars, doubtless gave rise to many acts of wrongdoing that never came to light, or, if they came to light, never happened to receive wide public attention. For example, one of the most infamous atrocities committed by American troops in Iraq, the group rape of a fourteen-year-old Iraqi girl and the brutal execution of her and her family in Mahmudiyah, might never have come to light as an American atrocity if a single soldier, SGT Tony Yribe, had not made an offhand reference months later to "murderers" during a conversation with another, newly arrived soldier in the unit, PFC Justin Watt.[18] Similarly, U.S. atrocities in the Vietnam War rarely came to the public's attention except through relatively unusual chains of events.[19] If anything, U.S. troops in Vietnam might be seen, at least at first glance, as generally less complicit in any wrongs from that war than U.S. troops in Iraq, because the latter troops volunteered, while many of the former were drafted.[20]

A more likely explanation for the dramatically different treatment of American veterans returning from Vietnam and Iraq can be found in the cultural changes that took place between the two wars, and that the historian and retired Army colonel Andrew Bacevich has described as the rise of a "new American militarism."[21] Bacevich details how the military failures, atrocities, and losses of the Vietnam era, along with a "poisonous civil-military climate," eroded the U.S. military's reputation and cultural prestige. From within the officer corps, "the American profession of arms" appeared to have been "thoroughly discredited and even dishonored in Vietnam by events such as the My Lai Massacre and by soldiers such as Lieutenant William Calley and those who had conspired to cover up his crimes." "[B]y war's end," the United States in general displayed "a mood of pervasive and seemingly permanent anti-militarism." The decline in the military's reputation did not reverse itself during the presidency of Jimmy Carter, the "least militaristic of recent presidents" despite being a nuclear submariner and U.S. Naval Academy graduate, and reached a symbolic nadir in Operation Eagle Claw, Carter's aborted attempt to rescue American hostages held in Iran.[22]

But the 1980s saw the beginning of "a powerful reaction from Americans who refused to accept the [Vietnam] war's apparent verdict and who viewed with alarm the changes the war gave birth to or encouraged." Chief among these Americans was President Ronald Reagan, who "[c]elebrate[ed] the American in uniform, past and present" through "a sanitized version of U.S. military history and...a romanticized portrait of those who made it." In his speeches, Reagan also reinterpreted the history of the Vietnam War, telling the guests at a Medal of Honor ceremony for a Vietnam veteran:

> Several years ago, we brought home a group of American fighting men who had obeyed their country's call and who fought as bravely and as well as any Americans in our history. They came home without victory not because they'd been defeated, but because they'd been denied permission to win.
>
> They were greeted by no parades, no bands, no waving of the flag they had so nobly served. There's been no "thank you" for their sacrifice.

Turning the tables on the accusation that crimes like the My Lai massacre had dishonored those who served in the Vietnam War, Reagan instead presented Vietnam veterans as the victims of those who treated them like criminals, as well as of those officials who, in revisionist accounts of the Vietnam War, prevented the troops from achieving victory. More importantly, by emphasizing that the American troops in Vietnam "fought bravely and as well as any Americans in our history," Reagan encouraged his audience to view the veterans not just as victims but as heroes—the kind of heroes that awards like the Medal of Honor are meant to recognize.[23]

Reagan was not alone in attempting to revive the narrative framework of the warrior-as-hero and to apply it to members of the American military. As Bacevich notes, some of the most popular films of the 1980s, such as *An Officer and a Gentleman*, *Rambo: First Blood Part II*, and *Top Gun*, offered a glorified, heroic portrait of "soldiers, military life, and war itself" that closely resembled Reagan's views and "would have been either unthinkable or unmarketable in the immediate aftermath of Vietnam."[24]

The militarism that Reagan helped to promote, "manifesting itself in a romanticized view of soldiers, a tendency to see military power as the truest measure of national greatness, and outsized expectations regarding the efficacy of force," long outlasted his presidency.[25] It retains a prominent position in the American political landscape today. For the purposes of this book, one of its most significant effects may be to protect members of the U.S. military from any general association with wrongdoing, and especially from the kinds of allegations of criminality that sometimes greeted veterans returning from Vietnam. Even for those critics of the Iraq War who view the war as a source of great wrongs against the people of Iraq, it remains taboo to suggest that ordinary U.S. troops may have been complicit in these wrongs. Criticisms of political and even military leaders are acceptable. Criticisms of the troops are not. The troops are to be thanked for their service. They are heroes or victims of the war, or both, but not complicit in the war's harms.

It is not the aim of this book to question these social conventions, and certainly not to suggest that there is any reason to return to the attitudes associated with the Vietnam era. Rather, for anyone attempting to make sense of American fiction about the Iraq War, it is important to understand the conventions because of the significant role they play in shaping cultural representations of the Iraq War. In one of the rawest passages in the Iraq War veterans' fiction published so far, for example, the narrator of Kevin Powers' *The Yellow Birds* explains in a stream-of-consciousness monologue why he has trouble accepting the kind of gratitude conveyed in routine statements like "thank you for your service." As discussed in greater detail in Chapter 5, the narrator worries that he will

> give away that I don't deserve anyone's gratitude and really they should all hate me for what I've done...because there isn't any making up for killing women or even watching women get killed, or for that matter killing men and shooting them in the back and shooting them more times than necessary to actually kill them and it was like just trying to kill everything you saw sometimes...[26]

The simple narrative of the soldier-as-hero—suggested, however faintly, in the expression of gratitude for a soldier's service—is not something that Powers' narrator can straightforwardly accept, because he believes that he has done wrong, and been complicit in the wrongs of others. To the extent that he feels that he was personally responsible for his choices, and not merely an inanimate cog in the machinery of war, viewing himself merely as a victim might seem inadequate as well.

In an insightful study of attitudes toward killing in World War I, World War II, and the Vietnam War, the historian Joanna Bourke notes the prevalence of the rationale that combatants "were 'merely obeying orders.'"[27] But she also observes:

> While civilians in the past and present have been anxious to exonerate servicemen from responsibility for their actions in battle, combatants themselves were often anxious to accept their own agency and to judge and be judged for their deeds. Historians have been rightly cautious about passing judgement on people in the past, but this must be done if we are to grant to servicemen and -women in the past an active, creative role in the making of their own histories.[28]

To deny that servicemembers are responsible for their actions may be to deny their agency, and thus a part of their humanity. Many veterans have found such a response inadequate as a way of addressing moral concerns.

The journalist Sebastian Junger, one of the most perceptive observers of the experiences of the veterans of the United States' post-9/11 wars, makes a similar point when he observes that, at least in some contexts, it can delay soldiers' recovery when they are encouraged "to see themselves as victims rather than as perpetrators." He suggests that after soldiers have committed acts of violence in a war, and feel guilty about doing so, it may be counterproductive to encourage them to view themselves as "victims," and thus not ultimately responsible for their violent acts. Junger contrasts the pervasive contemporary narrative of the soldier-as-victim with "more accurate and meaningful understandings of violence," such as the thinking of the Mende tribe in Liberia:

> Mende combatants often described combat as something that makes the heart "heat up," transforming a fighter to the point where he is thought to have literally become someone else. In that state he is capable of both

> great courage and great cruelty. Such a state...means that the moral excesses of the battlefield don't necessarily have to be brought home.[29]

Of course, Junger is not suggesting that Iraq War veterans should or even could simply replicate the Mende way of thought. The post-Nuremberg blurring of the lines between war and crime—as discussed in greater detail in Chapter 4—suggests that it is no longer feasible to excuse atrocities and other wrongs in war merely by asserting that the soldier becomes a different person in battle. Junger's insight is, rather, that encouraging soldiers to think of themselves as passive victims may be as psychologically problematic or unworkable as encouraging them to think of themselves simply as heroes, at least when they believe they have been the perpetrators of wrongs.

Marlantes, the novelist and Vietnam veteran, also suggests that the reintegration of veterans into peacetime society should include some recognition of moral sacrifice, of the wrongs that take place in war, rather than consisting entirely of celebration:

> Returning veterans don't need ticker-tape parades or yellow ribbons stretching clear across Texas. Cheering is inappropriate and immature. Combat veterans, more than anyone else, know how much pain and evil have been wrought. To cheer them for what they've just done would be like cheering the surgeon when he amputates a leg to save someone's life. It's childish, and it's demeaning to those who have fallen on both sides... There should be parades, but they should be solemn processionals...They should be conducted with all the dignity of a military funeral, mourning for those lost on both sides, giving thanks for those returned.[30]

Just as Junger suggests that treating soldiers as passive victims is often unhelpful, so Marlantes suggests that greeting soldiers simply as heroes is often an insufficient response. In both cases, the narrative framework leaves out a coming to terms with the soldier's active participation in what would at least ordinarily, and sometimes in war as well, be considered wrong, or even criminal.

Inviting soldiers to make sense of their actions simply by judging whether they were legal or not seems similarly unsatisfactory. The legal scholar David Kennedy has drawn attention to the potential distance between what is legal under international humanitarian law—the usual contemporary term for what used to be called the laws of war[31]—and what is just or capable of being embraced without anguish. "I was struck," he writes, "that Iraq War reporting was filled with anecdotes about soldiers overcome by remorse at having slaughtered civilians—and being counseled back to duty by their officers, their chaplains, their mental health professionals, who explained that what they had done was necessary, proportional, and therefore just."[32] ("Necessity" and "proportionality" are two of the basic criteria for evaluating the legality of a use of force in an armed conflict under international humanitarian law.[33]) Compliance with the law alone is not sufficient to provide soldiers' experiences with a meaning that will allow them, and others, to make sense of what American soldiers did in the Iraq War.

Each of the works of fiction addressed in this book attempts to tell a story of the Iraq War from the perspective of Americans who served in the military there. Each is an attempt to construct a narrative that works in various ways that a simple story of the soldier-as-hero or the soldier-as-victim apparently will not work, at least for many of the veterans of this war. In the process of making this attempt, each work of fiction notably struggles with the specter of criminality, the looming, often unacceptable thought that U.S. soldiers in the Iraq War were complicit in something deeply wrong. After the United States' disavowal of the ungrateful treatment of Vietnam veterans, a story that presents American soldiers as shrouded in criminality would seem to be a story that cannot be told. At the same time, it has apparently turned out to be impossible for veteran writers and those writing about veterans to exclude the question of criminality from a central place in Iraq War fiction.[34]

OTHER PERSPECTIVES ON IRAQ WAR FICTION

By focusing on narratives of criminality, I necessarily pay less attention to other distinctive aspects of the U.S. literary fiction of the Iraq War. Many of these aspects have already been addressed in prior literary criticism,[35] and some of them reflect widely recognized, distinctive features of the Iraq War itself. Because this book aims to contribute not only to the study of American war culture,[36] but also to the historical study of war literature, it may be useful to summarize a few of the distinctive aspects of Iraq War fiction that will not be emphasized elsewhere in the book.

For example, as is widely known, American military casualties in the Iraq War were more likely to have resulted from improvised explosive devices ("IEDs") than from the close-range enemy fire that often caused combat casualties in the Vietnam War.[37] The prevalence of IEDs, the psychological consequences of living with their threat, and the conflict between that threat and traditional notions of war and heroism, are thoroughly reflected in the literary fiction of the Iraq War.[38] Deaths or injuries in Iraq War fiction often come from insurgent mortar fire as well.[39]

Other relatively distinctive aspects of the war and its fiction include the ease of communication with family and others at home, thanks in part to email and the Internet;[40] the ever-growing presence of women serving alongside men, including in roles that were combat positions in all but name;[41] the ever-higher proportion of troops in support as opposed to combat roles;[42] the fact that the military was an all-volunteer force, although one featuring many reservists who did not anticipate being called to active duty, and eventually soldiers whose service was involuntarily extended through "stop-loss" orders;[43] the unprecedented use of often lavishly paid security contractors;[44] the many barriers and misunderstandings created by American soldiers' ignorance of Iraqi history and culture, and the important role played by interpreters ("terps");[45] the extravagant comforts and security available to some Americans in the Green Zone and on certain well-fortified Forward Operating Bases ("FOBs");[46] the frequent lack, especially early in the war, of obviously needed protective equipment, such as armor for Humvees;[47] the increased rates of survival after serious injury, resulting in fewer deaths relative to the number of wounded, but also more veterans living with amputations and other permanent injuries, including Traumatic Brain Injuries ("TBIs") resulting from IEDs;[48] the overprescription of medication to returning veterans;[49] the extremely common experience of PTSD and other forms of psychological trauma, including among soldiers who did not experience combat;[50] the prevalence of suicides by returning veterans;[51] and the severity of the sense of disconnection between those serving in Iraq and the civilian world at home, which is often presented in Iraq

War fiction as self-indulgently consumerist and either naively supportive of or willfully blind to the war.[52] Above all, as the Iraq War journalist George Packer notes in an insightful literary survey, Iraq War fiction contains a remarkable emphasis on the experience of homecoming, almost as though homecoming presented a more difficult, and less easily resolved, challenge than the war itself.[53]

A different book might also have interpreted Iraq War fiction as the literature of a war in the "neoliberal" era. If the transformation of politics and economics through what Wendy Brown calls "neoliberal rationality" has been one of the defining developments of the last several decades, then it should not be surprising if certain aspects of the Iraq War, and of Iraq War literature, reflect these developments.[54] In fact, as Brown and a number of commentators have suggested, Paul Bremer and other members of the U.S. occupation leadership attempted to transform Iraq itself into a kind of neoliberal fantasy-state based on the elimination of public goods and services; the sudden sale of state-run enterprises; severely weakened labor rights; low, regressive taxation; and unrestrained global financial speculation, "making Iraq a new playground of world finance and investment."[55] The frequent use of cash payments in an attempt to buy the backing or acquiescence of Iraqis, as well as the U.S. government's privatization of its own military functions through the hiring of private contractors, might also support an association of the Iraq War with neoliberalism.[56] A book written along these lines might have dedicated chapters to the bureaucratic satire of David Abrams' *FOBBIT* or the critique of for-profit patriotism in Ben Fountain's *Billy Lynn's Long Halftime Walk* rather than the works discussed in the chapters below.[57]

Ultimately, however, it is doubtful that neoliberalism provides the most helpful framework for understanding what is distinctive about the fictional portrayal of U.S. military service in the Iraq War. War and military service are, in fact, aspects of the United States that significantly conflict with the ostensible neoliberal reduction of all things to economic rationality. Even if it is accepted that the "free market" emphasis of neoliberal rhetoric leaves room for strong states, extractive economic imperialism, weaponized Keynesianism at home, and military worship as a more business-friendly alternative to other forms of communal solidarity, one can imagine a far more neoliberal military than the one that existed during the Iraq War and is portrayed in Iraq War fiction. On the contrary, in many ways the U.S. military—during the Iraq War, and to this day—resembles a kind of socialist refuge inside contemporary market society, with health care provided by the state through the Department of Veterans Affairs, state housing and schools on military bases, family welfare programs, a remarkable degree of job security, limited consumer choice and heavy subsidies at base commissaries, and all the ancillary benefits of military service, from subsidized child care to tuition assistance.[58] Many features of military life resemble stereotypes of life in a socialist state: the emphasis on obedience as opposed to individual initiative; the enforced solidarity through manufactured rituals; the effacement of individual identity through, for example, the wearing of uniforms; the wide, empty, Soviet-style roads dotted with plain, functional buildings on many military bases; and the uncanny homogeneity of those bases across the United States and around the world. In any case, while the expansive and often contested concept of "neoliberalism" leaves ample room for a neoliberal account of the Iraq War and its literature, that will not be the focus of this book.

Trauma theory is probably the most common framework used by literary scholars to make sense of Iraq War fiction. As Patrick Deer, a leading contributor to this literature, has written: "In the absence of compelling official narratives or a cohesive place in American popular memory, the invasion and occupation of Iraq...has often been understood and represented through the lens of trauma."[59] Roger Luckhurst, another prominent exponent of trauma theory, describes "the belatedness...of traumatic registration" as "the dominant influence on contemporary war fiction." He notes, in particular, that "literature deploying the trauma narrative often focuses on...the maladjustments of the veteran returning to the American domestic sphere after deployment."[60] Not surprisingly, trauma theory often approaches the soldier in Iraq War fiction as a traumatized victim. The Iraq War veteran novelist and literary scholar Roy Scranton famously, and critically, endorsed this reading of early Iraq War fiction in a 2015 essay in the *Los Angeles Review of Books*.[61] Scranton describes fictional works such as Kevin Powers' *The Yellow Birds* and Phil Klay's *Redeployment* as reflecting what he calls the myth of the "trauma hero," a view of soldiers that turns "a killer into a victim." Echoing James Campbell's critique of "combat gnosticism" and Yuval Noah Harari's scholarship on "flesh witnessing,"[62] Scranton describes how the view of ordinary soldiers as heroically traumatized victims developed in the twentieth century and now "dominates critical and scholarly interpretation of war literature, war movies, and the visual culture of war." Scranton criticizes the use of the trauma hero myth in Powers' and Klay's writing, but especially in Clint Eastwood's film *American Sniper*,[63] because the myth "serves a scapegoat function, discharging national bloodguilt by substituting the victim of trauma, the soldier, for the victim of violence, the enemy."

Against Scranton's influential interpretation, the central argument of this book is that Iraq War fiction distinguishes itself from the literature of earlier American wars precisely because of its unprecedented departure from the longstanding literary view of ordinary soldiers as victims. This book argues that Iraq War fiction is noteworthy for the extent to which it has answered Scranton's call to attend to the victims of American military violence, and to consider the moral responsibilities of ordinary American soldiers for that violence. Iraq War fiction by American writers, including not only Scranton's *War Porn*, but also the earlier works by Powers and Klay, treats harms to Iraqi civilians with greater moral solemnity than can be found in comparable works written in the years during and shortly after previous American wars. As Chapter 3 will argue, the contrast is especially clear when Iraq War fiction is compared to American fiction about World War II. Chapter 10 considers the closer case of American fiction about the Vietnam War. The chapter concludes that Vietnam War fiction prefigures the developments associated with Iraq War fiction in this book, but that the early American fiction of the Vietnam War remains primarily concerned with the victimization of American soldiers rather than reckoning seriously with the moral responsibility of American soldiers for harms to the Vietnamese. As Katherine Kinney argues in *Friendly Fire*, one of the leading works of scholarship on American representations of the Vietnam War, "[t]he idea that we fought ourselves, literalized in the repetitious image of Americans killing Americans, is...virtually the only story that has been told by Americans about the Vietnam War," with the result that the Vietnamese "typically serve as little more than the exotic backdrop for the American encounter with the 'heart of darkness' within itself."[64]

In other words, while Scranton criticizes early American representations of the Iraq War for telling stories that portray soldiers as victims, rather than grappling with more troubling questions such as why those soldiers "had to kill thousands upon thousands of Iraqi civilians,"[65] this book argues that Iraq War fiction is noteworthy in the history of American war literature for the extent to which it *does*, in fact, concentrate, often with apparent moral anguish,[66] on the ways that ordinary American troops harmed Iraqis.

In a valuable recent work, Joshua Pederson suggests a way of resolving the tension between, on the one hand, the tendency of literary criticism influenced by trauma theory to approach soldiers as victims, and, on the other hand, the uncomfortable presentation of soldiers in Iraq War fiction not as victims but as wrongdoers or perpetrators. Pederson argues that the pain of perpetration should often be understood not as trauma but as "moral injury," using a phrase that has become increasingly prevalent in the discussion of veterans' psychological wounds, especially as an alternative to the overuse of the label "PTSD."[67] Moral injury has been defined as "the lasting psychological, biological, spiritual, behavioral, and social impact of perpetrating, failing to prevent, or bearing witness to acts that transgress deeply held moral beliefs and expectations."[68]

In any case, my aim in this work is not to arrive at a just, holistic description of wrongdoing in war, or outside of war. My aim is above all to describe how American literary writers have made sense of the Iraq War through the stories they have chosen to tell.[69]

METHODOLOGICAL NOTE

A final piece of scholarly context may be useful before turning to this book's central arguments. At a time when the academic study of literature is often portrayed as being in crisis, and when it has apparently lost some of the influence that resulted in an earlier generation of historians, legal scholars, and social scientists routinely incorporating ideas from recent literary theory into their thinking, this book attempts to grapple with a topic that may be of relevance both inside and outside the community of literary scholars.

From a purely literary-historical point of view, there is a value to investigating and contextualizing new developments in the field of war literature. As a study focused on (mostly) fictional accounts of the experiences of soldiers, this book might also be seen as contributing to the nascent interdisciplinary field of "veterans studies," which has a plausible claim to exist alongside more well-established, and sometimes intersecting, fields and schools of inquiry such as African American studies, Native American studies, gender and sexuality studies, disability studies, and so on.[70] If American veterans are not a historically subordinated identity group, especially in the wake of the "new American militarism," there are nevertheless ways in which veterans constitute a kind of discrete and insular minority, and have been marginalized even as they have been celebrated. Many veterans—and their families—have certainly felt isolated from the larger civilian community in the United States.[71]

The book also attempts to look outward, beyond the community of literary scholars. Rather than responding to challenges to literary scholarship's relevance by drawing on a fresh vocabulary and set of assumptions from a critical theorist, or by imitating the quantitative methods of the social sciences, my investigation starts from the analysis and historical contextualization of narrative structures in literature, such as the "warrior-as-hero" and "soldier-as-victim" narrative templates discussed in the next chapter.[72] The results of such narrative investigations are often relevant beyond the community of literary scholarship, and even to those who have no interest in literature, because the stories we tell ourselves through literature about a given subject can reveal a great deal that is significant to anyone interested in the subject.[73]

Narratives matter. Narratives of war are particularly important, for at least three reasons.

First, politically, the narratives used in telling the stories of a war often lie in the background of future political decisions to use military force, or to refrain from doing so.[74] If, when members of the public think of war, the first thing that generally comes to mind is a generation of young men cut into raw meat for no apparent reason, the public will be much less enthusiastic about military intervention than if the default picture of war is a heroic adventure in which young men defend the nation's honor through virtuous displays of bravery and strength. The analysis of narrative structures in Iraq War fiction can help us become more aware of the stock narratives that often lie in the background of political discussions of military force.[75]

Second, for soldiers who participate in an armed conflict, narratives can be deeply significant in at least two ways. On the one hand, the narrative expectations about war that a soldier has before entering a conflict—which will inevitably have been shaped by narratives of prior wars to which the soldier has been exposed through conversation, reading, films and TV, video games, and other media[76]—may not only influence the soldier's attitude and behavior during the conflict, but may shape the soldier's experience of the conflict itself. The psychologist Jerome Bruner, drawing on works of narratology, studied and described some of the ways in which we make sense of our experiences as if they were literary works.[77] In doing so, we inevitably draw on narrative templates to which we have been exposed.

On the other hand, it can interfere with a veteran's reintegration to peacetime life if the veteran is unable to make narrative sense of his or her experience of war. Many psychologists have concluded that the ability and opportunity to tell a story of one's wartime experience to a sympathetic and supportive audience is often an important factor in recovering from wartime trauma.[78]

Third, for civilians, reading fictional war narratives can be a meaningful way of narrowing the troubling civilian–military divide in the contemporary United States. The divide has resulted from a variety of factors, including the transition to an all-volunteer military; the general lack of interest in military service in many parts of society, with the result that most members of the military today come from families with a tradition of military service; the isolation of most active-duty military families on largely self-contained bases; the increase in geographic "sorting" by political affiliation; and the inherently conservative aspects of the military—an institution committed to hierarchy, communalism, sacrifice, and violence in a culture increasingly committed to egalitarianism, individualism, self-actualization, and empathy.[79] Attempting to close or lessen the civilian–military divide is valuable for a wide variety of reasons, chief among them the many dangers of a powerful military that is not representative of or responsive to the nation it serves—or, even worse, a military that views the civilians it serves with contempt.[80]

At this point, it might be objected that many of the arguments above for the value of studying war narratives would apply just as well, if not better, to memoirs, documentaries, and other nonfiction narrative works about the Iraq War, as well as to popular fictional works such as TV series, movies, and genre fiction. Why focus this book for the most part on literary fiction?[81]

Two responses might be offered. First, it is necessary to define some limits around the subject matter in a book-length study. A book dealing with all of the narrative media noted above would be unwieldy, and would sacrifice the depth that can come from comparing multiple narrative works produced in a similar form. In addition, it would be fairly easy to apply the framework used to analyze novels in this book to other works in different narrative media. An analysis of, for example, fictional films about the Iraq War would likely find as much of a struggle with the inadequacy of narratives of heroism and victimhood, and as much ambivalence toward narratives of U.S. soldier criminality, as this book finds in the narratives of the novels it analyzes.[82]

A second response might begin by conceding that it is probably the case that Iraq War literary fiction written by veterans offers a view of the war that is skewed in certain ways. After all, not every veteran is the kind of veteran who would be interested in producing a work of literary fiction. There is a suspicious abundance of protagonists in these works who have an interest in literature, and who sometimes feel alienated from those around them by their literary and intellectual inclinations. In Kevin Powers' *The Yellow Birds*, the narrator mentions that people pushed him around in high school "because you liked to read books and poems sometimes and they'd call you fag."[83] In Christopher Robinson's and Gavin Kovite's *War of the Encyclopaedists*, the officer-protagonist is told that his men view him as a "weirdo" because he reads "highbrow shit" like *The Canterbury Tales* instead of *Maxim*.[84] Other examples could be offered.[85] By contrast, literary readers tend to get fewer intimate internal portraits of the less highbrow characters who appear frequently in works of journalism like the book *Generation Kill*.[86]

But whatever Iraq War literary fiction, especially by veterans, lacks in representativeness, it makes up for in deliberateness of narrative construction. Even an insightful and powerfully written memoir like Dexter Filkins' *The Forever War* is less likely to offer the interpretive richness and depth of potential meaning provided by a carefully crafted literary narrative.[87] The memoirist is limited by what happened to her, or what she is willing to say happened to her, and may also feel compelled to include especially significant but isolated details that do not necessarily contribute to a single, larger story. The novelist or short story writer, on the other hand, starts with no fixed constraints. To read a work of Iraq War fiction is to encounter an author's at least theoretically unhindered choices about what a story of the Iraq War should contain. Fictional literary narratives such as novels and short stories tend to offer the best available materials for studying the attempt to impose narrative structure on American soldiers' experiences of the war in Iraq.

AN OUTLINE OF THE ARGUMENT

The central argument of this book is that American fiction about the Iraq War reflects the troubled emergence of a new narrative template for war literature: the story of the ordinary soldier not as a hero or a victim but as a morally culpable wrongdoer. Iraq War fiction is haunted by depictions of harms to Iraqis and expressions of unresolved guilt. The book argues further that the emphasis on criminality in Iraq War fiction can be partly explained by the rise of moral cosmopolitanism and its blurring of the traditional conceptual lines between war and crime.

Chapter 2 begins by placing Iraq War fiction in the broader history of war literature. Synthesizing a range of historical sources and works of literary criticism, the chapter draws attention to two "ideal types" of war narrative. Pre-modern epics were often focused on the figure of the warrior-as-hero, while modern war literature has increasingly focused on the figure of the soldier-as-victim. Even today, for anyone writing a war story, the two ideal types exist as resources to be drawn upon or struggled against. Yet American authors of fiction about the Iraq War have often, apparently, found both the traditional heroic war narrative and the modern anti-war narrative with its focus on the traumatized soldier-victim to be inadequate.

Chapters 3 and 4 turn to the question of why the specter of criminality looms so persistently over Iraq War fiction. Through a comparison with American fiction about World War II, Chapter 3 considers and rejects the possibility that criminality plays such a prominent role in Iraq War fiction because the war itself was characterized by exceptional wrongdoing. Chapter 4 considers ways in which changing conceptualizations of war, morality, and law might have contributed to the perception of criminality in the Iraq War and the literary responses to it.

Chapters 5 through 9 illustrate the prominence of wrongdoing by ordinary soldiers in American narratives of the Iraq War through close readings of several works. Chapter 5 addresses Kevin Powers' *The Yellow Birds* (2012), which has a plausible claim to being, as of today, the canonical American novel of the Iraq War, at least among novels written by U.S. veterans. The chapter argues that Powers' narrative choices reveal, at the structural core of the novel, an evasion of a confrontation with criminality, while also noting a brief but powerful moment of recognition.

The eleven short stories in Phil Klay's *Redeployment* (2014), the subject of Chapter 6, present a variety of perspectives on U.S. military and civilian service in the war, each delivered through the voice of a first-person narrator. Even though Klay's collection is arguably the greatest achievement of American literary fiction about military service in the Iraq War, as of this writing, his work also illustrates the limitations of realist, "program-era" fiction as a way of making narrative sense of the war.

Chapter 7 turns to Helen Benedict's *Sand Queen* (2011), one of the first American novels of the Iraq War. *Sand Queen* portrays U.S. soldiers as engaged in a largely criminal enterprise. Both of the novel's two central narratives present the U.S. military as, in essence, the "bad guy" in the story of the Iraq War. Benedict focuses on two young women as protagonists: an Iraqi woman named Naema, and an American soldier named Kate. The U.S. military is the villain to Naema's hero and the criminal to Kate's victim.

Unlike the other works about the Iraq War discussed in this book, Chris Kyle's *American Sniper* (2012), the subject of Chapter 8, is a best-selling memoir rather than a work of literary fiction. I include Kyle's book in part because it appears to be the most widely read narrative work about military service in the Iraq War. Through a detailed close reading, the chapter argues that Kyle's book suggests the practical difficulty, or perhaps even impossibility, of telling a story of American military service in the Iraq War as a traditional hero story.

Finally, Chapter 9 discusses Roy Scranton's *War Porn* (2016), one of the most fully realized expressions of the shift in American war literature away from a focus on narratives of soldier victimization and toward narratives of soldier wrongdoing. The novel tells three stories about the Iraq War. Misconduct by U.S. soldiers plays a central role in each story. Yet the novel's thematic critique of the morality of military service in the Iraq War sits awkwardly beside its aesthetic elevation of violence and cruelty.

In conclusion, Chapter 10 finally addresses the comparison between Iraq War fiction and the fiction of the Vietnam War. The chapter concludes that the early American fiction of the Vietnam War reflects, although often in a nascent form, the shift away from the literary representation of ordinary American soldiers as victims, and toward their representation as, in some paradigmatic cases, morally responsible wrongdoers. But Iraq War fiction takes this development further through its greater moral scrutiny of relatively lesser wrongdoing. Iraq War fiction continues a transformation in war literature that is prefigured, but not yet as fully realized, in the fiction of the Vietnam War written by American authors in the years during and shortly after the war.

CHAPTER TWO

FROM HEROISM THROUGH VICTIMHOOD TO CRIMINALITY

In order to make sense of the narratives of U.S. soldier criminality in American fiction about the Iraq War, it is useful to set Iraq War fiction against the background of earlier war literature. This chapter begins by providing a schematic picture of two ideal narrative types from the history of war literature: the paradigmatically ancient narrative of the warrior-as-hero and the paradigmatically modern narrative of the soldier-as-victim.

THE WARRIOR-AS-HERO

Histories of attempts to represent war in narrative form typically begin with ancient and medieval epics such as *The Iliad*, *Beowulf*, and *The Song of Roland*.[1] Often derived from earlier, oral traditions, these metered stories of armed men frequently feature heroic battles and sit at or near the foundation of the linguistic literary traditions to which they belong. It is worth noting a few fairly common features of the epics as a background against which war literature continues to be written today.

First, the protagonists of the epics tend to be *heroes* in several possible senses of that term. The protagonist tends to embody, in an extreme form and under extreme circumstances, what the surrounding culture perceives as some of its highest ideals. The protagonist thus serves as a kind of model, if an unattainably grandiose one. He—and the primary warrior-protagonists of these works are nearly always male—is also a hero in the sense of shaping the world around him through his deeds.[2] What he does makes a profound difference to the course of events. He is thus a "hero" or "great man" in Carlyle's sense. Finally, some of the protagonists of the epics are also heroes in the sense of having life stories that fit the patterns of hero narratives identified by scholars of mythology and folklore.

Second, the cultural ideals embodied by the heroes of the epics are not just any ideals. They are the ideals of pre-modern *aristocratic warrior societies*, the societies that produced the epics. These chiefdoms, early states, and empires existed in an insecure world defined in part by the pursuit of glory and the defense of honor through violence. Practical necessities likely drove the production and reproduction of these constantly threatened, generally resource-poor communities' cultural ideals. The highest source of glory for a man in such a culture tended to be bravery in battle, and those with the highest social status were often expected to be warriors. The aristocracy tended to be defined not only by ties of kinship but by control over and ability to deploy expensive arms and men. If a chiefdom or early state had not possessed something like these militaristic, aristocratic ideals, it would have been at greater risk of being overtaken by a community that did. There is thus a practical logic behind the fact that so many cultures from such disparate times and places all happened to produce epics of battle among their first long-form, written literary works, and the fact that we have no record of an ancient or medieval epic that presents pacific trust and universalist-egalitarian cooperation between all peoples as the highest, heroic ideal.

Third, as already suggested, episodes of *battle* tend to play a central role in the narrative structures of these epics. The narratives of works such as *The Iliad* and *The Song of Roland* are primarily about war. But even those epics, such as *The Epic of Gilgamesh* and *Beowulf*, that do not depict war, at least in the paradigmatic sense of organized mass killing between communities, feature narratively pivotal scenes of battle.[3] The battle might be between the primary hero and another individual, such as Enkidu in *Gilgamesh*, or between the hero and a mythological creature, such as Humbaba in *Gilgamesh* or the monster Grendel in *Beowulf*. All epics share an emphasis on the great deeds of heroes, and it is very often through battle that the hero demonstrates his heroism.

Whether we view the epics' focus on battles as a response to an innate audience demand for scenes of violent conflict and dominance or, to the contrary, an attempt by warmongering elites to foster an appreciation for battle among an audience whose young men might be called upon to put their lives at risk for the elites' benefit, the decision to dwell on battle scenes within epic narratives is a noteworthy and pervasive one. It also draws attention to the fact that the epics offer not only stories about heroes. To the extent that the epics focus on battles, they also offer, necessarily, stories about the hero's enemy or enemies, his opponents in combat.

Fourth, the epics tend to *celebrate* war and violent combat. Far from viewing war as something that only wastes and degrades, and that we should strive to eliminate from the world, the epics present war in part as a vehicle for glory. The epics celebrate physical aggression, and tend to view the turning away from violence contemptuously, as a sign of weakness or cowardice, as in the pathetic depiction in Book X of *The Iliad* of Dolon, who begs for his life. Again, there may be a reason that the surviving epics so often contain celebrations of mastery in battle. Regardless of how the underlying myth or legend in an epic developed, it is unlikely that those with the power and resources to support a poet-performer in the militaristic, hierarchical societies that produced epics would have supported the performance of an epic that presented heroic ideals as illusory, encouraged young men to refrain from fighting the community's ostensible enemies, or denied the distinction between enemies and friends in favor of an ideal of universal community.

THE SOLDIER-AS-VICTIM

If we leap ahead from the pre-modern epics to many of the most widely studied works of war literature in the twentieth century,[4] or at least some of the works most widely studied and read in the United States in the later twentieth century, nearly everything seems to have changed with regard to each of the four points above. In novels such as Virginia Woolf's *Mrs. Dalloway*, Erich Maria Remarque's *All Quiet on the Western Front*, Ernest Hemingway's *A Farewell to Arms*, Dalton Trumbo's *Johnny Got His Gun*, Joseph Heller's *Catch-22*, Kurt Vonnegut's *Slaughterhouse-Five*, Leslie

Marmon Silko's *Ceremony*, or Tim O'Brien's *The Things They Carried*, the narrative template based around the warrior-as-hero has been shattered and replaced with something radically different.[5]

It is worth making explicit some of the basic differences between these two types of war literature, even if doing so inevitably simplifies the actual diversity of the literature to a few idealized characteristics. The exercise can provide a counterpoint to the tendency in writing about war literature and war culture to emphasize the admittedly remarkable continuities that exist across history and cultures.[6]

First, and most importantly for this book's concerns, the protagonist-warriors of the now-canonical works of twentieth-century war literature tend to be presented as *victims* at least as much as heroes. As one historian of war culture has observed, scholars studying war memoirs "have reached the almost unanimous conclusion that in the twentieth century, at least in the West," the image of soldiers "has partly changed from that of heroes to that of victims."[7] In the modern tale of the soldier-as-victim, soldiers are often conscripted or duped into war by nationalist ideals that are later revealed, often through the soldier's revelatory battlefield experiences, to be illusions or even lies. Far from serving as pivotal historical actors or "great men," these soldiers are the disposable pawns of powerful masters far from the battlefield, or of impersonal historical forces. Their own conduct hardly matters to the outcome of the war, and instead of being idealized paragons of the culture's virtues, they are often deeply flawed or at least ambiguous both morally and in terms of their competence. They are, in other words, not so much heroes as "antiheroes."

In addition, rather than presenting life stories that fit the template of a mythological hero's journey, these works often focus on the stripping away of illusory ideals through the experience of combat—what Harari refers to as "battlefield revelation."[8] The closer we come to the present day, the more the soldier's individual psychological experience of trauma is emphasized as a central narrative arc.

It may be worth pausing to note a feature of the widely acknowledged shift from viewing soldiers as heroes to viewing them as victims. The hero and the victim do not exist in a binary conceptual relationship. They are not opposite members of a pair. Rather, the usual contrasting term for the hero is *the villain*. The usual contrasting term for the victim, at least today, is *the criminal*. It is the criminal, or the perpetrator of a crime, who victimizes the victim. Thus, the movement from a war literature focused on the warrior-as-hero to one focused on the soldier-as-victim has not been a simple reversal. It has been, rather, a change of conversation, the adoption of a new orientation. The new orientation involves shifting attention not only toward victims, but also toward any criminals who might have caused their suffering.

Second, instead of arising out of an aristocratic warrior culture, twentieth-century war literature reflects the cultural trends of modernity. In order to highlight the contrast with the aristocratic warrior culture of the epics, we might consider the very general aspects of modern culture emphasized by writers such as Max Weber and Charles Taylor. They portray the world since the early modern period in the West as increasingly legal-rationalistic, secularized, egalitarian, and market-focused.[9] Reflecting the growth of egalitarianism, the protagonist in twentieth-century war literature is often an enlisted soldier or junior officer rather than the higher-ranking contemporary equivalent of one of Tolstoy's counts or princes, not to mention pre-modern warrior-chiefs like Achilles or Agamemnon. As in the paintings of Bruegel, the focus has shifted from the aristocratic elite to the common person, the representative of the people.

Reflecting the search for individual meaning that has gone hand in hand with the growth of secularism, twentieth-century war literature is far less concerned with the values at the center of the ancient epics, such as honor and glory, and far more concerned with the soldier-protagonist's personal development, the story of his "*Bildung*."[10] Also reflecting the secularizing processes of modernity, the supernatural elements of the epics have disappeared. Gods no longer intervene in the story, the soldier-protagonist lacks any divinity, and there are no longer monsters to combat, at least not literally. In most twentieth-century war literature, there are only human beings, killing one other.

The shift toward viewing soldiers as victims can also be seen as reflecting a more general cultural reorientation. The historian Enzo Traverso notes that the contemporary era has been defined "as the 'age of the witness', emphasizing the attention paid today to the accounts of past actors, and especially those of one particular category: the *victims*, who in today's vocabulary have become synonymous with witnesses." Traverso observes a "shift in gaze, directed previously at heroes and now at victims."[11] The growing cultural emphasis on victims rather than heroes is reflected even in the use of the words "hero" and "victim" in English-language books. While the use of the term "hero" fluctuated on a generally downward trajectory over the period from 1800 to 1980, with some recovery since then, the use of the word "victim" started lower but then began a remarkable rise around 1960 that quickly led it to surpass the use of "hero."[12]

The rising use of "victim" coincided with several cultural developments that might be seen as related: the increasing acceptance of psychiatry as a scientific and legitimate form of medicine, along with psychiatry's treatment of trauma as a diagnosable condition related to the human condition of victimhood; the emergence of second-wave feminism, and with it increased attention to the ways the victimization of women has been historically effaced or ignored; the emergence of other social movements advocating for the rights of subordinated identity groups who could likewise invoke the discourse of victimization, such as the gay rights and disability rights movements; and the growth, especially in Europe, of a culture of remembrance for the victims of the Holocaust. The simultaneous, interwoven rise of emancipatory rights discourse and victim consciousness even resulted in the development, beginning in the 1970s, of a "victims' rights" movement in the United States: a social movement dedicated to securing and defending the rights of crime victims as such.

Third, while episodes of battle continue to play a central role in many twentieth-century works of literature dealing with military experiences of war, the focus of narrative attention increasingly turns to the social, psychological, and political *contexts* of war, including soldiers' difficulties reintegrating into civilian society. There is a relative shift in narrative emphasis from the spectacle of battle itself to war's causes and consequences. Why men go to war and kill one another becomes a puzzle that calls out for explanation, an ill that calls out for diagnosis, rather than simply being an unquestioned, universal given of human experience. Battle, when it appears, appears more often as a vehicle for the further victimization of soldiers than as a proving ground for their courage or manhood.

Fourth, rather than celebrating war, twentieth-century war literature tends to *condemn* it as a general matter. It is as much anti-war literature as it is war literature. In line with modernity's general shift away from the valorization of the heroic violence of aristocratic warriors and toward a post-heroic, market-based culture that presents work, romantic and familial love, aesthetic experience, and consumption as the primary sources of human meaning and satisfaction, these works generally assume that the world would be a better place if there were no war. They are not concerned that a world without war would offer fewer opportunities for glory. This is especially true of twentieth-century war literature produced in Western liberal democracies after World War II. Even the popular movies of Bacevich's "new American militarism," like *Top Gun* and *Rambo: First Blood Part II*, not to mention the superhero movies that have often filled theaters early in the twenty-first century, celebrate military strength and prowess rather than war itself. They do not suggest that we should invite the prospect of a war because of the opportunities for proving toughness and vigor that a war would provide. The long tradition of delivering unabashed paeans to the virtues of war for its own sake, which renewed itself in the years before World War I, has virtually no foothold in contemporary mainstream American culture, and especially not in high literary culture. Instead, the most common perspective on war in literature that has artistic ambitions is probably the one suggested by Harari in his analysis of narratives of "materialist disillusionment": war is a pointless, obscene slaughter that reveals human beings to be nothing but meat, and that results in trauma for those who survive.[13]

CIVILIANS AS VICTIMS OF CRIMINALITY

It goes without saying that the history of war literature cannot be reduced to the two ideal types sketched above, and no lasting work of literature will entirely fit either type. Ancient epics such as *The Iliad* often reveal an ambivalence regarding their own heroic ideals, and a concern for the victims of others' heroic violence, as in the lamentations for Hector in *The Iliad*'s final book. Conversely, much of the twentieth-century literature that presents soldiers as victims also makes room for various kinds of heroism. In its time, *A Farewell to Arms* may have seemed to be a startling repudiation of earlier literature glamorizing war, but from a contemporary perspective its own portrayal of war is remarkably romantic, and its protagonist embodies an idealized masculinity that continues to depend on wartime displays of competence and courage.

But for anyone writing a war story today, the two ideal types exist as resources to be drawn upon or struggled against. They also embody expectations and narrative demands that audiences may have for literary writing about war. The Iraq War veteran and fiction writer Roman Skaskiw has noted that when he attended the Iowa Writers' Workshop, there was "'[s]o much expectation that you will be a victim or a hero.'"[14]

The legal scholar and former Defense Department official Rosa Brooks has compared the choice between viewing the September 11 attacks as an act of war or as a criminal act to Wittgenstein's "duck–rabbit" picture.[15] The eye perceives the picture either as a duck or as a rabbit, but not as both simultaneously. There seems to be no option of a compromise between the two, and there is no general, neutral basis for declaring one perception to be the "correct" one. Something similar might be said about the moral image of military service in contemporary American culture. The idea of soldiers as heroes, and the seemingly incompatible idea of soldiers as victims, both seem to be live options.

For example, the author Phil Klay, whose short story collection *Redeployment* is discussed below in Chapter 6, has described the formation of his own perceptions of military service in the 1990s, when as a teenager he read anti-war fiction like Joseph Heller's *Catch-22* and Tim O'Brien's *The Things They Carried*, which portrayed "war as pointless suffering, absurdity, a spectacle of man's inhumanity to man." At the same time, nonfiction about World War II by Stephen Ambrose and movies like *Saving Private Ryan* portrayed war as "a vision of remarkable heroism in a world that desperately needed it." As in the picture of the duck–rabbit, Klay's novels and histories "were sending very mixed signals."[16]

O'Brien's "How To Tell a True War Story" could not be clearer about which side is correct:

> A true war story is never moral. It does not instruct, nor encourage virtue, nor suggest models of proper human behavior, nor restrain men from doing the things men have always done. If a story seems moral, do not

believe it. If at the end of a war story you feel uplifted, or if you feel that some small bit of rectitude has been salvaged from the larger waste, then you have been made the victim of a very old and terrible lie. There is no rectitude whatsoever. There is no virtue. As a first rule of thumb...you can tell a true war story by its absolute and uncompromising allegiance to obscenity and evil.[17]

From this perspective, the notion of war as anything other than obscenity, and thus military service as anything other than an opportunity for moral debasement, would seem to be a grand illusion. To know war is to become disillusioned, to feel the scales fall from one's eyes, to experience the revelation of a truth that was hidden behind the veil of militarist ideology. The idea of soldiers as heroes, in particular, would seem to be almost laughably deluded from this perspective, or grotesque, like viewing human sacrifice or slavery as noble institutions deserving of celebration. Those who have read, or taught, O'Brien's story as the oracular, apodictic pronouncement of a flesh-witness of war might see the analogy to the duck–rabbit as itself horribly misguided, because it suggests a moral relativism in which militarists and their opponents have equally valid perspectives.

As a contrast to the view of military service as nothing but an invitation to moral corruption, we might turn to the militaristic pronouncements of one or another contemporary war lover rattling his saber as though nothing in particular had changed in the last two hundred or two thousand years. But even if we reject such atavism, the more measured words of the philosopher Charles Taylor might be offered. He writes that even in the twentieth century,

war has been the occasion, as well as of unspeakable horrors, of actions of great nobility...Belonging to the generation which were children going on teenagers during the Second World War, it still seems to me undeniable that, even taking account of the full complexity and murkiness of human motivation, there were people who laid their lives on the line so that others could be free, and even greater horrors avoided...[A]s things stand now, the end of war would remove an important occasion for human excellences: heroism, dedication, the defense of the weak...Nor can I accept the

> comforting view...that war breeds nothing but horrors and destruction, although plainly it does a lot of this.[18]

Whether Taylor or the narrator of O'Brien's story has the more defensible position is not a question that this book will attempt to resolve. What is clear is that it remains possible for many observers in the contemporary West to see participation in war as O'Brien's duck or Taylor's rabbit. Indeed, the apparent incompatibility and yet viability of the two perspectives on military service expressed by O'Brien's narrator and by Taylor is one of the defining conditions of contemporary war literature.

But these perspectives on participation in war are not the only ones. Authors of fiction about the Iraq War have often seemed to find both the traditional heroic war narrative and the modern anti-war narrative with its focus on the traumatized soldier-victim to be inadequate. Suggestions and echoes of the warrior-as-hero and the soldier-as-victim pervade Iraq War fiction, yet sit uncomfortably beside explorations of a contrasting narrative in which criminality plays a powerful role. The victims of this often elusive criminality are primarily civilians.

In that sense, Iraq War fiction can be seen as bringing together the tradition of war literature focused primarily on the experiences of soldiers, a tradition that encompasses both the ancient epics and the twentieth-century war novels discussed above, with another longstanding tradition that focuses primarily on the suffering of civilians. Examples of the latter tradition include Euripides' *The Trojan Women* and Aristophanes' *Lysistrata*, as well as a proliferation of more recent works from Voltaire's *Candide* to Bertolt Brecht's *Mother Courage* and Chimamanda Ngozi Adichie's *Half of a Yellow Sun*.[19] It is surely no coincidence that women's perspectives have predominated in works about civilian suffering, as female civilians have so often been the unmemorialized victims of war.

It is surely also no coincidence that war literature focused on civilian victims has become more prevalent as women have gained more power to tell their own stories, within and outside literature, over the last century, and as the death rate of noncombatants in armed conflicts has risen.[20] Fittingly, two of the first widely reviewed, book-length English-language works of Iraq War fiction were written by women and feature mostly female protagonists: Helen Benedict's *Sand Queen*, discussed in Chapter 7 below, and Siobhan Fallon's short story collection *You Know When the Men Are Gone*, both published in 2011.[21] But as this book will suggest, acute attention to the civilian suffering caused by American soldiers' acts is a characteristic feature of most Iraq War fiction.

CHAPTER THREE

WRONGDOING IN FACT AND FICTION: IRAQ VERSUS WORLD WAR II

Why does the question of criminality, and in particular the concern with criminality among American soldiers against Iraqi civilian victims, suffuse so much of Iraq War fiction? One response, which may appeal especially to critics of American power on the Left, is that the Iraq War was an especially illegitimate, immoral, and unlawful military engagement. The invasion of Iraq was, after all, at least arguably a violation of the UN Charter's rules for initiating war.[1] In addition, the planning of the war might be seen as so incompetent as to be similar to the kinds of reckless acts that in other contexts routinely result in criminal liability.

With regard to wrongful acts by U.S. forces in Iraq, the introduction already noted that various atrocities by U.S. forces came to light during the war, including the torture and other abuses at Abu Ghraib prison and the rape and murders in Mahmudiyah. The introduction also noted that these crimes only came to the public's attention through fairly narrow chains of contingencies. It is likely that U.S. forces in Iraq, like military forces in virtually any conflict, but especially in a foreign counterinsurgency operation, were probably responsible for numerous crimes that entirely escaped investigation and prosecution, and left no trace in the public record.[2]

Yet if war and atrocity have gone hand in hand throughout history, it is not the case that the fiction of every war, or even of every American war in the last century, has been haunted by the specter of soldier wrongdoing in the way that Iraq War fiction has been. Based on the works published so far, including those analyzed in this book, Iraq War fiction dwells far more intently on the suffering of Iraqis caused by U.S. forces than, for example, World War II fiction by American writers dwelt on the suffering of the Germans or the Japanese. A case could surely be made that the literature about a war featuring the firebombing of Japanese and German cities by U.S. and Allied forces, the atomic bombing of Hiroshima and Nagasaki, the failure by the United States to take available actions to impede the Holocaust,[3] the rape of thousands of European and Japanese women by U.S. forces,[4] and whatever complicity in Red Army atrocities can be said to result from the U.S. alliance with Stalin, should have been at least as concerned with U.S. military victimization of civilians as the literature of the Iraq War.

Looking back further, early American literature about conflicts between white settlers and Native Americans from the seventeenth to the nineteenth century displays even less of a moral reckoning regarding the settlers' repeated "attacks upon and...destruction of noncombatants, villages, and agricultural resources."[5] Instead, in the words of the literary historian Richard Slotkin, "the Indian fighter and hunter emerged as the first of our national heroes."[6] The literary reaction to the Indian Wars was the development of the American hero myth embodied by the figure of Daniel Boone, "the solitary, Indian-like hunter of the deep woods."[7] In the hunter myth, "the destroyer of the Indian...comes to know the Indian only in the act of destroying him."[8] In early American literary mythology, the white killer of Indians is very much a hero rather than a criminal.[9]

In the interest of simplicity, however, let us focus on World War II and its literature as a point of comparison with the Iraq War and the literature discussed in this book. The remainder of this section will suggest that the quantity of militarily unjustifiable suffering deliberately caused by the U.S. military and its soldiers in World War II was most likely significantly greater than in the Iraq War. Yet the American novels written about World War II, especially in the years immediately after the war, gave significantly less attention to this relatively greater suffering than American fiction about the Iraq War has done.

In the Pacific theater, in particular, atrocities by Allied forces were apparently fairly widespread. How prevalent can never be precisely quantified, of course, in part because the killing of surrendered enemy soldiers and the collection of grisly souvenirs will often escape memorialization in official records, and any witnesses or participants may be hesitant to discuss what they have seen or done. But the historian John W. Dower has collected a range of anecdotal evidence supporting the conclusion that the American killing of surrendered Japanese soldiers, and sometimes groups of them, was not rare; and that neither was the collection of Japanese gold teeth, ears, and sometimes other body parts as trophies. In addition to evidence from memoirs, Dower notes that "*Life* published a full-page photograph of an attractive blonde posing with a Japanese skull she had been sent by her fiancé in the Pacific." Similarly, *Time* magazine enthusiastically described the massacre of Japanese survivors after a three-day battle in the Bismarck Sea in March 1943. Exterminatory and genocidal rhetoric regarding the Japanese was widespread.[10]

In Dower's estimation, "most fighting men" in the Pacific theater "had personal knowledge" of "souvenir hunting" from the bodies of Japanese war dead, and "over wide reaches of the Asian battleground it was everyday practice" to take no prisoners—that is, to murder any enemy soldiers who surrendered. Dower describes the diaries of the aviator Charles Lindbergh, who served for several months in 1944 as a civilian observer in the Pacific. Lindbergh's writing suggests the routine nature of atrocities by U.S. forces: "Our men think nothing of shooting a Japanese prisoner." On one occasion, Lindbergh was informed of an incident in which American forces allegedly used machine guns to massacre thousands of Japanese prisoners on a flying field. He heard of torture, the frequent ransacking of Japanese corpses for gold teeth, and, in one instance, "the slaughter of all inmates of a Japanese hospital." An American general described to Lindbergh "an unsuspecting Japanese prisoner [who] was given a cigarette and then seized from behind and had his throat 'slit from ear to ear' as a demonstration of how to kill Japanese." Toward the end of his tour, Lindbergh learned that "on some islands Marines actually dug up dead bodies in their search for gold teeth. Elsewhere they collected noses as well as ears, teeth, and skulls."[11]

Yet unlike in the American literature of the Iraq War, the prevalence of atrocities and war crimes by U.S. forces is not, generally speaking, the central or even a central theme in American literary fiction about World War II produced shortly after the war. Although it would be impossible to generalize about the 1500 to 2200 American novels that have apparently been published about World War II, most of them between 1945 and 1958, it can safely be said that many of the most prominent early works of World War II fiction by American writers essentially portrayed American soldiers in a heroic light, or as the suffering victims of the brutality of war.[12]

Today, in the wake of the Vietnam War and the cosmopolitan transformations of war culture described in the next chapter, we tend to think of the canonical American works of World War II fiction as grim, violent works such as Norman Mailer's *The Naked and the Dead* (1948) and James Jones' *The Thin Red Line* (1962), as well as the increasingly irreverent and surreal works of the 1960s such as Joseph Heller's *Catch-22* (1961), Kurt Vonnegut's *Slaughterhouse-Five* (1969) and, later, Thomas Pynchon's *Gravity's Rainbow* (1973).[13] But if we look at the Pulitzer prizes as an indication of the most esteemed novels published shortly after World War II, a very different picture emerges.

Several World War II novels won the Pulitzer prize for fiction in the years after the war, beginning with the journalist John Hersey's *A Bell for Adano* (1944), the winner in 1945.[14] *Adano*, which was later adapted into both a Broadway play and a movie, tells the story of U.S. Army Major Victor Joppolo's benevolent efforts to bring peace and democracy to Adano, a small, fictional Italian town full of colorful locals. The first line of the novel's foreword states, without irony, that Major Joppolo "was a good man" (v), and the remainder of the novel sets about demonstrating, in Hemingway-flavored prose, the accuracy of this assessment. Major Joppolo is in charge of the occupation of Adano. The Fascists had taken away the town's bell to melt it down for gun barrels (23). After the townspeople convey to Major Joppolo how central the bell was to their lives, he dedicates great efforts to delivering a new bell. At the end of the novel, the new bell arrives, and the townspeople show their gratitude by painting a portrait of Major Joppolo and giving it to him (256). The novel does not portray the Americans as without flaws. There is a vignette of drunken property destruction by some good-hearted and repentant American soldiers (120–39). The uncaring, authoritarian General Marvin, echoing an actual incident involving General Patton, orders the shooting of a peasant's mule because it is blocking the road (52). In a mild echo of the soldier-as-victim, General Marvin relieves Major Joppolo for disobeying his command not to replace the town's bell (237). But because of its focus on the "good man" Major Joppolo, *Adano* is above all a story of the American soldier as well-meaning hero. After a local child dies in a vehicle accident while chasing after caramels thrown by the GIs, Major Joppolo explains to the dead child's mother that the Americans are, if anything, "'too generous'": "'If the Americans did not throw candies to them, they would not keep on running beside the trucks and begging'" (245).

In a similarly heroic spirit, the Pulitzer winner in 1948 was James Michener's *Tales of the South Pacific* (1947).[15] Despite a penultimate chapter portraying a brutal but heroic battle against "the Japs," most of the novel focuses on cross-cultural misunderstandings, racism, and thwarted romance. It was later adapted into a hit Broadway musical by Rogers and Hammerstein and a popular 1958 musical film. The next year, instead of Mailer's *The Naked and the Dead*, James Gould Cozzens' *Guard of Honor* (1948) took home the Pulitzer prize, after also receiving generally better reviews. Cozzens' novel celebrates the senior leadership on a Florida military base for deftly accommodating white supremacists who threaten rebellion if the base is integrated according to regulation.[16] Finally, Herman Wouk's *The Caine Mutiny* (1951), which displaced *Tales of the South Pacific* on the best-seller lists, won the Pulitzer in 1952, and was soon adapted into a Broadway play and a popular film. In *The Caine Mutiny*, as in a number of other popular World War II novels of the era, including *Adano*, *The Naked and the Dead*, and James Jones' *From Here to Eternity* (1951), the primary victims—to the extent that there are victims, a question that the novel treats with some ambiguity—are ordinary American soldiers and sailors abused by authoritarian, sadistic, or incompetent superiors.

Not until 1960 and after does the emphasis of some World War II literature begin to shift toward harm to foreign civilians, as in Heller's depiction of the Allied bombing of an undefended Italian village and Vonnegut's portrayal of the Allied firebombing of Dresden. James Jones' *The Thin Red Line*, recognized at the time of its publication for its exceptionally graphic attention to misconduct and atrocities by U.S. soldiers, also did not appear until 1962.[17]

Norman Mailer's *The Naked and the Dead*, published to mixed reviews but great commercial success in 1948, represents a partial exception to the emphasis of early World War II literature on U.S. soldier heroism and victimhood rather than wrongdoing. The novel prominently features a scene in which an American NCO murders a Japanese prisoner, and another scene in which an American soldier scavenges gold teeth from a Japanese corpse. One of the novel's final pages notes in passing that it became standard operating procedure for the Americans to murder wounded Japanese soldiers left behind in retreats, "smashing their heads with rifle butts or shooting them point-blank."[18]

Yet these atrocities occupy only a handful of the novel's more than seven hundred pages. *The Naked and the Dead* dedicates far more space to the anti-Semitism of American soldiers and the authoritarianism of American officers than it does to any American mistreatment of the Japanese. Moreover, the NCO who murders the Japanese prisoner in *The Naked and the Dead* is a moral outlier rather than an ordinary or representative American soldier. He is SSG Croft, a nearly demonic sadist who, later in the novel, crushes with his bare hands a tiny, wounded bird that the soldiers have rescued. The narrative core of Mailer's novel is the vivid description of a grueling, ultimately pointless reconnaissance march up a mountain. The general portrait of American military service that the novel offers is one of ordinary American soldiers suffering at the hands of unfeeling superiors and bigoted compatriots, interspersed with moments of camaraderie and heroic endurance—in other words, a traditional post-World War I portrait of the soldier as victim, and to some extent traumatized hero, rather than a representation that emphasizes soldiers as wrongdoers who are or should be haunted by guilt for the harms they have caused to strangers.

To get an initial sense of the contrast between early fictional representations of World War II and of the Iraq War, we might compare the relatively heroic, or at least largely non-criminal, portraits of military service in the World War II-era Pulitzer Prize winners discussed above to the portrait of service in the Iraq War offered by Nico Walker in his semi-autobiographical 2018 novel *Cherry*, which has since been adapted into a film. Walker dropped out of college, served as a medic in Iraq in 2005 and 2006, then became addicted to heroin, robbed a series of banks in Ohio, and wrote the novel with the help of several editors while in federal prison.[19] The section of the novel set in Iraq places casual substance abuse and the gratuitous, sometimes sadistic harming of Iraqis at or near the core of the enlisted U.S. military experience in Iraq, alongside relentless orders to carry out pointless missions and the ever-present risk of being injured or killed, usually at random, often by IEDs.

The narrator's unit arrives in Iraq to take over for a Mississippi National Guard unit that had assembled the "pictures of their kills...into a PowerPoint slide show called 'Towelhead Takedown'" (102). Iraqis are referred to indiscriminately as "hajis" (125). The narrator goes on nighttime raids, kicking in doors and finding "the ubiquitous women and children, the ubiquitous old man" (124). When injuries inevitably result, and, for example, a soldier breaks the leg of a naked young Iraqi man, the first sergeant shows no concern: "'No harm, no foul'" (124–25). During the day, the narrator patrols with "[t]ough guys" who "said they wanted to kill somebody, really anybody if it came to it" (131). In a central scene, shrouded in unknowns, the unit seems to kill a young Iraqi man simply because he is sleeping outside of his house, and then accidentally kills his mother in the confusion that follows (140–47). Meanwhile, the narrator fires repeatedly at the family's cow (143–44). By the end of his tour, "those of us who'd been kicking in doors and tearing houses up and shooting people, we were psychotic," and the narrator refers ambiguously to "occasional murders"—whether by Iraqis or Americans or both is left unstated (175). Some members of the narrator's unit have taken to filming elaborate "snuff films" with mice (177), and the narrator joins in the widespread abuse of inhalants, narcotics, marijuana edibles, cocaine, prescription drugs, and alcohol shipped from the United States or purchased from Iraqis (155, 171, 183). In general, U.S. military wrongdoing of various kinds is presented as the central thread in *Cherry*'s account of the war.

As the more detailed discussion of Iraq War novels in subsequent chapters suggests, *Cherry* is not exceptional in its emphasis on misconduct and criminality, even if it takes this emphasis to an almost parodic extreme. In the words of the Iraq War veteran and novelist Brian Van Reet:

> When I first heard of [Walker] and his autobiographical novel, I confess my reaction to it was not-so-gentle bemusement. Oh great, I thought. An Iraq-veteran-junkie-bank-robber novelist. We have truly jumped the shark in this genre...I feared the rest of us, in the wake of his book, would now have to deal with its confirmation of a damaging stereotype about this generation of veterans: that we are no more than mindless thugs who, by virtue of our participation in a criminal war, are criminals at heart, if not by the letter of the law.[20]

But Van Reet also observes that Walker's narrator acknowledges what some of the novel's reviewers have not: "[t]he narrator's drug use, thrill-seeking and criminality predate his PTSD. They predate even his enlistment in the [A]rmy."[21] Looking back at the wreck of his life, the narrator rejects the idea that his heroin addiction and armed robberies were solely the result of his military service: "I'd been born that way...and it was only a coincidence that I had been to a war and the war probably hadn't had much to do at all with my being fucked in the head" (198). Against the impulse to understand Walker's novel as the story of a traumatized soldier-victim, the novel itself suggests something different. The narrator's military experiences in Iraq are presented as just another chapter in a tale of destruction and self-destruction, coming before the narrator's heroin addiction and bank robberies but after other drug-fueled adventures (17). The novel implicitly frames the narrator's military service as just one more episode in a life of criminal escapades.

***

Let us provisionally assume that Chapters 5 through 9 succeed in showing that narratives of criminality do, in fact, play an unusually prominent role in American fiction about the Iraq War. Let us also assume that many of the celebrated American novels of World War II written shortly after the war paid notably less attention to U.S. wrongdoing toward foreign civilians and soldiers, despite the apparent frequency of such wrongdoing, especially in the Pacific theater. How can the disparity be explained? The next chapter will suggest that the heightened attention to U.S. military wrongdoing in Iraq War fiction may result in part from a shift in cultural understandings of war and crime. But before reaching this argument, it may be useful to address an alternative explanation for the attention to U.S. wrongdoing in Iraq War fiction.

It might be argued that the remarkable prominence of narratives of criminality in fiction about the U.S. forces in Iraq reflects something about the nature of American military service there, even if that service was not defined by an exceptional frequency of wrongdoing. Perhaps there were recurring elements in the experiences of U.S. soldiers in the Iraq War that made it difficult to tell stories in which these soldiers appeared either as traditional heroes or as pure victims.

The simplest way to convey a sense of these recurring elements may be to combine them into a brief story:

> *You are an American soldier in Iraq. You are not entirely sure why you are here. It is clear that the war is not going as planned, and whatever you are doing is not helping.*
>
> *Your life is an endless series of miseries. The unbearably hot days. The stench of burning garbage, open sewage, and days-old sweat. Bad food. Dehydration. Begging children. Heavy equipment. Filthy toilets, or no toilets at all. You do not speak the language or understand the culture.*
>
> *You spend your days driving a Humvee around on patrol through a city of people who hate you, or who at least do not care enough about your life to risk their own by helping you. At any moment, you or your friends could be killed by an IED, or some other source of death arriving randomly and without warning. Or you spend your days at a checkpoint dealing with angry people whose language you cannot understand. At any moment, you or your friends could be killed by a suicide bomber, or a VBIED, or something else. Or you spend your days in a convoy, jostling along in a Humvee that could be blown up at any moment. When you are not outside the wire, you sit in a poorly protected FOB where you and your friends could be killed by mortar fire at any time.*
>
> *You spend weeks or months in a continuous state of high alert. You have seen gaping wounds, severed limbs, and random obscenities like a spine separated from its body.*

There are no big battles against an enemy. It is usually impossible to tell the Iraqis who are trying to kill you from those who are not. Because the insurgents pretend to be civilians, it is more or less impossible to protect your fellow troops without sometimes mistakenly killing innocent Iraqi civilians.

There will be cars that approach your checkpoint and for whatever reason fail to stop quickly after a warning shot. Or cars that approach your convoy and fail to back off quickly after a warning shot. Or there will be men holding cell phones ambiguously and watching your patrol pass. Or unclear reports of enemy fire from a location where there might or might not be civilians. If you spend enough time at a checkpoint, or in a convoy, or on patrol, the tactics of the insurgents make it basically inevitable that you will either shoot an innocent Iraqi who appears to be an insurgent, or you will fail to shoot someone who will turn out to be an insurgent and who will then kill or wound your friends.[22]

While you experience all of this, other soldiers sit in comfortable, safe bases with Burger Kings. The soldiers in the Green Zone enjoy a disco and two Chinese restaurants. Private contractors rake in money while the Army did not armor your Humvee or provide you with effective body armor.

When you email your family, it is clear that no one has any idea what is going on, and you do not know how to tell them.

You just want to go home.

Shortly before your tour is set to end, the mission is extended.

It has been said that there is no such thing as an anti-war film.[23] It is true that many war movies, no matter how grim and disillusioned they might try to be, end up presenting war as a sublime departure from ordinary experience. The more horrific and surreal the portrayal of war, the more of a departure war represents from the presumed meaningless banality of the ordinary viewer's life.

It is difficult to imagine anyone reading the story above, however, and wishing to share in the experience, much less applying terms like "sublime," "transcendent," or "revelatory" to it.[24] The story's lack of appeal may, in fact, go some way toward explaining the poor box-office performance of every movie about the Iraq War prior to *American Sniper*—which, as discussed in Chapter 8, is in many ways a traditional hero story, and contains relatively few of the elements in the story sketched above.[25]

More importantly for the purposes of this book, the story above offers hints of why fiction about the Iraq War partially or wholly from the perspective of U.S. soldiers might be haunted by the question of criminality. The practice of urban counterinsurgency will almost inevitably lead to soldiers killing civilians that they mistakenly believe are part of the insurgent threat. By blending in with the civilian population and refusing to comply with the laws of war, insurgents often deliberately invite such mistakes and tend to benefit from them, because the killing of civilians, mistaken or not, tends to turn a population against those doing the killing.[26] It is not surprising that stories about soldiers caught in the virtually unwinnable trap of an occupation-based counterinsurgency might end up haunted by guilt.

The practice of urban counterinsurgency will also almost inevitably lead to some soldiers resenting, or even violently hating, local civilians for failing to identify and separate themselves from the insurgents. If the counterinsurgent forces perceive themselves as having a sharply distinct identity from that of the local population—as will likely happen in an occupation where the occupier has a different national identity, language, majority religion, and majority ethnicity than the occupied—then it will be very easy for resentment against uncooperative and apparently complicit civilians to bleed over into a sense that the local population more or less as a whole is the enemy. At that point, it becomes more likely that soldiers will use force against civilians not only by mistake, but intentionally—as a precautionary measure, or out of hatred or a desire for revenge. If soldiers believe they have actually identified an insurgent, the potential for criminal abuses, such as through the execution of the wounded or detainees, or the mutilation of a corpse, will loom even larger.

If the story sketched above had some redemption at the end, a sense that the soldiers and civilians who were wounded and killed had suffered these fates for some reason, then it might be easier for soldiers to look past any criminality during the struggle as a regrettable excess, but one mitigated by the good intentions and overall beneficence of the mission. It is one thing for soldiers to commit crimes in a war that results, for example, in the liberation of Europe from Hitler; it is something else for crimes to take place in an unprovoked war that strengthens the nation's enemies, results in a new birth of terrorism, and virtually destroys the country it is intended to liberate. American veterans returning from World War II had available to them a source of comforting rationalizations, an argument for the mitigation of any wrongs, that American veterans of the Iraq War tragically do not have. In that sense, it would be reasonable to see the focus on narratives of soldier criminality in Iraq War fiction as in part a reflection of facts about the war, or at least of a widely shared view of the war as a failure.

Nevertheless, the features of the Iraq War and of U.S. soldiers' experiences in it noted above would probably not have been *sufficient* to result in the prominence of soldier criminality in Iraq War fiction discussed in the chapters below. The next chapter suggests that something else was necessary, a shift in the culture of war, and especially in cultural understandings of the relationship between war and crime. Without the changes in values described in the next chapter, it is easy to imagine the American fiction of the Iraq War having been far less focused on soldier wrongdoing and harms to Iraqi civilians. Storytellers could simply have created new variations on the narrative template of the soldier-as-victim, emphasizing the suffering of ordinary American soldiers while largely ignoring any sufferings they might have caused.

CHAPTER FOUR

THE COSMOPOLITAN TRANSFORMATION OF WAR AND CRIME

The distinction between war and crime, although neither universal nor obvious, can be seen to underlie a great deal of conventional modern thinking about the morality of violence.

To begin with, nearly every culture has drawn normative lines between praiseworthy and blameworthy violence, and some of these lines have often corresponded to boundaries between "in-groups" and "out-groups."[1] It may be true that in many tribal societies, as the historian Azar Gat has argued, "[o]ur state-based distinction between external war and internal peace had scant validity."[2] Gat's research suggests that in stateless societies, there has often been less of a clear sense that the contrast between "us" and "them," wherever that line was drawn at any moment, correlated with a contrast between the absence of group fighting ("peace") and its presence ("war").

But the rise of the state facilitated a particular articulation of the distinction between praiseworthy and blameworthy violence. In essence, the paradigmatic example of blameworthy violence became one member of the state killing another, while the paradigmatic example of praiseworthy violence became members of the state, together, killing others from outside the state.[3] The centralization and hierarchy that define states as political organizations tend to sharpen the boundary between those who are "inside" and "outside" of the state's authority, making possible the now intuitively familiar distinction "between murder and feud, on the one hand, and war, on the other."[4] Murder typically involved the killing of one member of the state by another, and was generally condemned; war typically involved the killing of those outside the state, and was often celebrated.

A poetic expression of the state-based opposition between righteous external war violence and egregious internal criminal violence appears toward the conclusion of Aeschylus' *Oresteia*, which tells the mythologized story of the founding of Athens' homicide court, the Areopagus. The chorus of Furies, now transformed into "the Kindly Ones" (Eumenides), declares:

> [M]ay the dust not drink the black blood of the citizens
> and through passion for revenge
> speed on the ruin to the city
> wrought by murder in return for murder!
> But may each give joy to each,
> in a spirit of love toward the common weal,
> and may they hate with one accord,
> for many are the sorrows among mortals that this can cure.[5]

In the Schmittian view of the Eumenides, even as it was right for Athena to establish a homicide court to prevent murderous blood-feuds *within* the Athenian community, uniting in hatred toward enemies *outside* of the community should be embraced as well.[6]

Similarly, in Book V of the *Republic*, Plato draws a contrast between "war" (*polemos*) against "natural enemies" (that is, barbarians), which he does not have Socrates condemn, and "civil war" (*stasis*) against "natural friends" (that is, other Greeks), which Socrates condemns as "sick."[7] In modern times, Hobbes' defense of the state as a source of security, in opposition to the "[w]arre of every one against every one" in the anarchic state of nature, as well as his call for submission to state authority as a better alternative to the horrors of civil war, associates internal peace with the foundations of the state's legitimacy.[8] Max Weber's definition of the state in terms of its monopoly on the legitimate use of force likewise suggests that the maintenance of internal peace—against both internal and external threats—is central to the identity of the state.[9]

In sum, the rise of the state brought with it the idea that the dividing line between peace and war should generally coincide with the boundaries of the state—or coalition of states, in the case of a federation or alliance. There should be peace within, and any violence—other than, of course, any state violence necessary to ensure internal peace—should be directed externally. This vision of "internal peace" and "external war," to use Gat's terms again, expresses the state-focused articulation of the moral distinction between blameworthy and praiseworthy violence. The paradigmatic form of praiseworthy violence becomes "war," which involves organized violence against external enemies of the state; while the paradigmatic form of blameworthy violence becomes "crime," or more specifically "assault" or "murder," which involves unauthorized violence between members of the state.

Thus, "war" and "crime" have come to serve as two separate and morally distinct conceptual boxes into which most acts of violence can be placed.[10] According to this state-based categorization of violence, if someone were asked to offer a moral evaluation of an act of violence described in the abstract—for example, "the deliberate killing of another human being, not in self-defense"—the first question that the respondent might want to ask is whether the killing took place as part of a war. If not, it was probably a crime; if so, it very well might not have been.

If we put ourselves in the shoes of someone not accustomed to thinking in terms of the distinction between war and crime, the positive judgment of violence in war and the negative judgment of violence in crime might seem shocking. After all, violence is violence—why should any killing not be condemned? But as Barbara Ehrenreich notes in *Blood Rites*, her wide-ranging study of war culture, "War not only departs from the normal; it inverts all that is moral and right: In war one *should* kill, *should* steal, *should* burn cities and farms, should perhaps even rape matrons and little girls."[11] Acts that in ordinary life would be grave wrongs or, in a legalized society, violations of the criminal law—such as murder, rape, and theft—have often been treated as acceptable, desirable, or even imperative in war, as when Moses commands the Children of Israel to massacre all the men and adult women of Midian, but "all the women children...keep alive for yourselves" (Numbers 31:7–9, 31:17–18). Retired Army lieutenant general and moral philosopher James Dubik, who served as a commander in Iraq from 2007 to 2008, notes that in war, "the morally repugnant *is* the morally permissible, and even the morally necessary...War justifies—more importantly, demands—what, in peacetime, would be unjustifiable: the destruction of the lives and happiness of others."[12]

It is true that critics of war throughout history, including, for example, the ancient Chinese writer Mozi, have questioned why the murder of one person should be viewed as a crime, and the murder of ten should be seen as an even worse crime, but the murder of thousands in a war should be treated as no crime at all, or even as a cause for celebration.[13] But the very fact that such arguments tend to be phrased and seen as provocations, rather than reflections of a broadly shared cultural assumption, suggests the general strength and pervasiveness of the distinction between what is moral in a state of war and what is moral in a state of peace.

Just as the rise of the state enabled the opposition between war and crime, however, political, cultural, and legal developments in recent centuries, and especially in the last several decades, have begun to undermine that distinction. One of the arguments of this book is that the focus on U.S. military criminality in Iraq War literature is in part a product of the eroding of the distinction between war and crime. The novels discussed in this book reflect the growth of an increasingly "criminalized" view of war, a view of war as a site of criminality, in contrast to the traditional state-based conception that holds war violence and criminal violence apart from each other, in carefully insulated conceptual and moral boxes—so far apart, in fact, that it might simply never occur to a civilian observer to compare soldiers killing in battle to murder.[14]

Three developments in particular have contributed to the recent erosion of the conventional distinction between war and crime. Each of the developments can be seen gaining momentum unevenly over the last two hundred and fifty years, and each is particularly well-documented in the last seventy-five years. First, over the last two and a half centuries, but especially in the last seventy-five years, the relative rise in the cultural strength of moral cosmopolitanism has made earlier moral defenses of violence in war based on dehumanizing xenophobic or racist distinctions between "us" and "them" increasingly hard to defend. Second, the relative decline of martial values in favor of commercial values has stripped war itself of much of its cultural prestige, weakening the normative valuation of war that helped to support the moral contrast between war and crime. Third, the development of what Ruti Teitel has called "humanity's law," and in particular international humanitarian law, human rights law, and international criminal law, has made it increasingly feasible to conceptualize war as already or potentially subject to criminal regulation, against the argument that war is in some sense inherently lawless.[15] In the following sections, I will very briefly address each of the three developments in turn. In each case, by necessity, I offer a radically condensed summary. A less schematic account could of course draw attention to the innumerable fluctuations, reversals, and local variations that have taken place within the larger trends, the difficulty of measuring public values, and the pervasiveness of conflicts between values and behaviors. A history of the rise of cosmopolitan values could just as well be told as a history of hypocrisy.

THE RELATIVE RISE OF MORAL COSMOPOLITANISM

First, despite the many critiques that have been offered of celebratory accounts of the rise of "human rights," the legacy of "the Enlightenment," or the triumph of "liberalism," the evidence remains overwhelming of a long-term shift in many parts of the world over the last two and a half centuries in the direction of more cosmopolitan and egalitarian values.[16] The evidence of the shift over the last seventy-five years is especially well-documented. To take just one example, Gallup polling found that 94% of the American public supported interracial marriage in 2021, as opposed to only around 40% as recently as 1980, and only roughly 5% in 1960.[17] Over the last several decades, global polling such as the World Values Survey has found with remarkable consistency that increases in material security have led, usually after a generational lag, to rises in cosmopolitan and egalitarian values.[18]

It is sufficient for my argument to note that, within the United States, racism and other anti-cosmopolitan values have declined over the last several decades, which has made it increasingly difficult to dismiss the moral weight of harms to non-Americans caused by the U.S. military in war. The conventional moral distinction between praiseworthy violence in the context of war and blameworthy violence in the context of crime becomes harder to sustain once moral cosmopolitanism begins to undermine moral distinctions between the populations of different states. Just as it would probably have been inconceivable during World War II for *Life* magazine to have published an admiring photograph of a young American woman with a German or Italian skull sent by her fiancé, although the magazine had no qualms publishing such a photograph featuring a Japanese skull, today it would be inconceivable for any mainstream American publication to publish such a photograph involving the skull of any enemy soldier, regardless of race or ethnicity. The circle of moral recognition has expanded to include all of humanity, at least to this minimal degree.

It is surely no coincidence that the growth of cosmopolitan and egalitarian values in the United States has coincided with the changes in U.S. war literature described in this book. To the extent that Americans, and especially the kinds of Americans who tend to write and read literary fiction, have become less willing to discount the suffering of others based on differences of race, nationality, or religion, it is not surprising that this growing moral cosmopolitanism would be reflected in a growing attentiveness to the suffering of foreign civilians, and even foreign fighters, in fiction about America's wars—and especially to the uncomfortable exploration of U.S. responsibility for those harms.

THE RELATIVE DECLINE OF MARTIAL CULTURE

Second, the war-crime distinction has also likely been eroded by the decline of martial culture and values, a decline that in recent decades has tended to proceed in tandem with the rise of moral cosmopolitanism and egalitarianism.[19]

We have already seen, in Chapter 2, the centrality of warrior values in ancient aristocratic cultures. The caste-like medieval notion of the "three estates"—a social order defined by "those who pray (monks and ecclesiastics), those who fight (nobility), and those who work (peasants)"[20]—continued to identify nobility with martial prowess, and to place war near the center of culture. Hirschman notes the continuity between medieval chivalric ideals and the celebration of the pursuit of glory in the Renaissance.[21]

But critiques of the valorization of war gained prominence in the seventeenth and eighteenth centuries, even as the prevailing view continued to be that killing in war was "not only lawful but glorious."[22] The nineteenth century saw Benjamin Constant's dismissal of "the spirit of conquest" as an anachronism in the "age of commerce, an age which must necessarily replace that of war," as well as the growth of an international, evangelical Christian peace movement.[23] Just as talk of the "rights of man" gave way to biological racism and imperialism by the end of the nineteenth century, however, so the critique of war often gave way in the later nineteenth century to the romantic militarism and nationalism that culminated in World War I.

As already noted in Chapter 2, the horrors of World War I contributed to the idea of soldiers as victims that dominated war literature throughout much of the twentieth century. But the prestige of war still had further room to fall. In the United States, the Vietnam War and the antiwar movement brought military service into disrepute, and even undermined the confidence of military officers in their own chosen careers. Since then, what Andrew Bacevich calls the "new American militarism" has restored the U.S. military's standing in the eyes of the American public. But despite the war fever that followed the September 11 attacks and helped to fuel the Iraq War, and notwithstanding the committed, ongoing militarism of various factions in U.S. politics, the overall trend both in the United States and globally over the last several decades has been a decrease in individuals' willingness to fight for their countries.[24] Inglehart attributes the apparent shift against militarism to the continuing rise of what he calls "individual-choice values," which in turn are strongly linked with increases in material security, gender equality, and declining rates of violence.[25]

The decline of martial values, like the rise of cosmopolitan and egalitarian values, facilitates the blurring of the distinction between war and crime. To the extent that war is no longer perceived as a glorious adventure, it becomes easier to evaluate the violence of war through the same moral frameworks used for violence outside of war.

THE INCREASING CRIMINALIZATION OF WAR

Third, the last two centuries have witnessed the transformation of the legal distinctions between war and crime, especially in the period since the end of World War II. A brief history here could begin by noting that in the seventeenth century, European states started adopting an understanding of the legal rules of war proposed by theorists such as Hugo Grotius, Samuel von Pufendorf, and Emer de Vattel. As critics have observed, these theories of what would eventually become known as "international law" were often more concerned with establishing rational procedures for distributing the gains from conquest than with preventing war or imposing legal constraints on the conduct of war. From an internal legal perspective, in fact, the early modern laws of war were notable for the clarity with which they established the legal authorization for mass killing. As Oona Hathaway and Scott Shapiro observe, "[t]he soldier's right to kill in war…is of such antiquity that it is almost impossible to find an explicit statement of it before Grotius."[26] Grotius formulated the rule that came to be adopted by European states, according to which soldiers enjoy an absolute immunity from prosecution for killing enemy soldiers, provided that there has been a proper declaration of war, and regardless of whether the declared war is just or unjust. Echoing the longstanding recognition of a moral difference between killing in war and killing in peace, discussed above, Grotius asserted that there is a legal difference as well.

But regardless of the motives of Grotius and those who adopted and developed his ideas, the "legalization" of war—the growing acceptance that war was bound by law, however permissive the laws were initially said to be[27]—laid the foundation for the eventual imposition of more meaningfully humanitarian legal constraints. The latter project accelerated in the nineteenth century with the creation of the Red Cross, the foundation of the modern laws of *jus in bello* in the Lieber Code issued by President Lincoln, and the attempts of international lawyers to prevent and limit wars through multilateral treaties in the later nineteenth and early twentieth century.[28]

Efforts to constrain war through international law and international legal institutions continued after World War I through the League of Nations and the Kellogg-Briand Pact, and again, more enduringly, after

World War II through the establishment of the United Nations, the restrictions on the use of force in the UN Charter, and the 1949 Geneva Conventions. Finally, the modern idea of the "war crime," a term coined by Lieber but "rarely referenced before the mid-twentieth century," gained broad recognition through the Nuremberg trials, "the first time in history that an international tribunal heard cases of war crimes, crimes against the peace, and crimes against humanity."[29] The traditional distinctions between war and crime continued to erode.

Indeed, if one views the killing of human beings as at least presumptively criminal, then war in general may come to seem an exercise in criminality. This is how the early-twentieth-century anti-war activist lawyers in Hathaway's and Shapiro's history viewed war. Salmon Levinson, who pushed for the outlawing of aggressive war between states through the Kellogg–Briand Pact, compared war to dueling. Just as dueling came to be seen as "plain murder under our laws," so war might be outlawed: "it would be branded as a crime and the force of the world would be organized to deal with the criminal." James Shotwell, who ghostwrote the Pact and helped develop the UN Charter, similarly argued that "aggressive war is an international crime."[30]

Despite the questionable legality of some aspects of the war crimes prosecutions after World War II, they offered a warning to all future warmakers, suggesting that anyone initiating or engaged in a war might find himself, one day, on trial for criminal violations of international law. After Nuremberg, the choice to go to war, once seen as virtually definitive of state sovereignty and beyond the reach of any higher legal authority, increasingly came to be seen as subject to meaningful legal constraints, and potentially punishable as a criminal act.

Among many other innovations, the Nuremberg trials also cast a shadow of potential criminality over future military conflicts by rejecting the validity of two possible defenses against war crimes charges: first, that the defendant's act was legal under domestic law; and second, that the defendant was simply "following orders." In both cases, these "Nuremberg principles" reflected the cosmopolitan view that there exists a binding international law above the sovereignty of individual states, including criminal prohibitions that no state, and *a fortiori* no military commander, may abrogate.

As further evidence of the expanding role of law in war, the U.S. military bureaucracy embraced international humanitarian law in the years after Vietnam, and legally trained JAG (Judge Advocate General) officers began to have significant roles in planning and operations during the invasion of Panama and the Gulf War.[31] Especially after the end of the Cold War, the application of international criminal law to conduct in armed conflicts also continued to grow. In 1993 and 1994, the United Nations established ad hoc tribunals for prosecuting various international criminal law violations in the conflicts in the former Yugoslavia and Rwanda. In 1998, over a hundred states signed the Rome Statute establishing the International Criminal Court ("ICC").

A final reflection of the blurring of the traditional moral and legal lines between violence inside and outside of war can be found in "revisionist" challenges to traditional just war theory, such as in the work of the philosopher Jeff McMahan. McMahan has attacked the dominant view that "in a state of war, the practice of killing is governed by different moral principles from those that govern acts of killing in other contexts," as well as the assumption that "moral responsibility for the wrongful killing that occurs when an unjust war is fought lies solely with the political leaders whose decision it was to go to war."[32] In other words, McMahan's approach would bring the moral analysis of war much closer to the moral analysis of crime.

***

The interrelated developments described in this section—the rise of cosmopolitan values, the decline of martial culture, and developments in international criminal law—have all contributed to the erosion of the traditional distinction between praiseworthy violence in the context of war and blameworthy violence in the context of crime. Instead, an increasingly "criminalized" view of war has taken hold in significant parts of contemporary culture, both in the United States and in other countries.

The blurring of the line between war and crime is reflected even in the doctrines and training of many militaries around the world, including the U.S. military. As the legal scholar David Kennedy has noted, "[l]aw has crept into the war machine. The battlespace is as legally regulated as the rest of modern life."[33] Military operations are routinely preceded by a military lawyer offering a briefing on the rules of engagement ("ROEs").[34] Lawyers at higher levels of command have crafted these rules to comply with the laws of armed conflict, and to avoid the commission of war crimes. In terms of doctrine and training, the U.S. military simply accepts that it is bound by constraints on its behavior under international law.

THE IRAQ WAR AND MORAL COSMOPOLITANISM

The Iraq War took place against the background of the developments described above: the growth of moral cosmopolitanism, the decline of martial culture, and the increasing criminalization of war. In the 1990s, the cosmopolitan discourse of "human rights" became the dominant framework for a variety of international debates, activities, and institutions. At the same time, the memorialization of the Holocaust became a powerful, unifying aspect of European culture, as well as a prominent feature in the moral landscape of Western culture more generally. Although the term "genocide" did not exist before World War II, and the attempted extermination of Europe's Jews was not specifically charged at Nuremberg, the idea of the Holocaust as the ultimate crime took hold.[35]

Against the background of post-Cold War debates about human rights, humanitarian intervention, globalization, the importance of transnational non-governmental organizations, and even the term "cosmopolitanism" itself, the world also experienced a dramatic increase in attention to and prosecution of war crimes. If it is correct that moral cosmopolitanism and the criminalization of war are related, then it is no coincidence that the flourishing of cosmopolitan discourse in the 1990s and early 2000s was accompanied by the creation of the first standing court existing solely for the prosecution of international crimes, nor that the four categories of crime within the ICC's jurisdiction—genocide, crimes against humanity, war crimes, and crimes of aggression—generally or exclusively take place in the context of armed conflicts. Where the view of humanity as a single community takes root, the criminalization of war seems to follow.

The administration of George W. Bush routinely expressed contempt for and flouted international law, from the signing of the 2002 American Service-Members' Protection Act, authorizing an invasion of the Hague if the ICC ever attempted to arrest an American soldier; to the legal approval of torture by government lawyers such as John Yoo and Jay Bybee, in violation of the UN Convention Against Torture; to the decision to invade Iraq at least arguably illegally, without clear UN authorization or a justification based on self-defense. Yet it is noteworthy that the Bush administration felt obligated to make a case to the United Nations at all, that lawyers were consulted about the legality of various methods of torture, and that Yoo and Bybee apparently felt compelled to present the torture they authorized as complying with the Convention Against Torture, rather than simply rejecting the validity or relevance of international law in the context of war altogether.

Indeed, as much as the promoters and planners of the Iraq War drew on illiberal rhetoric and emotional appeals to militaristic tribalism, prefigured in Bush's declaration to the world on September 20, 2001 that "[e]ither you are with us, or you are with the terrorists,"[36] the Iraq War was not introduced as a lawless battle to the death between existentially opposed friends and enemies. Rather, many of the war's proponents presented it, disingenuously or not, in part as a humanitarian intervention, an attempt to topple a tyrant in the name of cosmopolitan ideals such as human rights.[37]

Far from the kind of traditional war of conquest that was a standard feature of international relations until the end of World War II,[38] the Iraq War was apparently intended by its leading planners, such as Secretary of Defense Donald Rumsfeld, to be a brief and decisive military intervention followed by a quick U.S. withdrawal and handover of sovereignty to the Iraqi people. Even the neoconservatives mentioned in the introduction, above, relied in part on cosmopolitan assumptions, or at least cosmopolitan rhetoric. If they presented the Iraq War as a partial repudiation of the existing international order in the name of unchecked American supremacy, their arguments were also premised on an image of humanity in which all people desire freedom—and not just any freedom, but the same Western liberalism that they believed to be best for themselves, including the emancipation of women, the separation of church and state, and a general emphasis on the rights of individuals.

Thus, from the start, the Iraq War existed in an ambiguous, uncertain, and deeply incoherent relationship to both cosmopolitanism and the criminalization of war. The war repudiated cosmopolitan values in order to defend them. It scorned the international legal order, but made a point of engaging it, only to violate it. After any initial euphoria in Iraq resulting from the invasion had given way to anarchy and crime, and then to suicide bombings, insurgency, and civil war, the contradictions of the war continued to grow. American soldiers were invited to view the people of Iraq both as exactly like "us," in the sense of sharing our love for individual freedom and the rule of law, but also as unknowably different, and entangled in exotic Oriental traditions that required explanation through works such as Raphael Patai's infamous *The Arab Mind*. Iraqis were increasingly seen both as American soldiers' necessary allies in the war and as the enemies trying to kill them.

In his novel *Spoils*, Brian Van Reet captures some of the ambiguity in the U.S. military experience of the Iraq War when his soldier protagonist, Cassandra, recalls "a few lines of jogging cadence sung during early-morning physical training sessions at Fort Hood before they deployed":

> *Line a hundred Iraqis up against a wall.*
> *Bet a hundred dollars I couldn't kill 'em all.*
> *Shot ninety-eight till my barrel turned blue.*
> *Then I pulled out my knife and stabbed the other two.* (10)[39]

Alongside this traditional militarist invitation to revel in violence against an enemy, Cassandra notes, the soldiers were also "told, over and over, to the point of indoctrination, that one half of their mission was to free this country, that they would go down in history as the great liberators of the Iraqi people" (13). Another character, Sleed, who is a tank crewman, as Van Reet was, and whose passages are presented as first-person narration, is troubled by his tank commander, SGT Galvan, repeatedly committing a war crime by taking pictures of dead Iraqi troops without any legal justification. "'You ain't worried about those Geneva Conventions or nothing, huh, Sergeant?'" Sleed says to Galvan, who takes another picture and replies: "'Don't you know this whole fucking war is illegal?'" (53).

As already suggested in Chapter 3, in any counterinsurgency operation in a foreign country, there will be a tension between viewing the local population as an ally and as a threat. The same was often true for

American soldiers in Vietnam. But this tension was significantly heightened for the U.S. military in the Iraq War by the progress of moral cosmopolitanism and the increased attention to war crimes and human rights violations in the preceding decades. This is surely one reason that a much higher proportion of Iraq War fiction has attempted to take the perspective of Iraqi people or insurgents, compared to the proportion of Vietnam War fiction by American writers that attempted to take the perspective of Vietnamese people.[40] It appears to be harder today than it was in the 1960s and 1970s for American soldiers to avoid questioning how their presence and behavior might appear from the local population's points of view.

In sum, unlike the anti-war literature of the twentieth century, from Remarque to O'Brien, which tended to condemn war in general, often saw fallen soldiers on both sides equally as victims, and viewed the distinction between heroes and villains, "good guys" and "bad guys," as part of the illusion that battlefield experience strips away, Iraq War fiction is war literature written in the wake of Nuremberg. In the eyes of contemporary international humanitarian law, some states may be engaged in more criminal conduct than others—and if you find yourself on the side of criminals, simply "following orders" might make you a criminal as well. This perspective exists in tension with the deeply rooted desire of many in the military to believe that they are engaged in a profession sealed off from politics, one that is based on ostensibly apolitical values such as duty, courage, and discipline, where soldiers need not trouble themselves about individually making moral judgments—and where soldiers can trust in the legality of any orders that have passed a lawyer's review.

War fiction written in the spiritual wake of Nuremberg finds itself forced to grapple with the possibility—even if this possibility is ultimately rejected—that the soldiers on one's own side may not be the heroes in the story, or even the victims, but participants in a wrong, and perhaps even complicit in crimes. As the following chapters argue, this troubling possibility lurks throughout a great deal of Iraq War fiction, creating a constant threat of confrontation with the question of criminality, and effectively preventing Iraq War soldier-narratives from following the template of simple stories of heroism or victimhood.

CHAPTER FIVE

THE YELLOW BIRDS (2012)

The Yellow Birds has a plausible claim to being, as of this writing, the canonical American novel of U.S. military service in the Iraq War, at least among novels written by veterans.[1] Published in 2012, the novel was greeted with critical rapture, possibly suggesting a long-unsatisfied demand for a serious literary treatment of soldiers' experiences by a veteran nearly a decade after the war's start.[2] In the ten pages of blurbs at the front of the 2013 paperback edition, luminaries of Anglophone literary culture from Michiko Kakutani, Tom Wolfe, and Dave Eggers, to Colm Tóibín, Robert Olen Butler, Edna O'Brien, and Hilary Mantel place *The Yellow Birds* in the company of the classics of war literature, comparing it to *All Quiet on the Western Front* (twice), *The Red Badge of Courage* (twice), *The Things They Carried* (twice), and *The Naked and the Dead.*[3]

What characters and what events does this foundational novel of the Iraq War choose to place at the center of its story of the war?

The Yellow Birds takes as its narrator and protagonist Private John Bartle, a twenty-one-year-old from a small town in Virginia who joins the Army because he "wanted to be a man" (145) or perhaps because he "got fed up with nothing" (44). Bartle deploys to northern Iraq in 2004 and commits war crimes under the influence of his masterful but sadistic superior, Sergeant Sterling, including aiding in the premeditated murder of an Iraqi civilian. Upon returning to the United States, Bartle remains traumatized by his guilt and flees from a military investigator. He eventually allows himself to be arrested and court-martialed, and he finally finds a measure of peace after serving a prison term.

Based on this description of the novel's plot, it might seem that *The Yellow Birds* has moved beyond both the idea of war as a vehicle for heroic acts, and of war as a vehicle for the victimization of soldiers, to a sense of war as a vehicle for crime. The narrative template seems to be based on sin and redemption through atonement, a type of story familiar not only from religious models but from fictional and nonfictional accounts of reformed gang-members and other criminals. In the latter stories, a rebellious boy may ignore the warnings of his mother—as Bartle does—and fall in with a violent crowd. He gradually loses touch with the righteous values of his upbringing, and commits shameful acts, but in the end finds some kind of redemption through the purifying forces of punishment and repentance. *The Yellow Birds*' plot, based on the summary above, would seem to be a story of crime and punishment—very much in the tradition of Dostoevsky's novel, which also concludes with a vision of penal redemption.

There is certainly something significant in the fact that one of the most prominent literary works of the Iraq War places the crimes of soldiers at its narrative center. As we saw in Chapters 2 and 3, this is simply not the case in the canonical literature of, for example, World Wars I and II, much less the canonical literature of ancient wars. Something has changed in the view of war when war stories become stories of soldiers' crimes, and punishment for those crimes.

Yet upon closer inspection, the approach to the Iraq War in *The Yellow Birds* is more complicated and suffused with unresolved internal tensions than the deliberately partial sketch above would suggest. A more detailed analysis of the novel might begin by noting that it presents two, never reconciled and arguably incompatible, perspectives on the war. Neither is focused on a moral evaluation of the war itself. In fact, contrary to what one might expect if the narrative were truly grounded in a view of the Iraq War as fundamentally wrong or tainted by criminality, any harms caused to the people of Iraq by the U.S. invasion and occupation are a largely peripheral concern.

One of the two overarching perspectives on the Iraq War in *The Yellow Birds* comes through its narrative structure. The other comes through various non-narrative formal aspects of the novel, as well as the protagonist-narrator's reflections on the war and his actions in it. I will discuss the former first.

AMERICAN VICTIMS OF THE IRAQ WAR

Viewed in terms of its narrative structure, *The Yellow Birds* is in fact a story of crime and punishment. But unlike the deliberately partial sketch of the plot above, it is not a story of a crime with an Iraqi victim. The primary victim is eighteen-year-old Private Daniel Murphy ("Murph"), a small boy from rural Virginia who worked in a mine before enlisting. His mother, LaDonna Murphy, can be seen as a secondary victim. During Murph's and Bartle's training in Fort Dix, New Jersey in December 2003, Sergeant Sterling pairs them together, giving Bartle responsibility for protecting the smaller Murph (33). From that moment onward, Murph is Bartle's "[b]attle" (60). (The term is short for "battle buddy," an Army expression for members of a pair of two soldiers who keep track of and watch out for each other.) Later, at a pre-deployment celebration, without thinking, Bartle elevates his perceived responsibility for Murph further by making a promise to LaDonna: "'I promise I'll bring him home to you'" (47). In September 2004, Bartle's and Murph's unit fights its way into the fictional town of Al Tafar in the northern Iraqi province of Nineveh.[4]

By October 2004, Murph has become increasingly withdrawn and finds solace only in observing a female Army medic, a "beautiful girl" who seems to represent a last refuge of compassion in his world (165). After she dies in a mortar attack and Murph sees her corpse, he suffers a breakdown and deserts the Forward Operating Base ("FOB") where his unit is located. He wanders naked and bleeding through Al Tafar, where he is captured and tortured to death by unidentified Iraqis who finally toss his mutilated, eyeless, nearly decapitated body from a minaret (205–6). When Sterling and Bartle find him, the rest of their platoon is out of view (202), and they agree to dispose of Murph's corpse in the nearby Tigris river rather than allow the body to be shipped home, where Murph's mother might one day open his casket (207). They also burn down the minaret (210). In order to leave no witnesses, Sterling murders the Iraqi "cartwright" who helped them (211).[5] Apparently as part of their attempt to cover up these events, Bartle later writes a letter to Murph's mother, pretending to be Murph (185). Bartle and Sterling also apparently construct a "bullshit story" for their superiors about Murph being killed in action, for which Murph receives posthumous "bullshit medals" (69).

After Bartle's service obligation ends, he returns to Virginia and lives with his mother, trying to avoid his guilt and traumatic memories by spending his days drinking (131, 135). Largely uninterested in living, he wanders in a daze into a river and nearly drowns (146). Meanwhile, Murph's mother does not believe the official story of Murph's death, and accuses the Army of covering up the truth (179). When Bartle learns that an investigator from the Army's Criminal Investigation Division is looking for him (148), he moves to an abandoned gasworks building at the edge of a nearby river (177). The investigator finds him. During the arrest scene, the reader receives fragmentary information suggesting that Sterling has committed suicide while under investigation, perhaps in part for the killing of other Iraqi civilians, and that the Army is arresting Bartle in part based on his fraudulent letter to Murph's mother. The Army still does not know what really happened to Murph and apparently does not care (182, 185–9).

In prison, Bartle takes responsibility within himself for breaking his promise to LaDonna: "[Murph's] absence from the family plot was my fault" (219). When LaDonna visits Bartle, he confesses what really happened to Murph, although the reader does not know what Bartle tells her specifically (223). After Bartle's release, he moves to a cabin, where he has apparently written the work that we are now reading (11)—although Bartle as the narrator never explicitly states that what we are reading is his written story. Since arriving at the cabin, Bartle seems to have found a degree of peace that was lacking from the post-deployment scenes before his arrest. The novel ends with Bartle's poetic, imagined vision of Murph's scattered bones being swept out to sea from the Tigris (226). Instead of suggesting guilt, the concluding vision suggests a quasi-religious sense of the smallness and finitude of human beings and their choices beside what endures in nature.

The preceding paragraphs, in any case, outline the story of crime and redemption through confession and punishment that provides the narrative backbone of *The Yellow Birds*. Bartle fills the role of the fallen and then at least partially redeemed criminal, and Murph, along with his mother, fills the role of victim. The novel's narrative structure—that is, the way it tells the story above—strengthens the sense that this story is the novel's ultimate narrative concern. The novel consists of eleven chapters divided into two narrative threads. The first thread—consisting of chapters 1, 4, 6, 8, and 10—takes place between September and October 2004 in Al Tafar, and chronologically tells the story of Bartle's "crime," above all his failure to prevent Murph's death. From its earliest pages, the novel gestures obscurely toward the fact of Murph's death and its importance to Bartle (for example, 4, 12–14, 25), building a sense of suspense that is finally resolved when the novel reveals, in its penultimate chapter, the gruesome details of Murph's death and its aftermath.

The second thread—consisting of chapters 3, 5, 7, 9, and 11—tells the chronological story of Bartle's return home, from his March 2005 arrival in Kaiserslautern, Germany, to his November 2005 arrest in Virginia, to his release from federal detention at Fort Knox, apparently in April 2009 (213). This thread tells the story of Bartle's "punishment": the consequences that unfold in Bartle's life as a result of his failure to prevent Murph's death, and his actions with Sterling after the death. By placing Bartle's arrest in chapter 9, before the reader is finally shown the scene of the crime in chapter 10, the novel further heightens the sense of suspense surrounding the crime. Chapter 2, the only chapter lying outside the chronological progressions in the two threads above, takes place during Bartle's and Murph's training at Fort Dix in 2003. It plants another seed of suspense when the narrator refers obliquely to his writing "a letter to a dead boy's mother" in the dead boy's name (30), and states that doing this was a "terrible thing," among various "other terrible things I think about" (31). The chapter culminates in Bartle's promise to LaDonna Murphy to bring Murph home (47). This is, of course, a promise that Bartle breaks by failing to prevent Murph's death, and by preventing his body from being repatriated.

In sum, *The Yellow Birds* presents the narrative of Bartle's actions leading up to and following Murph's death as a gradually revealed story of crime and punishment, with Bartle as the criminal or figure of guilt (166), and Murph and his mother as the victims. It is almost as though *The Yellow Birds* is structured as a mystery with the details surrounding Murph's death as its resolution. Murph's death is the novel's narrative center, the essential event that the rest of the plot either leads to (as in the first narrative thread above) or follows from (as in the second thread).

A LYRICAL VIEW OF IRAQI DEATH

As suggested above, however, the narrative structure of *The Yellow Birds* exists in tension with various formal aspects of the novel other than the plot, as well as many of the narrator's own explicit meditations on the war and his role in it. Instead of emphasizing the causal significance of human action and the weight of personal responsibility, as one would expect in a story of crime and punishment, many of the novel's formal choices and the narrator's statements suggest a vision of a world governed by vast, impersonal, and apparently random forces, such that the events of the world are both necessary, at least in the sense of lying beyond human control, and yet adhere to no meaningful design or pattern.

Indeed, from the novel's opening sentence to its final pages, *The Yellow Birds* returns continually to this vision of a world in thrall to inhuman causal forces, and a corresponding sense that human beings are not in fact responsible for what might appear to be the consequences of human actions. The celebrated first sentence of the novel—"The war tried to kill us in the spring" (3)—is not simply a lyrical flourish, but the opening statement of an extended personification of "the war" as a source of causation, a conceit developed explicitly over the next two pages and, arguably, implicitly over the remainder of the novel. The war prays, fasts, makes love, and gives birth (3). The war not only tries to kill U.S. soldiers, it succeeds in killing thousands of Iraqis whose "bodies lined the pocked avenues at irregular intervals" (4). Here we are far from the sense of guilt and personal responsibility that Bartle feels in relation to Murph's death. No one in particular, it seems, has caused the deaths of these Iraqis who have died in the wake of the U.S. invasion and occupation. Rather, their deaths are the result of a faceless, inhuman abstraction: "the war."

The figurative language and imagery of *The Yellow Birds* repeatedly downplays the significance of human agency. The clearest examples appear in the context of violence toward Iraqis. It is common in battle scenes in modern war literature for the author to attempt to convey the sometimes dissociative aspects of the experience of combat by presenting a disorienting succession of extreme sensory stimuli, often connected by no apparent logic or sense. *The Yellow Birds* employs this technique in its descriptions of battle against Iraqis, as when the narrator notes that after one battle started, "[i]t seemed as if the movement of one moment to the next had its own trajectory, a thing both finite and expansive, like the endless divisibility of numbers strung out on a line" (11). Even when Bartle himself fatally shoots an armed Iraqi, the action happens at a distance, as though in a dissociative state, not as a result of his own agency: "I realized with a great shock that I was shooting at him and that I wouldn't stop until I was sure that he was dead" (21). For a moment during the firefight, Bartle had wondered, "'What kind of men are we?'" (21), but the moral questioning passes without a trace along with all the disconnected sensations. Again, after the soldiers enter Al Tafar, Bartle presents them as "seeming to follow the destruction as it spread rather than spreading it ourselves" (123), as though some disembodied universal force of entropy had caused the damage to the city, rather than the weapons of the U.S. soldiers and their Iraqi opponents. In battle, according to the language of *The Yellow Birds*, one moment seems to cause the next, without human intervention.

The Yellow Birds also seems committed to extending the dissociative mode of representing battle to experiences outside of battle, and even to translating the dissociative perspective into a kind of general theory of nature. The narrator occasionally makes explicit his vision of a universe governed by faceless, random necessity, in which human choices do not matter, as in the invocations of mathematics above (11), or when he states of himself and Murph: "Our biggest error was thinking that it mattered what we thought" (13). Likewise, when the unit approaches an orchard outside Al Tafar, "[i]t all seemed in that moment to be the conclusion of a poorly designed experiment in inevitability" (115). Everything that happens, happens because "it was necessary" (11), perhaps in a way analogous to the necessity of statements in mathematics, as in the narrator's claim that an individual soldier in war is "nothing...a uniform in a sea of numbers, a number in a sea of dust" (12). The narrator seems to offer a general disavowal of moral agency when he observes, after a battle, that "we had no alternative" but to proceed to the next mission, because "our course was certain then, if unknown" (24). Back in the United States, as the investigator closes in, and Bartle's mother asks Bartle what he did, the narrator considers what brought him to this point. The narrator concludes not that he was responsible for anything, or that anyone was responsible, but that "[t]he dominoes of moments, lined up symmetrically...showed only that a fall is every object's destiny" (148, and cf. 189). Once again, human agency plays no role. All is the necessary result of impersonal, even mathematical, and utterly meaningless forces.

The intense lyricism that is one of the defining features of *The Yellow Birds* can also be seen to reflect the novel's guiding vision of a world dominated by inhuman forces. Iraq appears for the most part as a desolate if beautiful landscape, emptied of individualized human beings with lives and histories. The narrator's lyrical eye dwells incessantly on abstract forms and colors. The light fell in Al Tafar "beyond thin shapes of rooflines and angled promenades in the dark. It fell over buildings in the city, white and tan" (4). "Mere outlines took shape, and the city, vague and notional at night, became a contoured and substantial thing before us" (15). The city appears "as a blurred patchwork of shapes stretched in white and tan beneath a ribbon of blue sky" (75). When the narrator comes under fire, he notes that he was "still thinking that the only shadows I had seen in the war had been made of angles: hard blurs of light falling on masses of buildings" (117). It sometimes sounds as though the Iraq of *The Yellow Birds* exists primarily as a series of color-fields, like a desert-based Richard Diebenkorn painting.

The narrator's abstract, aestheticized approach to Iraq also, incidentally, echoes the dehumanizing myth of the American frontier, envisioned as an empty wilderness inhabited at most by a shadowy, unknowable Other. It is fitting that the novel's first page describes the U.S. soldiers approaching Al Tafar "like pioneers" (3). A later passage refers to Iraq as "an unknown corner of the world" (206), as though it were some unmapped territory in a colonial adventure-story, a blank space beyond the reaches of civilization, rather than the home of some of the world's first states.[6]

On several occasions, the narrator offers multi-sensory aesthetic appreciations of the dead bodies of Iraqis, their shapes and smells, "broken and shattered and bent, their white shifts gone dark with blood. A few smoldered among the junipers and spare tufts of grass, and there was a heady mix of carbon and bolt oil and their bodies burning in the newly crisp air of morning" (5). Later, Bartle and Murph "stood over a field of worn and pale bodies scattered in the sun like driftwood" (62). At one point, the narrator puzzlingly observes that "[t]he ash from the burning of clay bricks and the fat of lean men and women covered everything" (24). There is no indication that the statement is not meant literally, but also no explanation of how it could be true. Have so many Iraqi corpses burned in the conflict that their ashes cover the landscape?

On another occasion, the bloated corpses of decaying Iraqi bodies are literally reduced to abstract form by being described as "an echo of some morbid geometry" (123). Mathematical figures abound in the narrator's lyrical descriptions of Iraqi corpses: "There was a wet spot where the body had been and its remnants were scattered in pieces, some small and some large, others appearing infinite like the pieces we found near our feet..." (126). In general, there are many "[b]odies...scattered about" (5), but rarely faces, much less individualized Iraqi human beings. The only named Iraqi in the novel, an interpreter named Malik, is killed shortly after being introduced (8–11). Fittingly, when Bartle's unit first clears a building in Al Tafar, "[t]he building was empty...There were no people" (8). Later, the faceless Iraqis leaving the city "were a speckled line of color in the dark" (15).

Even after Bartle and Murph witness Sterling apparently murder an elderly Iraqi couple in a car, and the woman crawls out of the car before dying, Bartle's perceptions remain lyrically focused on visual abstractions: "The holes in the car funneled light...Her old blood mixed with the ash and dust" (22). Viewing the scene from his typical aestheticizing distance, the narrator marvels that after the killing, "[t]here was no judgment made" (22). The reader senses that the narrator is fascinated by the amorality of his own lyrical perceptions, by how detached they are from any evaluation of the morality of his and the other soldiers' acts. It seems entirely appropriate that the scene in which Bartle apparently commits his first war crimes, initially by repeatedly shooting a wounded Iraqi who is crawling away from his weapon, then by standing next to the man's corpse and firing multiple magazines into it, is also the scene containing perhaps the most unrestrained lyricism of any in the book: "In that moment, I disowned the waters of my youth...*Noctiluca*, I thought, *Ceratium*, as the tracers began to show themselves in sifted twilight..." (125). The coalescing of lyricism and atrocity against an Iraqi might be seen as the culmination of the novel's aesthetic strategy of reconceiving the Iraqi landscape and its people, and above all Iraqi corpses, as constellations of shape and color, occasions for lyrical improvisation. The episode featuring Bartle's initial war crime ends with faceless Iraqis, like shades, returning to bury their dead while the sun, in a final flourish, "went down purple and red, painting the city softly" (127).

To be fair, Bartle does imagine at a later point what it will be like for the Iraqis to return to Al Tafar when the fighting is over, and he grants his imagined figures a degree of unindividuated humanity (84). But for the most part, Iraqis are envisioned in *The Yellow Birds* more as abstract forms than personalized agents. Even the insurgents who kill Murph are strangely reconceived as lacking agency. Echoing the extended personification of war at the start of the novel, the narrator describes Murph's death not as a result of the killers' actions but as Murph "surrender[ing] fully to the war" (80).

In fact, the narrator seems to acknowledge and make no apologies for his lack of concern for Iraqis as individual human beings, because "we only grieved those we knew. All others who died in Al Tafar were part of the landscape, as if something had sown seeds in that city that made bodies rise from the earth, in the dirt or up through the pavement like flowers after a frost, dried and withering under a cold, bright sun" (124). The narrator seems to recognize that he is engaged in a project of lyrically aestheticizing Iraqi corpses, and he accepts the amorality of his perspective as unavoidable.

THE EVASION OF CRIMINALITY

The Yellow Birds can thus be interpreted as presenting two overarching and apparently incompatible perspectives on the Iraq War, and on Bartle's role in that war. The first perspective, largely reflected in the novel's narrative structure, views Bartle's story as a tale of crime and punishment, where Bartle is the criminal and Murph and Murph's mother are the victims. Bartle's sin, in this story, is his failure to protect Murph after promising Murph's mother that he would bring Murph home. By confessing the truth to Murph's mother, and by accepting the military's punishment, Bartle finds a measure of peace.

The second perspective, largely reflected in the narrator's painterly observations, lyrical prose, and some of his explicit meditations on the war, views the world as a whole, including the war, as a semi-abstract landscape governed by impersonal, uncontrollable forces. To the extent that this view of the war denies or at least minimizes the significance of human agency—for example, by attributing the violence of the war to "the war" rather than to individual human actors in the war—it rests in tension with the narrative of crime and punishment, which emphasizes the moral consequences of human choices. In fact, the narrator's semi-abstract view of the war arguably rests in tension with *any* standard narrative approach, in the sense that it presents the war not as a series of events with a narrative logic—a beginning leading toward an end, where "leading toward" implies a kind of *telos*—but rather as a largely disconnected field of sensory perceptions, one thing beside another, like daubs of paint on an abstract canvas.

What are we to make of the incompatibility of the two approaches to Bartle's Iraq War in *The Yellow Birds*? Rather than simply observing, in the spirit of an earlier generation of literary theory, that the unbridgeable aporia between narrative structure and lyrical form provides yet another illustration of the "impossibility of reading," I would propose a possible explanation for the coexistence of the conflicting perspectives in *The Yellow Birds*. Specifically, the two perspectives may result from the novel's attempt to avoid confronting the complicity of the novel's U.S. soldiers in general, and Bartle in particular, in the suffering of the Iraqi people.

To begin with, *The Yellow Birds* provides a wealth of evidence that might be used to support the conclusion that Bartle and his unit are neither heroes nor victims but often bigoted aggressors and even sometimes war criminals. The narrator does not shy away from offering up this evidence. We have already seen how Bartle's and Sterling's response to Murph's death culminates in the premeditated murder of an innocent Iraqi civilian, the poor man with the cart (211). We have also seen how the most lyrically elevated passage in the entire novel contains a depiction of Bartle committing two apparent war crimes by, first, killing a wounded Iraqi fighter who is crawling away from his weapon and thus *hors de combat* and not a legal target; and, second, desecrating the fighter's corpse by shooting several magazines of ammunition into it (126).[7]

Sterling and Murph also participate in the latter atrocity, and Sterling applauds it as a model of how they should behave. "'Now you've got it, Privates. Thorough, thorough is the way home'" (126), he ominously declares. In fact, Sterling repeatedly encourages the soldiers to violate norms, as when he announces: "'There's only one way home for real, Private. You've got to stay deviant in this motherfucker'" (156). More generally, Sterling encourages an attitude of aggressive, dehumanizing hate, relishing how "'we fucking kill the hajji fucks'" (17), ordering his men to "'Shoot these hajji fucks!'" (19), inviting Bartle to "'[f]ind that nasty streak'" (42), and reminding Bartle that any conflict is their enemies' "'idea every time. They ought to kill themselves instead of us'" (42). Sterling practices what he preaches, gleefully shooting at a car containing an elderly Iraqi couple after it approaches the unit's position (21–22), as noted above, and apparently desecrating Iraqi corpses after a battle (94–95). (He also carries his violence out of Iraq, assaulting a waitress at a brothel in Germany (66).)

In a story concerned with crime and punishment, we might expect Sterling to be presented as a criminal, or even as the primary villain of the story, with the people of Iraq as his primary victims. But the narrator ultimately makes no moral judgment of Sterling in relation to his war crimes and other misdeeds. To the contrary, although the narrator states that "I hated the way [Sterling] excelled in death and brutality and domination" (19), the narrator ultimately seems to believe Sterling was "necessary" (19), because without Sterling's leadership, Bartle himself would have been too much of a "coward" (19) to fight.

One has a sense that the narrating Bartle, even in the narration's present tense, long after his return from Iraq, has a kind of awed admiration for Sterling's character, all things considered: "I trusted that he was brave...It was a kind of elemental self-sacrifice, free of ideology, free of logic" (43). Setting aside the odd claim that Sterling's homicidal rage and violence toward "hajjis" and women is "free of ideology," the most baffling aspect of the narrator's presentation of Sterling may be the reluctance, in a narrative fixated on guilt and wrongful acts, to subject Sterling's war crimes to the same scrutiny that the narrator imposes on his own arguably far less egregious act of breaking a promise. On at least one occasion, the narrator even evades moral condemnation of Sterling by presenting Sterling's violence as the consequence of impersonal forces. The narrator describes Sterling as suffused with "the whole rage and hate of these few acres, alive and spreading, in and through him" (20). Why does the narrator exclude Sterling's violence against Iraqis from moral evaluation by presenting it as the necessary, inhuman product of a possessed landscape, while treating his own breaking of an arguably absurd promise as an exemplary occasion for moral scrutiny?

Nor is the narrator's treatment of Sterling an aberration. Fairly late in the novel, the narrator notes in passing: "We were unaware of even our own savagery now: the beatings and the kicked dogs, the searches and the sheer brutality of our presence...I didn't care" (159). The atrocities that the narrator has described in detail are apparently part of a larger pattern of abusive practices by the platoon as a whole. Not only are the practices encouraged by Sterling, the soldiers' superior, but the novel suggests that higher levels of command in the Army approve of Sterling's leadership, or at the very least have put in place no effective system for uncovering criminal misconduct. After the fight featuring the war crimes against the wounded Iraqi fighter, members of the unit receive citations, and the Army not only promotes Sterling but gives him a Bronze Star for valor (153). Indeed, one of the novel's few glimpses of American civilian opinion suggests that the American public is likewise unconcerned with misconduct against Iraqis. An American bartender suggests to Bartle that the United States should "'nuke those sand niggers'" (106). Although Bartle certainly does not endorse this view, he also fails to use it as an occasion for subjecting the war as a whole to the kind of moral evaluation he carries out so thoroughly in response to his single broken promise.

With one notable exception to be discussed below, Bartle almost entirely avoids a moral examination of his own misdeeds toward Iraqis as well, including his complicity in Sterling's murder of the man with the cart. The narrator echoes Sterling's language when he notes after a battle that the "platoon had done well" when it "killed a lot of hajjis" (151). It seems that "hajjis" include not only enemy fighters, but all Iraqis, as when the narrator later notes that "[o]n the knoll above me, the hajjis arranged themselves supplicant, clutching at their wooden prayer beads" (169). These are simply ordinary Iraqis praying, not participants in the hostilities. Even if Bartle's casual use of the ethnic slur is set aside, his general lack of moral concern (as opposed to aesthetic concern) for Iraqi corpses throughout the novel at the very least raises questions about how strongly his sense of moral concern extends to Iraqis at all.

In sum, the narrating Bartle appears to feel compelled to provide the evidence of his and other U.S. soldiers' crimes and other misdeeds toward Iraqis. He could have avoided mentioning these incidents to the reader at all, but he does not. Instead, he often seems to draw attention to them. At the same time, however, the narrator appears unable or unwilling explicitly to confront the possibility that the troops committing the misdeeds, including Sterling, might be morally culpable—might even be *criminals* in some sense. The narrator of *The Yellow Birds* appears quietly haunted by the bad behavior of U.S. troops toward Iraqis, or perhaps troubled by his failure to be sufficiently haunted, but also incapable of taking the unthinkable step that *Sand Queen* and *War Porn* take and presenting these troops as in some sense belonging among "the bad guys" in the story of the war.

The two, conflicting perspectives on the war discussed above—the narrative of Bartle's crime and punishment, and the anti-narrative of impressionistic natural forces—follow naturally from the tension between the narrator's acute discomfort with U.S. soldier misconduct toward Iraqis and his inability to subject that misconduct to an open moral critique. On the one hand, the narrator tries to evade coming to terms with the wrongful acts of the U.S. military by viewing the war as a whole as the product of impersonal forces. On the other hand, a sense of guilt seems to linger. The view of the war as a kind of natural disaster, as nobody's fault, does not seem to put the narrator's conscience to rest. Because the narrator remains unable or unwilling to identify this surplus of guilt with wrongs committed by U.S. soldiers against Iraqis, he must find a more acceptable, less taboo source for his guilt. He settles on his failure to fulfill his promise to Murph's mother.

Even the narrator sometimes seems to recognize how bizarre it is to place so much moral weight on such an isolated and unrealistic promise. On more than one occasion, the narrator expresses uncertainty about the precise nature of his guilt. Before Murph's death, Bartle seems to feel responsible for his friend's deterioration, but also attempts to evade responsibility by tracing the deterioration back to "one cause, to one thing I would not be guilty of" (155), then abandons the effort to seek causes as futile. After Murph's death, Bartle continues to wonder "what it was I was guilty of" (166). All he knows is that "I was guilty of something, that much was certain" (179).

It is strange that of all the morally problematic acts Bartle commits in the novel, he ultimately identifies the elusive source of his guilt as a promise to a new friend's mother to bring him home safely. Of course, anguish at having survived while a comrade in battle died is one of the most powerful and frequently recurring themes in all of war literature.[8] But this is not, specifically, what Bartle identifies as the source of his guilt. The source of his guilt is his promise to Murph's mother.

Yet the promise was unplanned, and no amount of effort could have ensured that he would keep the promise. As a result, it would have required magical thinking to take the promise seriously. Nor is there any evidence that he caused Murph's breakdown and death, or even that there were steps he could have taken that would clearly have prevented it. The only sense in which Bartle intentionally broke the promise was by casting Murph's body into the Tigris, thereby preventing it from being repatriated. However misguided this act was, it was at least intended to spare Murph's mother from greater suffering. Despite all of these mitigating factors, however, the narrating Bartle's self-imposed narrative of crime and punishment presents his violation of his promise to bring Murph home safely as though it were his central sin, the origin of the guilt that threatens to destroy him after he leaves Iraq.

The inexplicable moral weight that *The Yellow Birds* places on Bartle's promise becomes more understandable if it is interpreted as an evasion of placing moral weight on the wrongful acts toward Iraqis portrayed in the novel. By substituting an American-soldier victim (Murph) for the unmourned Iraqi victims of the war (such as, most notably, the murdered "cartwright"), *The Yellow Birds* substitutes a tale of punishment and redemption after a highly mitigated "crime" (Bartle's breaking of his promise to Murph's mother) for a tale of actual war crimes and other unpunished misconduct toward Iraqis (the wrongful acts described above). The narrator of *The Yellow Birds* appears able to tolerate a confrontation and moral reckoning with the former tale, but not the latter. By locating his guilt in the broken promise, he is able to overcome his guilt and move on. Perhaps he feels that locating his guilt in his and others' actions toward Iraqis would not be so easily overcome.

But why should responsibility or complicity in wrongs against Iraqis be so difficult to confront, as opposed to ostensible wrongs against a fellow American soldier and his mother? *The Yellow Birds* is a novel suffused with guilt, such intense guilt that it leads Bartle to prolonged isolation, alcoholism, and an apparent attempted suicide.[9] What prevents the narrator from fully, openly confronting one particular category of wrong?

One answer might be that the experience of survivors' guilt by soldiers is recognized and accepted as a common form of trauma, while presenting an ordinary soldier as guilty for crimes against Iraqis might come uncomfortably close to violating the post-Vietnam taboo against associating U.S. servicemembers in general with criminality. Another, less interesting answer might be that Bartle simply does not care about the suffering of Iraqis, and mentions his platoon's wrongs against them mostly out of a fascination with his own lack of moral concern. But a more compelling interpretation could also be offered.

It is possible that a thorough moral confrontation with the misconduct toward Iraqis portrayed in *The Yellow Birds* would have rendered the lyrical form of the novel—one of its defining features, and surely one of its reasons for existing—untenable. If the narrator had dwelled at length on the morality and immorality of his platoon's treatment of Iraqis, and of the war as a whole, it is difficult to see how the narration could have returned to the detached, lyrical aestheticization of Iraqi corpses and empty Iraqi landscapes described at length above. Once the full, individualized humanity and moral worth of Iraqis is acknowledged, such an approach risks seeming grotesque. It is questionable enough as a general matter to adopt a lyrical perspective that detaches itself from the causes and consequences of the suffering of other human beings, and instead views those sufferings merely as one more object of aesthetic contemplation. But it would be difficult not to recoil from a narrator or speaker adopting such a perspective toward sufferings that he himself has caused or been complicit in. Even if one believes that no aspect of human experience should be excluded from art, and that poetry should continue to exist even in the wake of the worst horrors, it would be hard not to be repelled by the spectacle of someone who participated in atrocities turning them to artistic benefit for the spectatorial enjoyment of a literary audience—especially when the audience itself might have shared some complicity in the atrocities through its political action or inaction.

By having the narrating Bartle avoid a thorough moral reckoning with the wrongs of U.S. soldiers, including Sterling and himself, toward Iraqis, *The Yellow Birds* obscures what might have seemed most objectionable in its lyrical treatment of the war. Assuming the novel began at least in part from a lyrical impulse, a desire to explore the landscape and experiences of the war in heightened, lyrical prose, it arguably had to evade a confrontation with the wrongdoing of the American protagonists toward Iraqis. The acceptance of complicity or responsibility would have undermined the lyrical exercise.

A BRIEF RECOGNITION

If *The Yellow Birds* is guided by a moral vision, it is not the half-hearted, somewhat confused traditionalist morality that seems to inform Bartle's narrative of crime and punishment for his broken promise. Nor is the novel's morality the utterly disillusioned, "materialist" perspective that Harari has found so often in twentieth-century war narratives. There is certainly something materialist about Bartle's vision of a world of inhuman, random causal forces. But rather than emphasizing the obscene materiality of destroyed human flesh, *The Yellow Birds* revels in the spectacle of man's and the world's materiality, and the violence that can be inflicted on it, finding in violence and its surroundings the potential for great beauty.

The Yellow Birds departs from most modern war literature in representing the spectacle of war more as beautiful than sublime. There is little sense of awe or terror at the incalculable grandeur of war, and more a sense of a disoriented appreciation of the shifting surfaces, the drifting colors and shapes.

Although I have argued that many of the conflicting and arguably troubling elements of *The Yellow Birds* can be explained by the novel's commitment to lyricism and aestheticism, I will close by noting a passage in the novel that offers an exception to this rule. The passage is a testament to the virtues of negative capability. It is probably the most powerfully insightful section in the novel, yet an editor striving for stylistic and thematic consistency might have argued for its excision.

In fact, the passage is exceptional in several ways: it is the only extended use of stream-of-consciousness narration in the novel, it contains virtually no lyricism, and it is the closest the novel comes to a moral reckoning involving misconduct toward Iraqis. It occurs midway through the novel, after Bartle has returned to Virginia. He observes, unseen, from a distance as some childhood friends play in a nearby stream. He attempts to articulate the guilt that holds him back from approaching them:

> Why didn't I just wade out to them? What would I say? "Hey, how are you?" they'd say. And I'd answer, "I feel like I'm being eaten from the inside out and I can't tell anyone what's going on because everyone is so grateful to me all the time and I'll feel like I'm ungrateful or something. Or like I'll give away that I don't deserve anyone's gratitude and really they should all hate me for what I've done but everyone loves me for it and it's driving me crazy." Right.
>
> Or should I have said that I wanted to die...like wanting to be asleep forever because there isn't any making up for killing women or even watching women get killed, or for that matter killing men and shooting them in the back and shooting them more times than necessary to actually kill them...[B]y the end you failed at the one good thing you could have done, the one person you promised would live is dead...[Y]ou want to burn every goddamn yellow ribbon in sight, and you can't explain it but it's just, like, Fuck you, but then you signed up to go so it's all your fault, really, because you went on purpose, so you are in the end doubly fucked...and, really, cowardice got you into this mess because you wanted to be a man and people made fun of you and pushed you around in the cafeteria and the hallways in high school because you liked to read books and poems sometimes and they'd call you fag and really deep down you know you went because you wanted to be a man... (144–45)

Here, in a flood of colloquial language, stripped of aspirations to poetry or profundity, the narrator confronts the moral questions of responsibility for and complicity in the tragedy in Iraq that so much of the novel seems dedicated to evading. The focus of Bartle's guilt is presented not primarily as the mysteriously weighty broken promise to LaDonna, and not only as Bartle's failure to prevent the death of the friend who depended on him, but also as the wrongs he committed and saw committed against the women and men of Iraq. If Bartle had been drafted, or even deceived, by a patriotic lie, he might have been able to resolve the violent misdeeds he witnessed, and in which he participated, into a narrative in which he and the other soldiers were victims, rather than criminals. But he believes he enlisted for selfish reasons, and cannot blame deception. He implies that he may even have enlisted in part to perform the kinds of violent deeds that would prove he is not a coward, but that now torment him.

It is because of Bartle's consciousness of these wrongs, and his inability to make sense of them—to place them in a satisfactory narrative frame, a story with an ending that can somehow allow him to move on—that the yellow ribbons and the expressions of civilian gratitude are intolerable. It is because of these wrongs that he finds himself unable to go on, and soon wades into the river, inviting death.

CHAPTER SIX

REDEPLOYMENT (2014)

Phil Klay's short story collection *Redeployment*, published to great acclaim in 2014, sits comfortably at the center of the canon of American literary fiction about military service in the Iraq War. The eleven stories in the book present a variety of perspectives on U.S. service in the war, each delivered through the voice of a first-person narrator. Except for a single story in which the narrator is a male Foreign Service Officer heading an embedded Provincial Reconstruction Team ("Money as a Weapons System," 77), all of the narrators are men who have served or are serving in the U.S. military in the Iraq War. Most of the narrators are marines, as was Klay.[1] Although *Redeployment* sometimes turns its attention to members of the infantry in combat (for example, "Frago," 17), more often the stories focus on what comes before and after combat, and on members of the military who serve in support roles—again, like Klay, who was a Public Affairs Officer. Specifically, the reader meets:

- an infantry marine veteran of the Second Battle of Fallujah struggling with the disorientation of homecoming ("Redeployment," 1),
- a mortuary affairs marine who was responsible for collecting remains in Iraq ("Bodies," 53),
- a marine NCO responsible for paying compensation to Iraqis ("OIF," 73),

- a young enlisted marine visiting a strip club while on leave from Iraq ("In Vietnam They Had Whores," 119),
- a marine chaplain troubled by hearing of atrocities and other misconduct in Iraq ("Prayer in the Furnace," 129),
- an Arab-American Coptic Christian Army veteran grappling with campus politics at Amherst after serving as a specialist in psychological operations in Iraq ("Psychological Operations," 169),
- a marine veteran going to a bar with a veteran friend who was disfigured in Iraq ("War Stories," 213),
- a marine adjutant who becomes a law student on the corporate track at NYU after serving in Iraq ("Unless It's a Sucking Chest Wound," 237), and
- a young artillery marine confronting the reality of violence and death in Iraq ("Ten Kliks South," 271).

Redeployment deserves its reputation as the most aesthetically accomplished work of fiction that has yet been written with a primary focus on the U.S. military experience of the Iraq War. If someone were looking to read a single book, fictional or not, in order to better understand what it was like for Americans to serve in various roles in or alongside the military during the Iraq War, Klay's story collection would be the obvious choice. In fact, it is difficult to imagine another book surpassing Klay's work as a single-author, realist literary exploration of American military experiences in Iraq.

But the "realist" qualification matters. Fussell suggested that the British literature of World War I was powerfully shaped by the popularity and prestige in England of a humanistic education based on the reading of the classics and English literature.[2] A similar observation might be made about the role of writing workshops in the literature of the Iraq War. The American literature of the Iraq War is largely the war literature of "the program era."[3] It is the product of writers who participated in creative writing workshops, and sometimes MFA programs. (Klay himself received an MFA from Hunter College.[4]) Program-era fiction is the fiction found in most issues of *The New Yorker*, as well as most literary journals from *Agni* to *Zoetrope*. Its formal roots can be traced back through commonly anthologized and assigned short story writers such as Chekhov, Hemingway, and Carver. Its contemporary ideal may be the writings of Alice Munro.

The paradigmatic work of program-era short fiction is an aesthetically restrained realist story—no fantastical excess or absurdity, no melodrama, no caricatured extremes of virtue or vice, no departures from narrative into non-narrative theory or linguistic experimentation—told from a first-person or close-third-person perspective, in a voice that uses just the right amount of vivid figurative language, while also displaying carefully curated concrete details and culturally localized diction—all to create the illusion that the author must have some intimate knowledge of the world being described. As Mark McGurl suggests in his history of the program era in American literature, two of the dominant principles of creative writing workshops are "write what you know" and "show don't tell."[5] Similarly, Eric Bennett has described how "the prevailing pedagogy" in creative writing programs often expresses a "triumph of the sensory, the personal, the individual, and the idiosyncratic," and a celebration of "concreteness" that may leave little room for critical abstraction.[6] The emphasis is on the empathetic exploration of the distinctive thoughts and cares of ordinary people, especially ordinary people from a cultural setting that the author happens to know based on her personal experiences. If larger historical events or forces appear, they appear through their effects on ordinary people. Every character, to the extent possible, is portrayed as a complex, three-dimensional individual with a unique life story. There is no stepping back to an omniscient authorial perspective to render final judgment, to spell out an ideological critique, or to provide a larger context drawn from history or the natural or social sciences.

Instead, the prototypical program-era short fiction narrative may culminate in a moment of heightened intensity—a trauma, a decisive act, an epiphany—and then end, shortly after, on a scene or detail whose precise meaning is unclear. Because the scene or detail is placed at the end of the story, it will seem to be charged with significance. But because it does not constitute a resolution of whatever problem drove the story, the nature of its significance will remain elusive. The reader is left with an enchanting sense of meaningfulness ungrounded in any particular meaning. The academic reader may attempt to resolve the dissonance between meaningfulness and meaning by interpreting the story in such a way that the ending is somehow a natural resolution of or commentary on all that came before. But ending on an open, unresolved note of captivating dissonance is itself one of the defining features of the program-era short story.[7]

Klay's *Redeployment* shows the great value, but also the limits, of program-era fiction as a mode of writing and a way of thinking about the U.S. military experience in Iraq. As Sam Sacks already noted in a perceptive 2015 essay in *Harper's* on "[w]hat's missing in contemporary war fiction," Iraq War fiction in general and *Redeployment* in particular continually seem to return "to the confined viewpoints of individual soldiers who can't comprehend what they've experienced." Drawing on Bennett's work,[8] Sacks observes that "the workshop philosophy" and its emphasis on concrete, particularistic, personal experiences seems to leave little room for "placing the Terror Wars within a larger political or ideological context." Without such context, the program-era fiction of the Iraq War seems curiously uninterested in questions such as: "Why did we fight these wars, and what were we trying to achieve? Did we succeed or did we fail? What consequences have we wrought on the countries we attacked? What, if anything, have we learned?" Instead, the program-era workshop encourages a focus on "personal stories," and in particular "the veteran's expected journey from trauma to recovery."[9]

At the same time, the aesthetic virtues of the workshop approach should not be ignored. There is a richness and subtlety to the detail of *Redeployment* that makes other works of Iraq War fiction seem less fully imagined by comparison. Reading *Sand Queen*, for example, or the portions of *War Porn* dealing with the lives of Iraqis, one sometimes has the sense that if the narration were to turn its attention too far in a different direction, there might only be a blank, or a hazy guess. Through all the marvelous artifices of well-crafted program-era fiction, by contrast, Klay achieves the consistent illusion that his narrators live in complete worlds, and are only offering a few select details from what they could say, only Hemingway's "tip of the iceberg."

Moreover, unlike some of the characterizations criticized in other chapters of this book, the voices of Klay's characters, to this reader at least, uniformly ring true, as though they were based on actual people that the author had encountered. This is not to say the characters were in fact based on actual people. Klay deployed as a Public Affairs Officer to Anbar province from January 2007 to February 2008. He saw one narrow slice of the war, but writes about many others. As he states in his acknowledgments, *Redeployment* is based as much on his reading about others' experiences in Iraq as it is on his own. But Klay's stories achieve the illusion of authenticity, giving readers the sense that they have had a glimpse, however small, of—for example—what someone suddenly at home after extended combat in Fallujah might have thought or felt.

"REDEPLOYMENT"

Homecoming is one of the central themes of *Redeployment*, as its title suggests. But there is another theme that is just as insistently woven into the stories of *Redeployment*: the theme of storytelling. Again and again, the reader hears the voices in Klay's stories attempting to make sense of their experiences in Iraq, and very often the attempt at sense-making takes the form of struggling to tell a story, or struggling to avoid doing so. The characters in *Redeployment* try, repeatedly, to fit their experiences of the Iraq War into narrative frames—including the various frames that have been discussed throughout this book: variations on the story of the warrior-as-hero, the soldier-as-victim, and the soldier-as-criminal. The stories in *Redeployment* are not only attempts to tell the story of the Iraq War from the perspectives of various Americans who served there. They are stories about the attempt to tell such stories. The first and title story in the collection, "Redeployment," provides a particularly good illustration.

"Redeployment" is a first-person account of a marine NCO's return to the United States after serving in Iraq for seven months, where he participated in the Second Battle of Fallujah, and where at least three of his fellow platoon members died (12, 13).[10] The narrator, SGT Price, speaks in a stylized imitation of conversational informality and intimacy: "So here's an experience..." (12). At one point near the story's end, he even seems to address the reader directly, as though he has been telling the story to an individual all along (16). The reader has the sense that SGT Price is still very close to the events he describes. One of the underlying stories of "Redeployment" is the narrator's difficulty in telling the story that we are reading, which moves back and forth between fragmentary anecdotes and observations about his time in Iraq and the disorientations of his return from Iraq. The story we are reading is of course a highly polished work of realist fiction, but it artfully presents an act of personal storytelling that is still very much a work in progress.

In broad narrative outline, "Redeployment" begins with an anecdote about SGT Price shooting dogs in Iraq, and ends, symmetrically, with SGT Price back in North Carolina shooting his chronically ill dog, Vicar, in an act of euthanasia. Along the way, SGT Price describes in sparse but vivid detail various surreal and anxiety-producing experiences he had in Iraq, and the difficulties of returning to a peaceful home life with his wife, Cheryl.

Why is it difficult for SGT Price to tell the story we are reading?

As in so much of the Iraq War fiction discussed throughout this book, SGT Price seems to struggle above all with a sense of moral discomfort. There are elements of warrior-heroism in the stories he tells—for example, in the almost superhuman intensity of his perceptions after he realized, in Iraq, "that everybody's life, everybody's, depends on you not fucking up" (12): "You take in every piece of the environment, everything. I could spot a dime in the street twenty yards away. I had antennae out that stretched down the block. It's hard to even remember exactly what that felt like" (13). There are also elements of the soldier-as-victim in the stories SGT Price tells. For example, the preceding description of intense perceptions arrives in a passage where SGT Price finds himself unable to turn off his "amped up" vigilance even when he and Cheryl are shopping at an American Eagle Outfitters (12–13). The reader is invited to conclude that SGT Price may be suffering from some form of psychological trauma.

But "Redeployment" neither starts nor ends on a note of heroism or victimhood. It begins on a note of moral discomfort based on a sense of wrongdoing: "We shot dogs. Not by accident. We did it on purpose, and we called it Operation Scooby. I'm a dog person, so I thought about that a lot" (1).[11] In the opening lines of the title and first story of this central work in the canon of Iraq War fiction, the focus is squarely on an American servicemember's responsibility for acts perceived as somehow morally troubling. The language goes out of its way to convey intent, rather than accident or even recklessness, as though attempting to establish the necessary state of mind for a prosecution. Of course, there is no literal prosecution, or even crime. But SGT Price's apparent inability to arrive at a satisfactory moral reckoning haunts the rest of the story.

After explaining that the "open season on dogs" began when the marines saw "a skinny brown dog lapping up blood the same way he'd lap up water from a bowl" (1), SGT Price emphasizes that he and the other marines felt no guilt at the time. "The thinking comes later, when they give you the time" (1), when the marines leave Fallujah for a logistics base, then Kuwait, and then a commercial airliner home. "[Y]ou sit there, and close your eyes, and think" (2):

> The problem is, your thoughts don't come out in any kind of straight order. You don't think, Oh, I did A, then B, then C, then D. You try to think about home, then you're in the torture house. You see the body parts in the locker and the retarded guy in the cage. He squawked like a chicken. His head was shrunk down to a coconut.
>
> ...
>
> I tried to think of other things, like my wife, Cheryl. (2)

"But thinking of Cheryl," SGT Price concludes, "made me feel guilty," because it reminded him of the three marines in his platoon who died (2–3). The narrator is comfortable using the word "guilty" to describe how he feels about surviving while fellow marines died. That is a familiar story and one that he knows how to tell. But he seems less able to tell a story about the Iraqi dogs, much less to admit guilt. He cannot yet place the dog-killing in a narrative from "A" to "D," beginning to end, perhaps because connecting a beginning to an end requires some kind of purpose or meaning. What was the meaning of shooting the dogs?

How to tell the story of Operation Scooby is the problem that initiates the story of "Redeployment." The story insists on this point by having the narrator circle back to the shooting of the dogs after he mentions his fallen friends. "So I'm thinking about" the death of friends, SGT Price states, and remembering the strange and horrible things he has seen. "But here's the thing. I'm thinking a lot, and I mean a lot, about those fucking dogs" (3). He thinks about the dogs, and about his own dog, "all the way home" (3).

In Kenneth Burke's terms, the shooting of the Iraqi dogs is the "Trouble" that sets the narrative of "Redeployment" into motion. There are well-established narrative frameworks for making sense of seeing enemy atrocities during war, and for the familiar phenomenon of survivor's guilt among veterans. It seems to be less clear to SGT Price how to make narrative sense of the mass killing of Iraqi dogs in which he was complicit. Is what he did wrong? If so, why did he do it? What did it have to do with his service in Iraq?

SGT Price ventures a tentative explanation for why he is so fixated on the shooting of the dogs: "Maybe, I don't know, you're prepared to kill people," but not dogs (3). But then he seems to undermine the explanation by noting that some of the marines' targets are called "dog targets," although they do not look like dogs, and his attention soon turns to an officer in his company who murdered an already-dying Iraqi by slitting his throat with a KA-BAR (3–4). "On the flight, I thought about that, too," he notes (4). SGT Price's juxtaposition of his gratuitous killing of dogs and the war crime by his company's XO strengthens the sense that in SGT Price's mind, the two may belong in the same category.

Narrative theorists from Aristotle to Burke to Jerome Bruner have suggested that the end of a story typically involves "some sort of resolution" of the problem, the "breach in the expected state of things" that set the story into motion.[12] This is the reader's intuitive expectation, trained into us by the countless stories, fictional and otherwise, that we have heard since learning language. In "Redeployment," as SGT Price recounts the jarring transition from violent combat in Fallujah, to fratty rejoicing during a refueling stop in Ireland, to his nervous and disoriented homecoming to Cheryl, he also increasingly turns his attention to the health problems of his dog Vicar (9, 11, 13). In the story's emotional climax, SGT Price leads Vicar to a stream and shoots him with an AR-15, the civilian equivalent of the M16 he used to kill the dogs in Iraq (15).

But in the moment before he fires, SGT Price hesitates, and he remembers a similar hesitation when he and some other marines found an insurgent hiding in "a cesspit, basically a big round container filled a quarter way with liquid shit," "hiding beneath the liquid and only coming up for air" (15). The other marines fired into the cesspit, but SGT Price hesitated and did not, because he had a feeling "like, something in me is going to break if I do this" (15). Finally, SGT Price pulls the trigger three times and kills Vicar (16).

The overarching narrative logic of "Redeployment," then, might seem to be something like the following. SGT Price participated in the gratuitous killing of dogs in Iraq, even though he is someone who likes dogs generally, and he does not know how to make sense of his acts. He feels something like guilt, but does not know how to fit his actions into a coherent story. At the end of "Redeployment," he resolves his uncertainty and moral confusion by killing his own dog. The appropriately named "Vicar" stands in, vicariously, as a substitute for the Iraqi dogs he killed. In line with Klay's Catholicism, and with the invocation of Catholicism in the name "Vicar," the story of SGT Price's struggle to tell his story ends by fitting everything into a familiar narrative frame: the purgation of sin through violence. Vicar is the bloody sacrifice that SGT Price makes in an attempt to cleanse himself of his wrongs.

If "Redeployment" ended with Vicar's death, we might question whether its narrative of sacrificial purgation makes any sense. Certainly, it was difficult for SGT Price to kill the dog he loved. But Vicar was in pain, and the pain was only going to get worse. How does an act of euthanasia serve as a substitute or moral recompense for the gratuitous mass killing of Iraqi dogs? More generally, we might wonder why an act of violence should bring about any purgation or catharsis at all—especially if we see the Iraqi dogs as vicarious stand-ins for the Iraqi people in general who have been harmed by the American invasion.[13] SGT Price has neither sought nor received forgiveness from the recipients of any harm in which he was complicit. In fact, he never states explicitly that he believes he was complicit in anything wrong. Why should his killing of Vicar be seen as a cathartic act, rather than just as one more act of destructive violence to add to all the others?

Maybe, as Roy Scranton has suggested, a story like "Redeployment" should dwell more on the consequences of SGT Price's actions for Iraqis, and less on how difficult it is for him to come home to his comfortable, peaceful life in the United States.[14] But accepting Scranton's objection would probably require "Redeployment" to be a different kind of story. If it is implausible to imagine SGT Price rapidly arriving at an explicit ideological critique of his service in Iraq, then it would be inappropriate for a work of program-era realist fiction to attempt to shoehorn such a critique into the story of SGT Price's homecoming.[15] As Sacks has emphasized, fiction like "Redeployment" stays close to the plausible individual consciousness.

The final line of "Redeployment," however, powerfully suggests an awareness of such limitations. As SGT Price stares at Vicar's corpse in the dimming light, he realizes: "I couldn't remember what I was going to do with the body" (16). This is not a statement of resolution. Even if the violence of killing Vicar was intended to bring some personal catharsis for SGT Price, or some degree of closure to the problem with which the story began—his inability to come to terms with his killing of the dogs in Iraq, or with his participation in the violence there more generally—it has also created an unresolved supplement to the narrative logic of the story: a new corpse, out of place.

The closing sentence of "Redeployment" could be interpreted as a preemptive response to any attempt to offer a positive, redemptive story of the Iraq War, especially a story that draws on the supposedly numinous or transcendent power of violence. After each attempt, there will still be the corpse to deal with. There will still be a body that has not been accounted for, and the problem will remain unresolved.

"PRAYER IN THE FURNACE"

A number of other stories in *Redeployment* similarly take the telling of stories about the Iraq War as a central object of concern. Often, as in "Redeployment," an elusive sense of guilt regarding wrongdoing in Iraq seems to prevent the storyteller from resting easily with a story of soldiers as heroes or victims.

The marine chaplain narrator of "Prayer in the Furnace," to take another example, serves in a unit led by a sadistic commander, Captain Boden, who encourages bigotry and brutality toward Iraqis (131, 135, 141, 143, 163). A marine named Rodriguez hints to the chaplain that he and others may have killed Iraqi civilians (139). The chaplain, a former boxer (129) who seems to view his role partly as offering moral reassurance to the marines after they kill (139), decides, with a note of insecurity, that he must "talk to someone or be a coward. Less than a priest. Less than a man" (140). Envisioning himself as a kind of moral hero, he tries to raise the issue of the unit's possible war crimes with officers who might initiate an investigation, but nothing happens (144, 146).

The wrongdoing seems to continue. A lance corporal tells the chaplain "'[t]he only thing I want to do is kill Iraqis...They're all insurgents'" (148). The chaplain struggles to make sense of what he is hearing. He had thought "there would be nobility in war" (150) based on stories he had heard. In other words, he came to Iraq with something like a heroic narrative in mind. But now he seems uncertain about what attitude he should take toward the marines' atrocities, if they are real. He struggles with the extent to which he should view them as wrongdoers, criminals—in a religious register, sinners—or instead as victims of their difficult circumstances. "If men inevitably act this way under stress, is it even a sin?... [N]obody expects sainthood, and it's offensive to demand it" (150). The chaplain instead attempts to assert a cosmopolitan Christian morality in a sermon to the marines, telling them that "being Christian means we can never look at another human being and say, 'He is not my brother'" (159).

But the situation does not improve, and in the years after the marines return home, several end up engaging in crimes and substance abuse, and some commit suicide (162–63). One appears at a protest event and presents photos and videos along with his testimony:

> He claimed to have abused Iraqis and shot some just to take out aggression. He claimed Captain Boden congratulated every Marine on their first kill and told everyone that if a Marine got their first kill by stabbing someone to death, they'd get a ninety-six-hour pass when they got back. It sounded right. (163)

The story concludes with the chaplain's resigned advice to Rodriguez that Christianity promises only that "'we don't suffer alone'" (167). Rodriguez spits into the grass and says: "'Great'" (167).

"Prayer" is the story in Klay's book that is most explicitly focused on the problem of U.S. military wrongdoing in Iraq, and how to address it, or not, in a narrative of military service in the war. The Catholic chaplain's unresolved questions echo the questions of a veteran at a documentary screening Klay himself has reported attending shortly after ISIS seized

Fallujah and Ramadi: "Was I part of an evil thing? Because if I was, then I don't know who I am anymore. I don't know what my identity is."[16]

What may be most striking about the story, however, given its narrator's identity, is what it does not contain: any consideration of the radical, pacifist rejection of war on the basis of Jesus' teachings. Of course, military chaplains are not pacifists. But "Prayer" incessantly draws the reader's attention to the manifest inadequacy of the chaplain's responses to the wrongs committed by the marines in Charlie Company. It is a testament to the marginal status of pacifism as a moral position in contemporary American culture that the chaplain does not even grapple with it as a possibility. He does not consider that his service as a moral facilitator of war might be fundamentally wrong, or out of accord with Jesus' message.

Again, however, Klay's exclusion of this possibility from the story rings true. The fact that pacifist thought appears nowhere in *Redeployment* faithfully reflects the current status of such thought in the aspects of our culture that the book portrays.[17] It is difficult to imagine a program-era short story successfully showing a chaplain struggling to reconcile the U.S. military's activities in Iraq with, for example, the teaching from the Sermon on the Mount that one should turn the other cheek rather than strike back, or the call to love one's enemies. A straightforward reading of the Sermon might suggest that Jesus of Nazareth was engaged in a revolutionary overturning of the values of aristocratic warrior cultures, including the violent, hierarchical, kinship-based values reflected in much of the Old Testament. By presenting the meek, the merciful, and the persecuted as blessed, rather than praising violently dominant warrior-heroes, the Sermon might seem to pose a challenge to central aspects of the traditional military ethos.[18] But presumably any Christian marine chaplain in Iraq would already have embraced one or another familiar way of reinterpreting the Bible to resolve such tensions.[19] Even if it were plausible to imagine a chaplain in Iraq still seriously struggling with the compatibility of the Beatitudes and the military pursuit of dominance over the enemy through force, depicting the struggle would probably require too much "telling" and not enough "showing."

Certain perspectives on the Iraq War may simply be difficult to incorporate into a work of program-era fiction. It would violate the conventions of the MFA workshop to write a story that explored the Iraq War by incorporating essayistic digressions on the anthropology of violence, economic theory, or political history, just as it would run against the grain of program-era methods to write a story on the Iraq War with George W. Bush as its central protagonist, treating his shifting thoughts, feelings, and passing interactions with the same subtle sympathy and attention to detail that Klay gives to unnamed, ordinary marines. When powerful figures enter program-era fiction, they tend to appear through the eyes of someone off to the side—not the president, but the president's wife; not the torturer, but the torturer's assistant.

OTHER STORIES

Several other stories in *Redeployment* grapple, like "Redeployment," with the difficulties of constructing a narrative about military service in the Iraq War. In "Unless It's a Sucking Chest Wound," the marine adjutant narrator's job in Iraq was in part to translate marines' experiences into narratives to be used for military awards. Although the narrator is attending law school with an eye toward a well-paying corporate job, no longer considers himself a marine, and flaunts a cynical attitude, he continues to believe that true stories of traditional heroism can sometimes exist in the Marine Corps. "[O]ur unit had one no-shit hero," the narrator observes, a marine named Julian Deme (239). "IEDs don't let you be a hero," the narrator notes later. "Without the rare stories like Deme's, who'd sign up?" (269). The narrator himself still yearns to have been a decorated warrior, for reasons he cannot describe, like an animal "in thrall to stimuli" (269). He remains captivated by warrior stories, even as he has seen and participated in their construction through extreme artifice.

As the title of "War Stories" suggests, it too deals with the difficulty of making narrative sense of American military experiences in the Iraq War. The narrator, a marine veteran, accompanies his severely burned marine veteran friend, Jenks, to a bar to talk with an actress who wants to use Jenks' story in a play for the Iraq Veterans Against the War (221). The narrator expresses frustration at his own past exploitation of Jenks' story of heroic victimhood to attract women, and at the fact that it works (215). The narrator seems repulsed by the way he and the playwright are both making use of Jenks' trauma for instrumental ends, but also uncomfortable with Jenks' own humble acceptance of others' attention and concern. At the end of the story, the narrator lies and declares that before the IED, Jenks "'was a worthless piece of shit. No subject for a play, that's for sure... Good thing he caught on fire, right?'" (236). Because the narrator is portrayed as both loyal and obnoxious, and conflicted in his own attitudes, the story comes across as an ambivalent critique of the exploitation of stories about veteran trauma. But just as "Chest Wound" ultimately refuses to reject the possibility of traditional stories of heroism taking place in the Iraq War, so "War Stories" ultimately refuses to reject the notion that a narrative of soldier victimhood involving trauma and sometimes heroic perseverance has a significant place in understanding American military service in the Iraq War.

Finally, in "After Action Report," the narrator's MRAP comes under attack. His friend Timhead instinctively shoots and kills a teenaged boy holding an AK-47 (31). It turns out that Timhead has a little brother, aged sixteen, who is in juvenile detention for lighting "a couple fires" (40)—in other words, for "dumb shit" that may not be so different from a teenaged Iraqi boy picking up a rifle (41). Timhead seems disturbed by his shooting of the Iraqi boy, and he encourages the narrator to take credit for the killing (34), to be "'[t]he big fucking hero'" (38). Strangely, the narrator then proceeds to share Timhead's concerns with a Staff Sergeant and chaplain, as though the concerns were the narrator's own. It is as though the narrator wishes he were not only a killer, but a traumatized killer—perhaps a "trauma hero," to use Scranton's term. Over the course of the story, we see the narrator trying on different narrative poses, but none of them seem satisfactory. Finally, at the end of the story, he lashes out at Timhead and suggests that anyone who has suffered through service in Iraq should be free to "'say what he wants'" (52). The narrator's frustration with his inability to arrive at a satisfactory telling of Timhead's story has apparently led him to a kind of narrative nihilism in which any story, or no story at all, will do equally well.

***

Despite its exceptional craft and insights into the matters it chooses to address, the limitations of *Redeployment* illustrate the more general limitations of a program-era approach to writing and thinking about the Iraq War. In essence, a mode of writing based on the dictum "write what you know" will tend to result in a body of war fiction that focuses on individual experiences rather than attempting to make sense of any larger historical or social context. Program-era war fiction will also necessarily downplay the perspectives on military service of those who did not participate in the war.

Indeed, *Redeployment* almost seems to confront its own inability, as program-era fiction based on "writing what you know" and "showing not telling," to give a voice to the people most affected by the Iraq war: Iraqis. It is fitting that Klay's book, the most fully realized program-style work on the Iraq War, is not one of the many works of American fiction about the Iraq War that attempts to speak in an Iraqi voice.[20] Writing from an Iraqi perspective would be to risk "writing what you do not know," even more than writing from American perspectives on the war that the author did not personally experience.[21]

The final story in the collection, "Ten Kliks South," functions as an allegory of the distance between American soldiers' and Iraqis' experiences. As Joshua Pederson notes, "Ten Kliks South" may be the closest Klay comes in *Redeployment* to addressing some the larger political questions that Scranton and Sacks have criticized the book for evading, because "the structure of the piece requires that the reader move from observing one service member's moral pain to reflecting more broadly on civilian culpability for that pain."[22]

In the story, a nineteen-year-old Lance Corporal serving in an artillery unit participates in what he believes to be his first killing, helping to fire "about 270 pounds of ICM on a smuggler's checkpoint ten kliks south of us" (272). One marine states that "[i]t feels good," because "[w]e just killed some bad guys." Then another wonders, "[i]f we used a howitzer to kill somebody back in the States...what crime they'd charge us with." The discussion turns to questions of shared liability, and another marine asks whether the marines who supplied the ammunition would be "responsible" as well. But in that case, "[w]hy not the factory workers who made the ammo?...Or the taxpayers who paid for it?" Undermining any provocation to the reader, however, the speaker continues: "You know why not? Because that's retarded" (274).

After initially sharing in his unit's excitement, the Lance Corporal finds himself preoccupied with the unknowable fate of the Iraqis that the unit targeted: "I know ten kliks south of us is a cratered area riddled with shrapnel and ruined buildings, burned-out vehicles and twisted corpses. The bodies. Sergeant Deetz had seen them on his first deployment, during the initial invasion. None of the rest of us have" (280). The Lance Corporal goes to SGT Deetz and asks whether they should patrol out and find the bodies of any survivors. SGT Deetz replies that as artillerymen, they "'*provide* the bodies. We don't clean 'em up'" (282). Then the Lance Corporal goes to "PRP: personnel retrieval and processing, aka Mortuary Affairs" (282). The Gunnery Sergeant there explains that they only handle U.S. casualties (284). Finally, the Lance Corporal goes to Fallujah Surgical and thinks about the corpses of American servicemembers being transported back home with reverence (287–88). By the end of the story, in other words, the distant reality of Iraqi corpses has faded from the Lance Corporal's imagination, and he thinks only of the American dead. Iraqi death fades away into an abstract distance, "ten kliks south."

Redeployment offers the most compelling fictional representation to date of veterans of the Iraq War attempting to make sense of their service and their homecoming. The stories that the veterans in *Redeployment* tell themselves about the war remain unsettled: aspects of traditional heroic stories and modern stories of soldier-victimhood sit uncomfortably beside intimations of wrongdoing, complicity, and guilt. *Redeployment* reflects the unresolved state of many Americans' attempts to make sense of the Iraq War and military service in it. As a work of program-era fiction, the book vividly illustrates the impasse rather than attempting to offer a way through it.

CHAPTER SEVEN

SAND QUEEN (2011)

At the start of her 2009 book *The Lonely Soldier: The Private War of Women Serving in Iraq*, investigative journalist and novelist Helen Benedict describes attending a March 2004 candlelight vigil in New York City "to honor the citizens and soldiers who had died in the first year of the Iraq War." Benedict is "taken aback" when a recently returned veteran gives a speech criticizing how the war is being fought. The veteran states that "'we're being used as cannon fodder. We're being sent into war without body armor or decent vehicles to protect us. And most of the people who are dying in this war are civilians.'" Benedict recalls her surprise at hearing the veteran's words at a time when "it was unpopular for anyone to criticize the way the war was being run...Surely this young soldier was going to be called a traitor by his comrades."[1]

An observer of the history of war literature, including American war literature, might be similarly surprised upon first encountering Benedict's 2011 novel *Sand Queen*, one of the first American novels of the Iraq War.[2] The novel tells two partly interwoven stories, one a story of heroism and the other a story of victimhood. Who is the hero, who is the victim, and what is the relation between the two?

If we were forced to guess answers to these questions based on the history of war literature, we might guess that the hero of one of the earliest American novels of the Iraq War would be an American soldier who has come to liberate the victimized people of Iraq from their oppression under Saddam Hussein's tyranny. This would, in any case, be the most traditional approach. The community tells the tale of a war by celebrating the glorious deeds of a hero-champion. Or, if we assume that an early American novel of the Iraq War would take a more modern approach, we might guess that the victim in the story will be a young soldier, perhaps deceived by the illusions of militaristic nationalism, who becomes disillusioned through battle and experiences a revelation of the futility and obscenity of war in general.

In fact, however, the hero of *Sand Queen* is a young Iraqi woman and medical student named Naema Jassim. As described below, her story in the novel fits the template of a hero narrative, and in that narrative, the U.S. military is the villain, causing incalculable, senseless destruction to Iraq and its people. Naema's heroism expresses itself precisely in her struggles against the injustices of the U.S. occupation, especially the occupier's imprisonment of her innocent father and her little brother, Zaki.[3]

In the other primary narrative in the novel, the narrative of victimization, the victim is a young soldier, as one might expect in a modern war novel. But unlike the protagonists of nearly all such novels, the young American soldier here is a woman, Kate Brady, and her victimizers are not callous, incompetent generals or a bloodthirsty nationalist public. Rather, Kate is primarily made a victim by the sexual predations of the male soldiers in her unit. They ostracize her because she is a woman, sexually harass her, sexually assault and attempt to rape her, then ensure that she is denied any justice. Other female soldiers receive similar treatment, and the Army as a whole appears to have turned a blind eye, or worse.

Thus, both of the two narratives of *Sand Queen* present the U.S. military as, in essence, the bad guy in the story of the Iraq War. The U.S. military is the villain to Naema's hero and the criminal to Kate's victim.

What was the response to this literary attack on the U.S. military in a time of war?

Sand Queen was positively reviewed, or at least reviewed positively enough to provide its paperback edition with several bold blurbs. The *Boston Globe* announces that "[t]his is *The Things They Carried* for women in Iraq." Of a novel that clearly seems intended as a political intervention, Robert Olen Butler notes: "Every war eventually yields works of art which transcend politics and history and illuminate our shared humanity. Helen Benedict's brilliant new novel has done just that..." It is a sign of how far elite culture has traveled in the United States from the values underlying the traditional warrior-hero epics that it attracted little attention when one of the first widely reviewed American literary novels about the Iraq War presented the U.S. military not as a force of virtuous heroes but as something very close to a gang of criminals.

Benedict's message about the victimization of female soldiers also found a large and receptive audience. Far from being charged with sedition or hounded out of her teaching position at Columbia University by patriotic mobs, Benedict has helped to change the way the American public thinks about sexual harassment and assault in the U.S. military. Her 2007 article in *Salon*, "The Private War of Women Soldiers," partly inspired the 2012 documentary *The Invisible War*, in which Benedict prominently appears. *The Invisible War* in turn played a pivotal role in building pressure among the public and elected officials such as Senator Kirsten Gillibrand for reforms in the way the military deals with sexual misconduct. As the acknowledgments to *Sand Queen* make clear, "[m]uch of the material for this novel was culled" (313) from Benedict's research for *The Lonely Soldier*, the book mentioned above, which itself grew out of the earlier *Salon* article. Far from representing a fringe perspective, Benedict's emphasis on narratives of U.S. military criminality in *Sand Queen*, like her journalism, reflects a prominent mainstream point of view in American culture, one that is powerful enough that it has forced the military to change its policies for handling sexual harassment and sex crime accusations among soldiers.

Although *Sand Queen* itself has not received the attention or achieved the influence of Benedict's journalism—few novels do—and although in some ways it follows the melodramatic formulas of genre fiction, the novel nevertheless deserves attention in the context of a survey of Iraq War fiction because it so clearly illustrates the narrative framing of war in terms of crime, which, as this book suggests, is one of the central developments in recent war literature. Indeed, the novel's weaknesses as a work of literature arguably become strengths when it is approached as a reflection of the cultural attitudes that have contributed to the rise of criminality as a framework for understanding war. The works discussed in other chapters, most of them written by veterans of the Iraq War, are often driven by an ambivalent struggle with the possibility of viewing the story of the Iraq War as a story of crime. *Sand Queen* displays no such ambivalence. It not only embraces a criminalized perspective on the Iraq War, but can be seen as a work of frank political advocacy for the wider adoption of such a perspective.

USES OF AND DEPARTURES FROM GENRE CONVENTIONS

One of the features that generally distinguishes writing identified as "genre fiction" from "literary fiction" is the former's greater adherence to narrative templates. Action thrillers or romance novels reproduce formulaic plot structures to a far greater degree than, say, the kind of short fiction published in *The New Yorker*, much less the more formally ambitious work published in some small-circulation literary journals. Of course, even literary fiction often draws upon familiar narrative formulas such as the story of the victim overcoming oppression, the hero defeating an enemy, or the criminal achieving redemption. But the interest and interpretive productivity of literary fiction partly results from the ways in which it does not *simply* reproduce the narrative formulas it draws upon. By disrupting, subverting, defamiliarizing, or otherwise manipulating standard story templates, literary fiction raises questions about why it has done so. The attempt to answer such questions is one of the ways in which literary fiction tends to give rise to richer and more varied interpretations than genre fiction.

Sand Queen in some ways resembles a work of genre fiction.[4] Its characters are largely one-dimensional. The villains, such as the serial rapist Staff Sergeant Kormick, are uniformly and predictably villainous. The heroic Naema is unwaveringly virtuous, as is for the most part Kate's supportive friend Jimmy Donnell. The protagonists' inner voices, as reflected in Naema's and Kate's first-person narration, are mannered and wooden. Both voices sound very much like the product of dutiful journalistic research—which, based on the author's note and acknowledgments, they apparently were (311–15)—and create little of the illusion of elusive, many-layered, responsive inner life expected from characters in a realist novel.

In Kate's narration, the reader is frequently treated to the uncomfortable sense of listening in on a grown-up's attempt to imitate the speech of younger people, as in the voiceover from a well-intentioned sexual harassment training video for high schoolers. The narration contains heavy doses of often outdated colloquialism and jarringly tame vulgarity: "We've just pulverized their towns, locked up their men and killed their kids, and one GI Jane with sand up her ass is supposed to make it okay?" (8). "Every boy I'd tried dating had turned out to be either a two-timing dipshit or stunningly dumb" (10). "I'm getting freaked. No matter how much I yell and try to shoo away...these damn locals, they won't budge" (20).[5] When Kate meets Naema, or in her words "some Iraqi chick" (22), Naema insists that her detained father and brother are innocent, leading Kate to think: "*Yeah, right. So's everybody in this whole friggin' sandbox, according to you people*" (21). Even more puzzlingly, the narration appears to be addressed conversationally to an unspecified listener, as when Kate explains what the heat in Iraq is like—"I'm not kidding. Imagine putting your oven on that high to heat up a pizza..." (25)—but at the same time is delivered in the present tense, not the tense that someone would ordinarily use when recounting past events to another person.

Naema's voice is also unpersuasive, but instead of being defined by its faux-youthful colloquialism, it is characterized by an unchangingly breathless passion—sometimes expressing moral outrage, sometimes intense affection, and always spiced with exotic local color. Although *Sand Queen* for the most part alternates between chapters narrated by Kate and chapters narrated by Naema, Naema's chapters are generally shorter and there are fewer of them. It is in the chapters narrated by Naema that *Sand Queen* comes closest to pure melodrama, as when Naema's ill-fated fiancé, Khalil, says goodbye to her before her family flees Baghdad. "We clung to each other in shock. 'I'll count every minute until we can be together again,' he said urgently, holding me tightly to his chest. 'And as soon as the war ends and we're reunited, *inshallah*, we will celebrate our new freedoms, our new Iraq, right, my love?'" (31). Later, Naema notes how Khalil's "fine dark eyes, curly black hair, sturdy shoulders, these pulled me to him as the moon pulls the tides...His lips were so warm, little pillows of tenderness" (90). Naema sometimes uses even more elevated and exoticized language: "What else do I have, oh comfortable, blind and selfish American? What else could any Iraqi have but dreams?" (92).

If the characters and language of *Sand Queen* sometimes seem closer to genre fiction than literary fiction, the same could also be said of its plot. *Sand Queen* reflects the conventions of a melodrama of social injustice, in the tradition of *Uncle Tom's Cabin*. Events often seem to happen either in order to instruct the reader about how various forms of injustice operated during the Iraq War, as discussed in more detail below, or in an effort to manipulate the reader's sympathies on behalf of the victims of those injustices.

But if *Sand Queen* in some respects follows the conventions of a melodrama of social injustice, in other respects it is something quite new. It is a piece of war fiction that defies the conventions of war fiction by making its hero a civilian woman from the country being occupied by the military forces of the author's (and presumably most of the expected audience's) home country. Equally rare, of course, it is a piece of war fiction in which the primary military protagonist is a female soldier. In that sense, for all the narrative simplicity of *Sand Queen*, and its transparent intentions as a work of political advocacy, it shares with literary fiction the defiance and subversion of narrative conventions—in this case, the conventional focus of the American war novel on the heroic or traumatic combat experiences of male, American soldiers.

KATE AS VICTIM

The previous section asserted that *Sand Queen* presents Naema as a hero, struggling against a villainous U.S. military occupation, and Kate as a victim of the same callous and cruel military machine. The remainder of this chapter will attempt to support these claims through a structural analysis of the dual narratives of *Sand Queen*, with two objectives in mind: first, to provide a more detailed consideration of the structure of hero and victim narratives than was possible in Chapter 2; and second, to provide an especially clear example of a narrative in which the United States appears as "the bad guy" in the story of the Iraq War—the villain, the criminal—partly to serve as additional context for the discussion of narratives of criminality in Iraq War fiction in other chapters.

I will begin with Kate's story of being victimized by the U.S. military's failure to protect female soldiers, and then turn to Naema's story of heroic struggle against the injustices of the U.S. military occupation.

Kate's story is in essence a fictionalized compendium of the many outrages against female soldiers described in nonfiction works such as *The Invisible War* and Benedict's *The Lonely Soldier*. Kate is a kind of synthesized model of the female American soldier-as-victim, and many elements of her story appear chosen in order to fit the narrative prototype of victimization. To begin with, *Sand Queen* makes clear that Kate cannot be blamed for her decision to join the military—in her case, the Army Reserve. She decides to enlist "back in March 2000, way before 9/11, so none of us was thinking about war" (41). Even if a reader believes that war in general, or the GWOT in particular, or even more particularly the Iraq War are manifestly unjust, the novel mitigates Kate's complicity in them by showing that she did not enlist in order to participate in them. Instead, she is persuaded by a recruiter at her school "talking about how noble it is to serve your country," and by the fact that "half the kids in my school were enlisting—the half who got the most respect" (40).[6]

Like the volunteers in so many tales of soldiers-as-victims since World War I, *Sand Queen* suggests that Kate was duped into enlisting in part through manipulative appeals to patriotism and peer pressure. "'The recruiter said I'll be traveling the world and keeping the peace,'" Kate explains to her pacifist boyfriend, who tries to dissuade her by showing her "scary movies about Vietnam" (42). (The notion that Kate, or the author, might find popular American movies about the Vietnam War to be a reason *not* to enlist in the military hints at the radically divergent perspectives on war in contemporary American society.) It is only after Kate is indoctrinated at her "summer boot camp" that she embraces, or at least plays at embracing, the military ethos of toughness and the celebration of violence (43). When she is finally deployed to Iraq to serve as an MP, she draws upon her family's evangelical Christian heritage to tell herself that she will be, like the Lord, lifting up the downtrodden and casting the wicked to the ground (44, see also 202)—where "the wicked," in her mind, may be somehow related to the 9/11 attackers (43).

These early stages in Kate's story are essential to her narrative arc as a victim. In order for her to be a model of the female soldier-as-victim, it is necessary for her to enter the military more or less innocently, or at least with plentiful mitigating factors. The perfect victim should have clean hands, so that her victimization cannot be misunderstood as a just punishment for some wrong. Ideally, victimization should be entirely unearned. Its injustice is a central part of its tragedy, and why stories of victimhood so often call out for the punishment of others—of the one responsible for the victimization: the criminal, the victimizer. Accordingly, if one approaches the U.S. military and its wars through the framework of criminality, as *Sand Queen* does, Kate *must* be oblivious to this criminality when she decides to enlist.

We see further evidence of Kate's naturally good character in her instinctive discomfort at the sight of the Iraqi women who congregate outside the wire perimeter of Camp Bucca, the large but ramshackle U.S.-run detention center for Iraqis where Kate works (25). As Kate approaches the camp's entry checkpoint at the start of the novel, she sees the crowd of Iraqi women—"[m]others and sisters, wives and daughters looking for their men"—and feels a "deep-down ache...again," concluding: "I hate this" (7). Later, the suffering on the women's faces "makes something crack inside of me," and Kate exposes herself to an accusation of disloyalty by disavowing the war to Naema, who has volunteered to serve as an interpreter at the checkpoint (72). Kate quickly develops a tenuous bond with Naema, showing her ability to empathize across cultural fault lines, and soon after criticizes a fellow soldier for using the word "hajji" (75). When Naema asks Kate why she became a soldier, Kate offers an innocent explanation: "'In my country, a lot of people have to be soldiers to pay to go to college'" (73). Oddly, *Sand Queen* did not present this as one of Kate's reasons for enlisting, but it does echo a point sometimes made by opponents of the Iraq War who wish to distinguish their criticism of the war from criticism of the troops. If one assumes that the U.S. military is the bad guy in the story of the Iraq War, as *Sand Queen* does, but wishes to avoid the politically counterproductive excesses of Vietnam-era anti-war criticisms of U.S. soldiers as, for example, "baby killers" (a phrase that Kate's pacifist, anti-Bush friend applies to her, saying she "signed up to be a baby killer" (256)), it is essential to provide excuses for why the U.S. soldiers in the Iraq War volunteered to serve in the military.[7]

All of this is to emphasize that *Sand Queen* lays an extensive foundation for Kate's victimhood by presenting her as, initially at least, largely innocent and good-natured. At the same time, *Sand Queen* does not present Kate as an idealized hero. Although Kate is less hateful toward the Iraqis than many other soldiers in her unit (see, for example, 158, 159), she shares some of their ignorance and casual bigotry, thinking of the Iraqi masses outside the Camp Bucca gate as "damn locals" and viewing them with suspicion (20–21). She seems to view the country as backward, expressing surprise when she learns that Iraqi women are allowed to study medicine (73). She responds to the trauma of her victimization—as described below—not by heroically overcoming it, but by growing increasingly frustrated, anxious, and finally criminally violent.

Most of Kate's story is taken up with the parade of injustices to which the novel subjects her. It seems appropriate simply to list these injustices, in part because their rapid sequencing bears some resemblance to a checklist:

- Three months into her deployment (10), Kate is subjected to unfair criticism by her squad leader, Kormick, apparently because she is a woman (7, 25, 27, 46), one of only three in her platoon (36).
- In general, rather than treating her with camaraderie and as a member of the in-group, the male soldiers harass, exclude, and ignore her, calling her "Tits," reading pornography in front of her, watching her urinate, making lewd comments to her, and above all refusing to talk to her (26, 27, 35, 38, 45–46, 59, 69, 86, 103, 155, 208, 255, etc.).
- The male soldiers in Iraq are such a threat to the female soldiers that the Army has ordered females not to walk alone to the latrines at night "so we can protect each other from getting raped by one of our own fine comrades" (55).[8]
- At least one of the other female soldiers in Kate's platoon blames Kate for the male soldiers' hostility toward her, explaining that she has failed to choose between the only options for a woman in the Army, being a "bitch or a slut" (56, cf. 60).[9]

- The Army has failed to provide sufficient materials to secure the checkpoint where Kate works (8), and has also apparently failed to provide an interpreter to help deal with the crowds of anxious Iraqis massing outside the checkpoint (23).
- Kate's ostensible "battle buddy," the male soldier Rickman, leaves her alone at the checkpoint to chat with another male soldier, violating protocol and placing her at risk (12, 27). But unlike Kate, Rickman is never reprimanded for his missteps (25).
- Kate's living conditions are unhealthy, with the result that she has lost twelve pounds and stopped menstruating, her fingernails are falling off, her hair is "falling out by the handful" (25), she has incessant stomach cramps (38), and she has already had two urinary tract infections and fainted from dehydration three times (27, 38, 39), although some of the latter may be a result of her desire to avoid "the four stinky Porta-Johns" (38).
- Shortly before Kate is to be transferred to a different assignment, Staff Sergeant Kormick and PFC Bonaparte ("Boner") attempt to rape her, and then violently attack her when she resists (78–80, 83).
- After the assault, which is interrupted only through the fortunate intervention of Kate's supportive friend Jimmy, most of the soldiers ostracize Kate further, calling her "party girl" (86) and creating graffiti about her rumored promiscuity. The graffiti refers to her as "SAND QUEEN," a derogatory term for, in Kate's words, "an ugly-ass chick who's being treated like a queen by the hundreds of horny guys around her because there's such a shortage of females" and who "lets herself be passed around like a whore at a frat party, never realizing that back home those same guys wouldn't look at her twice" (104–5).
- Kate is victimized further by the practical difficulties of bringing her aggressors to justice. The Army has created an institutional setting where Kate has many reasons and incentives not to report the crimes against her, including the risk of retaliation, shame at not having defended herself, and the harm she might do to the careers of supportive witnesses such as Jimmy (100, 130).
- Increasing her isolation, Kate's parents refuse to listen or understand when she calls them over a bad connection and seeks their sympathy (105).

- Some of the detainees at the camp discriminate against Kate for being a woman as well, not only throwing spiders and other bugs at her guard tower, but calling her "cunt," masturbating in front of her, and throwing their excrement at her (122, 126–27, 157, 288), something that Jimmy recognizes they would not do to a male guard (128).
- Kate is traumatized further when she learns that Kormick and Boner have gone on to rape one of her friends, a lesbian in the platoon nicknamed Third Eye (138), something that Kate believes might not have happened if Kate had reported their attempted rape of her (145).
- When Kate finally attempts "to do something right for a change" and report Kormick's and Boner's assault, in the hope of preventing future crimes against women (146), she must ask permission from her attempted rapist, Kormick, to see her platoon leader, SFC Henley, who is friends with Kormick and greets her story with hostility. Henley insists that Kormick be present to hear any accusations, and notes that Kormick has already secretly accused Kate of "indecent behavior" that "will lead to trial by court-martial" if she persists in accusing Kormick. Henley announces: "'We can't waste our time...on whiny snivelers like you...Now call Staff Sergeant Kormick in or shut the fuck up and go away'" (151–53).
- As Kate's traumatization continues, she grows more open to the idea of taking revenge by punishing the detainees who expose themselves to her (157, 174), although she continues to disbelieve reports from the Red Cross that U.S. soldiers are violently abusing the detainees in violation of the Geneva Conventions (174).
- Finally, Kate becomes violent toward the detainees:
  - first by firing, with ambiguous legality, into a crowd that is throwing stones at her (180–81);
  - then, with clear illegality, by using her boot to grind the head of a cuffed man she believes to be the masturbating detainee ("the jerk-off")—only to discover in a melodramatic twist that the man is in fact Naema's long-lost father, who has apparently gone mad after U.S. soldiers killed Naema's little brother Zaki (190–91, 282). This prompts Kate to exclaim in inexplicably Victorian diction: "'You mustn't hurt him!'" (192).

- In another illustration of the Army's revictimization of victims of sexual assault, when Kate finally goes to report Kormick's and Boner's crimes to a female Equal Opportunity Officer, the officer listens sympathetically to her story at first (225–26), but later turns mysteriously against Kate and does not intervene when Henley retaliates by reassigning Kate and her friend Yvette to serve in high-risk positions as shooters on a convoy (230–31).
- Compounding Kate's guilt, Yvette is then killed in a mortar attack during the convoy's first mission (258–59), in part thanks to the Army's failure to provide a siren system or mortar-proof bunker (275). Kate also suffers a traumatic brain injury (259, 273, 298).
- Still intoxicated by medications, and feeling increasingly hateful—now thinking of Iraqis as "camel jockeys" and "*towelhead[s]*" (264–65)—Kate takes a further step into criminality by shooting a poor young Iraqi boy's donkey for no reason. She also contemplates shooting the boy (265–66).
- At the peak of Kate's transformation into a criminal who views nearly all of those around her, U.S. military and Iraqi alike, as robots (275–76, 282–83), she shoots and mangles the groin of the masturbating detainee. Then she passes out from dehydration and falls from her guard tower, injuring her back (289, 297–98).
- After returning home, heavily medicated for her injuries (299), Kate shoots out her dining room windows in a fit of PTSD-induced delirium, all while her little sister April watches in horror (213).
- Kate is confined as a psychiatric patient in a military hospital, where she is medicated even more heavily, but her traumatic memories continue to return (81).
- The Army discharges her on medical grounds, but also for "failure to adjust," a stigmatizing term (132).
- Finally, bringing the arc of Kate's victimization to its end, she visits Jimmy, who has himself been victimized by his war experiences, and is retreating into alcoholism (294). Kate learns that Third Eye, her lesbian friend, has committed suicide—the ultimate consequence of Third Eye's victimization during the war (304). The novel ends with Kate mired in guilt, with no end in sight (305).

This admittedly laborious schematic rendering of the outlines of Kate's victimhood makes clear that *Sand Queen* offers something that is quite different from the prototypical narrative of the twentieth-century war novel. As Chapter 2 argued, the narrative prototype for the war novel had become by the end of the twentieth century a story of the soldier as victim, as seen in canonical works by Remarque, Heller, and O'Brien, often woven together with a story of the soldier's disillusionment through battlefield revelation, as described by Harari. The two stories fit together well because the soldier who enters a war based on illusions, whether patriotic or otherwise, may become disillusioned as a result of being victimized and witnessing the victimization of fellow soldiers.

In some ways, Kate's story fits both of these standard arcs. She enlists based on a recruiter's portrait of the nobility of patriotic military service, just the kind of stirring call to arms that so many twentieth-century works attempted to present as a lie. Kate's loss of her friend Yvette in the quasi-combat of the convoy attack delivers her a battlefield revelation that "[w]e soldiers are nothing more than work and killing machines," that is, "robots," so "[f]uck valor and honor" (275). Kate is, in other words, thoroughly disillusioned by the senseless violence of war. "I can't stand the waste of human lives," she thinks soon after (276). Kate arrives, just as in the twentieth-century prototype, at a dehumanized, "materialist" vision of the world, to borrow Harari's term.

The primary difference between Kate's story of victimization and disillusionment and the standard twentieth-century version might seem, at first glance, to be merely that she articulates her materialist disillusionment in the language of *machines* rather than the language of *meat*, perhaps reflecting the rising salience of computers and other technologies in the years leading up to the Iraq War. In a *Farewell to Arms*, Hemingway's narrator states that in war, "I had seen nothing sacred, and the things that were glorious had no glory and the sacrifices were like the stockyards at Chicago if nothing was done with the meat except to bury it" (161). In *Catch-22*, Heller describes the "raw muscles inside" a dying soldier's leg wound twitching "like live hamburger meat," and then the soldier's "insides slither[ing] down to the floor in a soggy pile" containing his "liver, lungs, kidneys, ribs, stomach and bits of...stewed tomatoes" (438–40). Searching for a metaphor of what is close to the human but is used and discarded as though it lacked a soul, Kate arrives at the imagery of robots rather than of livestock.

But in other ways, Kate's story of victimization and disillusionment is remarkably different from the standard twentieth-century model. There is of course the obvious fact that she is a female rather than a male soldier, and the related fact that she experiences her battlefield revelation while serving in a nominally non-combat position—indeed, while legally excluded from serving in combat positions.[10] It may also be noteworthy, against the background of Harari's emphasis on the portrayal of battle as the "ultimate experience," that a desire to experience the extremes of human existence, to confront and overcome the fear of death, or even simply to engage in a challenging, high-risk adventure, played no role in Kate's decision to enlist. Her motives, as we have seen, were patriotic and humanitarian.

But for the concerns of this book, *Sand Queen*'s most significant innovations lie elsewhere. In earlier soldier-as-victim narratives, the soldier tends to be victimized by propagandists and demagogues who lead nations into support for war, or by incompetent and unfeeling officers who order soldiers to risk their lives unnecessarily in operations against a foreign enemy. In neither of these cases, for the most part, does the entity responsible for the soldier's victimization act with the ultimate goal of victimizing the soldier. The victimization of soldiers—their sufferings, traumas, and deaths—are the byproduct of other goals. The general who orders another futile charge into no man's land, or the patriotic schoolteacher who encourages young men to volunteer for the Great War, does not do so *because* he wishes to see his nation's soldiers killed. In both cases, he would be content if the soldiers could live and avoid suffering—provided that his overriding aim of victory or national glory could still be achieved. In the standard twentieth-century version of the soldier-as-victim story, the victimizer responsible for the soldier's victimization is reprehensible because he is willing to sacrifice young men's lives for a purpose that is worth less than their lives—not because he specifically intends, as his ultimate goal, the deaths of these young men.

Drawing very loosely on the way that the law analyzes liability, we might say that the victimizer's culpability in these standard twentieth-century stories is based on his mental state of negligence or recklessness, rather than intent. He is negligent or reckless with young men's lives, but he does not intend, at least as his final aim, to see them suffer and die. To the extent that the criminal law considers intent to be the most culpable mental state, we might question whether the victimizer's acts deserve to be classified as "criminal," even figuratively.

In *Sand Queen*, by contrast, Kate's victimizers often intend to harm her, and their acts are sometimes literally criminal. Kormick and Boner commit prosecutable, criminal acts when they assault and attempt to rape her. Henley and the Equal Opportunity Officer at least arguably engage in obstruction of justice—a crime under article 134 of the Uniform Code of Military Justice—when they cover up Kormick's and Boner's crimes by impeding Kate's attempts to report what happened. The novel presents the Army as a whole as willfully blind to the sexual harassment and assault of its female soldiers. (Willful blindness can usually serve as a substitute for culpable knowledge in criminal cases.) Unlike in the twentieth-century prototype of the victim-as-soldier narrative, in *Sand Queen* the primary victimizers of the protagonist soldier are presented as literally, legally criminal.

Even more significantly, the culmination of Kate's victimization arrives through her own transformation into a criminal. Toward the start of the novel, Kate notes with discomfort various aspects of the U.S. occupation that may result in Iraqi deaths. When an Iraqi mother at the checkpoint tries to hand her a limp, sore-covered baby, Kate registers that it is problematic that the wealthy, occupying nation is incapable of providing "a doctor...medicine...[or] a fucking hospital" (24). Soon after, she remembers being ordered by a convoy commander on the way to Camp Bucca not to provide water to the desperate, bare-footed children who beg for it "because those babies might be carrying bombs" (26). When she describes her team's "routine" during searches of passing vehicles, she highlights its arbitrariness and injustice, noting that the soldiers sometimes take "hoards of jewels and dinars" when they find them, "sometimes not," and "[t]hen we either arrest the men or send them on their way, depending on how they behave and our moods" (36). In other words, reflecting her basically morally good nature before its corruption by military service, Kate begins the novel with a degree of concern for the people of Iraq.

But by the end of the novel, in the wake of her multiple traumas, victimization, and disillusionment, Kate is consumed by hate toward Iraqis, and wants to kill them. "'Those people killed Yvette. They tried to kill all of us,'" she explains to Jimmy (283). She thinks to herself: "I know who I hate and I know who I want to kill" (283). Soon after, she commits the war crimes against Iraqis noted above: the abuse of the cuffed detainee who turns out to be Naema's father, and the shooting of "the jerk-off." During her downward descent, Kate also nearly stabs Kormick and threatens with apparent sincerity to shoot "Macktruck," a male soldier who has been sexually harassing her since their arrival at Camp Bucca (223, 286–87).

In the standard twentieth-century soldier-as-victim narrative, the peak of the soldier's victimization and the primary focus of the soldier's trauma tends to be his guilt over the death or wounding of his friends, or his suffering as a result of his own physical or psychological injury. In *Sand Queen*, by contrast, Kate's trauma and sense of guilt is not only focused on her sense of responsibility for Yvette's death, but also on her own violent acts toward Iraqis. Shortly after Kate assaults Naema's father, she begins experiencing traumatized flashbacks to the incident. The memories interrupt her budding romance with Jimmy and lead her to conclude that she does not deserve to be loved (204, 210, 285–86). After her return home, Kate remains tormented by traumatic memories and the threat of those memories being triggered back to life (213, 234). Kate's litany of the sources of her guilt includes Yvette's death, but is largely taken up with harms she caused or imagines she caused to Iraqis: "Yvette's blood, Zaki's blood, the jerk-off's blood, the blood of the Iraqi worker I let die in the mortar attack. The blood of that little boy's donkey. Naema's dad covered in it as I ground his face into the sand" (299). In her final words in the novel, back in the United States, Kate expresses her guilt to Jimmy. She expresses guilt not only for the role she feels she played in the death of Yvette and the suicide of Third Eye, but also for harming Naema's father and failing to protect her little brother: "'I've killed so many of them. Oh God, when will it stop?'" (305).

In other words, by the end of *Sand Queen*, the focus of Kate's ongoing psychological trauma is not only her sense of responsibility for the deaths of her friends, as in so many earlier works of war literature, but at least equally her sense of guilt over wrongful and sometimes criminal acts toward the people of Iraq. Her guilt can be seen as an illustration of the conceptual connection between cosmopolitanism and the perception of war through the lens of criminality. Unlike so many soldiers in twentieth-century war literature, Kate recognized the humanity of the people of Iraq from the moment of her arrival. Because she recognizes Iraqis as deserving of her moral concern, she cannot ultimately dismiss the harms she has caused them as acts authorized or excused by the special nature of war. Instead, her violent acts toward Iraqis leave her feeling like a criminal.

NAEMA AS HERO

The presentation of the Iraq War within the framework of criminality is, if anything, even clearer in the chapters of *Sand Queen* written from Naema's perspective. If Kate's story sometimes resembles an assembled catalogue of depredations suffered by female servicemembers in Iraq, Naema's story seems dedicated to cataloguing instances of the U.S. military's victimization of the people of Iraq. Naema's life has been a parade of horrors, nearly all presented as the result of actions or inactions by Americans: the Iran–Iraq War (92); the "Kuwait war," which "slaughtered hundreds of thousands of our people" with American weapons (92); the "ruthless deprivation" of American sanctions in the 1990s (92); Saddam's use of American weapons and sometimes support "to torture and murder us for decades" (92, but see 115); the bombing of Baghdad by the Americans in March 2003 (29); the failure of American soldiers, lounging in the sun after the invasion, to stop the looting of shops, homes, and museums, to provide security from criminals who kidnapped children for ransom and raped "[m]any girls and women" (30); and so on.

When American soldiers raid Naema's house in the middle of the night, arresting her innocent father and little brother without explanation, the soldiers appear as inhuman apparitions of violent masculinity: "Hideous in their bulky uniforms, their faces obscured by goggles and helmets, their huge guns thrusting, voices roaring fury and insults" (16). The soldiers "stamped their filthy boots down on the necks of Papa and Zaki" (16), which is presumably meant to be seen as an especially humiliating form of brutality where shoes are viewed as offensively unclean. When Naema approaches Camp Bucca and first sees Kate, she mistakes Kate for a tiny boy, noting: "But of course he is no child. He is a killer and an occupier" (18). Based on the experiences above, Naema naturally views American soldiers as presumptively criminal.

In the narrative scaffolding supporting this collection of outrages, as noted above, Naema is the hero. Her fight for justice exemplifies what *Sand Queen* presents as the highest moral values in wartime. She struggles against the villainous Americans "and their armies of thugs" (91). She adopts her heroic stance early on, declaring that after her father's and brother's abductions, "[i]t was up to me now, and me alone, to make sure my family survived" (34). Through the remainder of the novel, she undertakes valiant efforts, at great personal risk, to confirm that her father and brother are being held at Camp Bucca. Meanwhile, her grandmother Maryam's health deteriorates under the stress of the occupation. In Maryam's delirium, she confuses the Americans with Saddam's soldiers and arrives at the view of war as criminality that in some sense underlies the novel as a whole: "All soldiers are the same to her, whatever their uniforms, whatever their justifications. All are murderers" (65). Naema echoes Maryam's insight later on, noting that "[i]t is the business of war to be unjust and cruel...To imprison and kill the innocent" (195).

We also see glimpses of Naema's strength and independence in flashbacks to her behavior before the war. Exemplifying how a liberated woman should take control of her own life, Naema declines her lover Khalil's offer of marriage, declaring, "I need first to follow my own dreams" (91), such as traveling "to London and Paris, to Istanbul and Rome" and learning more languages and medical skills with which she can help her country (91).

In the climactic scene of Naema's hero-quest, she brings her dying grandmother to an understaffed, underequipped hospital full of the dead and dying, its floors splattered with blood, vomit, and urine, and she uses her skills learned from medical school to save these other Iraqi victims of the American war while her grandmother dies (219, 249–52, 278). This is Naema's equivalent to the scene of battlefield revelation, her glimpse of "hell on earth" (279). But rather than leaving her disillusioned with all ideals, she is inspired to further bravery. In the novel's final chapter, we see a transformed Naema, "beyond revulsion or pity...beyond any feeling at all" (307), draining the fluids from her grandmother's body and burying her. Naema's heroic "quest" (309) to find her brother and father will go on. She will continue to travel to Camp Bucca, "keeping an eye out for al-Sadr's thugs and the American soldiers and their merciless guns" (309).

Thus, *Sand Queen* closes on a juxtaposition of the Mahdi army and the U.S. Army, leaving the impression of both as criminal threats to the people, and especially the women, of Iraq. A civilian Iraqi woman has the novel's final word.

THE IRAQ WAR AS A CRIMINAL ENTERPRISE

The Iraq War veteran, essayist, and English professor Ray Scranton, whose novel on the Iraq War is discussed in Chapter 9, tweeted in 2016: "You know what would be awesome? More veterans whining about how nobody understands the moral complexity of being an imperial stormtrooper." A reviewer of Scranton's novel in *The New Republic* approvingly quoted this tweet and noted that "[t]he unwillingness of most veterans' fiction to cast soldiers in an unsympathetic light—even when they commit war crimes—is one of the most striking elements" of the first wave of Iraq War fiction, including novels like *The Yellow Birds*, discussed in Chapter 5. The reviewer predicted that a second wave of Iraq War fiction would, like Scranton's novel *War Porn*, grapple more openly with the complicity of U.S. soldiers in the more criminal, or at least morally problematic, aspects of the Iraq War.[11]

Sand Queen is a fascinating contribution to the early canon of Iraq War fiction precisely because it portrays U.S. soldiers as engaged in a largely criminal enterprise—both against Iraqis and against the female soldiers among themselves. In that sense, it anticipates later novels that are more critical of U.S. servicemembers, like *War Porn*. But *Sand Queen* also provides a rejoinder to the critique of early Iraq War fiction for focusing too much on the victimization of U.S. soldiers. To the extent that the critique assumes that U.S. soldiers in the Iraq War were more the cause of harm than harmed, and thus should be evaluated more within the frame of criminality than that of victimhood, *Sand Queen* offers a reminder through Kate's story—almost too clearly—that even someone participating in great harms, even a soldier who commits war crimes, may be understood as a victim. Indeed, as in the case of child soldiers, *Sand Queen* suggests that a victim's participation in criminality may itself be one of the ultimate realizations of her victimhood. To become a criminal through the character-distorting forces of war is to suffer not only physical or mental trauma, but a kind of moral trauma as well—not just the harming of the body or mind, but what might be seen as the harming of the soul: a moral injury.[12]

Yet if Kate can be seen as a victim in part by virtue of her criminality, could it be possible to view her victimizers as victims as well? If the logic of mercy can extend to Kate for her harms to Iraqis, it is unclear why it cannot also extend to those who harmed her. Kate's power over the Iraqis she harms is structurally analogous to her aggressors' power over her. It may be inconsistent to claim that her aggressors are not entitled to mercy simply because of their greater power.

Of course, we do not learn the stories of Kate's victimizers. But in the words of Jean Renoir, "everyone has their reasons"—or, as most participants in adversary criminal proceedings in the United States would recognize, every story of a criminal can become the story of a victim with enough empathy, and enough resources. Harmful acts can be redescribed as the product of conditions stretching back to the wrongdoer's childhood and beyond. A serious moral recognition of the wrongfulness of an act, and of the harms it has caused, is compatible with a recognition that all human behavior is shaped by conditions, and that harm often results from and gives rise to other harms. *Sand Queen* stops short of exploring what a war story about wrongdoing might look like if we extended a holistic view of responsibility to all who cause harm.

CHAPTER EIGHT

AMERICAN SNIPER (2012)

> *There is a class of men in whom is contained a distilled essence of the American spirit. Sturdy, taciturn and mysterious, these men tend to come from places like Virginia, Georgia, Texas. They have a devout attachment to guns, which are, to them, Old Testament swords of righteousness. Their seriousness of purpose seems archaic. They are our warrior class. Women find them irresistible; lesser men salute, if they are wise, or scoff, if they are not...After 40 years of Hollywood counterpropaganda telling us war is necessarily corrupting and malign, its ablest practitioners thugs, loons or victims, "American Sniper" nobly presents the case for the other side.*
>
> (*From a review of American Sniper in the* New York Post)[1]

> *[A] mawkish, fawning tribute to a diseased serial killer [based on] a biography in which the killer himself spells out in appalling detail his own disgusting sickness.*
>
> (*From a review of American Sniper in* CounterPunch)[2]

Unlike the other works about the Iraq War discussed in this book, Chris Kyle's *American Sniper*, first published in 2012, is a best-selling memoir rather than a work of literary fiction. In form, it resembles a cross between a military-themed action-thriller, a patriotic pro-war manifesto, and a motivational autobiography.

Like many popular thrillers, *American Sniper* begins with an action-packed vignette, a sample of the book's offerings that is presumably intended to hook potential readers while they browse the best-seller stand. In a high-tech sans serif font, the prologue announces its title—"EVIL IN THE CROSSHAIRS"—and sets the scene in Hollywood action-movie fashion—"LATE MARCH 2003. IN THE AREA OF NASIRIYA, IRAQ"—before plunging into the story of Kyle's first killing as a sniper: "I looked through the scope of the sniper rifle, scanning down the road of the tiny Iraqi town..." (1).[3] Two pages later, Kyle saves a marine foot patrol by shooting and killing an Iraqi woman who is holding a Chinese grenade. It was "the first time I'd killed anyone while I was on the sniper rifle," and "the only time...I killed anyone other than a male combatant," he assures the reader (3). The remainder of the 377-page memoir unfolds in short, easy-to-digest sections, each only a few pages long and heavy on action, drama, and folksy observations: "Shooting the big machine gun was *fun*!" (70). Frequent subheadings like "JUST A COWBOY AT HEART" (7), "GETTING MY ASS KICKED" (26), and "LOVE" (40) minimize the risk that a distracted reader will grow bored.

In other words, *American Sniper* is not, and does not try to be, a work of high literary art. Because the book is also not a work of fiction, it might not seem to be an appropriate subject for a chapter in a book on American literary fiction about the Iraq War. In order to understand why the inclusion of *American Sniper* is not only appropriate, but almost indispensable, it will be helpful first to provide some background on Kyle's life and contested legacy.

THE PLACE OF *AMERICAN SNIPER* IN THE CANON OF IRAQ WAR LITERATURE

Kyle was a sniper in the Navy SEALs. He deployed to Iraq four times between 2003 and 2008. According to Kyle, "[t]he Navy credits me with more kills as a sniper than any other American service member, past or present. I guess that's true" (5).[4] After his retirement in 2009, Kyle undertook a variety of projects, including starting a security training company and a nonprofit for veterans, the Heroes Project. He also served as a bodyguard for reality television star and former Republican vice-presidential candidate Sarah Palin.

In early 2012, HarperCollins published *American Sniper: The Autobiography of the Most Lethal Sniper in U.S. History*. Kyle had written the book with help from ghost-writers Jim DeFelice, an author of popular military thrillers, and Scott McEwan, a trial attorney who helped negotiate Kyle's book contract. *American Sniper* describes Kyle's upbringing in Texas, his training to become a Navy SEAL, his many experiences in combat during his four deployments, and his post-Navy life focused on family, entrepreneurship, and helping other veterans. The book, which arrived less than a year after the killing of Osama bin Laden by members of SEAL Team Six, brought increased public attention to the SEALs and became a great success. It rose to the top of the *New York Times* best-seller list and reportedly sold 1.2 million copies in 2012 and 2013. Kyle became a celebrity, especially in conservative media, and appeared on a short-lived reality TV show, "Stars Earn Stripes." The actor Bradley Cooper purchased the film rights to the book. Although precise numbers are not publicly available, the book has by now sold well over two million copies, and seems destined to remain the most widely read book about the Iraq War.

As his fame grew, Kyle continued to help struggling veterans, including by taking them to shooting ranges as a form of therapy. On February 2, 2013, Kyle and a friend brought a severely mentally ill marine veteran named Eddie Ray Routh to a shooting range on a lodge in Texas. Routh then shot and killed Kyle and his friend. He was later sentenced to life without parole for the murders. An enormous memorial service for Kyle was held in Cowboys Stadium, and Tea Party groups funded the creation of a muscle-bound memorial sculpture of Kyle.[5]

After Kyle's death, the film version of *American Sniper* continued its development. Clint Eastwood took over from Steven Spielberg as director, and the movie was released in the United States on Christmas Day 2014. It became the first blockbuster film about the Iraq War, after a long series of financial disappointments. In fact, Eastwood's *American Sniper* became the highest-grossing film released in the United States in 2014, the highest-grossing war film of all time, and the highest-grossing film of Eastwood's career.[6]

The film provoked a great deal of ideological controversy and commentary, as suggested by the contrasting passages from two reviews used as epigraphs above. In the most extreme instances from social media, a comedy actor compared the film's celebration of Kyle to Nazi propaganda, and voices on the supportive Right suggested that the film had stirred up their desire "to kill some fucking ragheads."[7]

Meanwhile, various controversies surrounding Kyle continued. Jesse Ventura, a Navy veteran, former professional wrestler, and governor of Minnesota, successfully sued Kyle's estate for defamation based on a passage in *American Sniper* (not included in more recent editions) that described Kyle punching someone he later identified as Ventura for speaking disrespectfully of the SEALs. In 2016, *The Intercept* published a story alleging that Kyle had exaggerated his medal counts, leading the Navy to revise his official record.[8] Journalists also raised serious doubts about the accuracy of other stories that Kyle had told, such as the claim "that in the aftermath of Hurricane Katrina in 2005 Kyle and a friend went down to New Orleans and killed 30 thugs and criminals," and "that in 2009, shortly after he retired from the SEALs, he shot dead two thugs who tried to steal his truck."[9]

As the literary scholar Peter Molin has observed, "[i]t's easy to speculate" that if Kyle had lived, he "would be a conservative icon for like-minded veterans and members of the public, racking up millions of followers and thousands of likes proclaiming the virtues of a good-man-with-a-gun while 'owning the libs' with his well-aimed Twitter shots."[10] In a suggestion of what might have been, Kyle's friend and fellow SEAL Marcus Luttrell, who also published a best-selling, ghostwritten memoir of post-9/11 military service that was turned into a successful Hollywood movie, appeared at the Republican National Convention in 2016 to endorse Donald Trump, and later co-hosted a political talk show executive-produced by Glenn Beck.

American Sniper deserves a chapter in a book on American fiction about the Iraq War because it reflects a right-wing view of the war, and of military service in general, that is accepted by a large part of the American public, including some members of the military, but that rarely appears in contemporary literary fiction except as a subject of ridicule. Because there is no right-wing literary novel of the Iraq War that can be plausibly juxtaposed with the critical novels discussed in this book's other chapters—no pro-war *Storm of Steel* to set beside their *All Quiet on the Western Front*—it is necessary to turn to a type of writing other than literary fiction in order to explore the right-wing perspective on U.S. military service in Iraq. Without attending to that perspective, the book might be seen as offering a misleading picture of contemporary American cultural representations of the Iraq War.[11]

A comparison with Paul Fussell's *The Great War and Modern Memory* illustrates the risk of focusing too narrowly on one part of a community in studying how the culture of war has changed. Fussell's classic Vietnam-era work on the British literature of the trenches in World War I has been criticized for creating the impression that the war fostered an ironic rejection of nationalist militarism in British culture as a whole, when in fact the cultural transformation that Fussell describes happened much more gradually, and for the most part later. Fussell concentrated on the anti-militarist writings of a small portion of the British elite who served on the Western front. Later research showed that these writings were not representative of British public opinion, or even of the views of British soldiers as a whole.[12]

This book would be similarly misleading if, by focusing only on literary fiction about the Iraq War, it gave the impression that American culture as a whole has moved toward a concern with wrongdoing and criminality among American soldiers in war. To the contrary, the nationalist-militarist Right in the contemporary United States vehemently rejects the focus on soldier wrongdoing and guilt that pervades the literary fiction of the Iraq War, just as it in many ways rejects the moral cosmopolitanism that helps to motivate that concern.[13] Literary writers such as Klay and Scranton are a small but not insignificant part of an ongoing, potentially reversible development in the cultural understanding of war, just as Wilfred Owen and Sigfried Sassoon were in their time. Where the development will lead can no more be predicted today than it could have been in the 1920s. One goal of this chapter, in any case, is to suggest the great distance between most literary writers' views of military service in the Iraq War and the contrasting views that circulate in a large part of the surrounding American culture today.

AMERICAN SNIPER AS A SELF-UNDERMINING HERO STORY

In its narrative structure, *American Sniper* is in essence an attempt to tell a story of American military service in the Iraq War as a traditional hero story. Kyle not only rejects the figure of the soldier-as-criminal that haunts many works of literary fiction about the Iraq War. He also largely rejects the idea of the soldier-as-victim that has become customary in the canon of war literature over the last century. Kyle's commitments are explicit. In discussing his volunteer work with struggling veterans, for example, he notes that "[w]hat wounded veterans don't need is sympathy. They need to be treated like the men they are: equals, heroes, and people who still have tremendous value for society" (371). He named his veterans-services nonprofit "The Heroes Project." *American Sniper* is an attempt to renew the ancient narrative template of the heroic warrior that anti-war critics often assume was buried in the muddy trenches of Passchendaele, or at least lost in the jungles of Vietnam. The failure of Kyle's attempt, as described in this chapter, suggests that straightforwardly reviving a traditional warrior-as-hero narrative under contemporary conditions, but especially in a story of the U.S. engagement in Iraq, may not be possible.[14]

Kyle begins *American Sniper* by describing his "traditional values, like patriotism, self-reliance, and watching out for your family and neighbors" (7). He proclaims himself a Christian, and states that he has "a strong sense of justice" that is "pretty much black-and-white" (7). In sum, his priorities are "God, Country, Family," in that order, at least for most of the book (7–8, 117–18, 302).

Of course, these abstract labels could mean almost anything in practice. They certainly do not, by themselves, dictate a life largely devoted to armed killing. In order to understand the specific ideal of a man's life that Kyle seems driven to fulfill, it may be helpful to turn to an offhand remark he makes much later in the memoir, after describing his purchase of some pirated DVDs from a street stand in Baghdad. He buys "some Clint Eastwood, some John Wayne," and notes: "I love John Wayne. I love his cowboy movies especially, which makes sense I guess" (195). His love of cowboy movies "makes sense" on a superficial level because we know by this point that Kyle grew up in small-town Texas (7); rode horses, hunted, and raised steers and heifers (8, 10–11); participated in rodeo competitions in high school (12–13); and worked as a ranch hand in Texas and Colorado before joining the Navy (15–17). But it makes a much more significant kind of sense when we consider the values and language that structure *American Sniper*.

As David Buchanan notes in *Going Scapegoat*, his book on post-9/11 war literature, the racist myth of heroic cowboys fighting savage Indians has played a central role in U.S. military culture throughout its history, from the use of Native or pseudo-Native names for military equipment ("Kiowa," "Apache," and "Black Hawk" helicopters, "Tomahawk" missiles), to the description of enemies using Wild West imagery.[15] Kyle embraces the language of "cowboys and Indians," and the ideas behind it, with a passion. From the book's earliest pages, he introduces and defends his use of the epithet "savages" to describe those he fought: "Savage, despicable evil. That's what we were fighting in Iraq. That's why a lot of people, myself included, called the enemy 'savages'...I only wish I had killed more" (4). As the book progresses and becomes increasingly bloody and cavalier about killing, the language intensifies. "I hated the damn savages I'd been fighting. I always will," Kyle declares after noting that he has gotten a blood-red Crusader cross tattoo, to tell the world "I was a Christian" (219). By the end of the book Kyle is describing raids "deep into Injun territory" in Iraq "to look and wait for the bad guys...We were protectors, bait, and slayers" (267). Eventually, it almost seems as though the whole of Iraq outside of the Americans' bases is "Injun country" (291).

In other words, Kyle's values in many ways resemble the values of a John Wayne character in a cowboy movie.[16] Like in the portrayal of Wayne's Sheriff Chance in *Rio Bravo*—which Kyle says may be his favorite John Wayne movie (195)—the central narrative through-line of Kyle's self-crafted story in *American Sniper* is his aggressive protection of those who are close to him from violent enemies.[17] The hero-story that he wants his life to be is the story of using force to defend vulnerable friends from threatening enemies, especially criminals or members of a hostile out-group—and then, once the threat has been eliminated, returning to a life focused on love and wholesome patriarchal family values, like Sheriff Chance finally showing his affection for Angie Dickinson's Feathers at the end of *Rio Bravo*.

But as Chapter 4 suggested, values have changed in the United States since the release of *Rio Bravo*. For example, John Wayne was an openly committed white supremacist, something that is generally considered taboo today. In a 1971 *Playboy* interview, twelve years after the release of *Rio Bravo*, Wayne was still making public statements like the following: "I believe in white supremacy until the blacks are educated to a point of responsibility."[18] During his career, Wayne's white supremacism did not damage his popularity any more than his lifelong embrace of militarism, authoritarianism, or the celebration of America's ethnic cleansing of indigenous peoples. The year of Wayne's *Playboy* interview was the same year that he received a prize from the Marine Corps League for being the man "who best exemplifies the word 'American.'"[19]

Wayne's white supremacy is only a particularly stark illustration of the shifts in values that have occurred since the creation of the Westerns that helped shape Kyle's narrative aspirations for his life. To take another example, Kyle has nothing critical to say about his father's strict discipline, including the kind of corporal punishment that is now condemned by pediatric experts as harmful to children (9).[20] Kyle's casual acceptance or even celebration of once-common violence that many parts of American society would now consider harmful, if not criminal, is also reflected in his many unapologetic tales of hazing and bar fights, discussed below. Kyle's patriotism may appear equally old-fashioned, as he seems to recognize when he follows a solemn description of the raising of the American flag after a battle with the following comment: "I've lived the literal meaning of the 'land of the free' and 'home of the brave.' It's not corny for me. I feel it in my heart. I feel it in my chest" (85). Kyle also assumes old-fashioned patriarchal values and gender roles throughout the book, from his insistence that "my story is...about being a man" (6), to his largely untroubled acceptance of his wife's burdens in raising their children alone (196), to his joking insistence that his daughter will be "allowed to date...around the time she turns thirty" (368). Any doubts about Kyle's sensitivities regarding racial and sexual identity can probably be put to rest by an anecdote in a posthumous *New Yorker* profile. The article describes how a friend pranked Kyle by putting pro-Obama bumper stickers on his truck, and Kyle responded by putting a bumper sticker on the friend's truck that declared "I Love Black Cock."[21]

The purpose of drawing attention to Kyle's traditional values is not to suggest that he is an outlier in the contemporary United States. On the contrary, Kyle's story of his service in Iraq—his choices about how to structure the narrative, what to include and exclude, how to characterize and comment on people and places—is worth analyzing precisely because it appears to resonate with the values of a large part of the American public, as the extraordinary success of Kyle's memoir and Eastwood's film suggests. Understood in light of these traditional values, the U.S. invasion of Iraq represented a conflict between upstanding, heroic enforcers of the law and foreign savages. It was, in other words, a story of cowboys and Indians.

This is the story that Kyle tries to tell in *American Sniper*. Like a mythological hero, he was born, fortuitously, in the half-tamed wilds of Texas, and imbued with simple, upright Christian values from an early age. After a time of wandering in the wilderness as a lonesome cowboy, he faced and overcame a transformative test to become a Navy SEAL. When his nation was attacked on September 11, 2001, he joined the band of righteous warriors who retaliated by setting out for the frontier, on a crusade to a savage land. He slaughtered the shadowy evildoers there. Like a modern Achilles, he achieved excellence in battle. Having fulfilled his duty with honor, he returned home to dedicate himself to his family and to others he loved. The savages of the frontier would think twice before attacking his great nation again.

But the story will not tell. Tensions, contradictions, and silences assert and reassert themselves, undermining the heroic narrative template. The next two sections describe, first, the tension between Kyle's presentation of his military service as straightforwardly heroic and his wife Taya's emphasis on his failure to place her and his children above his enjoyment of being a sniper; and, second, the tension between Kyle's attempt to present his service as unambiguously good and the hints of wrongful violence that appear throughout the narrative.

In order to prevent what is already a long chapter from becoming even longer, I do not explore a third tension: the questionable logic of Kyle's political reasoning about the Iraq War, which provides part of the foundation for his portrayal of his own actions as heroic. Despite Kyle's conventional and reasonable suggestion that he and other soldiers should not be blamed for an unpopular war—"I do not choose which battles I go to. Ya'll send me to them" (118)—he in fact offers frequent defenses of the Iraq War, including through the argument that Saddam Hussein possessed weapons of mass destruction (47, 50, 69, 88, 89, 130). Because Kyle does not believe that Iraqi democracy is possible and in general does not give a "flying fuck" about the people of Iraq (194), he also naturally rejects the underlying premises and goals of the U.S. counterinsurgency strategy (250–54, 299–300).

Kyle's sense of the ultimate purpose of the Iraq War is not entirely clear. Perhaps it is the argument, frequently asserted by the war's supporters but rarely explained in detail, that it was necessary to fight "them" "over there" so that "we" would not have to fight "them" "here." Similar arguments were offered in defense of U.S. military involvement in Vietnam.[22]

THE HERO'S FAMILY AS VICTIM?

The aristocratic warrior epics were written before modernity, and thus before the general, ongoing rise of women's political, economic, and cultural power that has done so much to shape the course of modernity, especially over the last two centuries. In an epic such as *Beowulf*, the concerns of women usually play a peripheral role, often limited to uniting warring clans through marriage, giving birth to children who can carry on dynastic rule, performing ceremonial duties like Wealhþēow's carrying of the hostess's cup, and mourning the fallen men who are close to them. Women generally do not become warriors, and male warrior-heroes generally are not portrayed as engaging in childcare or domestic work.[23] When the aging Beowulf, now a king, defends his people by going to battle a dragon, the poem does not consider the possibility that he might be abandoning his family in a selfish quest for further glory.

By framing his service in Iraq as, in effect, a "cowboys and Indians" story focused on killing "savages," Kyle places himself in a tradition of masculine warriors that stretches back to the ancient epics. He even uses archaic diction with roots in Old English when he speaks of "slaying" the enemy and of their "slaughter" (244, 267, 271, 297). But Kyle also perceives, and explicitly struggles with, the conflict between traditional warrior values and other, traditionally more feminine commitments. In *American Sniper*, these commitments appear under the term "family." Kyle initially presents his priorities as God, then Country, then Family, but toward the end of the book he notes that "these days I've come around to believing that Family may, under some circumstances, outrank Country" (7–8; see also 117–18, 302, 322–23). His priorities differ from those of his wife, Taya, who in her words has "*always believed that your responsibility is to God, family, and country—in that order*" (213, 359). This statement appears in one of several lengthy italicized passages written in the voice of Taya, and presented as though they are based on interviews with her (for example, 41).

It might be argued that the traditional warrior-hero is honored in part because he is willing to risk his life to defend others. He places their lives ahead of his own, and in that sense is selfless. But the details in *American Sniper*, including Taya's italicized commentaries, give the sense that Kyle actually *prefers* to be deployed to Iraq, where he can engage in the killing that is his true passion, rather than living at home with his family. Like a comic-book illustration of Bourke's historical research showing that many soldiers find great pleasure in killing, Kyle returns incessantly to his enjoyment of the war.[24] Being a SEAL was "the time of my life" and "fun" (6). "*Fuck*," Kyle thinks to himself once he finally experiences "the thrill of battle" (71), "*this is great. I fucking love this*" (74). The start of the war is a "high" (80). "*Man, this is going to be good*," Kyle thinks later. "*We are going to kill massive amounts of bad guys. And I'm going to be in the middle of it.*" (131; see also 77, 118). "We were thrilled to be getting into a real battle" (135). "I wanted to shoot someone," Kyle notes shortly before the beginning of the Second Battle of Fallujah (142). When insurgents try to cross a marsh using beach balls, Kyle shoots the balls one by one: "Hell—it was a *lot* of fun. The insurgents were fighting among themselves...The ones who couldn't grab on promptly sank and drowned" (178). When he is not killing, Kyle quickly gets "bored" (161), just as he says all SEALs are jealous when they miss out on action—in other words, on "all the fun" (181–82, 184; see also 80, 83, 84). "Even with the pain, I loved what I was doing. Maybe war isn't really fun, but I certainly was enjoying it" (191). "I like war, and I love doing my job" (323). Kyle sees himself as "one lucky motherfucker" because he has had the opportunity to kill so many people

(192). When "[w]e had contact every time we went out," "[w]e loved it" (240). "I was loving what I was doing…I was getting to use my rifle, and killing enemies" (245). Eventually, Kyle's passion for killing takes on sexual overtones: "The pace was hot and heavy. It made us want more. We ached for it" (271).

By contrast, Kyle expresses little passion for his family responsibilities. As he leaves his newborn first son, he notes: "I felt bad about leaving Taya. She was still healing from the birth. But at the same time, I felt my duty as a SEAL was more important…I wanted to go to war" (117). He concedes that early on, "while I loved my son, I hadn't yet bonded with him…I still hadn't experienced the real depth of what being a father is all about" (118). Kyle's expression of love for his son is all the more perfunctory when placed beside the intensity of his love for killing in Iraq. In general, his accounts of his family life between deployments are relatively sparse and unenthusiastic, like necessary but often frustrating pauses in the action. In a chapter titled "FAMILY CONFLICTS," he highlights his disagreements with Taya and his increasingly "explosive" temper (202, 204). When Kyle is at home while Taya is pregnant with their second child, he "missed the excitement and the thrill. I loved killing bad guys" (220). "I was excited about doing my job again" (220). Later, Kyle does not object to yet another deployment, because "I still loved war" (324). In fact, "it felt good to be getting back to war…I was ready to kill some more bad guys" (329). When Taya finally persuades him not to reenlist by threatening a separation, Kyle seems to come around only grudgingly, and continues to have deep reservations about not having attempted to join the ultra-elite SEAL Team Six, the unit that would go on to kill Osama bin Laden (320–23, 356).

In light of Kyle's evident devotion to killing and his lack of any comparably intense feeling for family life, his multiple deployments to Iraq seem less heroic than they otherwise might, at least to the extent that heroism implies self-sacrifice. The reader has the sense that it would have been far more difficult, in fact, far more of a personal sacrifice and burden, for Kyle to remain at home and focus on supporting Taya and their children. Taya's devastating observations drive the point home, especially as she comes to accept what the reader has seen from the start: "*I realized I wasn't the most important thing in his life*" (312). The following exchange, recounted by Taya, is difficult to reconcile with the notion of Kyle as a selfless hero, willing to sacrifice his interests for the good of others:

> *He thought dying on the battlefield was the greatest. I tried to tell him differently, but he didn't believe it...*
>
> *I tried to explain that he was irreplaceable to me. When that didn't seem to faze him, I tried another equally valid point. "But you've got our son," I told him.*
>
> *"So what? You'll find someone else and that guy will raise him."* (196)

Even a battlefield death—sacrificing one's own life in battle—seems less selfless if it is pursued in the interest of personal glory or for the love of military adventure, with no concern for loved ones who will suffer. *American Sniper*'s juxtaposition of Taya's perspective with Kyle's sometimes suggests that the memoir may be deliberately attempting to undermine the authority or reliability of Kyle's version of events. One passage in which Kyle boasts about "lov[ing]" getting contact "every time we went out," for example, is followed by an abrupt transition to Taya stating: "*I had a hard time with the kids after Chris deployed...I'd sit there and cry*" (240). In any case, the inclusion of Taya's perspective interferes, deliberately or not, with the reader's ability to embrace Kyle's commitments as unambiguously good.

Through a series of awkward transitions in its final pages, *American Sniper* attempts to reconcile Kyle's and Taya's values, presenting Kyle as implausibly transformed into a devoted husband and father who has finally embraced his domestic responsibilities. One moment, Kyle notes with startling sensitivity that "I'd just forgotten what it means to be in love—the responsibilities that come with it, like truly listening and sharing" (320). The next moment, he concedes that he has secretly been in communication with another woman: "Soon my old girlfriend and I were talking and texting regularly" (320). Shortly after drunkenly totaling his truck, Kyle declares: "I have gotten to a point where being a SEAL no longer defines me. I need to be a husband and a father. Those things, now, are my first calling" (373). Then another passage in Taya's voice calls into question how much has changed, concluding with the lukewarm affirmation: "*We may love each other differently, but maybe that is a good thing. Maybe it is more forgiving and more mature, or maybe it is just different*" (375). This pronouncement, delivered as though through gritted teeth, is followed by an abrupt transition to Kyle announcing that his love for Taya has gotten deeper, and Taya suddenly returning in italics to note that "*I feel something coming from him that I hadn't felt before...I feel loved. And I feel the kids and I are important*" (375). The neat transformation from qualified, uncertain love to love's rebirth over the course of a single page raises doubts that remain unanswered as the narrative suddenly ends.

What is clear, in any case, is that Kyle's inevitable neglect of Taya and their children during his four eagerly sought-after deployments threatens any attempt to present his story of traditional warrior-heroism as straightforwardly virtuous or good. The values surrounding masculinity, gender equality, and the duties of soldiers to their families have changed in such a way that a life dedicated entirely to voluntary self-exposure to combat, at the expense of family responsibilities that remain largely culturally gendered as feminine, can no longer be seen as unambiguously heroic, in the sense of embodying the culture's highest ideals. To reach this conclusion does not require importing liberal values from outside the book. The tension is on vivid display within the pages of *American Sniper* itself. In Kyle's attempted tale of heroic glory through the killing of foreign enemies, Taya ultimately comes across almost as a collateral victim. But as Chapter 2 noted, heroes are not supposed to produce victims. In our narrative traditions, it is wrongdoers, not heroes, who victimize.

THE HERO AS CRIMINAL?

American Sniper also complicates any attempt to portray Kyle as an unalloyed hero by offering frequent evidence of unapologetic wrongdoing, casual sadism, and even criminality. All of the evidence discussed below appears in an account that Kyle himself controlled and offered for public consumption and scrutiny. That is, even in Kyle's own preferred selection and construal of events, he seems to engage repeatedly in conduct that sits in tension with the traditional narrative template of the warrior-as-hero.

To begin with, it may be helpful to reiterate that one of the most important principles of international humanitarian law is the principle of distinction between combatants and civilians. The use of military force must not have as its ultimate purpose the killing of civilians. The rules of engagement ("ROEs") in a conflict are intended in part to spell out in practical detail how soldiers can use force without violating the principle of distinction.

In *American Sniper*, Kyle criticizes the ROEs he was forced to operate under in Iraq—repeatedly, and at length. In his most extended critique, he argues:

> The ROEs got so convoluted and fucked-up because politicians were interfering in the process. The rules are drawn up by lawyers who are trying to protect the admirals and generals from the politicians; they're not written by people who are worried about the guys on the ground getting shot...
>
> A lot of people, not just politicians, wanted to impose ridiculous fantasies on us, hold us to some standard of behavior that no human being could maintain...
>
> I'm not saying war crimes should be committed. I *am* saying that warriors need to be let loose to fight war without their hands tied behind their backs...
>
> According to the ROEs I followed in Iraq, if someone came into my house, shot my wife, my kids, and then threw his gun down, I was supposed to NOT shoot him. I was supposed to take him gently into custody.
>
> Would you? (299–300)

The full passage above is pervaded by contempt for American civilians, most of whom "can't take the reality of war," and who may be represented by "some fat-ass congressman sitting in a leather chair smoking a cigar back in DC in an air-conditioned office, telling me when and where I can and cannot shoot someone" (299). Against this background of distaste for the American public and democratic control over the military, Kyle seems to suggest that the ROEs are "ridiculous fantasies" that "no human being" could comply with—as though no soldier could realistically be expected not to murder a combatant who has surrendered. It speaks volumes that Kyle feels compelled to clarify that he does not believe war crimes should be committed. He correctly perceives that his comments might have raised doubts.

In any case, Kyle insists elsewhere that he did, in fact, comply with these ostensibly impossible and fantastical ROEs. In an unusually detailed explanation of his approach, he writes:

> The ROEs were specific, and in most cases the danger [justifying the use of force] was obvious.
>
> But there were times when it wasn't *exactly* clear, when a person almost surely was an insurgent, probably was doing evil, but there was still some doubt because of the circumstances or the surroundings—the way he moved, for example, wasn't toward an area where troops were. A lot of times a guy seemed to be acting macho for friends, completely unaware that I was watching him, or that there were American troops nearby.
>
> Those shots I didn't take.
>
> You couldn't—you had to worry about your own ass. Make an unjustified shot and you could be charged with murder.
>
> I often would sit there and think, "I know this motherfucker is bad; I saw him doing such and such down the street the other day, but here he's not doing anything, and if I shoot him, I won't be able to justify it for the lawyers. I'll fry." Like I said, there is paperwork for everything. Every confirmed kill had documentation, supporting evidence, and a witness.
>
> So I wouldn't shoot.
>
> There weren't a lot of those, especially in Fallujah, but I was always extremely aware of the fact that every killing might have to be justified to the lawyers.
>
> My attitude was: if my justification is I *thought* my target would do something bad, then I wasn't justified. He had to be *doing* something bad. (149)

The uncharacteristic detail in this passage suggests a mind returning repeatedly to an unresolved issue, as though Kyle wants to believe the answer is clear—he *never* took an unjustified or illegal shot—but continues to find his own reasoning, step after step, somehow not entirely reassuring. Kyle is clearly aware of accusations that American troops committed war crimes in Iraq, as when he notes "claims by the Iraqi government...that we were killing civilians" (340), or when he complains that some of "the only news stories we read were about atrocities" (300).

Later, Kyle dedicates an entire subsection, in effect, to his compliance with the principle of distinction. Under the heading "CIVILIANS AND SAVAGES," he writes:

> It's true that it can be difficult to sort out civilians from insurgents in certain situations, but here the bad guys made it easy for us...Terrorists going to attack Americans would give themselves away by moving tactically against approaching convoys or when coming close to a base. They'd sneak around with their AKs ready—it was very easy to spot them. (245)

On the surface, Kyle's account seems entirely plausible. If an Iraqi was sneaking toward an American convoy with an AK raised, he would surely be a valid target for a sniper. For targeting purposes, civilians effectively become combatants when they engage in "direct participation in hostilities."[25] But Kyle all but invites the reader to question his repeated insistence that he *never* killed a civilian, even mistakenly. It is hard to believe that, as Kyle claims, "my targets were always obvious" (298). Even if we temporarily set aside Kyle's openly expressed hostility to the laws of war in general, *American Sniper* raises doubts in a variety of ways about Kyle's compliance with legal requirements such as ROEs.

For example, Kyle blatantly misinterprets the ROEs in effect during the initial invasion to allow the deliberate killing of civilians: "Our ROEs when the war kicked off were pretty simple: *If you see anyone from about sixteen to sixty-five and they're male, shoot 'em. Kill every male you see.* That wasn't the official language, but that was the idea" (79). Obviously, compliance with such an ROE would be consistent with deliberately targeting civilians who are not directly participating in hostilities, and thus with war crimes. To the extent that Kyle flippantly misinterpreted ROEs throughout the war in a similar manner, his insistence that he complied with them might not imply that he avoided killing Iraqi civilians.

In addition, although Kyle's criteria for distinguishing between civilians and legitimate military targets may seem clear enough at first glance, the concepts are in fact troublingly imprecise and malleable. In the passage above, for example, he speaks of Iraqis "moving tactically against" a convoy or base (245). The technicality of the phrase might suggest that it has a precise meaning. But can a "tactical" movement always be distinguished from a civilian's attempt to avoid being shot? Is a young man who darts from one doorway to another in the direction of a convoy "moving tactically"? What if the young man has no weapon, but is speaking urgently into a cellphone? What if the young man is carrying an object that may or may not be a weapon? What if the young man is carrying a weapon, but may be an ally attempting to fight back against a shared enemy?

Of course, the laws of war accept that civilians will sometimes be mistakenly killed. International humanitarian law is not intended to be an expression of utopian moral idealism, but "is a compromise between military and humanitarian requirements."[26] It is entirely possible that every shot Kyle took was legally justified, or even that every person he killed was in fact a combatant. But as he himself seems to acknowledge when he discusses the young men "acting macho for friends" (149), there will inevitably be circumstances when someone's status is unclear. Waiting to see someone "*doing* something bad" (149) may not be enough to clarify the situation, if "doing something bad" includes vague or ambiguous behaviors like "moving tactically."

We can gain a better understanding of what is problematic in Kyle's language by drawing an analogy to domestic policing in the United States. The difficulties that routinely arise in attempting to distinguish civilians and combatants are in some ways similar to the difficulties that American police officers encounter in complying with the Fourth Amendment requirement not to stop someone without reasonable suspicion of criminal activity, and not to arrest someone without probable cause to believe the person has committed a crime. Empirical research and evidence from institutional litigation has cast serious doubt on the accuracy of police officers' subjective perceptions of criminality, and has also suggested that their perceptions are systematically biased against certain racial groups.[27] Given the life-or-death stakes of how a sniper draws the line between civilians and combatants, it is troubling to consider how much Kyle's defenses of the legality of his kills resemble the defenses that police officers have often made of stops and arrests that turned out to be based on mistaken perceptions of criminality.

For example, evidence in the class-action litigation in 2013 challenging the NYPD's stop-and-frisk practices showed that officers frequently stopped people based on imprecise categories such as "furtive movements" or having a "suspicious bulge" in a pocket.[28] The officers were trained to believe that "angling"—moving one's body at an angle to the police officer—was evidence of being armed, and that seemingly innocuous items such as flip-phones could in fact be disguised weapons, and thus could serve as a basis for proceeding further with a stop or frisk. Reliance on vague legal justifications and permissive training may have contributed to the unjustified stopping and often frisking of mostly African-American and Hispanic young men on millions of occasions.

Assuming that a term like "tactical movement" possesses a vagueness that is in some ways similar to the vagueness of a term like "furtive movement," it is reasonable to fear that Kyle, based on the number of his kills over the course of the Iraq War, would almost inevitably have sometimes misidentified a civilian as a valid target—especially given his dehumanizing biases against Muslims in general and Iraqi men in particular.[29] When Kyle notes that he "tried to help the new guys" by teaching them that "[y]ou could tell someone was an insurgent not just by the fact that he was armed but by the way he moved" (269), we might wonder how an Iraqi would have viewed Kyle's targeting criteria. Kyle marvels on more than one occasion at how "lucky" he was to encounter so many legitimate targets (192). "Sometimes it seemed like God was holding them back until I got the gun" (297), as when he took over for another sniper who had not "seen anyone" during a four-hour shift. "Not ten seconds later," he recounts, "an insurgent" with an "AK out" appeared. "I watched him move tactically toward an American position for a few seconds, confirming that he was within the ROEs," Kyle says. "Then I shot him" (298).

Again, it is possible that Kyle's identifications of combatants were unfailingly accurate. It is possible that his account of his unerring compliance with ROEs is equally true, despite the questionable reliability of some of his stories on other occasions. It is possible that he was simply, repeatedly, over a period of years, more "lucky" than other snipers. Although the laws of statistics would suggest that "luck" is unlikely to persist so consistently over so many rolls of the dice, it is also true that some sniper had to take the most fatal shots in Iraq.

But it is difficult not to wonder whether, on at least some occasions, the "insurgents" that Kyle shot after he saw them "moving tactically toward an American position" might have been perceived differently by some other snipers—much less by other Iraqis, and setting aside the ultimate question of whether the person was, in fact, participating directly in hostilities. In a subsection labeled "CLEAR CONSCIENCE," Kyle reveals that even some of his fellow SEALs would joke about the validity of his shots: "My guys would tease me: *Yeah, I know Chris. He's got a little gun cut on the end of his scope. Everybody he sees is in the ROEs*" (298).[30]

Kyle offers a final line of defense for the absolute legal validity of all of his kills. He insists that he always had a witness. "[T]he truth was, my targets were always obvious, and I, of course, had plenty of witnesses every time I shot" (298). "It would have been tough to go and just blatantly shoot people in Iraq," because "there were always plenty of witnesses around" (296). "I wasn't inventing the incidents—I had witnesses for all my shots" (191). In response to this claim, the reader might observe that it does not appear to be true, even based on Kyle's own account, that there were always other witnesses of *the circumstances and behaviors* that preceded and ostensibly justified Kyle's shots. Two pages after his claim about there always being "plenty of witnesses," for example, Kyle recounts a killing where the only other person in the room was a fellow sniper lying on the floor with a ball cap over his eyes, and there were apparently no other witnesses (298).

The reader might also question how often any American witnesses would have provided damaging information about one of Kyle's kills. Here, again, the comparison with American policing might give the reader pause. Investigations have repeatedly shown that police are sometimes willing to lie, even in sworn testimony, especially to cover up misconduct by fellow officers.[31] The circumstances of Kyle's service would have made witnesses of any questionable shots even less likely to report them. He was, after all, a fellow American servicemember helping to protect them from being killed. Especially within the tight-knit, fiercely loyal community of SEALs, it seems unlikely that many witnesses would have been inclined to provide information that might have led to an investigation of or charges against Kyle.

In fact, *American Sniper* itself shows that special operators are often willing to protect each other by lying to law enforcement officials if necessary. During one of Kyle's many drunken bar fights, discussed below, he ends up in the hospital next to "a kid...with his jaw wired shut" (328). "Next thing I knew, some MPs came over and started questioning me. 'This kid is claiming you broke his jaw,' said one of them" (328). Kyle lies to the police, telling them he broke his hand in a training exercise, then notes: "Not so coincidentally, all of the bouncers at the bar where we'd been were Army SF [Special Forces]; they would surely back me up if it came to that" (328). Kyle simply assumes, no doubt reasonably, that fellow members of the special operations community will likely be willing to lie to the police to cover up his apparent crime of assault. As one of Taya's acquaintances warns her with regard to SEALs: "*They're trained to lie*" (342).

Against Kyle's protestation that he would have faced serious consequences if he had strayed from the ROEs, the recent and highly publicized case of Navy SEAL Eddie Gallagher suggests some of the many layers of protection that might insulate a SEAL from discipline for misconduct in war. During a deployment to Iraq beginning in 2017, Special Operations Chief Gallagher allegedly murdered a number of Iraqi civilians, including multiple women and a school-age "girl in a flower-print hijab who was walking with other girls on the riverbank."[32] He boasted about his killing in general—including by reportedly claiming that he had "more kills than Chris Kyle"[33]—and may have committed other atrocities including stabbing a defenseless teenaged prisoner to death.[34] His platoon members said he "fire[d] rockets at houses for no apparent reason," emptied an armored "truck's heavy machine gun into neighborhoods on the other side [of the Tigris River] with no discernible targets," and "spent much of his time in a hidden perch with a sniper rifle, firing three or four times as often as other platoon snipers."[35] One platoon member later told investigators that Gallagher was "freaking evil," and another said "[y]ou could tell he was perfectly O.K. with killing anybody that was moving."[36]

The members of Gallagher's platoon apparently spoke up repeatedly, but nothing happened for months. Then they reported Gallagher to their commander, a longtime friend of Gallagher, who warned them not to speak out any further. Meanwhile, Gallagher continued receiving praise and awards, including a Bronze Star. Only when the members of his platoon threatened to go to the media and senior Navy officials did their commanders formally report the allegations to the Navy Criminal Investigation Service, leading to Gallagher's arrest in September 2018.[37]

In preparation for his trial, Gallagher received supportive coverage from Fox News and other right-wing media, along with some members of Congress.[38] Disgraced former New York City Police Commissioner Bernard Kerik, himself a convicted felon, helped Gallagher to assemble a high-profile legal team including Marc Mukasey, the son of former Bush administration Attorney General Michael Mukasey, a defender of torture.[39] President Trump publicly tweeted in support of Gallagher, praised his military service, and may have considered preemptively pardoning him.[40] During the 2019 trial, a key Navy SEAL witness who had received immunity from prosecution contradicted his previous sworn statements and claimed that he, not Gallagher, had killed the teenaged prisoner. After eight hours of deliberations, the military jury found Gallagher not guilty of all the serious charges. Disregarding the testimony of the SEALs who risked their careers to report Gallagher's wrongdoing toward Iraqis, President Trump reversed Gallagher's demotion on the same day that he pardoned a former Army lieutenant convicted of murdering two civilians and another American officer charged with murdering an unarmed Afghan.[41]

The story of Gallagher's misconduct and its consequences calls into question the notion that if Kyle had made questionable shots in Iraq, or even if he had deliberately killed civilians, an investigation or charges would inevitably have followed. In fact, contrary to Kyle's claim that "[y]ou'd be crucified if you didn't strictly obey the ROEs" (298), on the following page he seems to describe marines committing war crimes, "putting a round in anybody they saw as they entered a house," and then not being charged after their apparent misconduct came to light (299).[42]

The details Kyle gives of some of his specific killings in Iraq provide further reasons to question his framing of his actions as unquestionably legal. For example, Kyle describes witnessing what he believed to be the beginning of a kidnapping. A group of "older teenagers and young adults" got off a bus, and a "young teenage kid" who was waiting for the bus "started walking very quickly in the opposite direction" (187). The group caught up with him, and "[o]ne of them pulled out a pistol and put his arm around the kid's neck" (187). Kyle then began shooting the teenagers and young adults. He killed "two or three" of them (187). Kyle apparently views his conduct as correct. But did he have the right under the ROEs to kill any Iraqi, without any investigation or legal process, that he suspected was engaged in armed kidnapping?

In one particularly disturbing passage, Kyle seems to hint that he may have killed Iraqis illegally in order to maintain his lead as the most prolific sniper:

> There was a little bit of a competition between myself and some of the other snipers during this deployment, to see who got the most kills. Not that we had all that much to do with the numbers—they were more a product of how many targets we had to shoot at. It's just the luck of the draw—you want to have the highest numbers, but there's not much you can do about it.
>
> I did want to be the top sniper. (264)

When it looks like another sniper is poised to break Kyle's record, Kyle continues:

> Well, things evened out real fast—all of a sudden I seemed to have every stinkin' bad guy in the city running across my scope. My totals shot up, and there was no catchin' me.
>
> Luck of the draw. (264)

Here, it almost sounds as though Kyle is hinting with a wink ("all of a sudden") that he began to kill Iraqis whom he might not have killed if his record as the top sniper had not been threatened. The insinuation would be less troubling if we did not know from the Gallagher case that such calculations have sometimes apparently led to the killing of civilians.

On several other occasions, Kyle admits or at least implies that he might have participated in less serious crimes while in uniform (53, 112, 125, 214–15, 217, 289–90).[43] Sometimes Kyle's admitted or implied misconduct is relatively more serious. Before the invasion of Iraq, for example, during a raid ("takedown") of a tanker carrying illegally loaded Iraqi oil, Kyle describes using the muzzle of his submachine gun to strike the captain, who had charged him (60). After the captain has been subdued through this unproblematic act of self-defense, however, Kyle adds: "Somehow, I managed to slip as well. My elbow flew out and landed straight on his face. A couple of times" (60). Kyle invites the reader to laugh along with his beating of the incapacitated prisoner.

Kyle also more or less openly admits a petty violation of international humanitarian law when he describes, during his first deployment, looting "a handheld Tiger Woods golf game" from an Iraqi apartment he was using as a sniper position (or "hide") (141).[44] Apparently aware that "acquisitioning" the game, as he puts it, would be illegal, he winkingly phrases the episode as a counterfactual: "If I *had* taken it, I would have played it the rest of the deployment. If I'd done that, it might explain why I am actually pretty good at the game now" (141).

Some of the most troubling details Kyle offers of his experiences in Iraq involve revenge for SEAL casualties. In 2006, after Kyle believes (mistakenly, as it turns out) that insurgents have killed one of his fellow team members, Ryan Job, Kyle's chief asks if he wants to "go get some payback," and Kyle enthusiastically agrees (283). "I just wanted blood for my guy," he states (283). The insurgents trick Kyle and the others into an ambush, and another member of the team, Marc Lee, is killed—remarkably, the first SEAL fatality since the beginning of U.S. combat in Iraq (288). Kyle retreats in a convoy of two tanks and four Bradleys that "went Winchester," that is, fired all of their ammunition. The entire neighborhood was reduced to "black smoke and ruined buildings" (284).

Whether or not this collateral damage to civilian property was "proportional" to any military objective—another key principle of international humanitarian law—Kyle finds the outcome to have been just: "They'd suckered us, and their entire neighborhood had paid the price" (284). But who is "they"? Had the entire neighborhood been complicit in attacking the SEALs? The details Kyle offers sound like the collective punishment of a civilian neighborhood for the actions of fighters who used the neighborhood as cover.

In the coming pages, Kyle's quest for revenge becomes even more indiscriminate. "Our attitude was, we're going out there and we're getting the guys who did this back. We're going to make them pay for what they did to us" (292). There is no indication that anyone had intelligence related to the specific insurgents who wounded Job or killed Lee. It is difficult not to read between the lines and wonder whether making "them" pay entailed the indiscriminate use of disproportionate force, in violation of the laws of war.

***

It is revealing that Kyle's platoon adopted as its symbol in Iraq the skull logo of the comic-book antihero the Punisher. Kyle used the Punisher skull again as part of the logo for Craft International, the "tactical" training company he founded (231, 366).[45] As Kyle recognizes, the Punisher is not known just for delivering justice. He delivers "vigilante justice" (231)—that is, justice defined by its lawlessness, or even more specifically, its criminality. The Punisher is a hero-criminal or criminal-hero, not a morally upright embodiment of uncontested virtues. The choice of symbol seems fitting for the ambiguous portrait that Kyle ultimately offers of himself.

If even Chris Kyle, a highly decorated member of one of the most elite units in the U.S. military, a beloved and profoundly mourned icon to many whose life story became the most popular book about the Iraq War and the most popular war movie of all time—if even Kyle could not persuasively present his life and his military service in Iraq as a traditional story of the warrior-as-hero, without also leaving pervasive hints of the soldier-as-criminal woven into his narrative, then it should not be surprising that narratives of criminality play a central role in the literature of the Iraq War more generally.

CHAPTER NINE

WAR PORN (2016)

One of the central arguments of this book is that American literary fiction about the Iraq War reflects a historical shift in American war culture away from a focus on narratives of soldier victimization and toward an emerging focus on narratives about the wrongdoing and moral injury of soldiers. Roy Scranton's novel *War Porn*, published in 2016, is one of the most fully realized expressions to date of this literary-historical shift. The novel tells three narratives about the Iraq War. Misconduct by U.S. soldiers plays a central role in each of the stories, which unfold across the five sections of the novel in a nested pattern, ABCBA:

A. The first and fifth sections of the novel tell the story of a barbecue outside Moab, Utah on Columbus Day, 2004 (7). A restless young woman, Dahlia, has grown tired of her tame, well-meaning software-engineer boyfriend, Matt (9–10, 14–15). One of Dahlia's friends arrives with a recently returned Iraq War veteran, Aaron (17). He soon gets into a fight with an anti-war hippie at the barbecue who compares him to a Nazi (28–34). Later, Aaron shows Matt his collection of "war porn," photos of sexually abused, tortured, and sometimes murdered detainees at the U.S. military prison where he worked in Iraq (306–22). At the end of the night, Aaron rapes Dahlia in a graphic scene spread across several of the book's final pages (330–34).

B. The second and fourth sections of the novel tell the story of SPC Wilson's service in Iraq. ("SPC" stands for "Specialist," an enlisted rank one step below "Sergeant" that is available to a soldier who has a college degree but enlists rather than being commissioned as an officer.) We learn in part through flashbacks that SPC Wilson used to be an aimless, unsuccessful poet with hippie friends (125–26, 274–78). Partly because he was unable to find a job, he joined the Army several months after the September 11 attacks (125–26). His time in Iraq gradually corrupts him, replacing his humanitarian ideals with bigoted rage (for example, 95–97, 116–18, 280). On the day SPC Wilson is scheduled to leave Iraq, his tour is extended for ninety days (272–73). In the final scene of his story, SPC Wilson observes his unit insulting and physically abusing an Iraqi family during a night-time raid that turns out to be based on bad intelligence (282–84).

C. The third and longest individual section of the novel tells the story of Qasim, an Iraqi mathematician living in Baghdad shortly before and during the American invasion (133). The section paints a portrait of the lives of ordinary Iraqis as Qasim and his family and university colleagues prepare for the American invasion. We see domestic squabbles, political arguments, the hopes and dreams of a teenaged girl, the meditations of a blinded victim of state torture, and Qasim's interrogation by Saddam's secret police. Finally, the invasion comes, "strewing metal and the screaming wounded" (219). (Later, in the fourth section of the novel, we see Qasim serving as an interpreter ("terp") for SPC Wilson's unit as the unit insults and harasses Iraqis (241, 244–46). We also see SPC Wilson have a brief, respectful conversation with Qasim (246–49). Finally, in the fifth section of the novel, we learn that the United States detained Qasim based on an Iraqi informant's lies, and that Aaron participated in torturing him (167, 320–21).)

War Porn can be read as expressing in narrative form the critical perspective on the role of U.S. soldiers in the Iraq War that Scranton has expressed in expository form elsewhere—for example, in an article for *Rolling Stone* published in July 2014, after visiting Iraq as a civilian. In that article, Scranton reveals a number of similarities between his own life story and the stories in *War Porn*.[1] Like SPC Wilson, Scranton joined the Army in 2002. Before enlisting, like SPC Wilson, he wrote poetry and was a "disillusioned radical." He lived in the Utah desert, like Dahlia and her friends. Just as it was for SPC Wilson, September 11 appears to have been a turning point for Scranton, although—like SPC Wilson—Scranton enlisted in part for financial reasons.[2]

Scranton's year in Iraq from 2003 to 2004 also appears to have resembled SPC Wilson's in a number of ways. He served with an armored division, at first picking up artillery rounds and then driving a Humvee, "looking for roadside bombs and snipers." He found the monotony and enclosed spaces of his time in Iraq "dehumanizing," and gradually became filled with hatred toward Iraqis:

> Over time, as we were shot at, mortared and sometimes blown up, fear and rage built up in us like toxins, until we were praying for reasons to shoot—not people, mind you, just fucking hajjis. We harassed and intimidated hajjis on the street. We humiliated hajjis in their homes. We ran hajji cars off the road when they got in our way. We locked hajjis up for being in the wrong place at the wrong time. Some of us did worse. Some of us did a lot worse.[3]

In other words, as in *War Porn*, so in Scranton's experience of the Iraq War, some U.S. soldiers behaved like criminals, with Iraqis as their victims. Also like SPC Wilson, Scranton's tour was "extended past its original end date, after the Jaish al-Mahdi uprising in April 2004."

> [D]uring our last months there, my anger, fear and frustration grew into an unbounded hate: I hated the constant threat of violence, the smell of oil, the despicable role I was forced to take on as an occupier and the resentment we drew in performing that role. I hated my commander, who was an idiot. I hated military logic, with its redundancy and regulations, and I hated military culture, with its puffed-up machismo and dumb aggression. I hated the explosions and the gunfire and the mortars. I hated the feel of the air. I hated the sand, the heat, the tents, the streets, the camouflage, the Iraqis, the Americans, the sky, the sun, the wind and the hands of the clock marking time.

Visiting Baghdad in 2014, as sectarian violence continued and ISIS expanded its territorial control, Scranton delivers a harsh verdict on the U.S. military's actions in Iraq, and his own complicity in them. "We let loose a grisly pandemonium in Iraq, then walked away and tried to wash our hands of the whole affair," he writes. When Scranton tells another journalist that what America did cannot have been "all by accident," he suggests that the disaster in Iraq was not merely a mistake, but in some sense intentional. He agrees with an Iraqi human rights activist that there may have been "an intention to keep Iraq weak." With regard to his personal responsibility, he states that if Baghdad had become a kind of hell, "it was a hell I helped create."

> We'd invaded a sovereign nation on a pretense, fucked up the lives of 30 million people, started a bitter, bloody civil war by pitting one religious sect against another, then left and pretended it had nothing to do with us...Whether or not breaking Iraq into pieces had been the plan from the beginning, as some evidence suggests, the war had been nothing but a murderous hustle. The politicians who ran the war had shown no higher ideals than robbery and plunder, and I'd been nothing but their thug.

In sum, Scranton writes of the Iraq War as a criminal enterprise and presents himself as a low-level conspirator and beneficiary:

> As an historical agent in the vast, crooked enterprise that was the Iraq War, I had helped cause immense suffering and I had profited by it. I had let it happen, and I had made it happen. And when I thought of the pride I'd taken in my service, the combat pay I'd spent vacationing in Paris, London and Berlin, and the blood money that had bought my college education, holding them up against the lives I'd seen shattered by violence, the hopes I'd seen trampled and the dreams for a better future I'd seen starved by neglect and choked by frustration, I could feel nothing but disgust and shame for having been an American soldier.[4]

Here we see a remarkably clear expression of the view of the U.S. soldier in Iraq as something like a criminal—not a victim, and certainly not a hero, but rather a participant in a grave wrong who should feel guilt for having participated, just as we would expect a former member of a criminal gang to express remorse. Scranton loudly violates the post-Vietnam taboo on blaming U.S. soldiers for the harms caused by American wars, not excluding himself.

Nor has time softened Scranton's critical perspective. In June 2019, the Iraqi author Sinan Antoon tweeted: "There should be a day in the US to celebrate war criminals." In a retweet, Scranton replied: "You mean in addition to Veterans Day, Memorial Day, Armed Forces Day, Patriot Day, Presidents Day, and the Fourth of July?"[5] More clearly than any other writer addressed in this book, Scranton seems willing to reject the view of U.S. soldiers as victims in favor of a view of U.S. soldiers as criminals, and more specifically war criminals.

In light of Scranton's critique of the U.S. occupation of Iraq and his role in it, it is unsurprising that *War Porn* reflects the shift toward the soldier-as-criminal narrative in war literature even more clearly than *Sand Queen*—whose author, incidentally, appears in Scranton's acknowledgments as the first name in his list of "early readers" of the novel (341). By placing *Sand Queen* and *War Porn* side by side, it becomes possible to begin observing some generalities about the underlying structure of soldier-as-criminal narratives, at least where the soldier is a U.S. servicemember in the Iraq War.

The prototypical story of the soldier-as-criminal is above all a story of the soldier's *corruption*. Just as Kate's experiences in Iraq erode her idealism and gradually transform her into the brutal figure who assaults Naema's father, so both SPC Wilson and Aaron are morally corrupted by their military service, as the following sections discuss.

A STORY OF CORRUPTION, I: SPC WILSON

Viewed from a distance, the unifying arc of SPC Wilson's story in *War Porn* is his moral corruption through military service. But the narrative clarity of SPC Wilson's downfall is muddied by the fact that he appears to be a deeply misanthropic and uncaring young man by temperament, and not only as a result of his military service. In fact, one of the remarkable features of SPC Wilson's story is the general lack of any deep sense of camaraderie with his fellow soldiers, outside of a brief period of solidarity after returning to Iraq from leave in the United States (235–37). The intensity of affective bonds between fellow fighters in war is one of the most consistent themes in the history of war literature, from Achilles' love for Patroclus in *The Iliad*, to Shakespeare's celebration of the "band of brothers" in *Henry V*, to the 2001 HBO mini-series of the same name. SPC Wilson's war, by contrast, seems to be a largely solitary one.

But even if the transformation of SPC Wilson's character is less straightforward than, for example, Kate's in *Sand Queen*, it remains discernable. SPC Wilson comes to the Army from a world of leftist hippies and artists, "*a fuzz of pot smoke, excuses, and superstition*" (277; see also 104), where skepticism toward American power leads some to question, after September 11, whether "*maybe we'd sort of caused it. Maybe we wanted it to happen*" (126). His acculturation to military life during basic training seems to have pushed him some distance away from whatever cosmopolitan and egalitarian moral ideals he might have held before enlisting, or at least away from politically correct language reflecting those ideals. Even at the start of his tour in Iraq, SPC Wilson plays along with the casual misogyny and racism of his fellow soldiers. He cheers as a female National Guard soldier removes her shirt (49; see also 75, 122), and fantasizes half-sarcastically about joining in the long American tradition of killing "the savages" (52) and bombing "*little brown people*" (54). At least initially, however, the hint of sarcasm places some distance between SPC Wilson's moral identity and the illiberal values that surround him. There remain ambivalent traces of "the poet I'd once been" (78).

Similarly, when SPC Wilson visits the UN Compound in Baghdad before it is bombed, he daydreams about becoming "a war correspondent or maybe some kind of humanitarian" (96). "I wanted to talk with these business-casual cosmopolitans about human rights and cultural programming, Michel Foucault and Zadie Smith" (96–97). He sees a woman in a skirt and wants "to corner [her], take her hands in mine, and convince her: I used to read *Whitman*. I used to read *Joyce*" (97). SPC Wilson may engage in racist and misogynist trash-talking, he may think of all Iraqis as "hadjis" (for example, 109), and as time goes on he may insult and threaten the Iraqis he is forced to deal with (109–12, 117, 244–46, 252–54).[6] But he is far from the worst or most enthusiastic abuser in his unit (for example, 92, 115, 120–22, 244–46, 251, 256, 265). His basic cultural and temperamental detachment from the chauvinistic militarism of the other soldiers is clear enough that he feels alienated from them, and they in turn do not trust him (115, 116). As the end of the first part of SPC Wilson's story (the second section of the novel) approaches, even as he continues to engage in casually misogynistic banter (122), it is clear that he remains an outsider based on his skepticism about the Iraq War (124). He has not yet been fully converted away from his pre-military, leftist political ideals.

The second half of SPC Wilson's story begins—at the start of the novel's fourth section—with hints of his persistent, underlying moral commitments. SPC Wilson has just returned from a brief period of leave in the United States. In an echo of so many veterans' discomfort with being thanked for their service in Iraq, a discomfort we already saw reflected in a passage from *The Yellow Birds*, SPC Wilson tells a fellow soldier: "'It's weird, man…[A]nytime anyone found out I was in Iraq, they…started thanking me and telling me what a great thing it was I was doing. I didn't know what to say. Like, hell yeah, fuck hadji! I mean, what the fuck?'" (238). As in *The Yellow Birds*, SPC Wilson appears to be nonplussed by expressions of thanks because of his moral discomfort with his participation in the war. We see his relative moral cosmopolitanism again in his brief exchange with the Iraqi mathematician Qasim, who is now serving as an interpreter. SPC Wilson engages Qasim with respect, trying to determine whether Qasim thinks the American invasion has made life better in Iraq (247–49).

If anything, for much of the fourth section of *War Porn*, SPC Wilson appears to be hardening in his leftist skepticism of the war and his rejection of the U.S. military in general. During a chat with an Iraqi security contractor, SPC Wilson insists over the contractor's objections: "'Bush no good…Bush Ali Baba…Saddam, Bush, same-same…Ali Baba, Ali Baba'" (262). (Throughout American writings on the Iraq War, Iraqis with limited English use the term "Ali Baba" to refer to "bad guys" in general, and especially to criminals.) It is perhaps in part because of SPC Wilson's perceived hostility to the U.S. presence in Iraq that he is sidelined within his unit, relegated to serving guard duty at a gate while most of the other soldiers go on patrols (256–57).

When SPC Wilson is asked what he did to piss off the officer who assigned him to gate duty, SPC Wilson states: "'I don't fucking know, man. I read a book one time'" (257). He jokes "'I hate freedom'" (253), mockingly echoing President Bush's explanation for why Al Qaeda attacked the United States. But unlike his partner at the gate, SPC Wilson does not seem to mind being separated from the other soldiers (256). When given the opportunity to volunteer for a convoy four days before his redeployment from Iraq, SPC Wilson does not raise his hand (269). Instead, we have already seen him reading another book—Noam Chomsky's *For Reasons of State* (265), a collection of the leftist activist's critical writings on the Vietnam War and American militarism. As the anticipated end of SPC Wilson's tour in Iraq approaches, it seems as though his service might even have sharpened his anti-militarist moral commitments.

His narration certainly shows no sympathy toward his commanding officer, CPT Yarrow, when the latter awards a Bronze Star for valor to a soldier for shooting and killing "a retarded kid throwing rocks" (265). CPT Yarrow jokes that the only thing the soldier did wrong was not shoot the child twice, in line with the soldier's training (265). SPC Wilson observes that CPT Yarrow "chuckled," while the soldier receiving the award "stared straight ahead" (265).

But SPC Wilson's story does not end with his planned redeployment. Instead, on the scheduled day of SPC Wilson's departure from Iraq, in the wake of rising insurgent violence, his unit's tour is extended for ninety additional days (268, 270, 272–73). The fourth section of the novel, and SPC Wilson's story, ends with his growing fury and its consequences. When the photos of the tortured and humiliated Iraqis at Abu Ghraib prison come to light, SPC Wilson's reaction shows little trace of the cosmopolitan sympathies that once seemed to set him apart, at least in his own mind, from the other soldiers:

> I know what I'm looking at, but at the same time, fuck 'em. Fuck 'em to their goddamned shitsucking hadji hell. They're shooting at us every day and I'm supposed to give a flying fuck about human rights? Fuck that. Once they quit chopping people's heads off and lighting dudes on fire, then maybe we'll talk. (280)

Here, in the brief, rhetorical nadir of SPC Wilson's moral transformation, he embraces the opposite of cosmopolitanism: violence against an indiscriminately defined ("hadji") out-group. It is typical of *War Porn*'s thematic transparency that SPC Wilson explicitly invokes, and rejects, "human rights" in his anti-cosmopolitan division of the world into "us" and "them." He adopts a tribalistic vision in which the demands of morality and legality end at the boundary between Americans and Iraqis.

In the final, brief scene of SPC Wilson's story, he assists in a night-time raid of an Iraqi home that turns out to be based on bad intelligence. The violent, humiliating behavior of the soldiers ("On your knees, motherfucker!" "Shut that bitch up" (282–83)) makes our final glimpse of SPC Wilson resemble a scene of robbery and kidnapping by a gang of armed criminals. By ending SPC Wilson's story on this note, *War Porn* suggests that moral corruption was the ultimate consequence of SPC Wilson's service in Iraq, despite whatever twists and turns the story may have taken along the way. SPC Wilson entered the military a relatively sensitive, if irritable, poetic soul in search of meaning, and the military transformed him, at least partly and temporarily, into a figure of bigoted rage, and made him forever complicit in something like a crime.

A STORY OF CORRUPTION, II: AARON

War Porn offers less insight into the background of Aaron, the recently returned Iraq War veteran who attends a barbecue in the Utah desert on Columbus Day, 2004, in the first and fifth sections of the novel, and exits the novel with the graphic rape scene noted above. But despite our limited knowledge of Aaron's life before his deployment to Iraq, it is quite clear—even excessively, didactically clear—that the story of Aaron's service is even more straightforwardly a story of corruption and criminality than SPC Wilson's was. Aaron is a literary epitome of the Iraq War veteran as criminal.

While the narration of the barbecue sometimes dips into the interior monologues of Dahlia and her boyfriend Matt, the reader is never offered a glimpse of Aaron's interior world. In fact, it is unclear whether Aaron's interior life could be plausibly rendered. There is something one-dimensionally demonic in his present character. What we learn of Aaron's past comes from remarks by Aaron and his girlfriend, Wendy. These clues are difficult to reconcile with each other and with the Aaron we encounter in 2004.

Aaron says that he grew up near Tucson and met Wendy in college, where he was studying history (26). He claims that he dreamed of fronting a punk-rock band (327), and Wendy confirms that he was in a band in college and had "stoner buddies" (309), although he has always been a "loner," and seems not to have had any close family (309). Although Aaron has an appropriately hardcore "anarchy" tattoo—"a crude circled A on his right shoulder" (20)—Wendy also describes him giving her a mix tape in college that features songs by PJ Harvey and Captain Beefheart (22), neither of which are punk.

It is noteworthy by itself that Aaron dated Wendy, an MFA student at the time and apparently friendly with hippies like those at the barbecue. All of these clues hint that Aaron was not always the stylized illustration of masculine American brutality who appears at the Columbus Day barbecue. The suggestion of some hippie side to Aaron's identity before his service in Iraq is strengthened by some of the language he uses, and by the fact that when he attempts to seduce Dahlia by lying about the war and portraying himself as a traumatized soldier-victim (or, one might say, "trauma hero"), he suggests that his plan is now to ride his motorcycle across the country "till I have a vision" (327).[7] The fact that Aaron arrives at this particular invented story, with its echoes of a magical hippie "vision quest" (see 26), implies at least a familiarity with hippie culture.

When Mel, the anti-war hippie who later accuses Aaron of being an "American Nazi" for refusing to admit that what he did in Iraq was evil (32), asks Aaron why he joined the military, Aaron replies nonchalantly: "College money, patriotism. Service, challenge, honor. Nine-eleven. Same things as anybody else" (30). Of course, as we gradually learn, Aaron is not a trustworthy or consistent narrator of his own story (see, for example, 296, 327). But the picture of a pre-Iraq War Aaron motivated by generally humane values is consistent with other glimpses of Aaron from before his deployment. He apparently told Wendy at the time that he expected to spend his tour sitting in the desert twiddling his thumbs "like in that book *Jarhead*" (308). When Mel criticizes Aaron for joining the Army by suggesting he decided to "kill people for money" (30), Aaron's sarcastic response suggests that this is not, in fact, the case: "Okay, you got me. I joined the Army so I could fucking kill people. Big secret: It's a blast" (30).

Wendy also suggests that when Aaron learned he would be deploying to Iraq with his Arizona National Guard unit, Aaron seemed to want "promises" that she could not make (308). Here we see another hint that before his deployment, Aaron might have had some attachment to traditional, bourgeois "family values," such as the desire to be in a faithful, monogamous relationship. Nothing could be further from the animalistic, misogynist nihilism Aaron proclaims to Matt upon his return from the war—as, for example, when Aaron offers the following summary of his relationship to Wendy: "We fuck...She's a liar and a cunt, but she fucks good" (296). Similarly, when Matt says he does not know what Aaron is "here for," Aaron explains: "Same thing we all are: kill, fuck, and die" (303). As Wendy notes: "Sometimes I get the feeling he just doesn't care what happens anymore. He didn't used to be like that" (313).

Thus, the Aaron we encounter in 2004 has been radically changed—in a remarkably short period of time—by his experiences in Iraq, in ways that will soon be detailed. But first, what were these experiences? We know that he was a military policeman with the Arizona National Guard, and worked "at several different internment camps," including the fictional "Camp Crawford" (presumably named after the Texas town where George W. Bush moved during his first presidential campaign). The "war porn" photographs that Aaron shows to Matt tell a tale of the unit's increasingly violent and humiliating treatment of detainees, partly based on the example and inspiration of CIA interrogators referred to as coming from "OGA" ("[o]ther governmental agencies") (307). As the back cover of *War Porn* helpfully explains, "war porn" can be defined as: "Videos, images, and narratives featuring graphic violence, often brought back from combat zones, viewed voyeuristically or for emotional gratification. Such media are often presented and circulated without context, though they may be used as evidence of war crimes."

Aaron explains to Matt that "our guidance with the OGA fucks was full cooperation" (314), and that his entire chain of command passed along verbal orders to participate in what he calls "the torture detail" (314). For the most part, Aaron speaks in a detached, casual tone as he describes the war crimes and other misconduct he photographed and sometimes carried out: the pimping out of a female detainee (309), the anal rape of male detainees with chemlights (311), other forms of sexual humiliation (317, 318), and various forms of torture ("Enhanced interrogation, technically" (312)), including punching detainees (318), slamming their faces into cell bars (310), kicking and beating them with batons (316–17), placing them in stress positions until they passed out (318), and simulated drowning (319). As Aaron notes, "sleep deprivation, hostile environment, loud music, stress positions, beatings, immersion" were "normal shit," "the basics," in contrast to the more unusual techniques shared by "one of our OGA dudes" based on his time at Abu Ghraib prison (318). Sometimes the torture resulted in death (318).

The disengaged tone of Aaron's descriptions of the atrocities seems to suggest that he gives no moral weight whatsoever to the suffering of the Iraqi detainees. He continues to care about his fellow American soldiers, and does not think it would be fair for them to get into trouble for the war crimes they committed—especially because those who are ultimately responsible, such as Bush, Rumsfeld, and the officers in charge, will never face prosecution (314). But with regard to Iraqis, or at least Iraqi detainees—most of whom were probably locked up by mistake, as he acknowledges (314)—Aaron is, like SPC Wilson in his fit of rage, the opposite of a moral cosmopolitan. As Aaron says, "[y]ou get real racist over there" (307). By the time we hear Aaron describe his abuse of Qasim, the novel has already made a point of offering a detailed, individualized portrait of Qasim and his family life, but Aaron presents him as a partially dehumanized object of amusement and domination (320–21). Toward the end of Aaron's tour, he explains, "a lot of shit we did 'cause we were bored" (318).

In case the reader might have any lingering doubt about Aaron's descent into criminality, there is of course the extended rape scene at the conclusion of the novel (330–34). It would be easy to dismiss the clinically detailed depiction of Aaron's rape of Dahlia as gratuitous. But the fact of the crime, at least, adds an important dimension to Aaron's criminality, and by extension to the emerging narrative template of the soldier-as-criminal. Aaron's moral corruption does not reverse itself with his return to the United States. His military service has transformed him into a violent, hateful sadist, and he remains one even after his service has ended. At one point, Aaron explains to Dahlia's boyfriend: "We're devils, Matthew" (297). Aaron has embraced his self-perceived identity as a force of evil, and he acts accordingly.

SOLDIERS AS CRIMINALS

In sum, *War Porn* presents in a particularly clear, even exaggerated, form the relatively novel war literature template of the soldier-as-criminal. The novel suggests, like *Sand Queen*, that a central part of this template may be the story of ordinary soldiers' moral corruption through their experiences in the military, and especially in war. As with the story of Kate's descent into criminality in *Sand Queen*, the stories of SPC Wilson's and Aaron's downward spirals suggest that there may remain an element of soldier-victimization in the story of the soldier-as-criminal. The soldier's corruption into criminality is itself a kind of victimization, an injury with a moral rather than exclusively physical or psychological form.

In *War Porn*, as in *Sand Queen*, there is also little doubt that the primary victims of soldier criminality are civilians: the Iraqi civilians who suffer from the American invasion, such as Qasim and his family; and also Dahlia, who becomes a collateral, indirect casualty of the war. Indeed, the portrayal of U.S. soldiers as criminals in *War Porn* is almost redundantly clear. The criminality of U.S. soldiers is both shown and told, narratively portrayed and thematically analyzed. The preceding sections dealt with the narratives. I now turn to the analyses.

In *War Porn*'s first section, as already briefly mentioned, we are treated to an extended conversation on the theme of U.S. soldiers in Iraq being similar to Nazis, one of the standard contemporary reference-points for soldier criminality. Mel, an anti-war hippie and daughter of a Vietnam veteran, asserts that the U.S. soldiers in Iraq are evil, "like the Nazis" (31). Mel's girlfriend, Rachel, responds by attempting to enforce the post-Vietnam taboo on treating U.S. soldiers as criminals: "You might as well have just called him a baby killer. We don't do that anymore. You know how messed up your dad is" (34). The sharp-witted, critical Dahlia, who is perhaps the most positively portrayed character in the novel, agrees. She insists that Aaron is "not a Nazi...He's a soldier who just got back from a war zone. He's a person" (34). Dahlia's response resonates with the idea of the soldier as a traumatized victim, even if part of the trauma results from complicity in wrongdoing. Earlier, she had wondered about Aaron: "What would it feel like...[to] [b]reak a world in two and walk away? Would it change you?" (9). While recognizing that the Iraq War is a disaster for the people of Iraq, Dahlia also conveys a concern for the effects of the war on American soldiers like Aaron.

Perhaps because of Dahlia's apparent acceptance of the idea that soldiers should be treated as the victims of unjust wars, she is primed to be tricked by Aaron's presentation of himself, late in the novel, as the humanitarian-minded, traumatized victim-hero of the horrors he witnessed in Iraq: "It's always the children that suffer the most," he explains, recounting how he tried to save seven children who bled to death after a VBIED attack (323). While Aaron early in the novel mocked the assumption that he must have PTSD (29), now, in his attempt to seduce Dahlia away from Matt, he speaks of the difficulty of homecoming, noting that when he returned to the United States, "[e]verything seemed changed. Unfamiliar. Disconnected" (324, 328). Aaron is like a demonic parody of Scranton's trauma-hero myth, exploiting Dahlia's sympathies toward soldier-victims in an attempt to isolate her from anyone who might protect her from his violence.

Naturally, *War Porn* is not content to stop with the reader's knowledge that Aaron is deceiving Dahlia. In line with the novel's general aesthetic of extremity and transparency, we must be graphically shown Dahlia's victimization as a result of her misapprehension of Aaron as a victim rather than a criminal.[8] The final words of the novel's narrative could be read as a simple allegory of the path that the reader is meant to have traveled. As Dahlia regains awareness, battered and dazed after her rape, the novel closes by stating: "Dahlia opened her eyes" (334). There is only a final, brief section of non-narrative, fragmentary poetry after this line (337–79).

The spell has been lifted. Dahlia sees now, as the reader is meant to see, that Aaron, the figure of the morally corrupted Iraq War veteran, is not a victim but a victimizer, a criminal. The ideology of the trauma hero has been stripped away—through violence.

VIOLENCE AS A SOURCE OF MEANING

But it is the role of violence in *War Porn* that finally complicates its apparent didactic intentions. Even if it would be uncharitable to describe *War Porn* merely as a work of political advocacy, the novel is, at the very least, consistent with Scranton's broader polemical project of critiquing the valorization of service in the U.S. military. At the center of that critique is a reversal of the widely assumed moral valence of American military service. In the usual post-Vietnam understanding, as we have seen, American soldiers appear paradigmatically either as heroes or as victims of wartime traumas caused by the misdeeds of those in positions of power, especially militarist political leaders. Scranton inverts the moral axis of military service, suggesting that American soldiers, rather than being victims or heroes, are criminals. They commit crimes against less powerful victims, such as the civilian victims of American violence in Iraq.

In this light, *War Porn* can be read as a warning to anyone who might be tempted to join the U.S. war machine. It presents a cautionary tale of the corruption that might follow from military service. To join the U.S. military, Scranton's work suggests, is to forfeit a significant degree of moral control, and thus to risk becoming an agent of evil. The potential recruit should be aware that he or she might not only be physically or psychologically wounded, but morally wounded as well. While trauma may be compatible with a certain idea of heroism (as in the portraits of "trauma-heroes" that Scranton has criticized), an agent of evil can surely never be the hero in a story of war. There are no heroes among the faceless stormtroopers in Star Wars, or the Nazi *Sturmabteilung* soldiers who inspired them.[9] They are criminals or the tools of criminals, and either way complicit in wrong. This, in any case, seems to be the view in Scranton's writings.

But while Scranton's critique of the valorization of U.S. military service is consistent with *War Porn*'s portrayal of service in Iraq as a source of moral corruption, the same cannot be said about *War Porn*'s apparent fascination with violence and cruelty. The novel's thematic critique of the morality of military service in the Iraq War sits awkwardly beside its aesthetic embrace of violence. In order to understand why this is, it will be helpful first to take a step back and consider or reconsider some theoretical perspectives on the meaning of violence in war.

As Scranton has recognized in his scholarly critique of the trauma-hero myth, a central element in the soldier-as-victim narrative that has increasingly dominated elite cultural understandings of military service over the last century and a half is the idea that the soldier gains *insight* through his trauma.[10] The literary scholar James Campbell famously described one form of this assumption as "combat gnosticism," "the belief that combat represents a qualitatively separate order of experience that is difficult if not impossible to communicate to any who have not undergone an identical experience."[11] Campbell's target was what he viewed as insufficiently critical analyses of the poetry of World War I.

Harari has persuasively traced the development of the more general idea of war as a source of revelation back to the "long" Romantic period from the mid-eighteenth to the mid-nineteenth century. In particular, Harari emphasizes how the rise of the revelatory interpretation of war accompanied the rise of the Enlightenment view of life as a process of inner development or education (*Bildung*). In the late modern era, "war became a *Bildungsroman*, in which the body taught the mind through a process of experiential revelation who one really was and what the world was really like. Instead of merely testing the soldiers, war began teaching and changing them."[12]

As Harari summarizes his argument, which draws in large part on his close reading of military memoirs and literature about war:

> By the first half of the nineteenth century, all the ingredients of the master narratives of late modern war experience were in place: The basic ideals of *Bildung* and of the sublime; the new language of nerves, sensations, and emotions; a set of key military experiences; and the maxim that "those who weren't there can't understand anything." When these ingredients were combined they resulted in a number of different and even contradictory master narratives, which nevertheless shared common assumptions and a common view of war as a process of experiential revelation.[13]

With regard to the content of the revelation available through combat, two opposed schools of thought predominated: idealists and materialists.

> The idealists, represented in particular by fascist writers, claim that ultimately mind (or soul) is superior to the body. During peacetime decadent ideas contaminate and clog the mind, and it is only these decadent ideas that are swept away in war by the body...Idealists accordingly tend to view war as a positive regenerating experience, in which body has an indispensable part to play, but which ultimately results in "the triumph of the will."[14]

The idealists had the upper hand until roughly World War II.[15] But since then, the materialist perspective has come to the fore: "In contrast to the idealists, materialistic veterans believe that there is nowhere to proceed beyond the body. Once the body takes over it remains in control, and no 'purer mind' is thereby liberated. According to the materialists, the deepest and most important truth revealed by war is simply that man is matter."[16]

Just as Scranton's critique of contemporary understandings of military service attacks the notion that U.S. soldiers in Iraq should be viewed as victims rather than victimizers, so the critique questions the assumption that soldiers who have experienced combat, or soldiers in general, have access to an esoteric truth that is not available to civilians.[17] Scranton rejects the idea "that veterans have learned something special through their encounter with violence, and civilians need to hear that sacred knowledge."[18] One passage in Scranton's later writing succinctly brings together the various threads of his critique into a single statement that includes a rejection of the revelatory interpretation of war:

> Cultural narratives about war that highlight the status of combatants as victims, sanctify combat experience as a revelation of transcendental truth, and disavow the recognition of complicity in favor of moralistic denunciation serve and have served to obscure serious consideration of the responsibilities of power, to efface and marginalize the suffering of others (particularly those targeted by our tragic trauma heroes), justify aggression, and excuse war crimes.[19]

War Porn, as a narrative exploration of how war can turn soldiers into something like criminals, straightforwardly supports Scranton's critical rejection of viewing "combatants as victims." But the novel stands in a far less comfortable relationship to his critical rejection of "combat experience as a revelation of transcendental truth," or at least of the revelatory interpretation of violence more generally.

It is true that the most notable portrayal of combat in *War Porn* appears as if designed to undermine the reader's assumption that war is a source of revelation. Before SPC Wilson has experienced combat, he finds himself berating an Iraqi subordinate, and then muses:

> This wasn't who I was, who I was meant to be. I was *sensitive*. I'd been a *poet*. The solution seemed obvious: if I just shot a hadji, it'd all be okay. If I just killed one hadji, anyone, someone, then all the black bile, hatred, and fear would flow out of me like blood and water pouring from the wounds of Christ. I'd be transformed, transfigured. Please Jesus, I prayed, let me fucking kill somebody. (118)

SPC Wilson's tone is, as usual, bitterly ironic. The obscene prayer to Jesus asking to kill obviously does not seem serious, and not only because SPC Wilson is an atheist (262). But beneath his caustic humor, SPC Wilson appears to be only half-mockingly considering something like a revelatory interpretation of combat, according to which killing an Iraqi might provide a quasi-religious transcendence and purification of the unwanted parts of himself.

Not surprisingly, in light of Scranton's critical commitments, when SPC Wilson soon has his chance to kill, it provides no revelation. His convoy is ambushed, and everyone in the unit appears to be delighted at the opportunity to use their weapons. A gunner named Porkchop fires a .50 caliber machine gun at the enemy Iraqis and howls with adolescent glee: "'Yeah, get some! Get some! Fuck yeah! How you like it? Get some!'" SPC Wilson fires his M16 rifle repeatedly at an Iraqi, "[m]y hadji" (120). It is unclear whether SPC Wilson hits anyone, but regardless the experience ends up unfulfilling. "I didn't feel any better," he thinks in the following days (122). The experience of combat has been utterly meaningless.

But if we look beyond combat narrowly defined to the larger question of whether *violence* can serve as a source of meaning, revelation, or transformation, *War Porn* tells a far more ambivalent story. It is not only that the novel could be interpreted as suggesting that Aaron's exposure to and complicity in the torture of Iraqi prisoners revealed the true, awful nature of the Iraq War to him—and thus that soldiers, even criminal ones, know something that civilians do not. More generally, *War Porn* displays a pervasive fascination with and attraction to violence that exists in an unresolved tension with its equally evident repulsion toward violence.

The vivid descriptions of the humiliation and harsh treatment of Iraqis by U.S. soldiers; the graphic depiction of torture in Aaron's "war porn"; and the placement of clinically detailed scenes of violence at narratively pivotal moments, including a physical struggle between Aaron, Mel, and her dog, but especially Aaron's rape of Dahlia at the book's narrative conclusion—all of these seem to suggest that violence *does* in fact carry a special significance. The remarkable weight and narrative emphasis that *War Porn* places on precise depictions of violence calls into question Scranton's blithe insistence, elsewhere, that the military is simply "a professional subculture with its own rituals, traditions and jargon," such that a "military-civilian gap" is no different than "a police-civilian gap, an oil rigger-civilian gap, a barista-civilian gap."[20] To the extent that the military's professional specialty is the production of violence, rather than coffee or oil, the treatment of violence in *War Porn* suggests that there might be something special, distinct, and worthy of attention about the military and its culture after all.

In fact, a fascination with witnessing violence that at the same time repels the viewer appears as a recurring motif in many of Scranton's writings. In his *Rolling Stone* piece, for example, he notes that he joined the Army in part because "I wanted to see what war was like." During his time in Iraq, he experienced "the thrill of danger and how it made me feel alive." When he returns to Iraq as a civilian, he prepares by watching war porn videos posted by ISIS on YouTube: "teenagers shot in the back of the head, a woman choked to death, a man crucified." While in Iraq, he interviews a man who shows him pictures of his executed children. "Both children had been shot in the head. Blood pooled around their limp bodies." Scranton continues: "I asked him if I could take pictures of the pictures of his dead children. It seemed necessary but inadequate, and I felt like a vulture. I had to keep retaking the pictures, again and again, from different angles, shifting the photos around the table. My reflection kept getting in the way."[21]

Again, in a radio interview, when the host asks Scranton why he has chosen the challenging title "War Porn" for his novel, Scranton replies that the title is supposed

> to confront the reader with their own appetite for a war story. They want to, you know, readers want to read about war. I did. I do. We love to hear the stories. And there's always something voyeuristic about it because it's storytelling...[T]hat title is a way of, in a, even a crude way, of putting that front and center.[22]

The compulsion to witness violence also pervades Scranton's writings on the environment in books such as *Learning to Die in the Anthropocene: Reflections on the End of a Civilization* (2015) and *We're Doomed. Now What?: Essays on War and Climate Change* (2018).[23] These works emphasize the catastrophic, even apocalyptic possibilities of climate change, and take the coming collapse of civilization as an occasion for ruminations on living under an existential threat.

It is surely no coincidence that the characters in *War Porn* also seem irresistibly drawn to thoughts about extreme violence and cataclysm. Early on at the barbecue, Dahlia's boyfriend Matt finds himself thinking back to the fears of chaos that arose before the turn of the millennium. Although "[t]he end of the world came and went" in that case, Matt has continued to work on a piece of software "whose main purpose was, jargon aside, to predict the apocalypse" (16). Later, while Dahlia is chatting with Aaron shortly before her rape, she spontaneously turns the conversation to a discussion of "the Ancestral Puebloans, and how recent evidence suggested they were cannibals. 'The Navajo name, Anaasází, means Ancient Enemy,' she said" (327). The incessant return in Scranton's writings to depictions of and meditations on violence is difficult to reconcile with the notion that violence in general is charged with no heightened significance, or by extension that the military is no different than any other profession.

If anything, the apparent fascination with violence as a locus of meaning in *War Porn* places the novel close to a tradition that is squarely opposed to Scranton's critique of militarism. The modern thinkers who have placed the greatest emphasis on the meaningfulness of violence have tended to be critics of cosmopolitan liberalism who display a deep nostalgia for the lost ethos of the aristocratic warrior-hero, like Friedrich Nietzsche in *On the Genealogy of Morals*, Ernst Jünger in *Storm of Steel*, or Carl Schmitt in *The Concept of the Political*.[24] They have often been right-wing proponents of war.

Those on the Left who have offered the most fervent arguments in favor of the *significance* of violence have also tended to favor the *use* of violence, as in Georges Sorel's writing in favor of the violent revolutionary socialist strike, Frantz Fanon's promotion of anti-colonial violence, or Jean-Paul Sartre's notoriously hyperbolic defense of such violence in his preface to Fanon's *The Wretched of the Earth*.[25] The theorists of violence who have more clearly opposed its use, by contrast, such as Hannah Arendt and Elaine Scarry, have tended to show little fascination with it or pornographic attraction–repulsion to its spectacle, and have also tended to downplay its ability to serve as a source of great political meaning. In Arendt's words, "Violence can destroy power; it is utterly incapable of creating it."[26] Scarry writes that "[p]hysical pain does not simply resist language but actively destroys it, bringing about an immediate reversion to a state anterior to language."[27]

It is not only in its repeated, graphic depictions of violence that *War Porn* appears to align more closely with the theoretical devotees of violence as a source of meaning, rather than with the critics of that position such as Arendt and Scarry. The structure of SPC Wilson's life story also suggests that there is something peculiarly meaningful in military service, regardless of the morality of such service. After all, SPC Wilson did not join the military only because he was unable to get a job and needed money (125–26). He also joined because his life lacked meaning or purpose: "*I didn't know what I was doing...I was killing time...[W]hen I went into town...I'd be the same aimless transient I was yesterday, still no goal, no point to my story*" (276). Unlike in the narratives of materialist disillusionment discussed by Harari, SPC Wilson does not enter the military with any particular illusions, and certainly not nationalist-militarist ones. If anything, he enlists in search of an illusion, a source of meaning that might provide direction in his life. He wants there to be a "point" to his story. The content of this point seems less important than its existence. SPC Wilson's purpose is simply to have a purpose.

As we have seen, *War Porn* tells a relatively clear story of SPC Wilson's moral corruption, muddied only by the aspects of SPC Wilson's personality that make it difficult to view his initial state as an ethical ideal from which to fall. The story of SPC Wilson's attempt to find meaning, by contrast, is more ambivalent.

On the one hand, as already noted, he gains no revelation through the experience of combat. In addition, the sections of *War Porn* dedicated to SPC Wilson's story consist for the most part of brief, fragmentary episodes arranged in chronological order. There is little sense of suspense or of a *telos*, of events driving toward a meaningful conclusion. The logic of the narrative is "one thing after another." Concrete details of military life receive attention for no evident reason, like items in a disordered catalogue (for example, 58, 61, 93). Some of the most prominent episodes in the narrative, appropriately, involve getting lost or losing something in Iraq. SPC Wilson falls asleep while driving and loses sight of his convoy (52). The Humvee gets lost again, repeatedly, when SPC Wilson's company commander fails to understand the route to their destination (63–72). The battery commander ("BC") loses his pistol, and the Humvee must leave the base again to search for it (73). And so on.

In a sense, then, SPC Wilson's duties in Iraq appear nearly as aimless and haphazard as his life was before he entered the military. Thus, it might seem that the story of SPC Wilson's military service, when viewed in terms of the search for meaning, is a story of failure. He enlisted in order to find a purpose, and found none. In the absence of purpose, he experiences boredom and anger, both of which contribute to the casual cruelty that he and his unit, like Aaron and his unit, display to varying degrees. One of the more memorable passages in *War Porn* involves SPC Wilson's unit staging fighting matches between scorpions and camel spiders (62).

On the other hand, it would be misleading to suggest that the novel portrays SPC Wilson's experiences as having *no significance*. It is not only that SPC Wilson's moral corruption itself provides a kind of meaning or *telos* for his service in Iraq, even if it is not one that he intended or would embrace. More significantly, SPC Wilson's experiences in Iraq are not *all* illustrations of aimless boredom. Even when he is getting lost in the Humvee, there is an intensity to the experience that is lacking in our glimpses of Wilson's earlier, civilian life. There are elevated stakes to driving a military vehicle through the streets of Iraq during a military occupation. It is in part because the stakes are elevated that CPT Yarrow's planning failures and the BC's incompetence seem so absurd.

If SPC Wilson's time in Iraq had simply been a meaningless chore, his thoughts on returning to Iraq after leave would make little sense. Iraq now seems "[n]ormal," while life in the United States, without a rifle and the threat of IEDs, seemed disorienting (236). SPC Wilson notes: "I was surprised by how eager I felt to see my fellow soldiers—I had to make sure they were okay, but as much as that I just wanted to see their faces. They understood" (235). "I wanted to scan rooftops. I wanted shots fired. I wanted ninja women in abayas, hadjis in man-dresses" (236). If, before enlisting, SPC Wilson had succeeded at getting a job at Goodwill, Denny's, or Walmart (126), and instead of going through basic training and deploying to Iraq he had spent a comparable period of time busing tables or stocking shelves, it is difficult to imagine him having a similar response. During a vacation from Walmart, he would not have been unconsciously reaching for his inventory scanner and finding himself unable to speak with friends about what it is like to work in retail. Something about SPC Wilson's time in Iraq has been significant enough that it has changed him, pushing him away from those who were not there. Perhaps there is an intensity to living with the risk of "shots fired" that makes the discomforts of SPC Wilson's Iraqi deployment not only bearable but something whose absence he misses.

More generally, there is a performative tension in any attempt by *War Porn* to deny the meaningfulness of SPC Wilson's experiences, or of military service in general and particularly combat experience. Simply by choosing to make SPC Wilson's experiences in Iraq one of the main subjects of a novel, *War Porn* suggests that there is something meaningful in them, something worthy of attention. If SPC Wilson had gotten a job at Walmart instead of enlisting, he might or might not have avoided moral injury, but it is hard to imagine that a novel about his experiences written in the manner of *War Porn* could have found a publisher. Furthermore, it is difficult to avoid the conclusion that a primary source of meaning in SPC Wilson's narrative is the risk of violence—either the ever-present threat of an attack against SPC Wilson and his unit, or the possibility that SPC Wilson and his unit will use violence against Iraqis. If there were no risk of violence, SPC Wilson's story would mostly be a story of sitting around in a foreign country, reading, and occasionally getting lost while driving. One can imagine such a story of boredom being truly meaningless, or in other words, without significant stakes.

Thus, *War Porn* gestures toward a troubling possibility within the narrative template of the soldier-as-criminal. Just as the idea of combat revelation permitted both materialist-pacifist and idealist-fascist variations, so the idea of soldiers-as-criminals is consistent with a continuing fascination with, and even embrace of, military violence. Criminals, after all, are not always the antagonists of popular narratives, and it is not inconceivable that stories of darkly appealing criminal soldier-protagonists could proliferate just as stories of darkly appealing domestic criminals play a significant role in popular culture today.

Contemporary screens frequently captivate audiences with depictions of criminal violence, sometimes by morally complex, ambiguously appealing criminal-heroes. Even when the depictions are gritty rather than glamorous, they retain mass appeal. Movies and TV series from *Bonnie and Clyde* and *The Wild Bunch*, through *The Godfather*, *Scarface*, and *Goodfellas*, up to *The Sopranos*, *Breaking Bad*, and the countless other less successful festivals of spectacular criminal violence on screens today may have been intended by some of their creators as moralistic condemnations of criminality. But their receptions suggest that audiences, and especially young men, often come for the violence and ignore any underlying moral judgment.[28]

The allure of the spectacle of violence can be seen not only in contemporary viewing habits and the massive consumption of first-person shooter videogames, but also in how soldiers recount their own experiences. As Bourke emphasizes, "[d]espite the statistical insignificance of face-to-face killing" in twentieth-century Anglo-American wars, stories of such killing "were of immense personal importance with combatants constantly emphasizing (and exaggerating) any rare moments of intimate killing."[29] The fascination with violence reflected in *War Porn* is enduring, widespread, and apparently largely independent from moral considerations.

Until violence has lost its fascination for spectators, and criminal violence is seen as not only immoral but also uninteresting—as it may already be to some, like Arendt and Scarry—any attempt to critique and devalorize military service may run up against the limits reflected in *War Porn*. The possibility of experiencing war will continue to exert some appeal as a source of meaning, as a way to experience the heightened existential risks that have perhaps always appealed disproportionately to young men. Military service, like criminal activity, will continue to draw in those seeking an escape from what Charles Taylor calls the "leveling" of secular modernity, or from triviality, boredom, and aimlessness in general. However moral or immoral it is in any particular context, war at least tends to involve decisions and actions that make some difference—if for no other reason than that violence and the risk of violence almost inevitably matter to everyone concerned.

CHAPTER TEN

CONCLUSION: *IRAQ/VIETNAM*

> *I thought dying for your country was the worst thing that could happen to you, and I don't think it is. I think killing for your country can be a lot worse.*[1]

The preceding chapters have argued that the American literary fiction of the Iraq War contains a remarkable emphasis on wrongdoing by American soldiers toward Iraqis, and often seems haunted by a pervasive sense of unresolved guilt. Against an ancient tradition that presents warriors as heroes, and a modern literary tradition that has focused on the victimhood of ordinary soldiers, Iraq War fiction seems drawn to a conception of ordinary American soldiers as wrongdoers, even as it often seems deeply uncomfortable with such a view. Whether we think of soldier wrongdoing in terms of "criminality," or more euphemistically in terms of "moral injury," the recurring attention in Iraq War fiction to wrongdoing by U.S. soldiers, especially toward Iraqi civilians, represents a notable departure from earlier American war literature. In particular, as Chapter 3 suggested, the emphasis on ordinary soldier wrongdoing in Iraq War fiction contrasts sharply with the emphasis on the heroism and sacrifices of soldiers in much of the early American fiction of World War II.

But before we can conclude that the focus on military wrongdoing in Iraq War literature is a new development in American war literature, it is necessary finally to address the literature of the Vietnam War. To what extent did the literary-historical development that this book identifies with Iraq War literature already take place in Vietnam War literature? To what extent did American fiction about U.S. military experiences in the Vietnam War, written during and in the first decades after the war, emphasize the wrongdoing of American soldiers, especially toward the Vietnamese?

In order to explore this question, it is helpful to begin by drawing a historical comparison between the actual harms to civilians caused by the U.S. military in Vietnam and in Iraq. If the military engaged in greater abuses in Iraq than it did in Vietnam, for example, then a greater emphasis on soldier wrongdoing in Iraq War literature as compared to Vietnam War literature would not imply a shift in the literary representation of war or military service. It might only reflect a difference in the historical materials used to create war fiction. Writers confronted with greater evidence of atrocities, war crimes, and other harms might simply have responded by foregrounding these themes in their writings about Iraq. If the evidence suggested, however, that the military engaged in greater abuses in Vietnam than it did in Iraq, and yet Iraq War literature placed more emphasis on soldier wrongdoing and guilt than Vietnam War literature did, then a stronger case could be made that a shift in cultural understandings of war has taken place.

In fact, the latter conclusion seems more likely than the former. Although it is difficult to imagine how a reliable, quantitative comparison of the military abuse of civilians in the Vietnam and Iraq Wars could be compiled,[2] historical sources certainly create the consistent impression that American forces engaged far more frequently in serious abuses in Vietnam than they did in Iraq. The difference between the most well-known scandals of the Iraq and Vietnam wars is illustrative. At Abu Ghraib prison, members of the American military and CIA employees humiliated, tortured, and sexually abused detainees, and in at least one known case (Manadel al-Jamadi) tortured a detainee to death.[3] Detainee abuse appears to have been fairly widespread in Iraq, but detainee deaths resulting from deliberate mistreatment were apparently rare—perhaps a matter of ones or tens rather than hundreds.[4] More than fifteen years after the invasion of Iraq, only a relatively small number of other incidents have emerged in which American servicemembers knowingly and deliberately murdered or raped Iraqi civilians, such as the notorious incident in Mahmudiyah.[5]

By contrast, in the My Lai massacre, the signature scandal of the Vietnam War, American soldiers murdered more than five hundred Vietnamese women, children, and elderly people "in close-up machine-gun barrages" or by burning them alive in their huts, "many women were raped and disemboweled," and some were scalped.[6] Moreover, there is evidence that My Lai was not an isolated atrocity in the Vietnam War, even if it was particularly extreme. Reports of widespread American atrocities and war crimes were controversially collected in the Winter Soldier Investigation conducted by Vietnam Veterans Against the War in 1971.[7] In 2006, journalists reported the discovery of a previously hidden Pentagon study, the Vietnam War Crimes Working Group, that had catalogued 320 substantiated incidents of American atrocities against Vietnamese and Cambodian civilians.[8] In fact, the relatively indiscriminate killing of large numbers of civilians appears to have been fairly routine in the Vietnam War in a way that it was not in Iraq, in part due to "rules of engagement" in Vietnam that often led to artillery and air strikes on peasant villages.[9] The command emphasis on "body counts" also likely encouraged indiscriminate killing.[10] Sexual violence against women also appears to have been far more widespread in Vietnam than it was in Iraq.[11]

The journalist Jim Frederick captures the apparent contrast between the degrees of misconduct in the Iraq War and in the Vietnam War when he writes:

> It is...a testament to the control and discipline now exercised by the Army how rarely crimes such as [the rape and murders in Mahmudiyah] are actually committed today...Although most Vietnam War movies are works of fiction, it is fascinating how often misconduct or outright felonies figure in them, sometimes just as subplots or secondary narrative devices. In contrast, today's soldiers are required to be nothing less than warrior monks. Frequenting whorehouses and drinking anytime not on duty (and sometimes when on duty) in a war zone used to be tolerated, if not condoned, by the Army until just a few decades ago.[12]

Even the desecration of enemy corpses appears to have been less severe and less frequent in Iraq than in Vietnam. We have already seen references to the unnecessary shooting of enemy bodies in Iraq, and it is clear that American troops not infrequently took inappropriate pictures of, or with, dead Iraqis. But these offenses seem tame in comparison with the apparently more routine collection of severed ears in Vietnam, the atrocity photo albums that journalist Michael Herr describes encountering with predictable regularity, and the far more outrageous atrocities such as a unit where "they were cutting off the heads of enemies, and anyone who presented it to the commander got an extra beer ration."[13]

The psychologist Jonathan Shay records a dialogue between two Vietnam combat veterans in a therapy group:

> *First Veteran*: Well, at first, I mean when I just come there, I couldn't believe what I was seeing. I couldn't believe Americans could do things like that to another human being...but then I *became* that. We went through villages and killed everything, I mean *everything*, and that was all right with me.
>
> *Second Veteran*: I was just lucky, that's all. There were never, never any civilians up where I was...We did some horrible, horrible things to NVA—but they were *soldiers*...Killing babies, young girls, I would have *killed* an American I seen raping a nine-year-old girl without giving it a moment's thought. But where we were in the A Shau, there just weren't any [civilians].[14]

No one could plausibly mistake this dialogue for the words of two Iraq War veterans, even with the relevant geographic details transposed. Even if it is the case that during the Iraq War, members of the U.S. military routinely harassed and sometimes mistakenly killed Iraqi civilians at checkpoints,[15] engaged in petty pillaging, physically abused Iraqi families during nighttime raids, and mistreated detainees, as well as killing and injuring civilians through the questionable use of long-range weapons or by erroneously targeting individuals after incorrectly identifying them as hostile,[16] these alleged abuses, harms, and errors would still, collectively, seem less egregious than what took place in Vietnam.[17]

Assuming it is correct that the American military carried out more frequent and more serious wrongdoing in the Vietnam War than it did in Iraq, has the literature about the two wars reflected this difference? In particular, did fiction about the U.S. military experience in Vietnam, produced in the years during and shortly after the war, contain a *greater* emphasis on soldier wrongdoing and guilt than the literature about the U.S. military experience in Iraq discussed in this book?

Although it is difficult to generalize about such a large body of literature—according to a bibliography published in 1995, at least 666 novels about the Vietnam War had already been published at that time—the answer to this question appears to be a qualified "no."[18] The presentation of American soldier wrongdoing toward the Vietnamese and the attitude toward that wrongdoing in the American fiction of the Vietnam War, is consistent with the idea, proposed in Chapter 4, that moral cosmopolitanism and anti-militarism have generally spread and deepened within American culture during the era since World War II, and that these values tend to have a positive association with sensitivity to wrongdoing in war.

It is true that early Vietnam War literature pays far greater attention to American atrocities than the early American literature of World War II. As one critic notes, "[w]hat seems different in the literature of the Vietnam War is how directly and minutely atrocities are described and how conscious the writer (witness or perpetrator) is of the horror and of the moral implications of the event and of its record in language."[19] Yet the dominant narrative focus of Vietnam War literature, especially early on, remains the victimization of American soldiers rather than a moral reckoning with any wrongdoing. Mark Heberle, one of the leading experts on American literature about the Vietnam War, states that "the great majority of serious American Vietnam fictions are conventional war stories."[20] As already quoted above, Katherine Kinney, another widely cited expert, argues that "virtually the only story that has been told by Americans about the Vietnam War" is "[t]he idea that we fought ourselves, literalized in the repetitious image of Americans killing Americans."[21] Stories of "friendly fire" will necessarily dedicate less moral attention to harms directed at the Vietnamese. Instead, the Vietnamese "typically serve as little more than the exotic backdrop for the American encounter with the 'heart of darkness' within itself."[22] Harari's words about war culture in the Vietnam era apply also to the early fiction of the Vietnam War: "[e]ven when Vietnam veterans were accused of heinous crimes, the dominant tendency was to absolve them from responsibility [for] these crimes. The soldier's crimes were really the fault of the generals and politicians who victimized him and placed him in an impossible situation."[23]

More importantly, the shift toward moral cosmopolitanism and the criminalization of war has gone even further in Iraq War fiction than it did in the fiction about the Vietnam War. We might begin by noting a contrast between the earliest literature of the two wars. Arguably the first American novel of the U.S. military experience in the Iraq War to leave a lasting imprint was Helen Benedict's cosmopolitan, anti-war, and deeply critical *Sand Queen*, discussed above. By contrast, the first widely read and reviewed American novel about the Vietnam War may have been Robin Moore's wildly successful *The Green Berets* (1965), the basis for a similarly commercially successful 1968 John Wayne movie.[24] The novel reflects a morally uncritical, heroic conception of American soldiers at war, offering (in the words of one critic) tales of "patriotism, adventure, secret-mission suspense and heroic individualism" as its "animated cartoon heroes" square off against enemy "'Communists...black hordes, monkeys,' or the Vietnamese in general—'gooks,' 'dinks,' female 'slant-eyes': inferior, sub-human creatures who...share the fate of their literary predecessors, the devilish 'injuns.'" If the hero-commandos of Moore's novel "seem much like the enemy in their use of deceit and brutality, they are...basically good comrades, with a soft spot for gentle women and helpless children."[25] Although the film based on Moore's novel was widely mocked by Americans who had spent time in Vietnam, and few literary works as caricatured as Moore's received critical attention in later years, relatively traditional heroic portraits of Americans serving in the Vietnam War continued to be produced.[26]

A more prominent and enduring thread of Vietnam War literature has been naturalist, "war-is-hell" fiction in the American tradition of Crane, Dos Passos, Hemingway, and Mailer, focused for the most part on the horrific experiences of ordinary American soldiers in Vietnam. The emphasis here is more on the victimization of American soldiers by the experience of war than it is on wrongdoing by American soldiers toward the Vietnamese, although the latter is often portrayed. Marine veteran James Webb's celebrated *Fields of Fire* (1978) is representative.[27] The novel tells the chronological, realist tale of three marines: Snake, Hodges, and Will Goodrich ("Senator"). The conclusion of the novel contains a didactic statement of its attitude toward U.S. wrongdoing in Vietnam. An antiwar activist named Kerrigan encourages Goodrich, who returns home with a mechanical leg, to speak at a protest about "how shitty it was in the Nam...The whole immorality bit. You know, the desecrations, the tortures, the atrocities. I'll bet in the Marines you saw a lot of that." Goodrich replies "[t]hat's all a bunch of shit":

> "I didn't say things don't happen. And I don't know anything about My Lai. But it's a bunch of shit to say it's regular or even condoned. Look, man. I fought with myself about this for *months*. I even turned a guy in for murder. I thought it was my duty. But I just *don't know anymore*...You drop someone in hell and give him a gun and tell him to kill for some goddamned amorphous reason he can't even articulate. Then suddenly he feels an emotion that makes utter sense and he has a gun in his hand and he's seen dead people for months and the reasons are irrelevant anyway, so *pow*...That isn't murder. It isn't even atrocious. It's just a sad fact of life."[28]

The fact that such a meditation on atrocity appears at all in the novel, much less as prominently as it does, suggests the distance between World War II fiction and the fiction of the Vietnam War. But the fact that the meditation culminates in an almost cavalier dismissal of the moral responsibility of U.S. soldiers suggests the distance between relatively early Vietnam War fiction and relatively early Iraq War fiction. The latter has tended to treat lesser wrongdoing with greater solemnity and a greater sense of guilt.[29]

Atrocities by American soldiers toward the Vietnamese often play an even larger role in formally less conventional works of Vietnam War literature such as Larry Heinemann's *Close Quarters* (1974), which takes a slang-heavy, incessantly riffing, impressionistic approach to the story of PFC Philip "Flip" Dosier's moral descent in Vietnam.[30] Toward the beginning of the novel, Dosier objects when a medic murders a dying Vietcong prisoner whose moaning threatens to give away the soldiers' position.

Soon enough, however, Dosier finds himself taking jockish glee in taunting "an old mama-san" (106) by gratuitously killing her buffalo with his shotgun (108–9). "[I]t all came on a whim," Dosier muses. "She was gook. The hooch was gook. The buff was a gook buff" (110). By the end of his time in Vietnam, Dosier murders a captured Vietnamese boy who had helped an older Vietnamese man detonate mines that killed an American soldier (213–16). "I wanted that smooth, smug, slant-eyed fucking face ground into meat, transformed into spray," Dosier thinks (219). When no one is looking, Dosier "blew the top of his head off" with a shotgun (219). Another soldier covers for Dosier, claiming "the gook panicked and grabbed the gun," and Dosier faces no consequences for his murder (220). He also experiences no regret, at least initially: "I hated [the boy] when he was alive and I hated his corpse...[T]he dink was dead" (220). A hint of a possible moral reckoning to come arrives in the narrator's subsequent allusion to all of the corpses and unfillable graves created by the drive for vengeance (220). Then the atrocities continue, including a graphically described gang rape of a Vietnamese prostitute (259–61). Toward the end of his tour, Dosier marvels at his lack of care and even his love of killing "dinks" (278–79). "I dug free-fire zones," he rhapsodizes, "because we could kill anything that moved, and all I wanted to do was kill and kill and burn and rape and pillage until there was nothing left" (279).

But by the end of the novel, even after Dosier's homecoming, the moral reckoning has never arrived. Dosier marries his sweetheart Jenny and eventually tells her about all that he has done, including apparently the gang rape and the killing of the captive teenager (321–22). This catalogue of wrongdoing, however, appears in a single paragraph of the twenty-two-page chapter describing Dosier's life back in the world (314–36). There is no suggestion that Dosier is haunted by guilt regarding what he has done to the Vietnamese. Instead, the focus is on Dosier's traumatized reaction to the death of his buddy, Quinn, in "that fucking dumb-ass war" (331). Despite its intermittent fascination with the violent excesses of American soldiers, the ending of *Close Quarters* suggests that it views American soldiers like Dosier as victims rather than wrongdoers. The novel ultimately seems far more troubled by the suffering of American soldiers than by the suffering they have caused to the Vietnamese, including through the criminal acts of rape and murder described in the novel.[31]

Why does formal innovation in Vietnam War fiction tend to correlate with attention to American atrocities and other misconduct? Perhaps there is some affinity between the authorial attitude that is interested in attempting formal experimentation, and thus in violating traditional narrative rules, and the political attitude that is willing to confront wrongdoing by one's own community against others, and thus to violate the traditional value of loyalty in favor of more modern, cosmopolitan values. But there is also something arguably distancing, or even self-protective, in the use of unorthodox literary devices to present American wrongdoing.

To say that American soldiers' experiences in Vietnam were impossible to write about using traditional, realist narrative techniques, or required the adoption of new, postmodern modes of description, can come close to suggesting that there is no ordinary way to make sense of these experiences—that the experiences are something new and inexpressible, or even insane in a way that places them beyond the ordinary sense-making operations of language. Kurt Vonnegut's experimental, Vietnam-era novel about the Allied bombing of Dresden in World War II, *Slaughterhouse-Five* (1969), echoes the apparent attitude of many experimental literary works toward American atrocities in Vietnam by stating that "there is nothing intelligent to say about a massacre" (24). But is there, in fact, nothing intelligent to say about a massacre? It seems as though it is often possible to say a variety of intelligent things about a massacre, such as: who was responsible, who was harmed, why the massacre occurred, and how the risk of such massacres might be reduced in the future. Far from defying description or comprehension, there are few things less novel in human history than groups of young men carrying out atrocities during a war. From a historical perspective, it would be harder to explain a lack of atrocities in war than it would be to explain their recurrence in the latest conflict. Iraq War fiction, in contrast to Vietnam War fiction, seems much less shocked by American wrongdoing, and much more interested in confronting it directly, as a moral problem.

Consistent with this book's assumptions regarding the gradual, uneven but discernable rise of moral cosmopolitanism since the end of World War II, early Vietnam War fiction contains fewer closely drawn portrayals of Vietnamese experiences than early Iraq War fiction does of Iraqi experiences. As we have seen, a remarkable number of Iraq War novels written by Americans have even offered lengthy sections written from the points of view and in the voices of Iraqi characters.[32] Perhaps American authors writing in the twenty-first century feel obligated to incorporate the perspectives of Iraqis, despite the extreme difficulty of doing so and the risks of cultural appropriation and misrepresentation. By contrast, very few American works of Vietnam War fiction written in the years during and shortly after the war attempted to adopt the first-person perspective of Vietnamese characters.[33] Heberle notes that despite the formal and thematic variety of serious Vietnam War fiction, "[i]t is also narrow in fundamental ways...It is marked by narrow and/or sexist subject positions—women figures are almost exclusively objects of desire, much of it degrading—and by domestic and xenophobic racism."[34]

In sum, the early American fiction of the Vietnam War reflects, although often in a nascent form, the shift away from the literary representation of ordinary American soldiers as victims, and toward their representation as, in some paradigmatic cases, morally responsible wrongdoers. Iraq War fiction, as this book has argued, takes this development further through its greater moral scrutiny of relatively lesser wrongdoing. The often-solemn tone of Iraq War fiction, and its emphasis on the troubled homecomings of soldiers who are haunted not only by physical but by moral injuries, continues a transformation in war literature that was already foreshadowed in early American fiction about the Vietnam War.[35]

COHORT, LIFE-CYCLE, AND PERIOD EFFECTS

Before concluding, and with the preceding comparisons between "Vietnam War literature" and "Iraq War literature" in mind, it may be useful to clarify more precisely what it means to speak of "the literature" of a war. Rather than treating all novels written about a given war as a single group, it may be useful to distinguish between these novels based on developments that could plausibly alter the way a war is represented in literature over time. I will discuss three: cohort effects, what might be called "life-cycle" effects, and period effects.[36] It is because of these effects that throughout this book, in my discussion of World War II, Vietnam

War, and Iraq War literature, I have primarily focused on literature written during or shortly after each war.

First, a generational "cohort effect" may affect views of war in general. Members of different generations may think of war in different ways, in part due to their experiences of war (or its absence) during young adulthood, when values and perspectives are more malleable than they are later in life.[37] One generation of Americans lived through World War II in young adulthood, while another generation lived through the Vietnam War. It should not be surprising if the literature about World War II written by the "Greatest Generation" who experienced it directly differs from the literature about World War II written by "baby boomers" for whom the Vietnam War was a formative experience. Because Thomas Pynchon was born in 1937, for example, *Gravity's Rainbow* can be viewed as a novel about World War II written by a member of a later generational cohort.[38] The novel arguably reflects the concerns and attitudes of a generation that came to view war not only as a horrific ordeal, but as an absurd, obscene product of military-industrial conspiracies and the apparently uncontrollable proliferation of destructive technologies.

Similarly, Viet Thanh Nguyen's Pulitzer Prize-winning *The Sympathizer* (2015) can perhaps be read as a novel of the Iraq War generation, although the novel takes the Vietnam War and its aftermath as its backdrop.[39] By giving voice to Vietnamese and Vietnamese-American perspectives on the war, and reckoning in a morally serious way with the pervasive criminality and moral corruption that often accompanies and follows military conflict, the novel displays some of the characteristics that, this book has argued, distinguish Iraq War fiction from the American war fiction produced by earlier generations.[40] Nguyen's morally cosmopolitan, criminalized view of war can be seen in his lack of sympathy, elsewhere, for the idea that Bob Kerrey, the former Senator and Vietnam veteran quoted at the start of this chapter, "is also a victim—of an unjust war and disastrous leadership...[S]uch a claim seems ironic, if not outright ludicrous, when one compares Mr. Kerrey's prominence to the obscurity in which the survivors of the attack he led and the relatives of those killed now live."[41] Because Nguyen's focus is on the silenced victims of U.S. military activities, he resists attributing victimhood to those who victimized them. Instead, he emphasizes the victimizers' culpability.

Second, the literary representation of any given war may be affected by a kind of "life-cycle effect," according to which temporal distance from the war tends to alter its representation in predictable ways, regardless of any changes in the surrounding culture.[42] (Although I use the term "life-cycle effect," I am referring to the cultural "life" of a war rather than to the life of any individual.) For example, it would not be surprising for literature written long after a war to be more likely to explore the humanity of opposing soldiers, and the misdeeds of one's own country, than literature written during or shortly after a war, while tempers—and hatreds—remain more raw. It may not be a coincidence that James Jones' *The Thin Red Line* (1962), with its graphic descriptions of American atrocities against the Japanese,[43] arrived a decade after his more romantic *From Here to Eternity* (1951), rather than the novels appearing in the opposite order.[44] In general, the well-known American novels about World War II published after 1960 present a harsher and more critical perspective on the war—including works such as *The Thin Red Line* and *Catch-22* that appeared before the "Vietnam era" meaningfully began, that is, before the United States sent large numbers of ground troops to Vietnam. A similar dynamic may be at play in the sequencing of Oliver Stone's trilogy of Vietnam War films, which begins with the perspective of the American infantry in *Platoon* (1986) and ends with *Heaven & Earth* (1993), based on a memoir by a woman born in Vietnam, Le Ly Hayslip.[45] Even Tim O'Brien's fiction about the Vietnam War may reflect a subtle shift over time toward greater attention to American harms to the Vietnamese. Such harms appear in *Going After Cacciato* (1978) but are not the narrative focus of the novel.[46] By contrast, at the center of O'Brien's *In the Lake of the Woods* (1994) are the consequences for a Senate candidate of the revelation that he participated in the My Lai massacre.[47] The novel is an investigation of criminality and guilt, offering a fictionalized account of the massacre, as well as quotations from William Calley's court-martial.

Third, perceptions of any given war may be altered by "period effects" based on events and cultural changes occurring subsequent to the war—although these effects would in most cases be difficult to distinguish from the first two kinds of effects. Robert Altman's *M*A*S*H* (1970), for example, is often viewed as a reflection of contemporary attitudes toward the Vietnam War, even though the film is ostensibly about medical personnel in the Korean War. Altman, born in 1925 and a veteran of World War II, was a member of an earlier generational cohort. To the extent that *M*A*S*H* reflects a Vietnam-era view of the Korean war, it may be that the events of the Vietnam War itself (a period effect) shaped the film more than Altman's formative experience of World War II (a cohort effect) or the distance in time from the Korean War (a "life-cycle" effect).[48]

Obviously, the mention of the effects described above is not intended to suggest that all differences in the literary representation of war result from broad sociological dynamics. Writers may produce countless, diverse literary perspectives on any war at any time—including stark outliers like William March's *Company K*, a novel about World War I written by a highly decorated marine veteran of the war and published in 1933.[49] If the novel's relentless focus on the violent obscenity of war foreshadows some of the war literature of the Vietnam era, its moralistic emphasis on acts of wrongdoing by ordinary U.S. troops, such as the murdering of wounded enemy soldiers, may even be said to foreshadow the war literature of the Iraq War era.[50]

NATIONAL FORGETTING

This book began with the question: "What might a memorial to the American veterans of the war in Iraq look like?" With the comparison to the Vietnam War in mind, it might be tempting to answer that this problem has already been solved, and that an Iraq War memorial could and should adopt a similar approach to the one taken by the Vietnam Veterans Memorial in Washington, D.C. The Iraq War might seem to share with the Vietnam War many of the troubling features that interfered with the construction of a traditional war memorial in the earlier case. Both wars came to be seen by large parts of the American public as morally wrong, and neither war ended in a victory that could be celebrated. The Vietnam War in particular divided the American public, and the Vietnam Memorial has often been praised for accommodating the conflicting political and moral meanings of the Vietnam War through its indeterminacy, "its capacity to honor the dead with an openness that allows visitors to impress upon it their own meanings, their own histories, their own memories."[51]

But there is something unsatisfying in repeating the gesture of the Vietnam Memorial. It is one thing to create a memorial with no determinate political meaning, once, when thousands of Americans die in a war whose moral sense turns out to be so opaque and disputed that there is no public agreement even on whether the war dead can be celebrated. It is arguably something else to repeat this gesture several decades later. The fact of repetition raises questions and problems that were not present the first time around. How could America find itself, once again, in a position where it is apparently unable to memorialize its war dead on the basis of any shared meaning? Was there a lesson that we failed to learn?

If something happens twice, it seems less of an inexplicable aberration, an anomaly whose internal contradictions can defensibly be papered over in the interests of communal healing, and more of a pattern whose origins and meaning should perhaps, finally, be squarely confronted. Moreover, in contrast to the Vietnam War, there seems to be greater agreement among Americans about the Iraq War, at least as of this writing. Virtually everyone agrees it was a mistake, if not worse.

Is it possible to create a memorial to those who died in such a war?

The military historian Martin Van Creveld suggests that there have been three basic types of war monument, loosely corresponding to the changes in the perception of war sketched above in Chapter 2. The earliest type of war monument, which often took the form of obelisks, columns, equestrian statues, or triumphal arches, recorded victories and unambiguously glorified the victor, who is portrayed as a hero. More recently, there have been monuments paying tribute to fallen soldiers, who may be portrayed as heroes or victims of the war, or some combination of the two. Finally, since 1918 there has been a rise in war monuments "whose purpose is to warn against war." In these monuments, if soldiers are portrayed at all, they are portrayed simply as victims, and war "as a final tragedy inflicted on the innocent through no fault on their part and to no possible purpose that might justify it."[52] While in Germany after World War I there were "many *Denkmale*, war memorials celebrating the sacrifices of German soldiers," after World War II "one sees *Mahnmale*, memorials to the victims of Hitlerian Germany."[53]

Throughout the world, there are few if any monuments to soldiers who are presented within the monuments as agents of injustice. Those perceived as wrongdoers are not honored with monuments. As scholars have noted, "'[a]lmost always a monument is an attempt to interpret an event in which those who have erected it take pride.' They are ways by which a specific culture names its heroes."[54]

This book has argued that literary representations of U.S. military experiences in Iraq have dwelled, to a remarkable extent, on the wrongdoing or complicity of American servicemembers. If the paradigmatic literary-cultural image of the Iraq War veteran is closer to that of a wrongdoer than that of a hero, then, whatever one thinks of the justice of this image, it might seem fitting that no heroic monument specifically dedicated to the Americans who served in Iraq has yet been built.[55] Can there be a memorial to the victims of moral injury? To those who have become victims in part by participating in harm?

There is no indication that such questions will be answered any time soon, perhaps in part because the political leaders who were most directly responsible for the Iraq War have never faced a public reckoning. It is difficult to imagine coming to moral terms with the experiences of U.S. soldiers in Iraq without finally addressing the responsibility of those who initiated the war. Yet despite the increasing criminalization of some aspects of war in recent decades, legal accountability for the initiation of the Iraq War remains far outside the realm of plausibility. Instead, over the last several years, one of the few points of political consensus in the United States seems to have been a desire to forget that the American invasion of Iraq ever took place. Rather than memorializing, we seem to be engaged in an ongoing project of national forgetting. Now that the twentieth anniversary of the invasion has come and gone, the most lasting memorial for the thousands of Americans who died in Iraq remains a collective silence.

APPENDIX

A BRIEF SURVEY OF OTHER LITERARY WORKS

The focus of this book is American fiction about the U.S. military experience in the Iraq War, especially fiction written by veterans of the war. The study consists primarily of the five close readings in Chapters 5 through 9. But additional support for the book's arguments can be found in many other works of memoir and fiction. In this appendix, I offer a brief survey.

In support of this book's claim that contemporary American war culture reflects a relatively cosmopolitan moral outlook in comparison to the dominant outlook during past wars, it is a remarkable fact that two of the earliest novels about the wars in Afghanistan and Iraq by American veterans feature an Afghan and an Iraqi narrator, respectively, rather than being narrated from the perspective of an American soldier. Even more remarkably, both of the narrators kill Americans and are nevertheless portrayed with empathy. Benjamin Buchholz's *One Hundred and One Nights*, which may be the first novel about the Iraq War written by an American veteran of the war, is narrated not by a U.S. servicemember but by an American-educated Iraqi shopkeeper who bombs an American convoy.[1] Similarly, Elliot Ackerman's *Green on Blue*, which may be the first novel about the war in Afghanistan written by an American veteran of that war, is narrated not by an American soldier but by an Afghan boy who joins a U.S.-backed militia. Ackerman's novel offers a compelling portrait of the struggles that ultimately lead the boy to kill the indistinctly sketched, somewhat sinister American adviser to the militia, "Mr. Jack."[2] Neither book was greeted with protest. Instead, Ackerman's book received a blurb from retired Admiral James Stavridis, who described it as "the best novel of the Afghan-Iraq wars to date." Ackerman went on to co-author two geopolitical thrillers with Stavridis.[3]

In support of this book's suggestion that literary treatments of the U.S. military experience in the Iraq War feature pervasive representations of U.S. soldier wrongdoing and guilt, a number of additional works might be cited. The title of Iraq War tank crewman Brian Van Reet's novel *Spoils* refers primarily to a female American soldier captured by an Islamist militia, but the novel also features an extended, narratively pivotal scene of looting by American soldiers, as well as a discussion of photographing dead Iraqis as "trophies" or "souvenirs."[4] *Youngblood*, a novel by Army infantry officer Matt Gallagher, begins as though it might be a mystery about an old-school, violently intolerant staff sergeant's rumored murder of an Iraqi civilian.[5] But by the end, the novel has instead developed into a generally heroic love story between an American lieutenant and an Iraqi woman. Nevertheless, the staff sergeant's bigotry and culpability remain a theme throughout the novel, including through his killing of an Iraqi child's goat, his "tweaking" of the ROEs to permit more uses of force, and his use of "drop weapons" to cover up the wrongful killing of Iraqis.[6]

Despite its satirical tone, Iraq veteran David Abrams' *FOBBIT* contains scenes of American soldiers recklessly or intentionally causing harm to Iraqis, such as when Captain Abe Shrinkle shoots and kills an intellectually disabled Iraqi civilian.[7] In line with Abrams' generally jaunty, Joseph Heller-influenced style, however, there is little moral gravity in the novel's treatment of the killing. It would be an exaggeration to say that the novel plays the killing for laughs, but the narration concentrates on the surreality of the victim's appearance in a parka and jester's cap, the absurdity of Shrinkle's delusions of heroism, and the effects of the killing on Shrinkle's career. Later, after Shrinkle appears to kill a second Iraqi recklessly with a grenade, he loses his command and spends his days "rereading care package letters from good, decent Americans who had no idea...that he was the perpetrator of Crimes of Atrocity."[8]

Consistent with the observations in Chapter 10 regarding the narrative changes that tend to take place over the "life-cycle" of a war, Abrams' second novel about the Iraq War, *Brave Deeds*, presents a relatively darker view of American soldiers in Iraq, including through the presence of a sadistic, racist, homophobic soldier named Fish who murdered someone before entering the military and unnecessarily knocks an Iraqi woman unconscious with his rifle butt during a raid.[9] Like the sadistic SSG Croft in Mailer's *Naked and the Dead*, discussed above, Fish is presented as an outlier, and not as representative of the ordinary soldier. But at the center of *Brave Deeds* is a heroic, deeply mourned sergeant who also commits an apparent war crime by executing four Iraqis: "That was our Sergeant Morgan: breaker of international law, stoically doing the right thing."[10]

Although *The Surge*, by Iraq War infantry veteran Adam Kovac, stands out from other Iraq War literature based on the depressed affect of its prose and the exceptional cynicism, boredom, and annoyance toward fellow soldiers expressed by its protagonist, CPL Larry Chandler, its narrative, ironically, comes far closer than many other works discussed in this book to a traditional tale of soldier heroism. After endless drudgery, the novel culminates in an unexpected battle scene in which Chandler (in the spirit of Raymond Chandler's cynical but heroic Philip Marlowe) displays bravery, competence, and even a self-sacrificing commitment to military objectives—despite the fact that he and his fellow soldiers, as he later learns, were simply being used as bait for a CIA drone strike.[11] Even in this tale of heroism, however, U.S. soldier criminality emerges, as when an NCO, SFC Flowers, uses his "war club" to smash the skulls of a row of insurgent corpses.[12]

U.S. military harms to Iraqis are not a central focus of *Fives and Twenty-Fives*, a 2014 novel by Michael Pitre, who served in Iraq as a marine officer working in logistics and communications. But the novel features a Navy corpsman, Lester "Doc" Pleasant, who becomes addicted to his own painkillers while in Iraq.[13] In a remarkable parallel, Brandon Caro's *Old Silk Road*, which appeared in 2015, tells the story of Norman "Doc" Rogers, a Navy corpsman who abuses his supply of painkillers in Afghanistan.[14] Caro's novel goes much further than Pitre's in exploring themes of U.S. criminality, culminating in Rogers' hallucinatory discovery that his superiors are involved in the production and smuggling of opiates.[15]

Memoirs written by veterans of the Iraq War are, if anything, even more replete with instances of soldier wrongdoing, often directed toward Iraqis. In *Eat the Apple*, the formally innovative memoir of marine veteran Matt Young's service in Iraq, Young describes repeatedly seeing interrogators slap detainees across their faces with rolled-up newspapers and with their hands. On one occasion, Young participates in an interrogation where an Iraqi interpreter presses a knife into a man's cheek and then cuts the man's hand while he screams. "Hours later the human intelligence exploitation team arrives, they speak with the guilty man for five minutes, and the man is found innocent."[16] Young concludes the chapter with an expression of submerged guilt, noting that "years later when trying to fall asleep we tell ourselves we did what we had to do."[17] On another occasion, Young refers to himself as a "person-thing" and describes how, in the aftermath of a suicide bombing, the person-thing finds the bomber's face, "blown completely from his skull," and holds the face "in front of its own and screams at the crowd [of Iraqis] through plump, blood-flecked lips, watching the crowd's reactions through empty eyeholes."[18] Again, the chapter ends with Young recalling his attempts to repress the memory while his eyes "well with tears for our once-lost humanity."[19] Toward the memoir's end, in an imagined dialogue with his younger self, Young concludes that "[e]nforcing the idea that every service member is a hero is dangerous...I worry about...creating a generation of veterans who believe everything they did was good."[20]

An even more explicit, detailed, and vehement condemnation of U.S. military wrongdoing appears in the West Point graduate Erik Edstrom's memoir *Un-American*, although because Edstrom served in Afghanistan rather than Iraq, his arguments are an additional step outside the focus of this book. Edstrom expresses a morally cosmopolitan perspective on war when he states, in his first sentence, that "[t]he decision to go to war should be accompanied by three visions," including "the vision of experiencing the war from the other side."[21] Edstrom repeatedly realizes this vision in his own writing, as when he recounts the consequences of approving a warning shot at an Afghan man on a motorcycle an hour after a soldier has been injured by a roadside bomb. The warning round ricochets off a rock and strikes the motorcyclist's femoral artery. Bleeding "like someone slaughtered a sheep," the motorcyclist is evacuated to Kandahar Airfield and survives. But looking back years later, Edstrom chastises himself for not having followed up to convey an apology to the motorcyclist. "If you were in the United States and hurt an innocent person...[t]he decent thing to do is to help them up, ensure they are OK, and, if you are responsible, pay for damages. Why should I have acted any different with an Afghan than an American?"[22] After Edstrom's unit leaves Afghanistan, the unit that relieves them carries out a series of civilian "[s]port killings"—according to CNN, "throwing grenades at civilians and then shooting them"—as well as keeping "finger bones, leg bones, a tooth, and a skull from a corpse as sick war trophies."[23] Not surprisingly in light of his morally cosmopolitan orientation, Edstrom views the war in Afghanistan as "not only a tragedy but a crime."[24]

Eric Fair's memoir *Consequence* is one of the clearest illustrations of this book's argument that the literature of the Iraq War, in comparison to the literature of earlier American wars, has often treated relatively lesser wrongdoing with relatively greater moral anguish. Fair was a civilian contractor in Iraq who conducted interrogations at Abu Ghraib. He did not work in "the hard site" where the most serious abuses took place, but he describes how he put his hands on detainees and shoved them into walls.[25] The memoir is written in the tone of a confession, as when he describes walking past a blindfolded man "bound to the Palestinian chair," gasping for air with a pool of urine at his feet: "I am silent. This is a sin...There will be no atonement for it...Witnessing a man being tortured in the Palestinian chair requires the witness to either seek justice or cover his face."[26] Fair's harsh treatment of his actions might be compared, for example, to the Vietnam veteran Philip Caputo's more ambivalent handling of far more serious harms, including the killing of innocent Vietnamese civilians, in his celebrated memoir *A Rumor of War*.[27]

Episodes of soldier wrongdoing play a more peripheral but still notable role in a number of other Iraq War veteran memoirs, including John Crawford's *The Last True Story I'll Ever Tell*, which portrays looting during a house raid, as well as the routine harassment of Iraqis.[28] After someone in a red Volkswagen Passat shoots at Crawford's unit, "[a]ll over the sector" soldiers begin stopping red Volkswagens, searching them, knocking out their windows, slashing their tires, "anything to make them feel like they had achieved some form of vengeance, but we caught no one."[29] As Crawford's deployment continues, he writes, "I found myself looking with greater disdain on the Iraqis we had come to liberate. I lived for any excuse to deliver violence on them. This isn't a confession; this is life."[30]

In *Shade It Black*, marine veteran Jess Goodell imagines the experiences of Iraqis during the initial invasion when marines "cleared a village": "There had to be some who refused to go…The people who refused to go were the corpses we saw as we drove through what had been their village. Killed. Splattered. There was blood on the walls. On the doors. In the streets. On the cars. It wasn't marine blood. It was civilian blood. There were bodies."[31]

Air Force EOD technician Brian Castner's widely praised *The Long Walk*, which was adapted into an opera in 2015, does not present Castner in a criminal light.[32] Yet he returns from the war mentally and emotionally damaged, under the sway of what he calls "the Crazy," unable to shake the sense that "[a]ll that my feeble actions until now have produced is misery for myself, my children, my wife, and the children of thousands I do not know."[33] The catalogue of Iraq War memoirs containing expressions of moral discomfort regarding U.S. military harms to Iraqis could easily be extended. Even David Bellavia, the first living recipient of the Medal of Honor for service in the Iraq War, states early in his gory memoir *House to House* that "I've done things that even [God] can never forgive." He also insists that he is "not a victim": he has "heard [his] conscience call for restraint" and he "told it to shut up."[34]

Finally, there is no shortage of fictional portraits of U.S. soldier criminality in Iraq by writers who did not serve in the war. *Sand Queen* is only an especially extreme and clear example of a large and varied group of fictional works. To note only a few of the many possible examples: in Roxana Robinson's heartbreaking and deeply researched *Sparta*, a marine lieutenant, after returning home, is driven to thoughts of suicide in part by his recurring memories of Iraq, including a memory of having mistakenly shot an unarmed civilian, and a memory of the aftermath of a marine massacre of an Iraqi household, where he saw the bodies of women, a young girl, and a little boy dressed in pajamas stained in blood.[35] As the lieutenant tries to explain to his brother in the novel's final pages, "'You have no idea...It's like I'm a secret criminal. No one here knows what I've done.'"[36]

Whitney Terrell's *The Good Lieutenant* uses a reverse chronological structure to emphasize the tragic corruption of a lieutenant through her military service. At the opening of the novel, she has betrayed one of her soldiers, become complicit in the torture of detainees, and played a role in causing multiple deaths, including through her own mistaken shooting of an innocent civilian Iraqi.[37] By the end of the novel, we meet the person she once was, someone so committed, or overcommitted, to moral rectitude that she once turned in her brother to the police after he stole a car.[38] In the novel's final pages, which return to the time period of the novel's beginning, the lieutenant looks at her platoon and wonders, abstractly: "Who will dare report her murders?"[39]

Atticus Lish's *Preparation for the Next Life* tells the love story of Zou Lei and Brad Skinner, a damaged Iraq War veteran. The novel, one of the great artistic achievements of post-9/11 American literature, is not primarily about Skinner's experiences in Iraq. But the reader's glimpses of Skinner's service are suffused with wrongdoing and harm. His unit "manned a checkpoint and shot up a car...Mom's head was gone."[40] The infantry murders civilians and then covers up the killings with "dropped wire or weapons on corpses." Skinner himself murders two civilian Iraqis, the second "in cold blood" as he writhes and shouts.[41] Later we learn about the many ways that Skinner and his unit desecrated corpses.[42]

Notes

CHAPTER ONE

1. All quotations in this and the next paragraph come from Chapter 2 of Andrew J. Bacevich, *The New American Militarism*, updated ed. (Oxford: Oxford University Press, 2013), with internal quotation marks omitted. For this paragraph, see pages 88, 92–93, 95. On the intersecting delusions and incompetence of the Bush administration officials who were ultimately responsible for the Iraq War, see Robert Draper, *To Start a War: How the Bush Administration Took America into Iraq* (New York: Penguin Press, 2020). For a contrasting account that "empathize[s]" with the perspectives of Bush administration officials, see Melvyn P. Leffler, *Confronting Saddam Hussein: George W. Bush and the Invasion of Iraq* (Oxford: Oxford University Press: 2023), xviii.
2. Bacevich, *New American Militarism*, 94–95.
3. In fact, as of this writing, Congress has authorized the planning of a Global War on Terrorism Memorial to commemorate the nearly 7,000 U.S. military deaths in the ongoing post-9/11 wars, including the Iraq War from 2003 to 2011. Elliot Ackerman and Jennifer Ballou, "Opinion: A Memorial to the War on Terror Is Coming. Here Is Why You Should Care," *Washington Post*, September 25, 2023. The framing of the Iraq War as part of a "Global War on Terrorism" ("GWOT") may provide a convenient solution to the problems discussed in this introduction. If the Iraq War can be seen as a response to the September 11 attacks, or to some indefinite global terrorist threat, then it may come to possess a public meaning that it currently lacks, a place in a

purposeful historical narrative. It is as though, instead of dedicating a specific memorial to the American servicemembers who died in the Vietnam War, the nation had decided to construct only a monument to the Cold War in general.

The trouble, of course, is that placing the Iraq War within the frame of a "Global War on Terrorism" risks entrenching the false belief, widespread at the time of the invasion and promoted by the Bush administration's language, that Saddam Hussein had a role in the September 11 attacks. Carroll Doherty and Jocelyn Kiley, "A Look Back at How Fear and False Beliefs Bolstered U.S. Public Support for War in Iraq," *Pew Research Center*, March 14, 2023. In doing so, the GWOT framing risks promoting long-discredited arguments that the war in Iraq was somehow justified as an act of self-defense. George W. Bush's role as honorary chairman of the Global War on Terrorism memorial foundation strengthens the concern that the memorial may serve to obscure the history of the Iraq War and rehabilitate the Bush administration officials who initiated it.

4. John Tirman, *The Deaths of Others: The Fate of Civilians in America's Wars* (Oxford: Oxford University Press, 2011), 324–36. As of August 2023, Brown University's Cost of War project estimated approximately 200,000 civilian deaths directly resulting from the Iraq War. The project also noted, however, that "[s]everal times as many more" civilians may have been killed indirectly "because, for example, of water loss, sewage and other infrastructural issues, and war-related disease." "Figures," Costs of War, Brown University, updated August 2023, https://watson.brown.edu/costsofwar/figures/2021/WarDeathToll.

   In what appears to be an implicit acknowledgment that the U.S. military has dedicated inadequate resources and attention to tracking, minimizing, and redressing civilian casualties, the Pentagon released a plan in 2022 including "sweeping changes aimed at reducing risks to civilians in U.S. military operations by fostering a culture in which those in the field view preventing such harm as a core part of their missions." Eric Schmitt et al., "Austin Orders Overhaul to Better Protect Civilians During U.S. Combat Operations," *New York Times*, August 25, 2022.

5. Joel D. Rayburn and Frank K. Sobchak, eds., *The U.S. Army in the Iraq War, Volume 2: Surge and Withdrawal, 2007–2011* (Carlisle Barracks, PA: United States Army War College Press, 2019), 639.
6. See Andrew J. Bacevich, *America's War for the Greater Middle East: A Military History* (New York: Random House, 2016), 245–46, 272, 276–77, 343. For a history of the rise of the Islamic State and its predecessors during the Iraq War, see Joby Warrick, *Black Flags: The Rise of ISIS* (New York: Doubleday, 2015).

7. See Jürgen Habermas, *The Divided West*, trans. and ed. Ciaran Cronin (Malden, MA: Polity, 2006), 28, 40; Thomas Ricks, *Fiasco: The American Military Adventure in Iraq* (New York: Penguin Press, 2006), 90–94; James J. Sheehan, *The Monopoly of Violence: Why Europeans Hate Going to War* (Boston, MA: Houghton Mifflin, 2007), xiii; "America's Image in the World: Findings from the Pew Global Attitudes Project," *Pew Research Center*, March 14, 2007.
8. Joseph E. Stiglitz and Linda J. Bilmes, *The Three Trillion Dollar War* (London: W.W. Norton, 2008). According to Brown University's Costs of War project, "[t]hrough Fiscal Year 2022, the United States federal government has spent and obligated $8 trillion dollars on the post-9/11 wars in Afghanistan, Pakistan, Iraq, and elsewhere." "Economic Costs," Costs of War, Brown University, updated September 2021, https://watson.brown.edu/costsofwar/costs/economic. A 2009 draft of an official history cataloguing the failures and waste of the reconstruction effort in Iraq began its concluding chapter with a quote from Charles Dickens' *Great Expectations*: "We spent as much money as we could, and got as little for it as people could make up their minds to give us." Office of the Special Inspector General for Iraq Reconstruction, *Hard Lessons: The Iraq Reconstruction Experience* (draft February 2, 2009).
9. Although I use the general term "servicemembers" here, sometimes in this book I will refer to U.S. military servicemembers collectively as "soldiers," despite the sensitivity that marines and other non-Army servicemembers sometimes express about being included within this label.
10. As the literary scholar Patrick Deer noted in a 2017 issue of *Modern Fiction Studies* dedicated to narratives of the contemporary U.S. wars, "[d]espite their long and bloody duration and vast scale, the wars in Iraq and Afghanistan are still conflicts with uncertain histories and without a secure place in history." Patrick Deer, "Beyond Recovery: Representing History and Memory in Iraq War Writing," *Modern Fiction Studies* 63, no. 2 (2017): 312, 313. Similarly, the literary scholar Roger Luckhurst has drawn attention to "the resistance to narrative or representation" of the Iraq War. Roger Luckhurst, "In War Times: Fictionalizing Iraq," *Contemporary Literature* 53, no. 4 (2012): 713, 722.
11. Sinan Antoon, "Opinion: Fifteen Years Ago, America Destroyed My Country," *New York Times*, March 18, 2018. Bush has painted a number of wounded American veterans of the Iraq War, but has apparently never painted an Iraqi victim. Adam Johnson, "What's Wrong with This Picture? Fawning Praise of Bush's Veteran Art Ignores Iraqi Victims," *FAIR*, April 21, 2017.
12. There appears to be no gender-neutral term for referring to members of the U.S. Air Force. The four least senior enlisted ranks in the Air Force, E-1 to

E-4, incorporate the masculine gendered "Airman" (Airman Basic, Airman, Airman First Class, Senior Airman).

13. Karl Marlantes, *What It Is Like to Go to War* (London: Corvus, 2011), 176–78.
14. Nancy Sherman, *Afterwar: Healing the Moral Wounds of Our Soldiers* (Oxford: Oxford University Press, 2015), 30–31.
15. Phil Klay draws on the routine assumption that Iraq War veterans have PTSD in a short story where a female law student acquaintance pulls the narrating marine veteran law student aside "to tell me the sorts of things...you tell only close friends or your psychiatrist." Klay, "Unless It's a Sucking Chest Wound," in *Redeployment* (New York: Penguin Press, 2014), 260, the collection that is the subject of Chapter 6 below. In fact, the veteran narrator does not have PTSD, never said he had PTSD, and largely spent his time in Iraq handling paperwork as an adjutant. Klay, "Unless," 239. When the female law student confides that eventually people realize, "'This one is damaged,'" the narrator notes: "That was absolutely what I was thinking." The female law student had "been through infinitely worse" than him. Klay, 260–61.
16. Throughout this book, I use the terms "criminal" or "criminality" not only to refer to violations of positive criminal law, but also to refer to especially egregious violations of moral principles. My primary focus is on acts of wrongdoing that are serious enough (from whatever moral perspective is being invoked) that state punishment could be defended as a morally appropriate response. I use the term "criminality" because it is the dominant term for discussing serious wrongdoing in our culture.
17. See, for example, Elizabeth D. Samet, *No Man's Land: Preparing for War and Peace in Post-9/11 America* (New York: Farrar, Straus, and Giroux, 2014), 77–81. Bacevich writes: "In the eyes of the American people, 'the troops' could do no wrong. To the last man and woman, they were heroes, to whom the nation owes an immense debt of gratitude." Bacevich, *Militarism*, 235. A 2011 survey found that three-quarters of Americans "say they [have] thanked someone in the military." "War and Sacrifice in the Post-9/11 Era," *Pew Research Center*, October 5, 2011.
18. Jim Frederick, *Black Hearts: One Platoon's Descent into Madness in Iraq's Triangle of Death* (New York: Crown, 2010), 305, 310, 312, 316–24. "PFC" is an abbreviation of "Private First Class," a junior enlisted rank just above Private.
19. Nick Turse, *Kill Anything That Moves: The Real American War in Vietnam* (London: Picador, 2013), 4, 108–9, 192, 258. Turse also notes that while "the U.S. military attempted to quantify almost every other aspect" of the Vietnam War, "it quite deliberately never conducted a comprehensive study of Vietnamese noncombatant casualties." Turse, 12.

20. The distinction may not be as clear-cut as is sometimes assumed. The psychiatrist Jonathan Shay mentions, for example, that "only about 10 percent" of the Vietnam veterans he treats were drafted. Jonathan Shay, *Achilles in Vietnam: Combat Trauma and the Undoing of Character* (New York: Atheneum, 1994), 9.

21. Bacevich, *New American Militarism*. For evidence that militarism in Western culture has generally declined over the last two centuries, see Azar Gat, *War in Human Civilization* (Oxford: Oxford University Press, 2006), 570–673; Steven Pinker, *The Better Angels of Our Nature: Why Violence Has Declined* (New York: Viking, 2011), 161–63, 242–43, 378–481; Martin Van Creveld, *The Culture of War* (New York: Ballantine Books, 2008), 188–208, as well as other sources discussed below in Chapter 4. For suggestive evidence that values associated with militarism have continued to decline even in the era of Bacevich's "new American militarism," especially in Europe but also in the United States, see Ronald F. Inglehart, *Cultural Evolution: People's Motivations Are Changing, and Reshaping the World* (Cambridge: Cambridge University Press, 2018), 102–13, 192–93; Pippa Norris and Ronald Inglehart, *Cultural Backlash: Trump, Brexit, and Authoritarian Populism* (Cambridge: Cambridge University Press, 2019), 32–36, 87–131.

Samuel Moyn claims that there was "a period of clarity in the early 1970s, when many people, far more than ever since, were prepared to see government officials and U.S. citizens themselves as potential and actual evildoers," and when "concerns about how the United States fought were explicitly linked to what justification the country had to fight at all (and what role it ought to play in the world)." Moyn, *Humane: How the United States Abandoned Peace and Reinvented War* (New York: Farrar, Straus and Giroux, 2021), 163. But he does not cite survey evidence. The claim rests in tension with Inglehart's public opinion research regarding the rise of postmaterialist values, cited above, as well as with anecdotal evidence such as the fact that George McGovern ran on an anti-war platform in the 1972 presidential campaign and lost every state except Massachusetts. By contrast, in 2004, John Kerry only narrowly lost the presidential election despite his criticisms of the Iraq War and his background as a Vietnam Veterans Against the War spokesperson. In 1971, in testimony before the Senate, Kerry had stated that American war crimes in Vietnam were "not isolated incidents but crimes committed on a day-to-day basis with the full awareness of officers at all levels of command." "Transcript: Kerry Testifies Before Senate Panel, 1971," NPR, April 25, 2006. (In the interest of transparency: I worked for the Kerry–Edwards field campaign in Ohio and West Virginia in 2004.)

The claim that Americans in the early 1970s were more critical of the government than Americans today also rests in tension with opinion polling that found the percentage of Americans "who say they trust the government to do what is right just about always/most of the time" declined from a high of 77% in 1964, to 53% in 1973, to 16% in 2023. "Public Trust in Government: 1958–2023," *Pew Research Center*, September 19, 2023. It is true that Americans' confidence in the military generally rose from 1980 to the 2000s, before declining since then, but this confidence may be distinct from support for militarism in general or faith in the justice of American military actions. "Confidence in U.S. Military Lowest in Over Two Decades," *Gallup*, July 31, 2023.

As Moyn shows, there is a wealth of anecdotal evidence of Americans condemning U.S. atrocities in Vietnam as criminal, including through the Vietnam Veterans Against the War's Winter Soldier investigation, the writings of journalist Neil Sheehan, and the former Nuremberg prosecutor Telford Taylor's best-selling *Nuremberg and Vietnam: An American Tragedy* (New York: Bantam Books, 1970). Moyn, *Humane*, 161–92. But other anecdotes can be offered of prominent Americans, such as John Wayne and Billy Graham, downplaying even the clearest atrocities in Vietnam, including what Wayne called "'the so-called My Lai massacre.'" Kristin Kobes Du Mez, *Jesus and John Wayne: How White Evangelicals Corrupted a Faith and Fractured a Nation* (New York: Liveright, 2020), 49–50, 57. Moyn notes that even after the use of torture in Vietnam became a public issue, "there was no torture debate in the Vietnam years, at first because the practice was tolerated." Moyn, *Humane*, 171.

By contrast, in publications since 2001, any number of American writers have condemned the Bush administration's post-9/11 foreign policy as potentially criminal, especially but not only its use of torture, as Moyn's own book illustrates. Moyn, *Humane*, 233–65; see also Jane Mayer, *The Dark Side: The Inside Story of How the War on Terror Turned into a War on American Ideals* (New York: Doubleday, 2008); Senate Select Committee on Intelligence, *The Senate Intelligence Committee Report on Torture: Committee Study of the Central Intelligence Agency's Detention and Interrogation Program* (Brooklyn, NY: Melville House, 2014). In an explicit echo of the Winter Soldier investigation, the organization Iraq Veterans Against the War published their own investigation of atrocities by American servicemembers in Afghanistan and Iraq, with much less public pushback. Iraq Veterans Against the War and Aaron Glantz, *Winter Soldier: Iraq and Afghanistan: Eyewitness Accounts of the Occupations* (Chicago: Haymarket Books, 2008). The present study as a whole, and in particular Chapter 10, provides further evidence in support of the conclusion that Americans, at least as judged by their literature, are more prepared to see their government and themselves as wrongdoers today than they were in the early 1970s.

22. Bacevich, *New American Militarism*, 34, 36–37, 104–5, 107; Bacevich, *America's War for the Greater Middle East*, xix–xxii. Bacevich's son, Andrew, was killed in the Iraq War in 2007 at the age of 27. Andrew J. Bacevich, "I Lost My Son to a War I Oppose. We Were Both Doing Our Duty," *Washington Post*, May 27, 2007.
23. Bacevich, *New American Militarism*, 34, 106–7, 110.
24. Bacevich, *New American Militarism*, 116. On the global popularity of "Rambo culture," see Barbara Ehrenreich, *Blood Rites: Origins and History of the Passions of War* (New York: Henry Holt and Co., 1997), 228.
25. Bacevich, *New American Militarism*, 2.
26. Kevin Powers, *The Yellow Birds* (New York: Little, Brown, 2012), 144.
27. Joanna Bourke, *An Intimate History of Killing: Face-to-Face Killing in Twentieth-Century Warfare* (London: Granta, 1999), xix.
28. Bourke, xix–xx.
29. Sebastian Junger, *Tribe: On Homecoming and Belonging* (New York: Twelve, 2016), 99–100.
30. Marlantes, *What It Is Like to Go to War*, 195.
31. According to Moyn, the widespread use of the phrase "international humanitarian law" can be attributed to the proselytizing efforts of the Swiss jurist Jean Pictet beginning in the mid-1950s. Moyn, *Humane*, 198. The U.S. military tends to refer to international humanitarian law as the law of armed conflict ("LOAC").
32. David Kennedy, "Speech: Modern War and Modern Law," *University of Baltimore Law Review* 36, no. 2 (2007): 193.
33. See Dieter Fleck, ed., *The Handbook of the International Law of Military Operations* (Oxford: Oxford University Press, 2008), 35.
34. Patrick Deer makes a related but distinct point when he argues that "recent war narratives appear to need the crime genre to impose coherence and interpretive order on their fictional worlds." Patrick Deer, "Crime Fiction and War," in *The Routledge Companion to Crime Fiction*, ed. Janice Allan et al. (New York: Routledge, 2020), 343. Deer's brief essay focuses not on themes of criminality but on works of war fiction that imitate the conventions of the crime genre, such as Matt Gallagher's *Youngblood* (New York: Atria, 2016).
35. In fact, many of the distinctive, recurring motifs of Iraq War fiction are already noted in the relatively early, non-academic summaries offered by

Michiko Kakutani, "Human Costs of the Forever Wars, Enough to Fill a Bookshelf," *New York Times*, December 25, 2014; George Packer, "Home Fires," *New Yorker*, March 31, 2014; Sam Sacks, "First-Person Shooters: What's Missing in Contemporary War Fiction," *Harper's*, August 2015. By far the best resource for researching the literature of the post-9/11 wars is a blog written by Peter Molin, a former active-duty Army officer and now literature instructor at Rutgers University. "Time Now: The Iraq and Afghanistan Wars in Art, Film, and Literature," *Time Now* (blog), accessed February 1, 2023, https://acolytesofwar.com. For two excellent and recent scholarly introductions to some of the characteristic themes of Iraq War literature, see Jennifer Haytock, *The Routledge Introduction to American War Literature* (London: Routledge, 2018), 153–71; Stacey Peebles, "The Forever Wars," in *War and American Literature*, ed. Jennifer Haytock (Cambridge: Cambridge University Press, 2021), 254–68.

36. Throughout this book, I use the term "war culture" simply to refer to the cultural phenomena related to war in any given community. To be clear, I do not use the term, as Patrick Deer does, to refer to "a dominant culture defined by militarism" or a "process of militarization of the general culture," with the implication that some communities "live in a war culture" while others do not. See Patrick Deer, "Mapping Contemporary American War Culture," *College Literature* 43, no. 1 (Winter 2016): 48, 52.
37. As of 2007, IEDs had caused three-fifths of all hostile deaths of coalition soldiers in Iraq. Sheila M. Bird and Clive B. Fairweather, "Military Fatality Rates (By Cause) in Afghanistan and Iraq: A Measure of Hostilities," *International Journal of Epidemiology* 36, no. 4 (2007): 841.
38. See, for example, Michael Pitre, *Fives and Twenty-Fives* (New York: Bloomsbury, 2014).
39. See, for example, Helen Benedict, *Sand Queen* (New York: Soho Press, 2011); Gallagher, *Youngblood*; Brian Van Reet, *Spoils* (New York: Little, Brown, 2017).
40. See, for example, Benedict, *Sand Queen*. Military bloggers were also a novel feature of the Iraq War, as Stacey Peebles highlights in her discussion of Colby Buzzell's blog and subsequent book, *My War: Killing Time in Iraq* (New York: G.P. Putnam's Sons, 2005) in Stacey Peebles, *Welcome to the Suck: Narrating the American Soldier's Experience in Iraq* (Ithaca, NY: Cornell University Press, 2011), 10, 12, 23–48.
41. See, for example, Benedict, *Sand Queen*; Pitre, *Fives and Twenty-Fives*. The sizable bookshelf of nonfiction works about women deployed in the post-9/11 military includes Helen Benedict, *The Lonely Soldier: The Private War of Women Serving in Iraq* (Boston: Beacon Press, 2009); Jess Goodell and

John Hearn, *Shade It Black: Death and After in Iraq* (Philadelphia: Casemate, 2011); Kirsten Holmstedt, *Band of Sisters: American Women at War in Iraq* (Mechanicsburg, PA: Stackpole Books, 2007); Helen Thorpe, *Soldier Girls: The Battles of Three Women at Home and at War* (New York: Scribner, 2014); Kayla Williams, *Love My Rifle More Than You: Young and Female in the U.S. Army* (New York: W.W. Norton and Company, 2005).

42. See, for example, David Abrams, *FOBBIT* (New York: Black Cat, 2012).
43. See, for example, Roy Scranton, *War Porn* (New York: Soho Press, 2016); Kimberly Pierce, dir., *Stop-Loss* (Hollywood, CA: MTV Films, 2008).
44. The Iraq War veteran novelist Brian Van Reet captures a common sentiment when he notes his resentment toward "civilian contractors, also sometimes known as mercenaries...[who] were doing basically the same job as I was but getting three or more times the pay." "The Red and the Blue: Writing War in a Divided America," *Brian Van Reet* (blog), last modified January 11, 2019. "Although precise figures are difficult to determine, by 2008 the number of personnel in Iraq under contract with the U.S. government roughly equaled or was greater than the number of U.S. troops on the ground." Deborah Avant and Renée de Nevers, "Military Contractors and the American Way of War," in *The Modern American Military*, ed. David M. Kennedy (Oxford: Oxford University Press, 2013), 136–37. According to Brown University's Costs of War project, more contractors (over 8,000) have died in the post-9/11 wars than U.S. servicemembers (over 7,000). "U.S. & Allied Killed," Costs of War, Brown University, updated July 2021, https://watson.brown.edu/costsofwar/costs/human/military/killed.
45. See, for example, Pitre, *Fives and Twenty-Fives*.
46. See, for example, Abrams, *FOBBIT*; Rajiv Chandrasekaran, *Imperial Life in the Emerald City: Inside Iraq's Green Zone* (New York: Vintage Books, 2007); Scranton, *War Porn*.
47. See, for example, Benedict, *Sand Queen*; Nathaniel Fick, *One Bullet Away: The Making of a Marine Officer* (Boston: Houghton Mifflin Company, 2005). At a December 2004 town hall with Secretary of Defense Donald Rumsfeld, SPC Thomas Wilson of the Tennessee Army National Guard explained: "Our vehicles are not armored. We're digging pieces of rusted scrap metal and compromised ballistic glass that's already been shot up...to put on our vehicles to take into combat." Ricks, *Fiasco*, 411–12. Rumsfeld responded: "As you know, you go to war with the Army you have. They're not the Army you might want or wish to have at a later time." Ricks, 412.
48. Tanisha M. Fazal, "Dead Wrong?: Battle Deaths, Military Medicine, and Exaggerated Reports of War's Demise," *International Security* 39, no. 1

(Summer 2014): 95. For the literary representation of survival after extreme injury, see Elliot Ackerman, *Waiting for Eden* (New York: Vintage Books, 2018); Brian Van Reet, "Big Two-Hearted Hunting Creek," in Scranton and Gallagher, *Fire and Forget*, 173–90; the character of Michelle Gomez in Pitre's *Fives and Twenty-Fives*; and the disfigured veteran in Phil Klay's "War Stories," in *Redeployment*, 213. The increased rates of survival after serious injury in the Iraq War continued a long-term trend. Already in the 1970s, Ron Kovic noted that someone with his injuries "would never have come back from any other war." Ron Kovic, *Born on the Fourth of July* (New York: McGraw-Hill Book Company, 1976), 177.

49. See, for example, Benedict, *Sand Queen*.
50. See, for example, Benedict; Junger, *Tribe*, 87.
51. See, for example, Phil Klay, "Prayer in the Furnace," in *Redeployment*, 129.
52. See, for example, Ben Fountain, *Billy Lynn's Halftime Walk* (New York: HarperCollins, 2012).
53. Packer notes that "the new war literature is intensely interested in the return home," so much so that the equivalent to the trenches in World War I literature is "a reunion scene at an airport or a military base—families holding signs, troops looking for their loved ones, an unease sinking deep into everyone." Packer, "Home Fires." Owen W. Gilman Jr. makes a similar point in *The Hell of War Comes Home: Imaginative Texts from the Conflicts in Afghanistan and Iraq* (Jackson: University Press of Mississippi, 2018), 7. The focus of Iraq War literature on the difficulties of homecoming echoes the *Heimkehrerliteratur* ("homecoming literature") that followed World War II in Germany, as soldiers of the Nazi regime returned home to a world in which it was impossible to tell many of the stories that they might once have hoped to tell of their military service.
54. Wendy Brown, *Undoing the Demos: Neoliberalism's Stealth Revolution* (Brooklyn, NY: Zone Books, 2015). For a more extended discussion of the term "neoliberalism" and some of the puzzles it has created for historiography, see Gregory Brazeal, "Markets as Legal Constructions," *University of Cincinnati Law Review* 91, no. 3 (2023): 595, 646–54. To the extent that the "neoliberal era" in the United States was partly defined by harshly punitive economic policies, it might be noted that the financing of the post-9/11 wars was not particularly "neoliberal." It could have been accomplished through calls for fiscal sacrifice, but was not. Instead, after the invasion of Iraq, Congress passed a massive tax cut in 2003.
55. Brown, *Undoing the Demos*, 142.
56. See Phil Klay, "Money as a Weapons System," in *Redeployment*, 77.

57. In terms of this book's primary categories of analysis, *Billy Lynn's Long Halftime Walk* presents soldiers not as wrongdoers but as victims. Despite a passing reference to "the state of pure sin toward which war inclines," the novel as a whole suggests that ordinary soldiers are not sinners but pawns whose lives are determined by larger forces, including the American public's demand for traditional stories of soldier heroism. Fountain, 45–46. As the young enlisted protagonist realizes in the novel's final pages, the "smiling, clueless citizens" "are the ones in charge...His reality is their reality's bitch." Fountain, 306.
58. Rosa Brooks, *How Everything Became War and the Military Became Everything* (New York: Simon & Schuster, 2016), 17–20.
59. Patrick Deer, "The Iraq War," in *The Routledge Companion to Literature and Trauma*, ed. Colin Davis (New York: Routledge, 2020), 418. For an introduction to the many uses of trauma theory in contemporary literary studies, see J. Roger Kurtz, ed., *Trauma and Literature* (Cambridge: Cambridge University Press, 2018).
60. Roger Luckhurst, "Iraq War Body Counts: Reportage, Photography, and Fiction," *Modern Fiction Studies* 63, no. 2 (Summer 2017): 355, 365. In influential works such as *Frames of War: When Is Life Grievable?* (London: Verso, 2009), and *The Force of Non-Violence: An Ethico-Political Bind* (London: Verso, 2020), Judith Butler has drawn on the psychoanalytic tradition more generally to redescribe the "selective and differential framing of violence" in contemporary war. From the perspective of this book's arguments, trauma theory reflects the transformations in value that have also contributed to the view of the "soldier as victim," as discussed in Chapter 2. In fact, Butler often seems to frame human life in general in terms of the human potential for victimization. In *Frames of War*, she proposes "a new bodily ontology...that implies the rethinking of," among other things, "precariousness, vulnerability, injurability, interdependency, exposure, [and] bodily persistence" (2). She calls for "the apprehension of a generalized condition of precariousness or, in other words, of the radically egalitarian character of grievability" (183). In many ways, Butler's attention to the unequal recognition of human lives overlaps with this book's discussions of moral cosmopolitanism. Moral cosmopolitanism, as discussed below, stands for the recognition that all human lives, regardless of group identity, are equally deserving of moral concern. But while Butler draws primarily on familiar figures from the pantheon of high literary theory, from Freud and Benjamin to Foucault, Barthes, Derrida, and Deleuze, this book attempts to bring into the critical conversation works of history, social science, and legal scholarship that are more empirically oriented, and that

may be relatively less familiar to literary scholars, especially those working outside the field of war literature.

Unlike this book, Butler's work could also be described as committed to developing new "vocabularies," in Richard Rorty's sense. See Richard Rorty, *Contingency, Irony, Solidarity* (Cambridge: Cambridge University Press, 1989). To be clear, this book's relative lack of engagement with some of today's more ambitious literary-theoretical vocabulary-building projects does not result from the assumption that the relatively familiar, status quo vocabularies largely used in this book are somehow natural or necessary. Inherited vocabularies are the products of contingent historical circumstances, and it is entirely possible that some unfamiliar way of talking might better serve our purposes than the current ways. But from a pragmatic perspective, the case for using a new vocabulary will usually depend on showing that it does, in fact, better serve our purposes than the present one—even after factoring in the risk that the new language will be exclusionary, like a priestly jargon, or will create confusion in a world where "the meaning of a word is its use in the language," and thus meanings often become clearer through more extensive use. See Ludwig Wittgenstein, *Philosophical Investigations*, trans. G.E.M. Anscombe (Oxford: Blackwell Publishing, 1953) § 43. Where I have felt that unfamiliar terms served some purpose within this project, such as in the discussion of holistic responsibility, or cohort, life-cycles, and period effects, I have used them. Otherwise, I have not.

61. Roy Scranton, "The Trauma Hero: From Wilfred Owen to 'Redeployment' and 'American Sniper,'" *Los Angeles Review of Books*, January 25, 2015.
62. Chapter 9 contains a more detailed discussion of Campbell's, Harari's, and Scranton's writings.
63. Clint Eastwood, dir., *American Sniper* (Burbank, CA: Warner Bros., 2014). Chapter 9 does not address Eastwood's film, instead analyzing the *American Sniper* book's attempts to tell a traditional hero story about service in the Iraq War. Like the book, the film incorporates many traditional heroic elements, but it also incorporates a trauma framing to a greater extent than the book, as Scranton suggests. In scenes that do not appear in the book, for example, Kyle nearly loses control and shoots a puppy at a child's birthday party, then meets with a doctor at a veterans' hospital. Patrick Deer notes that "*American Sniper* is perhaps the most obvious example of the appropriation of trauma discourse by contemporary US war culture." Deer, "Iraq War," 422.

    The 2011 trailer for the military-style video game Gears of War 3, which apparently sold over three million copies, provides an especially jarring illustration of the apotheosis of the traumatized hero-victim in popular culture. Ordinarily, a viewer might expect an advertisement for a video game promising simulated armed combat to feature an aggressive soundtrack—perhaps a heavy metal song such as Drowning Pool's "Bodies," a military favorite from the early years of the Iraq War that was also used in the torture of detainees at Guantánamo Bay. See Sarah Hepola, "A Violent Song's Latest, Ugly Encore," *Salon*, January 10, 2011; Mohamedou Ould Slahi, *Guantánamo Diary: Restored Edition* (New York: Back Bay Books, 2017), 232. Instead, the Gears of War trailer uses "Into Dust," a sensitive, mournful ballad by the 1990s alternative rock band Mazzy Star. It is as though the simulated experience of trauma, and grim perseverance through trauma, is itself the entertainment promised by the game.

64. Katherine Kinney, *Friendly Fire: American Images of the Vietnam War* (Oxford: Oxford University Press, 2000), 4, 6.
65. Scranton, "Trauma Hero."
66. In the related context of Iraq War veteran memoirs involving combat trauma, Geoffrey Wright has noted the particular prominence of "shame." Geoffrey A. Wright, "The Anatomy of Shame: Combat Trauma and the Undoing of the Self in Iraq War Memoirs," *PsyArt* 21 (2017): 159. For further discussion of Iraq War memoirs, see the Appendix below.
67. Joshua Pederson, *Sin Sick: Moral Injury in War and Literature* (Ithaca, NY: Cornell University Press, 2021). For examples of the growing use of "moral injury" as a framework for understanding the psychological wounds of Iraq War veterans, see Robert Emmet Meagher and Douglas A. Pryer, eds., *War and Moral Injury: A Reader* (Eugene, OR: Cascade Books, 2018); Robert Emmet Meagher, *Killing from the Inside Out: Moral Injury and Just War* (Eugene, OR: Cascade Books, 2014); and David Wood, *What Have We Done: The Moral Injury of Our Longest Wars* (New York: Little, Brown and Company, 2016). As Pederson notes, although Jonathan Shay coined the term "moral injury" in the 1990s, its current prominence can be traced back to the publication of Brett Litz et al., "Moral Injury and Moral Repair in War Veterans: A Preliminary Model and Intervention Strategy," *Clinical Psychology Review* 29, no. 8 (2009): 695. Pederson, *Sin Sick*, 8, 22.
68. Litz et al., "Moral Injury," 697. In light of the growing use of the concept of moral injury to make sense of the kinds of wrongdoing at the center of this book, the concept deserves a brief discussion. On the one hand, the language of "moral injury" might be seen as an appealing alternative to the language of "criminality." As critics have observed, the contemporary, domestic criminal legal system in the United States is largely based on a punitive ideology of individual blame and retribution. Gregory Brazeal, "Justice Theater in the

Criminal Law Curriculum," *Cardozo Law Review* (forthcoming). In narrative terms, the typical story of a crime in a law school textbook or a legal opinion pays little or no attention to the larger contexts that shaped the criminal act. Instead, the typical legal story of crime presents wrongdoing simply as the result of an isolated individual choice by an inexplicably bad person. Against this punitive background, a perspective on wrongdoing that, like the framework of moral injury, recognizes the humanity of wrongdoers, and the ways in which wrongdoers may themselves be victims, would for many observers be a welcome development. Perhaps viewing veteran wrongdoing in war through the lens of moral injury could even help lay a foundation for applying the moral injury perspective in the domestic criminal context, opening the door to greater treatment and understanding for domestic criminal defendants.

On the other hand, there is a risk that reconceptualizing wrongdoing as a moral injury to the wrongdoer might give inadequate attention to the person harmed, and to the harm itself—ignoring the actual victim while placing the victimizer in the victim's role. To state the matter very bluntly, the discourse of moral injury might be criticized as just another way of turning "a killer into a victim," in Scranton's words. Whatever the efficacy of moral injury as a clinical tool might be, as a moral or political vocabulary it may justifiably provoke resistance by inviting us to focus on the suffering of the wrongdoer rather than that of the person harmed by the wrongdoer. Moral injury discourse, at least in some of its forms, may not provide a sufficiently holistic perspective for thinking seriously about justice. (For a discussion of holistic perspectives on responsibility, including in the contemporary restorative justice movement, see Brazeal, "Justice Theater.")

A concrete illustration of the risks of moral injury discourse can be found in the journalist David Wood's *What Have We Done: The Moral Injury of Our Longest Wars*, an essayistic, in many ways insightful work that uses the concept of moral injury to make sense of the psychological struggles of Americans who served in Iraq and Afghanistan. The book begins with a brief "Author's Note" that recognizes the "physical and psychological trauma" of Afghans and Iraqis, but suggests that exploring their trauma is not an essential part of an account of the moral injuries of American servicemembers: "The moral injuries of the Afghan and Iraqi people are beyond the scope of this book but not, I trust, out of our thoughts." The book stays true to its word, as when Wood tells the story of a marine who, in the marine's words, shot a middle-aged Afghan man "'a couple of times with a SAW, and one of the bullets bounced off his spinal cord and came out his eyeball,'" turning it to "'pulp.'" Wood notes laconically that "[i]t turned out later that the man he'd killed might not have been a Taliban after all, maybe just a local farmer." The book describes the marine's retrospective thoughts and feelings in vivid, empathetic detail, but says almost nothing about the dead Afghan man, or his family or community. Wood's approach may have been unavoidable given his journalistic sources, but the effect is almost disorienting. How can we justify attending so empathetically to the moral wounds of the killer while attending so little to the world of the man he killed? How can we make sense of the marine's "moral injury" without first accounting for the scope of the harm that gave rise to the injury?

69. For any readers seeking additional scholarly context, I would like to acknowledge, finally, three other book-length critical works that deal with literary writing about the Iraq War: David A. Buchanan, *Going Scapegoat: Post 9/11 War Literature, Language, and Culture* (Jefferson, NC: McFarland and Company, 2016); Suman Gupta, *Imagining Iraq: Literature in English and the Iraq Invasion* (New York: Palgrave Macmillan, 2011); and Ikram Masmoudi, *War and Occupation in Iraqi Fiction* (Edinburgh: Edinburgh University Press, 2015).

    Buchanan's book may be the closest to my own concerns. It surveys some of the most prominent early Iraq War novels, offering chapters on Kevin Powers' *The Yellow Birds*, Ben Fountain's *Billy Lynn's Long Halftime Walk*, and David Abram's *FOBBIT*, all published in 2012. Buchanan approaches these works through a theoretical framework drawn from Kenneth Burke and focused on "a rhetorical examination of the scapegoating mechanism," with the aim of "subvert[ing] and redirect[ing] the dominant scapegoating metanarrative that the United States incorporates into its war fighting culture." Buchanan, *Going Scapegoat*, 9–10. Buchanan's emphasis on how "the painful history of our Indian Wars" has been "twisted into misused symbols time and again," including by American military leaders, provides an important and still relevant reminder about a central theme of American war culture. Buchanan, 13. But the dynamics of scapegoating have no necessary connection to the concerns of this study.

    Masmoudi's book deals solely with literature produced by Iraqis. She interprets these works through a theoretical framework drawn from the writings of Giorgio Agamben, who has become one of the leading political theorists for literary academics thinking and writing about state violence after 9/11. For other examples of the use of Agamben as a lens for interpreting literature about the Iraq War, see Deer, "Crime Fiction and War," 348; Mark Firmani, "At War with Monsters in Postwar Iraqi Literature," *Los Angeles Review of Books*,

February 24, 2018; Roger Luckhurst, "Not Now, Not Yet: Polytemporality and Fictions of the Iraq War," in *Trauma and Contemporary Literature*, ed. Marita Nadal and Mónica Calvo (New York: Routledge, 2014), 51, 59; Pederson, *Sin Sick*, 27. See also Mary L. Dudziak, *War Time: An Idea, Its History, Its Consequences* (New York: Oxford University Press, 2012), 4. As already suggested by my earlier footnote regarding theoretical vocabulary-building projects, there is little overlap between Agamben's approach and my own.

Incidentally, Firmani's article discusses Ahmed Saadawi's *Frankenstein in Baghdad*, trans. Jonathan Wright (New York: Penguin Books, 2018), which is one of the most powerful and lasting novels about the Iraq War that has yet been published in English. If I had expanded this study to include non-American authors or literary treatments of the war not focused on the U.S. military experience, Saadawi's novel would certainly have received a chapter. To borrow a phrase from Roger Luckhurst, *Frankenstein in Baghdad* also resembles other works by Iraqi writers, such as Hassan Blasim's *The Corpse Exhibition and Other Stories of Iraq*, trans. Jonathan Wright (New York: Penguin Books 2014) and Sinan Antoon's *The Corpse Washer*, trans. Sinan Antoon (New Haven, CT: Yale University Press, 2013), in the sense that it "seems expressly designed to bring the absent bodies back into focus." Luckhurst, "Iraq War Body Counts," 357. Luckhurst also mentions the profusion of severed body parts in Saad Z. Hossain, *Escape from Baghdad!* (Los Angeles: Unnamed Press, 2012), a novel by a Bangladeshi author.

In comparison to Agamben's prominence, it is noteworthy that Edward Said's theoretical writings have not played a more central role in the academic interpretation of Iraq War literature. Edward W. Said, *Orientalism* (New York: Vintage Books, 1978) was one of the most influential and widely cited works of literary theory in the United States in the decades before the Iraq invasion, and the book offers a framework for criticizing Western colonialism in the Middle East. In addition, as Pankaj Mishra has noted, "[a]fter the terrorist attacks of 9/11, [Said's] old adversary Bernard Lewis emerged as the chief theoretician of American wars in the Muslim world, and [Raphael Patai's] 'The Arab Mind' became a guidebook for military officers in Iraq." Pankaj Mishra, "The Reorientations of Edward Said," *New Yorker*, April 19, 2021; Said, *Orientalism*, 308–21. Perhaps Said's subtle critiques of Orientalist scholarship were not the most useful framework for understanding literary works that portray most of America's invading force as unfamiliar not only with Lewis, Patai, or Ernest Renan, but with the most basic facts about Iraqi society. For example, it is not necessary to draw on Said's refined theoretical apparatus in order to identify problems in the language of an NCO who encourages his soldiers to "'fucking kill the hajji fucks.'" Powers, *Yellow Birds*, 17.

70. For example, the peer-reviewed *Journal of Veterans Studies* was founded in November 2016. Related scholarship and literature can be found in a number of other publications including *Armed Forces & Society*; *As You Were: The Military Review*; *The Line*; *O-Dark-Thirty*; *War, Literature, and the Arts*; and *Wrath-Bearing Tree*.

71. Brooks, *How Everything Became War*, 14–22; Siobhan Fallon, *You Know When the Men Are Gone* (New York: New American Library, 2011). The literary scholar Joseph Darda has expressed skepticism toward the analogy between veteran and minority identity, at least in the context of literary culture, noting that "[v]eteran-writers may have more institutional resources available to them than any other group of emerging artists." He observes, in particular, that "[w]hite veteran-writers"—and it is a noteworthy fact that virtually all of the writers of Iraq War fiction addressed in this book, veteran or not, appear to be white—"may have recognized a strategic advantage to declaring their marginalization in American literary culture...An understanding of his own minoritization has allowed the white veteran-writer to reassert his relevance in an age of liberal multiculturalism." Joseph Darda, *Empire of Defense: Race and the Cultural Politics of Permanent War* (Chicago: University of Chicago Press, 2019), 172. Darda offers an early, explicitly racist illustration of a similar gesture when he notes that "John Wheeler, the chairman of the Vietnam Veterans Memorial Fund, which planned and financed the memorial on the Washington Mall," argued, after cataloguing veterans' grievances, that "'the Vietnam veteran was the nigger of the 1970s.'" Darda, 18.

    On the other hand, the apparent absence of a widely recognized literary novel about U.S. military service in the Iraq War by a non-white writer could change at any time. For a survey of recent African-American veteran writing, see Peter Molin, "Black Voices in Contemporary War-Writing," *Time Now* (blog), July 4, 2020. Dewaine Farria, an African-American marine veteran who served in Jordan and Ukraine, and then as a UN security advisor in Iraq and Afghanistan, recently published a prize-winning novel featuring an African-American Afghanistan veteran as one of its protagonists. Peter Molin, "Structures of Feeling in Adrian Bonenberger's *The Disappointed Soldier* and Dewaine Farria's *Revolutions of All Colors*," *Time Now* (blog), July 31, 2021; Dewaine Farria, *Revolutions of All Colors* (Syracuse, NY: Syracuse University Press, 2020). Christopher Paul Wolfe, an African-American Iraq War veteran, published a short story that juxtaposes racialized mass incarceration in the United States with the lack of punishment for a veteran narrator who failed to save an Iraqi detainee, as well as the apparent impunity of Bush administration officials. Christopher Paul Wolfe, "Another Brother's Conviction," in *The Road Ahead: Fiction from the Forever War*, ed. Adrian Bonenberger and Brian Castner (New York: Pegasus Books, 2017), 85–90.

A final, tangential factor in the shaping of the Iraq War literary canon that may be worth noting is the role of family. Remarkably, the very small community of authors who have written widely reviewed literary works about military service in the post-9/11 wars happens to include the son of the legendary literary editor Gordon Lish (Atticus Lish), the son of the celebrated novelist Frederick Busch (Benjamin Busch), and the son of the vice president of PEN International (Elliot Ackerman).

72. The book's attention to changes in the narrative templates of war literature, from the warrior-as-hero to the soldier-as-victim and beyond, might be seen as related to the empirical study of recurring plot structures in the works of formalists such as Vladimir Propp and Viktor Shklovksy. See Jonathan Culler, *Structuralist Poetics: Structuralism, Linguistics and the Study of Literature* (London: Routledge, 2002), 242–49, 260–61.

73. The psychologist Jerome Bruner explored what might be called (to borrow a phrase from Alasdair MacIntyre) "the narrative character of human life" in numerous works including *Actual Minds, Possible Worlds* (Cambridge, MA: Harvard University Press, 1987); *Acts of Meaning: Four Lectures on Mind and Culture* (Cambridge, MA: Harvard University Press, 1990); and *Making Stories: Law, Literature, Life* (Cambridge, MA: Harvard University Press, 2002). Similar arguments have been made by many other philosophers and social scientists, including Alexander Nehamas, *Nietzsche: Life as Literature* (Cambridge, MA: Harvard University Press, 1985). Although some literary theorists might reject on principle the attempt to develop simple, easily understood models of narrative structure for use in empirical explanation and prediction, the economist Robert Shiller's recent work illustrates the relevance that narrative analysis can have outside of literary study. See Robert J. Shiller, *Narrative Economics: How Stories Go Viral and Drive Major Economic Events* (Princeton, NJ: Princeton University Press, 2020). As Shiller noted in an earlier article, "[c]onsideration of narratives in economics brings us to an unfamiliar association with literature departments in our universities." Robert J. Shiller, "Narrative Economics," *American Economic Review* 107 no. 4 (2017): 967, 970. It may be indicative of the relative lack of usefully reductive narrative models in recent literary scholarship that Shiller turned to a popular how-to book from over two decades ago as a source of usable insights into narrative structure. Shiller, "Narrative Economics," 970, citing Ronald

B. Tobias, *Twenty Master Plots and How to Build Them* (Blue Ash, OH: Writer's Digest Books, 1999). In his later book, Shiller briefly notes more scholarly works of literary theory that deal with narrative, but also observes that attempts to model recurring narrative types have been rejected in contemporary theory as "'overly reductive and dehumanizing.'" Shiller, *Narrative Economics*, 16, quoting Mary Klages, *Literary Theory: A Guide for the Perplexed* (London: Bloomsbury Academic, 2006), 33.

For another example of a recent work of social science that emphasizes the importance of narrative but contains almost no references to contemporary literary theory or literary scholarship, see Lawrence Freedman, *Strategy: A History* (Oxford: Oxford University Press, 2013), 607–30. In his discussion of the role of narrative in military strategy, Freedman, like Shiller, resorts to citing a non-academic work that describes several simple narrative structures. Freedman, *Strategy*, 717, citing Christopher Booker, *The Seven Basic Plots: Why We Tell Stories* (New York: Continuum, 2004).

74. The "constructivist" school in international relations theory has emphasized the powerful role of cultural assumptions in shaping the menu of options considered by policymakers even in matters of war and peace. See, for example, Martha Finnemore, *The Purpose of Intervention: Changing Beliefs About the Use of Force* (Ithaca, NY: Cornell University Press, 2003). Some of the claims of constructivists about culture and beliefs could be redescribed in terms of narrative.

Victims' narratives also play a central role in human rights advocacy. For example, Diana Tietjens Meyers describes the standard narrative templates of the "pathetic victim" and the "heroic victim," and suggests caution in the use of these paradigms in human rights advocacy because they exclude "impure," morally compromised victims who may not qualify as "innocent." Diana Tietjens Meyers, *Victims' Stories and the Advancement of Human Rights* (New York: Oxford University Press, 2016), 32–40, 48, 62–64. Earlier, Red Cross founder Henry Dunant's artful narrative of soldier-victims' suffering after the 1859 Battle of Solferino helped motivate the development of the Geneva Conventions. John Fabian Witt, *Lincoln's Code* (New York: Free Press, 2012), 339. On the possible role of fictional narratives in the growth of empathy in certain aspects of eighteenth-century European culture, see Lynn Hunt, *Inventing Human Rights: A History* (New York: W.W. Norton and Company, 2007), 30–34.

More recently, Elizabeth Samet has considered whether the celebration of World War II as a mythologized "good war," especially in popular writings from the 1990s such as Tom Brokaw's *The Greatest Generation* (New York: Random

House, 1998) and Stephen Ambrose's *Band of Brothers* (New York: Touchstone, 1992), may "increase the likelihood" of "devastating, indecisive wars." Elizabeth D. Samet, *Looking for the Good War: American Amnesia and the Violent Pursuit of Happiness* (New York: Farrar, Straus and Giroux, 2021), 91. Even the U.S. military's counterinsurgency field manual, released to great publicity in 2006, highlights narrative as "[t]he most important cultural form for counterinsurgents to understand" and a "basis for strategies, actions, and interpretation of the intentions of other actors." Department of the Army, *FM 3–24: Counterinsurgency* (December 2006), 1–65 to 66, 3–49 to 50.

Incidentally, the captivating power of literary narratives may even have played a role in Saddam Hussein's miscalculations. Steve Coll has reported that by the time the United States invaded Iraq in 2003, Hussein, far from being focused on attacking the United States, "had lost much of his prior interest in military affairs and had become obsessed with writing novels." Steve Coll, "Opinion: Why Authoritarians Like Saddam Hussein Confound U.S. Presidents," *New York Times*, February 28, 2024.

75. In fact, standardized narratives also play a significant role in military planning. The military historian John Lynn has emphasized the recurring tension between the war that military leaders want to fight and plan to fight, and the war they actually end up fighting. John A. Lynn, *Battle: A History of Combat and Culture* (New York: Basic Books, 2003). Based on historical narratives and personal experience, military leaders often have a certain expectation of how events will proceed, and it can be difficult to accept when events diverge from the expected narrative. Bacevich describes, for example, how U.S. political and military leaders resisted the notion that the Iraq War had become a counterinsurgency campaign. Bacevich, *America's War for the Greater Middle East*, 270–94.

76. Bourke, for example, notes that many soldiers "idealized themselves as warriors similar to heroic figures in combat literature and films." Bourke, *Intimate History*, 359. From Alexander the Great allegedly sleeping with a copy of *The Iliad* under his pillow, to a generation of Army and Marine Corps officers reading Anton Myrer's *Once an Eagle* (New York: HarperPerennial, 1968), to contemporary soldiers viewing war through the lens of war movies, as documented at various points below, there is a long tradition of literary accounts of war influencing the ideas of those actually responsible for conducting wars.

In this light, it is deeply troubling that the only war novel among the top ten novels shipped to the war zone in Iraq, according to one prominent U.S. bookseller's 2006 analysis, was a work of neo-Nazi atrocity fiction, George Robert Elford's *Devil's Guard* (New York: Dell Publishing, 1971). John

Sutherland, "Under the Covers," *Telegraph*, January 27, 2008. The hero of the novel, which is presented as a true confession, is a German SS soldier who engages in genocidal adventures against sub-human Communists on the Eastern Front of World War II, and then fights for the French Foreign Legion against the sub-human Communist Viet Minh. "The novel, which glorifies Nazi military practices, describes counterinsurgency tactics such as mass slaughter and desecration and other forms of wanton violence as a means of waging psychological warfare against the 'savage' Vietnamese." Matthew Cole, "With Medal of Honor, SEAL Team 6 Rewards a Culture of War Crimes," *Intercept*, May 22, 2018. Cole notes that among the U.S. military readers of *Devil's Guard* were members of a troubled SEAL Team 6 squadron that allegedly desecrated enemy corpses in Afghanistan.

77. See, for example, Bruner, *Making Stories*, 9–10.
78. See, for example, Stacey Peebles, "Blood, Force, Influence: Studying the Representation of Violence," in *Critical Insights: Violence in Literature*, ed. Stacey Peebles (Ipswich, MA: Salem Press, 2014): 23, 27; Shay, *Achilles in Vietnam*, 188–93. The classic work on the role of personal narrative in recovery from trauma is Judith L. Herman, *Trauma and Recovery: The Aftermath of Violence—From Domestic Abuse to Political Terror* (New York: Basic Books, 1992), 254–85.

    If the sense of an ending is an important part of any story, then the seemingly limitless duration of the "forever wars" may have interfered with veterans' ability to make narrative sense of their experiences. See Samet, *No Man's Land*, 8, 28, 218. The potentially limitless duration of the post-9/11 conflicts was reflected at the time in titles like *The Long War Journal* and Dexter Filkins' *The Forever War* (New York: Vintage Books, 2008). For a history of the terms "long war" and "forever war," see Elizabeth D. Samet, "War and Memory," *American Literary History* 24, no. 4 (Winter 2012): 864–75. On the temporal boundaries of war in general, see Dudziak, *War Time*; Stephen M. Griffin, *Long Wars and the Constitution* (Cambridge, MA: Harvard University Press, 2013).

    But the term "forever wars" may be losing some of its salience. As of early 2023, the United States had withdrawn from Afghanistan and had roughly 2,500 troops in Iraq, as opposed to, for example, roughly 35,000 troops in Germany. The "most active element in the 'forever wars'" appeared to be a 450-member U.S. training force in Somalia. Eric Schmitt, "U.S. Commandos Advise Somalis in Fight Against Qaeda Branch," *New York Times*, February 27, 2023. Perhaps the United States could still be described as engaged in a permanent war that began on September 11, 2001 based less on the scale of current deployments and more on the readiness to deploy violence across the globe, at any time, from "over the horizon," especially through targeted killing via drone strikes, special operations raids, or attacks using new technology such as cyber weapons. For a critique of American uses of military force that focuses on such forms of violence, see Moyn, *Humane*, 3–5, 321–23. Since the publication of Moyn's book, however, the use of drone strikes by the United States appears to have fallen dramatically. "The overall number of declared US airstrikes...fell from 441 in 2021 to a minimum of 36 in 2022." Anna Zahn, Clarie Alspektor, and Sanjana Varghese, "US Airstrikes Fell to Historic Low in 2022, Despite Fresh Operations," *Airwars*, February 2023. See also Charlie Savage, "Biden Rules Tighten Limits on Drone Strikes," *New York Times*, July 1, 2023.

Incidentally, what may be the most widely discussed play about the Iraq War, George Brant's *Grounded* (London: Oberon Books, 2013), does not focus on ground forces in Iraq. It is instead about the ethics of drone warfare and the potential for drone operators to kill foreign civilians and experience moral injury.

79. For sources of the civilian–military divide, see Brooks, *How Everything Became War*, 14–22. For the distance between the values of aristocratic warrior cultures and contemporary liberal democracies, see Chapters 2 and 4 below. On the atavistic aspects of military culture, see, for example, Madeline Morris, "By Force of Arms: Rape, War, and Military Culture," *Duke Law Journal* 45, no. 4 (1996): 651. The status distinctions between officers and enlisted soldiers, including the obligation of enlisted soldiers to salute and refer to officers as "Sir" or "Ma'am," are among the most obvious remnants of legally recognized caste in contemporary American society.
80. For a portrait of military service creating disdain for civilian American culture, see Thomas Ricks, *Making the Corps* (New York: Scribner, 1997), 228–37. As the narrator of Klay's "Psychological Operations" notes, "The weird thing with being a veteran, at least for me, is that you do feel better than most people." Klay, *Redeployment*, 203, and related language at 12, 151. The potential for the civilian–military divide to result in military contempt toward civilians was illustrated by a press conference on October 19, 2017 featuring President Donald Trump's Chief of Staff, retired Marine Corps General John Kelly, the father of a Marine Corps lieutenant killed in Afghanistan. Kelly accurately drew attention to the relative isolation of the American military from some spheres of American society. Responding to allegations that President Trump had disrespected the mother of an African-American soldier killed in Niger, Kelly said of the "young men and women" in the military:

> They are the best 1 percent this country produces. Most of you, as Americans, don't know them. Many of you don't know anyone who knows any one of them. But they are the very best this country produces, and they volunteer to protect our country when there's nothing in our country anymore that seems to suggest that selfless service to the nation is not only appropriate, but required.

Callum Borchers, "John Kelly's Fiery Defense of Trump's Shot at Obama and Gold Star Phone Call, Annotated," *Washington Post*, October 19, 2017. (Kelly would later abandon his defense of President Trump, in part because of Trump's disparaging statements about military service and veterans. Maggie Astor, "John Kelly, a Former White House Chief of Staff, Confirms Trump's Disparaging of Veterans," *New York Times*, October 3, 2023.)

By contrast, shortly after stepping down as President Obama's Secretary of Defense, Robert Gates delivered a speech at West Point warning of military leaders developing a sense of distance from and moral superiority to "the civilian sector," which could ultimately pose a threat to American democracy. Bacevich, *New American Militarism*, 237.

81. The exception is Kyle's *American Sniper*, for reasons discussed below in Chapter 8.
82. In 2007, for example, the first two relatively mainstream, artistically ambitious movies about the Iraq War chose to approach the war through the following stories: Iraq War veterans murdering a PTSD-afflicted fellow soldier who also engaged in detainee abuse, the focus of Paul Haggis' *In the Valley of Elah* (Los Angeles: NALA Films, 2007); and the group rape and murders in Mahmudiyah mentioned above, the focus of Brian De Palma's *Redacted* (New York: Magnolia Pictures, 2007). Another early film was inspired by the marine killings in Haditha. Nick Broomfield, dir., *Battle for Haditha* (London: HanWay Films, 2007). The theme of veteran criminality has continued in films such as *Triple Frontier*, where a group of disillusioned Special Forces veterans decide to put their skills to use robbing a South American drug lord, and ultimately end up killing several civilian farmers. J.C. Chandor, dir., *Triple Frontier* (Los Angeles: Atlas Entertainment, 2019). Early on, one character suggests that the heist will not be their first foray into illegality, because in their military work they repeatedly violated the Geneva Conventions.
83. Powers, *The Yellow Birds*, 145.
84. Christopher Robinson and Gavin Kovite, *War of the Encyclopaedists* (New York: Scribner, 2016), 345.

85. See, for example, Abrams, *FOBBIT*, 346; Klay, *Redeployment*, 129–68; Pitre, *Fives and Twenty-Fives*, 12, 28–30; Scranton, *War Porn*, 48, 97. In the words of Malcolm Cowley, "[w]ar novelists are not…average soldiers…In military service, many future writers were men of whom their comrades said that they were 'always goofing off by themselves.'" Malcolm Cowley, *The Literary Situation* (New York: Penguin Books, 1947), 25. An early appearance of the sensitive intellectual soldier in American literature can be found in the Francophile pianist John Andrews in John Dos Passos, *Three Soldiers* (New York: George H. Doran Co., 1921).
86. Evan Wright, *Generation Kill: Devil Dogs, Ice Man, Captain America, and the New Face of American War* (New York: G.P. Putnam's Sons, 2004). Wright focuses his narrative on the perspectives of enlisted marines. The distance between their experiences and those of their officers can be seen by comparing Wright's reportage with the memoir of Dartmouth classics graduate Nathaniel Fick, who happened to serve in the same marine reconnaissance battalion where Wright was embedded. Fick, *One Bullet Away*, 17–18.
87. Filkins, *Forever War*.

CHAPTER TWO

1. Homer, *The Iliad*, trans. Robert Fagles (New York: Penguin Books, 1990); *Beowulf: A New Verse Translation*, trans. Seamus Heaney (New York: Farrar, Straus, and Giroux, 1999); *The Song of Roland*, trans. Frederick Goldin (New York: W.W. Norton & Company, 1978).
2. On the male gendering of violence in general, see Ehrenreich, *Blood Rites*, 123–31; Gat, *War in Human Civilization*, 79; Joshua S. Goldstein, *War and Gender: How Gender Shapes the War System and Vice Versa* (Cambridge: Cambridge University Press, 2001), 3–4; Richard Wrangham and Dale Peterson, *Demonic Males: Apes and the Origins of Human Violence* (Boston: Houghton Mifflin Company, 1996).
3. *The Epic of Gilgamesh*, trans. N.K. Sandars (New York: Penguin Books, 1972).
4. This is of course an enormous leap, passing by, among other things, all the modern transformations in war culture described by Yuval Noah Harari in *The Ultimate Experience: Battlefield Revelations and the Making of Modern War Culture, 1450–2000* (Basingstoke: Palgrave-Macmillan, 2008). Even the character traits associated with warrior-heroism have changed over time. Ehrenreich notes, for example, "the change in the ideal warrior personality wrought by the advent of guns in the fifteenth and sixteenth centuries, from 'ferocious aggressiveness' to 'passive disdain.'" Ehrenreich, *Blood Rites*, 9.

An especially important figure between the ancient epics and the modern war novel is the chivalrous knight of medieval European literature. Harari writes: "Though glorious façades for war have been constructed at least since Biblical times, the particular façade characteristic of the modern West is largely a product of the Renaissance, born out of the marriage of the old medieval chivalric ideals with the rising ideals of statehood and nationalism." Yuval Noah Harari, "Martial Illusions: War and Disillusionment in Twentieth-Century and Renaissance Military Memoirs," *The Journal of Military History* 69, no. 1 (January 2005): 49. The knight continued to serve as a notable, if increasingly archaic, reference point in the military imagination of the hero through at least World War I. Bourke, *Intimate History*, 46–47. As discussed in Chapter 8, below, the movies of John Wayne, and especially "Old West" movies about "cowboys and Indians," offer even more recent variations on the warrior-as-hero narrative that have enduring relevance in American culture.

In light of the themes of this book, it is also important to note that common soldiers were often viewed as more like criminals than heroes in the aristocratic culture of early modern Europe. As Hariri observes: "In no era of Western history was the status and image of the common soldier lower than in the seventeenth century and early eighteenth century." Harari, *Ultimate Experience*, 160. "Throughout the early modern period common soldiers were seen primarily as the criminal dregs of society," while "[r]espectable military heroes were almost always officers." Harari, 184. See also Nancy Isenberg, *White Trash: The 400-Year Untold History of Class in America* (New York: Penguin Books, 2016), 23. But in the era of the Thirty Years' War, the common soldier was perceived as similar to a criminal not because of the morally corrupting effects of military service or war. Rather, in the aristocratic, status-based culture of the time, before the rise of modern egalitarian and nationalist values, the common soldier was more likely seen as inherently morally debased because a man from the "dregs of society" was assumed to have a low character.

5. Ernest Hemingway, *A Farewell to Arms* (New York: Scribner, 1929); Joseph Heller, *Catch-22* (New York: Simon & Schuster, 1961); Tim O'Brien, *The Things They Carried* (Boston: Houghton Mifflin, 1990); Erich Maria Remarque, *All Quiet on the Western Front*, trans. A.W. Wheen (New York: Ballantine Books, 1982) [1928]; Leslie Marmon Silko's *Ceremony* (New York: Penguin, 1977); Dalton Trumbo, *Johnny Got His Gun* (Philadelphia: J.B. Lippincott & Co., 1939); Kurt Vonnegut, *Slaughterhouse-Five* (New York: Delacorte, 1969); Virginia Woolf, *Mrs. Dalloway* (London: Hogarth Press, 1925). Representations of common soldiers as victims can be found already in the nineteenth century.

See, for example, J. Henry Dunant, *A Memory of Solferino* [trans. unknown] (Geneva: ICRC, 1959) [1862]. Harari notes that "Stendhal's *Charterhouse of Parma*, Tolstoy's *Sebastopol in August, 1855* and *War and Peace*, Stephen Crane's *Red Badge of Courage*, and several short stories by Ambrose Bierce, all narrate the familiar story of how a young man full of romantic martial dreams is disillusioned by the cruel realities of war." Harari, "Martial Illusions," 69. For a prescient work portraying a common soldier as both victim and criminal, see Georg Büchner's 1836 play *Woyzeck*, in Georg Büchner, *Complete Plays, Lenz and Other Writings*, trans. John Reddick (New York: Penguin Books, 1993).

6. As Kate McLoughlin has noted, literary anthologies often emphasize "[w]ar's sameness." Kate McLoughlin, *Authoring War: The Literary Representation of War from the Iliad to Iraq* (Cambridge: Cambridge University Press, 2011), 115. The military historian John Lynn has similarly criticized historians for imagining a "universal soldier" and asserting "that only weapons and tactics have changed, not the men who have wielded them." Lynn, *Battle*, xiv. Even Joanna Bourke's exceptionally perceptive and useful history of intimate killing in World War I, World War II, and the Vietnam War gives relatively little attention to the enormous changes in war culture that took place over the course of the twentieth century. As she notes, she "has paid more attention to the similarities" between the wars she discusses than to their differences. Bourke, *Intimate History*, 363. Simone Weil's perceptive and frequently anthologized but ahistorical "The Iliad, or the Poem of Force" (1939) offers a more extreme example, mining Homer's epic for enduring psychological insights almost as though nothing essential had changed in the nature of war between the Mycenaean age and the Spanish Civil War. Simone Weil, "The Iliad, or the Poem of Force," *Chicago Law Review* 18 (1965): 5. Jonathan Shay similarly draws on the works of Homer for insights into the traumas of Vietnam War veterans. Shay, *Achilles in Vietnam*, xx–xxi.
7. Harari, "Martial Illusions," 43. As noted above, Scranton makes a similar point in his discussion of the myth of the "trauma hero." Jay Winter, one of the preeminent cultural historians of World War I, has noted that two of the most influential mid-century histories of war culture, Paul Fussell's *The Great War and Modern Memory* (Oxford: Oxford University Press, 1975) and John Keegan's *The Face of Battle* (New York: Viking Press, 1976), "moved the whole field in a tragic direction, one in which all soldiers were both the agents and the victims of war." Jay Winter, "Introduction," in Fussell, *The Great War*, ix, xi. Fussell's famous emphasis on irony arises in part against a background of assumed soldier victimization: "Every war is ironic because every war is

worse than expected." Fussell, 8. Bitter, disillusioned irony is an understandable response when one leaps into a war expecting to be a hero and instead emerges as a victim of a war that turns out to be a "hideous embarrassment." Fussell, 8.

8. Harari, *Ultimate Experience*; Harari, "Martial Illusions," 43.
9. For the picture of modernity suggested here and in Chapter 4, see works such as Benjamin Constant, "The Spirit of Conquest and Usurpation and Their Relation to European Civilization," in *Constant: Political Writings*, ed. Biancamaria Fontana (Cambridge: Cambridge University Press, 2010), 52–55; Norbert Elias, *The Civilizing Process: Sociogenetic and Psychogenetic Investigations*, trans. Edmund Jephcott (Hoboken, NJ: Blackwell Publishing, 2000), 365–75; Joseph Henrich, *The WEIRDest People in the World: How the West Became Psychologically Peculiar and Particularly Prosperous* (New York: Picador, 2020); Albert O. Hirschman, *The Passions and the Interests: Political Arguments for Capitalism before Its Triumph* (Princeton, NJ: Princeton University Press, 1977); Albert O. Hirschman, *The Rhetoric of Reaction: Perversity, Futility, Jeopardy* (Cambridge, MA: Belknap Press, 1991), 1–8; Inglehart, *Cultural Evolution*, 1–35; Pinker, *The Better Angels of Our Nature*; Alasdair MacIntyre, *After Virtue: A Study in Moral Theory*, 3rd ed. (Notre Dame, IN: University of Notre Dame Press, 2007); Charles Taylor, *A Secular Age* (Cambridge, MA: Harvard University Press, 2007), 90–145; Max Weber, *From Max Weber: Essays in Sociology*, trans. H.H. Gerth and C. Wright Mills (Oxford: Oxford University Press, 1946), 196–244, 253–66, 267–301.
10. See Harari, *Ultimate Experience*, 145–50.
11. Enzo Traverso, *Fire and Blood: The European Civil War 1914–1945* (Brooklyn, NY: Verso, 2016), 3, citing Annette Wieviorka, *L'Ère du Temoin* (Paris, France: Pluriel, 1998). In the context of war literature, Harari notes "a growing circular convergence between the war stories of combatants and non-combatants" in recent decades: "Combatants are increasingly seen as victims of war, which blurs the difference between them and non-combatants. On the other hand, the discourse of trauma and of military revelation, which originated with combatants, has subsequently been adopted by non-combatants as well." Harari, *Ultimate Experience*, 24. Similarly, the literary scholar Samuel Hynes observed that in the twentieth century, "for the first time," war stories were "written by the sufferers" in war, rather than by the agents of their suffering. Samuel Hynes, *The Soldiers' Tale: Bearing Witness to Modern War* (New York: Penguin Books, 1997), 223. This has added "to the usual story of army against army a different war story—of armies against humanity." Hynes, 223. His two examples are stories of the Holocaust and of Hiroshima. Hynes, 258–77.

12. More detailed data can be found through a search of the terms "hero" and "victim" on Google's NGram Viewer, https://books.google.com/ngrams.
13. Harari, *Ultimate Experience*, 16–17.
14. Michael David Lukas, "Workshopping the Next Generation of American War Literature," *VQR* 86, no. 2 (Spring 2010): 208–12. Similarly, Caleb Cage writes that "America's understanding of veterans in recent times can be reduced to two basic narratives: the hero narrative and the victim narrative." Caleb S. Cage, *War Narratives: Shaping Beliefs, Blurring Truths in the Middle East* (College Station: Texas A&M University Press, 2019), 79. In his memoir of service in the Iraq War, by contrast, Medal of Honor recipient David Bellavia anticipates the arguments of this book by observing: "The warrior class, bleeding in Iraq, has been painted with two brushes: that of the victim and that of the felon." David Bellavia, *House to House: A Soldier's Memoir* (New York: Free Press, 2007), 290.
15. Brooks, *How Everything Became War*, 222–24.
16. Phil Klay, *The Citizen-Soldier: Moral Risk and the Modern Military* (Washington, D.C.: Brookings Institution Press, 2016).
17. Tim O'Brien, "How To Tell a True War Story," in *The Things They Carried*, 64, 65–66.
18. Taylor, *A Secular Age*, 630. Recent historical writings have questioned the extent to which Americans embraced World War II as a defense of freedom against the global spread of tyranny. Samet argues that the American historical memory "of liberation focused largely on the European Theater" has obscured the "general American indifference to the fact that the world was on fire" prior to the attack on Pearl Harbor. Samet, *The Good War*, 50–51. "[M]any Americans understood the war not as sacrifice or even vengeance, but, more simply and practically, as deliverance from the miseries of the Depression." Samet, 70. By 1944, "two Americans out of every five still said they had no clear idea what the war was really about...[M]any began to see themselves as fighting for private and prosaic ends...The war correspondent John Hersey asked a group of Marines on Guadalcanal what they were fighting for. After an uncomfortable silence, one grunt said, 'Jesus, what I'd give for a piece of blueberry pie.'" Samuel Zipp, *The Idealist: Wendell Willkie's Wartime Quest to Build One World* (Cambridge, MA: Harvard University Press, 2020), 274–75. Any presentation of U.S. participation in World War II as a crusade for freedom against Nazi ideology would also have to confront the uncomfortable tension between this goal and the ongoing, violent tyranny of Jim Crow in the U.S. South, as well as the awkward fact that the Nazi government had drawn on U.S. race law as an inspiration for its own policies. James Q. Whitman,

Hitler's American Model: The United States and the Making of Nazi Race Law (Princeton, NJ: Princeton University Press, 2017).

19. Chimamanda Ngozi Adichie, *Half of a Yellow Sun* (New York: Knopf, 2006); Bertolt Brecht, *Mother Courage*, trans. Eric Bentley (New York: Grove, 1991) [1939]; Aristophanes, *Lysistrata*, in Aristophanes, *Lysistrata and Other Plays*, trans. Alan H. Sommerstein (New York: Penguin Books, 2003) [c. 411 BCE]; Euripides, *The Trojan Women*, in Euripides, *The Trojan Women and Other Plays*, trans. James Morwood (Oxford: Oxford University Press, 2009) [c. 415 BCE]; Voltaire, *Candide ou l'Optimisme* (Paris: Éditions Gallimard, 1992) [1759]. See also W.H. Auden, "The Shield of Achilles," in W.H. Auden, *Collected Poems* (New York: Vintage International, 1991).
20. It has been estimated that only 10% of those who died in World War I were noncombatants, while the figure rises to 50% in World War II, and as high as 90% for a conflict like the recent civil war in the Democratic Republic of the Congo. John Arquilla, "The Big Kill," *Foreign Policy* (online), December 3, 2012.
21. Fallon, *You Know When the Men Are Gone*.

CHAPTER THREE

1. See Oona A. Hathaway and Scott J. Shapiro, *The Internationalists: How a Radical Plan to Outlaw War Remade the World* (New York: Simon & Schuster, 2017), 372; Moyn, *Humane*, 255.
2. Chapter 10 compares atrocities in the Iraq and Vietnam Wars.
3. Gregory Brazeal, "Bureaucracy and the U.S. Response to Mass Atrocity," *National Security and Armed Conflict Law Review* 1, no. 1 (2011): 58.
4. One historian has estimated that American soldiers in Western Europe carried out over 10,000 rapes during World War II. David Wilson, "The Secret War," *Guardian*, March 27, 2007, citing J. Robert Lilly, *Taken by Force: Rape and American GIs in Europe during World War II* (London: Palgrave Macmillan, 2007). Another academic estimated American servicemen may have raped as many as 10,000 Okinawan women at the end of World War II. Calvin Sims, "3 Dead Marines and a Secret of Wartime Okinawa," *New York Times*, June 1, 2000. A recent book-length study speculates based on rough inferences from the available evidence that as many as 190,000 women living in the Federal Republic of Germany may have been raped by Americans between 1945 and 1955. Miriam Gebhardt, *Crimes Unspoken: The Rape of German Women at the End of the Second World War* (Cambridge: Polity, 2020), 22.
5. John Grenier, *The First Way of War: American War Making on the Frontier* (Cambridge: Cambridge University Press, 2005), 10.

6. Richard Slotkin, *Regeneration through Violence: The Mythology of the American Frontier* (Norman: University of Oklahoma Press, 2020), 18. On the common rationalization of killing in war through an analogy to hunting, see, for example, Bourke, *Intimate History*, 221–23. For a short story about the Iraq War that critiques the analogy to hunting, see Alex Horton, "Small Kill Team," in *The Road Ahead: Fiction from the Forever War*, ed. Bonenberger and Castner (New York: Pegasus Books, 2017), 29–44.
7. Slotkin, *Regeneration through Violence*, 21, 23.
8. Slotkin, 563–64.
9. Atrocities from other U.S. military expeditions outside the United States before World War II are also easy to find. For example, General Winfield Scott reported that the crimes of future president Zachary Taylor's men in the Mexican-American War were so heinous, they would "make Heaven weep...Murder, robbery, & rape on mothers & daughters, in the presence of the tied up males of the families, have been common all along the Rio Grande." Greg Grandin, *The End of the Myth: From the Frontier to the Border Wall in the Mind of America* (New York: Metropolitan Books, 2019), 90–91. The U.S. military also committed atrocities in the Philippines at the turn of the twentieth century, including water torture and the desecration of "the corpses of suicide warriors...by burying them with the carcasses of hogs." Elizabeth Schambelan, "Special Journey to Our Bottom Line: On Hazing and Counterinsurgency," *n+1*, no. 34 (Spring 2019). In 1906, Army General Joseph Duncan received a personal telegram of congratulations from President Theodore Roosevelt after leading "the slaughter of between eight hundred and one thousand Filipinos, the majority of them women and children." Grandin, *End of the Myth*, 329. For a general history of the use of torture in and by the United States, see W. Fitzhugh Brundage, *Civilizing Torture: An American Tradition* (Cambridge, MA: Harvard University Press, 2018).
10. John W. Dower, *War without Mercy: Race and Power in the Pacific War* (New York: W.W. Norton, 1986), 52–55, 65, 67, 71–73. A veteran wrote in the *Atlantic* in 1946 of American soldiers having "'boiled the flesh off enemy skulls to make table ornaments for sweethearts, or carved their bones into letter openers.'" Robert M. Sapolsky, *Behave: The Biology of Humans at Our Best and Worst* (New York: Penguin Press, 2017), 668. To be clear, the desecration of enemy heads had also occurred in earlier American conflicts. For example, in 1873, the Army executed Kintpuash, who had led the Modoc tribe's resistance to a genocidal campaign in California and Oregon. After Kintpuash's execution, "his head was severed from his body and sent to Washington in a box as a trophy." Moyn, *Humane*, 109–10.

11. Dower, *War without Mercy*, 66–71.
12. For the number of novels, see Walter Hölbling, "The Second World War: American Writing," in *The Cambridge Companion to War Writing*, ed. Kate McLoughlin (Cambridge: Cambridge University Press, 2009), 212.
13. Heller, *Catch-22*; James Jones, *The Thin Red Line* (New York: Charles Scribner's Sons, 1962); Norman Mailer, *The Naked and the Dead* (New York: Rinehart & Company, 1948); Thomas Pynchon, *Gravity's Rainbow* (New York: Viking Press, 1973); Vonnegut, *Slaughterhouse-Five*.
14. John Hersey, *A Bell for Adano* (New York: Knopf, 1944).
15. James A. Michener, *Tales of the South Pacific* (New York: Macmillan, 1947).
16. John M. Kinder, "The Good War's 'Raw Chunks': Norman Mailer's The Naked and the Dead and James Gould Cozzens' Guard of Honor," *Midwest Quarterly* 46, no. 2 (Winter 2005): 187, 189, 192–97; James Gould Cozzens, *Guard of Honor* (New York: Harcourt, Brace and Company, 1948). More recently, it may be worth noting, the U.S. military has become one of the most racially integrated institutions in American society. David M. Kennedy, "Introduction," in *The Modern American Military*, ed. David M. Kennedy (Oxford: Oxford University Press, 2013), 2. But it continues to struggle with a long legacy of racism and racial inequalities. On the use of military service to rehabilitate the white supremacist South during the Jim Crow era, see Grandin, *End of the Myth*, 134. On the role of Vietnam veterans in the post-Vietnam white supremacist movement, see Kathleen Belew, *Bring the War Home: The White Power Movement and Paramilitary America* (Cambridge, MA: Harvard University Press, 2018). On the persistence of racial disparities, monuments to the Confederacy, and pockets of white nationalism in the U.S. military, see Helene Cooper, "African-Americans Are Highly Visible in the Military, but Almost Invisible at the Top," *New York Times*, May 25, 2020. Recent years have seen the renaming of bases that honored Confederates, the correction of racial injustices in historical records, and greater attention to diversity in the highest ranks. See, for example, Chris Cameron, "Army Base Renamed for Native American War Hero, Replacing Confederate," *New York Times*, March 24, 2023; Helene Cooper, "After 246 Years, Marine Corps Gives 4 Stars to a Black Officer," *New York Times*, August 6, 2022; Michael Levenson, "Army Overturns Convictions of 110 Black Soldiers Charged in 1917 Riot," *New York Times*, November 13, 2023. But special operations forces remain particularly racially skewed. Although 40% of the Navy's enlisted force as a whole is Black, for example, only 2% of SEAL and elite combatant-craft crew officers are Black, and the same percentage applies among the enlisted. The officers of the Army's Special Forces are also only 2% Black. Lolita C. Baldor,

"US Military's Elite Commando Forces Look to Expand Diversity," *Military.com*, June 16, 2021.

The official Defense Department history of the integration of the armed forces now acknowledges, contrary to the portrait offered by Cozzens, that the embrace of Jim Crow on federal military installations "undermined the country's readiness for war and destroyed morale, introducing black recruits to a brand of hard-core racism many had not experienced in civilian life," and "'spread federally sponsored segregation into areas where it had never before existed with the force of law.'" "Editorial: Why Does the U.S. Military Celebrate White Supremacy?," *New York Times*, May 23, 2020, quoting Morris J. MacGregor Jr., *Integration of the Armed Forces, 1940–1965* (1981).

On the frequent erasure of racial politics in American war literature, see Roger Luckhurst, "War and Whiteness," in *War and American Literature*, ed. Haytock, 315.

17. See Orville Prescott, "Books of the Times," review of *The Thin Red Line*, by James Jones, *New York Times*, September 17, 1962, L29. E.B. Sledge's similarly grim memoir *With the Old Breed at Peleliu and Okinawa* (New York: Ballantine Books, 1981), which contains numerous examples of the desecration of corpses by marines, did not appear until the 1980s, and seems to have only gained in visibility since then, culminating in its adaptation as one source for the 2010 HBO miniseries *The Pacific*.
18. Mailer, *The Naked and the Dead*, 718–19.
19. Niko Walker, *Cherry* (New York: Vintage Books, 2018), 315–17; Scott Johnson, "How a War Hero Became a Serial Bank Robber," *BuzzFeed*, May 30, 2013; Anthony Russo and Joe Russo, dirs., *Cherry* (Culver City, CA: Apple TV+, 2021). Many other works of fiction that depict Iraq War veterans after their returns from deployment describe veterans engaged in criminal activity. See, for example, Luke Mogelson, *These Heroic, Happy Dead* (New York: Tim Duggan Books, 2016), 23, 131. The psychiatrist Jonathan Shay has noted that infantry combat experience may not provide helpful preparation for many careers, but one "career that war exactly prepares veterans for upon return to civilian life is a *criminal* career." Jonathan Shay, *Odysseus in America: Combat Trauma and the Trials of Homecoming* (New York: Scribner, 2002), 19–34.
20. Brian Van Reet, "A New Kind of Desert: A Reading of Nico Walker's *Cherry*," *Brian Van Reet* (blog), August 22, 2018.
21. Van Reet.
22. For a vivid illustration of this principle, structured as a Choose-Your-Own-Adventure short story, see Gavin Ford Kovite, "When Engaging Targets,

Remember," in *Fire and Forget: Short Stories from the Long War*, eds. Roy Scranton and Matt Gallagher (Boston, MA: Da Capo Press, 2013), 157.

23. In the words of François Truffaut: "[S]ome films claim to be antiwar, but I don't think I've really seen an antiwar film. Every film about war ends up being pro-war." Gene Siskel, "The Touch That Transcends Violence," *Chicago Tribune*, November 11, 1973, 6:3. Earlier, Truffaut stated that "it seems to me that war films, even pacifist, even the best, willingly or not, glorify war and render it in some way attractive." "The Issue: Questions and Answers on Peace and War," in Robert Hughes, ed., *Films of Peace and War* (New York: Grove Press, 1962), 154, 189. One of the most plausible candidates for an anti-war film, in Truffaut's sense, may be Jon Alpert, Ellen Goosenberg Kent, and Matthew O'Neill, dirs., *Wartorn: 1861–2010* (New York: HBO Documentary Films, 2010)," a documentary that focuses on the experiences of veterans of the wars in Iraq and Afghanistan.
24. Notably, when the Iraq and Afghanistan veteran writer Elliot Ackerman was asked whether he had "ever encountered anyone who chose not to fight [in the post-9/11 wars] and regretted that," Ackerman answered that he had not. Adrienne Westenfeld, "Author and Veteran Elliot Ackerman Reflects on the War That Defined His Generation," *Esquire*, June 11, 2019.
25. On the lack of commercial success for feature films about the Iraq War, see Deer, "Mapping," 50. Brian De Palma's 2007 *Redacted*, which earned only $780,000 at the box office based on a $5 million budget, may be the most extreme example. But even Kathryn Bigelow's *The Hurt Locker* (Santa Monica, CA: Summit Entertainment, 2008), winner of the Academy Award for Best Picture, only earned $49 million based on a $15 million budget. By comparison, *American Sniper* (2014) earned nearly $550 million based on a $59 million budget.
26. On counterinsurgency operations as, in Robert Lifton's words, "atrocity-producing situations," see Herman, *Trauma and Recovery*, 351.

CHAPTER FOUR

1. See, for example, Gat, *War in Human Civilization*, 47, 116–17, 135, 183–84, 406–9, 665. On the ease with which human beings form in-groups and out-groups, see the research by Henri Tajfel and others summarized in Ezra Klein, *Why We're Polarized* (New York: Avid Reader Press, 2020), 49–79; Sapolsky, *Behave*, 387–424.
2. Gat, *War in Human Civilization*, 183–84. In tension with Gat, the biological anthropologist Richard Wrangham suggests that the contrast between praiseworthy external violent aggression and blameworthy internal violence may have a basis that long precedes the formation of states. "[W]ithin our social

communities we have a low propensity to fight...compared to most wild mammals," Wrangham notes, while there is evidence "that humans evolved to enjoy killing unknown enemies," and that we retain "a high propensity for coalitionary proactive aggression." Richard Wrangham, *The Goodness Paradox: The Strange Relationship between Virtue and Violence in Human Evolution* (New York: Vintage Books, 2019), ix, 258, 276–77. For more empirical social science research on violence and group dynamics, see Sapolsky, *Behave*.

3. The celebration of war appears to have been central to the elite culture of the early palace states that were the first to assemble massive armies. An Assyrian ruler from approximately 1100 BCE offers a glimpse of his attitude toward war in a boast about his conquest of another city: "I cut off their heads like lambs," Tiglath-Pileser is recorded as saying. "[T]heir blood I caused to flow in the valleys and on the high places of the mountains...That city I captured; their gods I carried away; I brought out their goods and their possessions; and I burned the city with fire." Victor Davis Hanson, "Genesis of the Infantry," in Geoffrey Parker, ed., *The Cambridge History of Warfare*, 2nd ed. (Cambridge: Cambridge University Press, 2005), 16.
4. Gat, *War in Human Civilization*, 406–9.
5. Aeschylus, *The Oresteia*, trans. Hugh Lloyd-Jones (Oakland: University of California Press, 1979), 268.
6. The fascist legal theorist Carl Schmitt's discussion of existential group conflict in terms of "friends" and "enemies," while unhelpful as a basis for understanding what is ordinarily referred to as politics, captures something significant about the psychology of war. Carl Schmitt, *The Concept of the Political*, trans. George Schwab (1932; Chicago: University of Chicago Press, 1996). Indeed, Schmitt's use of the term "the political" seems to refer to a phenomenon that would ordinarily be associated precisely with war *as opposed to* politics—that is, the phenomenon of a group unifying in opposition to another group that poses an existential threat. The historical sociologist Charles Tilly notes "the surprising prominence of 'us-them' categorical distinctions in all varieties of collective violence," and describes how various mechanisms can "activate" a boundary between "us" and "them" such that violence between the groups becomes more likely. Charles Tilly, *The Politics of Collective Violence* (Cambridge: Cambridge University Press, 2003), 11, 21–22, 76–78, 226. The language of the law similarly seems to recognize the peculiarly destructive nature of group-focused hatred. Thus, "hate crimes" and "hate speech" refer not to hate toward individuals, but exclusively to hate toward certain identity groups.
7. Plato, "Republic," in *Plato: Complete Works*, ed. John M. Cooper (Indianapolis, IN: Hackett Publishing Co., 1997), 971, 1097. According to Hannah Arendt,

"the Greek *polis*, the city-state, defined itself explicitly as a way of life that was based exclusively upon persuasion and not upon violence...However, since for the Greeks political life by definition did not extend beyond the walls of the *polis*, the use of violence seemed to them beyond the need for justification in the realm of what we today call foreign affairs or international relations." Hannah Arendt, *On Revolution* (New York: Penguin Books, 1963), 12.

8. Thomas Hobbes, *Leviathan*, ed. Richard Tuck (Cambridge: Cambridge University Press, 2004), 88.
9. See Max Weber, "The Profession and Vocation of Politics," in *Weber: Political Writings*, eds. Peter Lassman and Ronald Speirs (Cambridge: Cambridge University Press, 1994), 309–11. As further support for the intimate relationship between the state and war, Tilly famously argued that, historically, "[w]ar made the state, and the state made war," in the sense that external conflict incentivized the development of state capacity, including through the extraction of resources and the centralization of power, which states in turn used to conduct wars. Charles Tilly, "Reflections on the History of European State-Making," in *The Formation of National States in Western Europe* (Princeton, NJ: Princeton University Press, 1975), 42. Earlier in the twentieth century, Randolph Bourne observed a different interdependence between war and the state when he argued that "[w]ar is the health of the state" because of the "passionate cooperation" and submission to collective values that war can bring about. Randolph Bourne, *Untimely Papers* (New York: B.W. Huebsch, 1919), 145.
10. An early scholarly exploration of the distinction between war and crime begins with the premise that "[c]rime is an individual action, war a group action." Hermann Mannheim, *War and Crime* (London: Watts & Co., 1941), 6. Similarly, the international relations theorist Hedley Bull writes: "Violence is not war unless it is carried out in the name of a political unit...[and] directed against another political unit." Hedley Bull, *The Anarchical Society: A Study of Order in World Politics*, 4th ed. (New York: Columbia University Press, 2012), 178. In *On the Social Contract*, Rousseau states: "War is not...a relationship between one man and another, but a relationship between one state and another." Jean-Jacques Rousseau, *The Basic Political Writings* (Indianapolis: Hackett Publishing Company, 1987), 145.

   In the wake of the September 11 attacks, the perceived need for legal and other responses to global terrorism prompted a renewed interest in the distinction between war and crime. See, for example, Brooks, *How Everything Became War*, 219–20; Lynn, *Battle*, 319; Moyn, *Humane*, 263–64. According to retired general James Dubik, non-nation-state entities such as Al Qaeda "wag[e] war in the space between crime and war," which has led to a broad rethinking of *jus ad bellum* principles. James Dubik, "Foreword," in Sherman, *Afterwar*, xi–xii. For an early contribution to the post-9/11 debate, see Noah Feldman, "Choices of Law, Choices of War," *Harvard Journal of Law and Public Policy* 25, no. 2 (2001), 457–86. Feldman proposes four intuitive distinctions between crime and war: "identity" ("[o]ur intuition tells us that states make wars and individuals commit crimes"), "provenance" (war generally involves an attack on a jurisdiction originating from outside the jurisdiction), "intentionality" (war generally involves a challenge to sovereignty), and "scale" (war tends to operate at a larger scale than crime). Feldman, "Choices," 458–62. Feldman would go on to serve as a legal adviser to Paul Bremer and his Coalition Provisional Authority in Iraq. Packer, *Assassin's Gate*, 138. After Arab satellite television stations reported that Feldman, who is Jewish, was advising the Iraqi constitution writers, Grand Ayatollah Ali al-Sistani issued a fatwa "stating that Iraq's constitution had to be written by elected representatives." Chandrasekaran, *Imperial Life*, 90–91.

The debate in the United States over whether to try terrorist suspects in military or civilian courts has remained politically contested. See, for example, William Finnegan, "Taking Down Terrorists in Court," *New Yorker*, May 8, 2017. In line with the arguments of this chapter, support for treating terrorists as criminals to be prosecuted, if possible, rather than combatants to be killed in war, seems to correlate with support for moral cosmopolitanism; support for the strengthening of international law, including international criminal law; and opposition to militarism.

It may be worth noting, in this context, that if the ideological trends described in this chapter continue, including the growth of moral cosmopolitanism and the accompanying tendency to apply concepts from criminal law to war, then political pressures may drive the practices currently categorized as war toward "a form of decreasingly violent...global policing." Moyn, *Humane*, 322–23. Moyn, writing as an abolitionist critic of war, emphasizes the dystopian potential of such a development, while Rosa Brooks, writing from a perspective of reformist pragmatism, suggests that such an outcome may be the least worst available alternative. See Brooks, *How Everything Became War*, 344–45, 351–52, 353–66. In practice, as in debates between abolitionists and reformers regarding domestic policing and prisons, the two sides may have wide areas of agreement.

11. Ehrenreich, *Blood Rites*, 12.
12. James Dubik, "Foreword," in Sherman, *Afterwar*, xiv.
13. Ehrenreich, *Blood Rites*, 19–20. Similarly, in the early Christian church, Cyprian condemned the fact that "murder, which in the case of an individual

is admitted to be a crime, is called a virtue when it is committed wholesale." Meagher, *Killing from the Inside Out*, 62–63. In line with this book's suggestion that moral cosmopolitanism tends to lead toward a criminalized view of war-killing, Mozi seems both to have described killing in war as murder and to have embraced a cosmopolitan outlook, writing: "What is the way of universal love and mutual benefit? It is to regard other people's countries as one's own." W.-T. Chan, *A Source Book in Chinese Philosophy* (Princeton, NJ: Princeton University Press, 1963), 213, quoted in Peter Singer, *One World Now: The Ethics of Globalization*, 3rd ed. (New Haven, CT: Yale University Press, 2016), 222. Similarly, in the nineteenth-century United States, Senator Charles Sumner, well-known for his morally cosmopolitan arguments for the abolition of slavery, also argued in 1845 that war is "'organized murder.'" Witt, *Lincoln's Code*, 110.

14. A famous exchange from *The Godfather* (incidentally, Saddam Hussein's favorite movie) illustrates the point. Michael Corleone, a decorated veteran of World War II whose father is a mobster, tells his girlfriend Kay Adams: "My father is no different than any powerful man, any man with power, like a president or senator." Kay responds: "Do you know how naive you sound, Michael? Presidents and senators don't have men killed!" Michael replies: "Oh. Who's being naive, Kay?" Francis Ford Coppola, dir., *The Godfather* (Hollywood, CA: Paramount Pictures, 1972). A longtime professor of ethics at the Naval Academy "has reported how nearly without exception her midshipmen and -women students have insisted on a clear distinction between killers and murderers. 'It is very important to them,' she writes, 'that I understand that while most warriors do *kill* people, they never *murder* anyone.'" Meagher, *Killing from the Inside Out*, 77.
15. Ruti G. Teitel, *Humanity's Law* (Oxford: Oxford University Press, 2011).
16. See again the sources cited in the discussion of the "soldier-as-victim" in Chapter 2. For the movement in modern thought away from hierarchical values and toward egalitarianism, see especially Taylor, *A Secular Age*. For the rise of egalitarian thought in the mid-eighteenth-century West, see, for example, Hunt, *Inventing Human Rights*, 30–34, 176–214. For a brief summary of the limited but nevertheless noteworthy expansion of civil rights beginning in the eighteenth century, political rights beginning in the nineteenth century, and economic rights especially in the twentieth century, along with the reactionary arguments that followed in each instance, see Hirschman, *Rhetoric of Reaction*, 1–8. For the movement to abolish slavery, perhaps the most powerful illustration of the developments described in this section, see David Brion Davis, *The Problem of Slavery in the Age of Emancipation* (New York: Vintage, 2014), xiii.

I note that throughout this book, I use the term "cosmopolitan" to refer to the rejection of the moral relevance of a familiar set of boundaries used to distinguish in-groups ("us") from out-groups ("them"), including race, ethnicity, nationality, and religion. These boundaries allow the imagined division of human beings into distinct, opposed communities. By contrast, I use the term "egalitarian" to refer to the rejection of hierarchical differences in status between various groups *within* a community based on, for example, gender, class, sexuality, or disability. The two terms are of course deeply related and will often overlap. The civil rights movement in the United States, for example, to the extent that it involved extending legal, political, and social rights to African Americans, could be described either as evidence of growing moral cosmopolitanism, or as evidence of growing egalitarianism, or both. If African Americans in the Jim Crow era are conceived of as a subordinated part of the national community, then the advances of the civil rights movement may register as advances in egalitarianism. If African Americans in the Jim Crow era are instead conceived of as excluded from the national community, then the civil rights movement's advances may register as developments in the direction of cosmopolitanism.

The common idea of an expanding (or contracting) "circle" of moral concern can perhaps be conceptualized more precisely as a series of expanding (or contracting) concentric circles, where each circle represents a specific expression of solidarity, and an expansion represents the extension of that degree of solidarity to new (perceived) identity groups. For example, in the time between World War II and the present day, most Americans have apparently extended to all human groups the minimal degree of solidarity that excludes the flaunting of that group's skulls as trophies, while during World War II many Americans apparently excluded the Japanese from even this degree of solidarity, as discussed in the body text; and most Americans have also apparently extended to all racial groups the slightly greater degree of solidarity that finds nothing problematic in intergroup marriage, while in 1940 nearly all white Americans excluded African Americans from this degree of solidarity. The image of progressively expanding circles of sympathy may have its origin in Hume. See Taylor, *A Secular Age*, 608. Peter Singer discusses the expansion of the "moral circle" or the "circle of altruism" in Peter Singer, *The Expanding Circle: Ethics, Evolution, and Moral Progress* (Princeton, NJ: Princeton University Press, 1981), 120–21. Martha Nussbaum traces the related idea that we have "special duties to our family, friends, and local context" from Cicero to Adam Smith's *Theory of Moral Sentiments* in Martha Nussbaum, *The Cosmopolitan Tradition: A Noble but Flawed Ideal* (Cambridge, MA: Belknap Press, 2019), 172.

17. Justin McCarthy, "U.S. Approval of Interracial Marriage at New High of 94%," *Gallup*, September 10, 2021.
18. Inglehart, *Cultural Evolution*.
19. Inglehart, *Cultural Evolution*, 102–13, 192–93. To be clear, none of the deliberately simplifying grand narratives sketched in this chapter should be misunderstood as a history of *natural* moral progress. The chapter does not make the Whiggish claim that any movements toward cosmopolitan and egalitarian values were inevitable or are guaranteed to continue. Even if Inglehart is correct and material security generally tends to promote, after a lag, postmaterialist values, it is entirely possible that the causal mechanism will break down, perhaps due to technological transformations affecting the public sphere; or that modernity will turn out to have been an isolated, fossil-fueled episode of sporadically increasing prosperity, peace, and postmaterialist values, followed by one or another form of global collapse and the return of survival values.
20. Taylor, *A Secular Age*, 123.
21. Hirschman, *The Passions and the Interests*, 11.
22. Hathaway and Shapiro, *The Internationalists*, xvi. Pinker notes critiques of the valorization of war in Pascal, Swift, Montesquieu, Samuel Johnson, Voltaire, Adam Smith, and Kant. Pinker, *The Better Angels of Our Nature*, 163–66.
23. Constant, "The Spirit of Conquest," 52–55; Mark Mazower, *Governing the World: The History of an Idea, 1815 to the Present* (London: Penguin Books, 2012), 31–38. For later developments, see Moyn, *Humane*, 47–77.
24. Inglehart, *Cultural Evolution*, 111–12.
25. Inglehart, 108, 111.
26. Hathaway and Shapiro, *The Internationalists*, 62.
27. There is a long tradition of viewing war, at least in some contexts, as largely or entirely lawless. See Gregory Brazeal, "Law, War, and Four Modes of Conflict," *Oregon Review of International Law* 20, no. 2 (2019): 532n2, collecting quotes from Thucydides, Clausewitz, Kennan, and others. The idea is often referred to using the phrase "*inter arma silent leges*," which Walzer translates as "in time of war the law is silent." Michael Walzer, *Just and Unjust Wars* (New York: Basic Books, 2015), 3.
28. Brooks, *How Everything Became War*, 185–89; Finnemore, *Purpose of Intervention*, 31–51; Mazower, *Governing the World*, 66–68; Witt, *Lincoln's Code*, 1–2. On the distinction between *jus ad bellum* and *jus in bello*, see Walzer, *Just and Unjust Wars*, 21. Although the Lieber Code contained some humanitarian constraints, Lieber himself was an ardent militarist and no friend of humanitarianism. Moyn, *Humane*, 29–30; Witt, *Lincoln's Code*, 170–96.

29. Oona A. Hathaway et al., "What Is a War Crime?," *Yale Journal of International Law* 44, no. 1 (2019): 53, 60, 64, 267; Hathaway and Shapiro, *The Internationalists*, 267. John Fabian Witt suggests that by imposing individual criminal liability on Mexican guerillas during the Mexican–American war, "Winfield Scott and the U.S. armies in Mexico [gave] life to the idea of a war crime," even before Lieber's use of the phrase. Witt, *Lincoln's Code*, 122–30.
30. Hathaway and Shapiro, *The Internationalists*, 109, 117.
31. Moyn, *Humane*, 195, 209–17.
32. Jeff McMahan, *Killing in War* (Oxford: Oxford University Press, 2009), vii. McMahan writes from a secular perspective, but somewhat similar arguments have been made from religious perspectives as well. For a critique of Christian just war theory that suggests the tradition betrays Jesus' teachings, see Meagher, *Killing from the Inside Out*. The "immunizing primacy of personal intent" in just war doctrine is "dangerous," Meagher suggests, in part because it provides "'a marvelous way...of making any action lawful. You only had to 'direct your intention' in a suitable way.'" Meagher, 94, quoting G.E.M. Anscombe, "War and Murder," in Walter Stein, ed., *Nuclear Weapons: A Catholic Response* (London: Merlin, 1961), 43–62. Meagher also offers a revisionist portrait of the deeply authoritarian bishop and just war theorist Augustine of Hippo, who, among other things, defended torture, so long as it was carried out with the right intent and "performed in love." Meagher, 71–84.
33. Kennedy, "Speech: Modern War and Modern Law," 175. As Stacey Peebles has observed, an early and innovative film about drone warfare, Gavin Hood, dir., *Eye in the Sky* (Toronto: Entertainment One, 2015), also dramatizes the significant role that lawyers and legal constraints currently play in targeting. Peebles, "Forever Wars," 260.
34. Filkins provides a detailed description of a legal adviser explaining the ROEs to marines before the Second Battle of Fallujah. Filkins, *Forever War*, 186–88. For a real-world example, see the 2005 standing ROE quoted in Wood, *What Have We Done*, 194–95. Wood also describes how the tactical ROEs issued by a combat commander might differ from the standing ROEs or even, based on his example, violate the laws of war. Wood, 195–96.
35. Hathaway and Shapiro, *The Internationalists*, 291–92.
36. President George W. Bush, Address to a Joint Session of Congress and the American People (September 20, 2001). The quote seems to echo Hermann Göring's declaration, "I know of only two types of people: those with us and those against us." Quoted in Hathaway and Shapiro, *The Internationalists*, 232.

37. The humanitarian argument for invasion is especially associated with the figure of Kanan Makiya, an Iraqi-American critic of Saddam Hussein's many atrocities. Packer, *Assassin's Gate*, 8–12. Makiya later wrote a didactic novel about the aftermath of the invasion. In terms of this book's narrative categories, Makiya's novel can be read as arguing that an excessive Shia idealization of victimhood led to Saddam Hussein's Shia victims becoming criminals after the invasion. As a result, the novel suggests, the Shia and not the Americans deserve the greatest blame for the collapse of Iraq into sectarian violence. Kanan Makiya, *The Rope* (New York: Pantheon Books, 2016).
38. Brazeal, "Four Modes of Conflict," 531, 537–38, 548–54.
39. Violent cadences appear repeatedly in writings about the Iraq and Afghanistan wars, including the following one, which Erik Edstrom heard as a seventeen-year-old at West Point in 2003: "*Left right, left right, left right KILL!...I went to the mosque, where all the terrorists pray, I set up my claymore, AND BLEW 'EM ALL AWAY!...I went to the playground where all the kiddies play, I pulled out my Uzi, AND I BEGAN TO SPRAY!*" Erik Edstrom, *Un-American: A Soldier's Reckoning of Our Longest War* (New York: Bloomsbury Publishing, 2020), 35. Later, Edstrom quotes another Army marching cadence: "*We shoot the sick, the young, the lame, [w]e do our best to maim, [b]ecause the kills all count the same, [n]apalm sticks to kids.*" Edstrom, 209. In another memoir, a marine veteran of the Iraq War describes being told to respond "*kill* in a loud bloodthirsty manner" in response to the references in a cadence to "Hajjis," "Muj," and "Targets." Matt Young, *Eat the Apple* (New York: Bloomsbury Publishing, 2018), 96. The title of Kevin Powers' *The Yellow Birds* comes from an Army marching cadence: "A yellow bird with a yellow bill was perched upon my windowsill. I lured him in with a piece of bread and then I smashed his fucking head." See Power, *Yellow Birds*, 1.

    Such cadences are not new. The Gulf War veteran Timothy McVeigh, who killed two Iraqis and received a Bronze Star before bombing the federal building in Oklahoma City in 1995, described being made to scream during his Army training until his "throat was raw": "Blood makes the grass grow! Kill! Kill! Kill!" Daniel Immerwahr, "A Fire Started in Waco. Thirty Years Later, It's Still Burning," *New Yorker*, May 1, 2023. Dave Grossman similarly recounts that during his Army basic training in 1974, one running chant was: "Iwanna RAPE, KILL, PILLAGE'n' BURN, annnnn' EAT dead BAAA-bies." Grossman, *On Killing: The Psychological Cost of Learning to Kill in War and Society*, rev. ed. (New York: Back Bay Books, 2009), 311–12. Lyle Jeremy Rubin describes a controversy in 1989 when "a senior drill instructor at Parris Island had his recruits march beside a picture of a naked woman and a guidon flag emblazoned with the words *rape, kill, pillage, burn.*" Rubin, who experienced both enlisted and officer marine training, notes that by the mid-2000s the latter involved "far less degrading language toward Muslims, Arabs, women, or anyone who wasn't a straight white male" than the former. Lyle Jeremy Rubin, *Pain Is Weakness Leaving the Body: A Marine's Unbecoming* (New York: Bold Type Books, 2022), 157.

It might be tempting to dismiss such cadences as self-parody rather than indoctrination or desensitization. But there is a long history of winking irony and comical exaggeration being used to facilitate actual violence, from the Muscadins of the French Revolution, a right-wing mob that dressed like dandies and beat political opponents with clubs they jokingly called "constitutions"; to the mocking speech that often accompanies violence during fraternity and other hazing rituals; to the "Boogaloo boys," who were known for wearing comically festive Hawaiian shirts and for plotting kidnapping, murder, and a coup in the United States in 2021. It is especially difficult to dismiss the embrace of atrocity in cadences as "just a joke" when Edstrom receives advice such as the following during his actual pre-deployment training: "All these people from Muslim countries—all they understand is force... You can't treat 'em like people 'cause they're not." Edstrom, 97.

40. For a comparison of American literary representations of the Vietnam War and the Iraq War, see the conclusion below.

CHAPTER FIVE

1. Phil Klay's *Redeployment*, as noted in Chapter 6, has a better claim to being the most celebrated book-length work of Iraq War fiction. But it is a collection of short stories rather than a novel.
2. As further evidence of such demand, see Matt Gallagher, "Where's the Great Novel About the War on Terror?," *Atlantic*, June 14, 2011.
3. For an early dissenting view primarily focused on the style of the novel's prose, see Theo Tait, "The Hemingway Crush," *London Review of Books*, January 3, 2013. In 2017, the novel was adapted into a languorous art film. Alexandre Moors, dir., *The Yellow Birds* (Los Angeles: Cinelou Films, 2017).
4. According to the back cover of the 2013 paperback of *The Yellow Birds*, the author served in the Army in 2004 and 2005 in Mosul and Tal Afar as a machine gunner. "Al Tafar," through which the Tigris river passes, as it does through Mosul, appears to be an amalgam of the two cities.
5. The narrator refers to this man as a "cartwright" (201, 202, 211) and a "hermit" (211). But he does not appear to be either a maker or repairer of carts or someone who has retreated from society to live in solitude. Rather, he appears simply to be a man living in extreme poverty on the streets of Al Tafar, with

"the whole of his earthly possessions" (202) consisting of a cart, its contents, and a three-legged mule with a wooden contraption in place of its fourth leg (201).

6. James C. Scott, *Against the Grain: A Deep History of the Earliest States* (New Haven, CT: Yale University Press, 2017), xiii.
7. Fleck, *Handbook*, 13, 337–39.
8. For an account of the *phília* between Achilles and Patroklos, as well as evidence from outside literature of the intense love between some soldiers in combat, and the devastation that can follow the loss of such a friend, see Shay, *Achilles in Vietnam*, 39–68. Remarkably, a psychological study of a sample of Vietnam veterans with PTSD found that their loss of friends in combat three decades earlier continued to result in levels of grief that (according to a standard measure) were on average higher than the grief scores of a sample of people whose spouses had died within the previous six months. Ilona L. Pivar and Nigel P. Field, "Unresolved Grief in Combat Veterans with PTSD," *Journal of Anxiety Disorders* 18, no. 6 (2004), 745–55, 751.
9. Powers has described his own isolation, alcoholism, and suicidal despair after his return from Iraq. Kevin Powers, "Opinion: What Kept Me from Killing Myself," *New York Times*, June 16, 2018.

CHAPTER SIX

1. Klay (rhymes with "sky") served as a Public Affairs Officer in the Marine Corps from 2005 to 2009, and deployed to Iraq from January 2007 to February 2008. "Bio," Phil Klay, https://www.philklay.com/bio. In an essay, Klay notes: "As a public affairs officer, working with the media and running an office of Marine journalists, I was never even in combat. And my service in Iraq was during a time when things seemed to be getting better." Klay, *Citizen-Soldier*. Given the continual increase in the ratio of military servicemembers in support as opposed to combat roles, it seems fitting that the most celebrated work of Iraq War fiction would be written by someone who experienced no combat.
2. Fussell, *Great War*, 170.
3. See Mark McGurl, *The Program Era: Postwar Fiction and the Rise of Creative Writing* (Cambridge, MA: Harvard University Press, 2009). For example, Matt Gallagher, Gavin Kovite, Phil Klay, Perry O'Brien, Roy Scranton, and Jacob (Jake) Siegel met at a veterans' writing workshop at New York University. Colum McCann, "Foreword," in *Fire and Forget*, eds. Roy Scranton and Matt Gallagher, vii, ix.

   The acknowledgment sections, blurbs, and reviews for many of the works of fiction and memoirs discussed in this book provide further evidence that the literary world of post-9/11 veterans features a dense network of personal and professional connections. For a profile of some of the central nodes in the network, including Matt Gallagher, Phil Klay, and Elliot Ackerman, see Lea Carpenter, "The Words of War," *Vanity Fair*, November 26, 2014. Carpenter herself wrote a literary novel about the Navy SEALs, *Eleven Days* (New York: Vintage Contemporaries, 2013), before going on to write the screenplay for an action thriller, Peter Berg, dir., *Mile 22* (Burbank, CA: STX Entertainment, 2018).

The connections and inside jokes sometimes continue within the works of fiction themselves, as when Phil Klay refers in one of his stories to a marine named "Kovite" who was killed, and Gavin Kovite returns the favor by describing a "PFC Klay" who died from "one of those concussion deaths where all your blood vessels burst and you bleed out internally." Klay, *Redeployment*, 124; Robinson and Kovite, *War of the Encyclopaedists*, 155. Even this book exists at the far periphery of the network of literary connections, in the sense that I once served in a legal operations unit in the Army Reserve with Gavin Kovite. I thank then-CPT Molly Kovite for drawing my attention to Klay's and Kovite's mutually fictionalized destruction.

Other intersections between works in the canon of Iraq War writings might also be noted. Elliot Ackerman, the future novelist and essayist, appears as a second lieutenant fighting in the Second Battle of Fallujah in Thomas Ricks' *Fiasco*, 403–4. George Packer's *Assassin's Gate* and Dexter Filkins' *The Forever War* contain overlapping first-person journalistic accounts of the same failed visit by Paul Bremer to a maternity hospital. Bremer had apparently hoped to tout his successes, but instead encountered a skeletal premature baby and other evidence of the increased child mortality that resulted from power outages after the American invasion. "'I don't like seeing this at all,' he said, and asked the photographer to stop taking pictures." Packer, 199. In his book, Filkins even notes Packer's presence. Filkins, 138, 350. Elsewhere, Packer dedicates a chapter to CPT John Prior ("The Captain"), who resurfaces years later in Nancy Sherman's writing as a veteran struggling to come to terms with guilt. Packer, 219–20; Nancy Sherman, *The Untold War: Inside the Hearts, Minds, and Souls of Our Soldiers* (New York: W.W. Norton & Company, 2010), 94–95.

Sherman also knew the late Ian Fishback, an Army officer and whistleblower whose protest against detainee abuses led to the passage of the Detainee Treatment Act of 2005, prohibiting the "cruel, inhuman or degrading treatment" of any "individual...under the physical control of the United States government." C.J. Chivers, "Ian Fishback's American Nightmare," *New York Times*, February 21, 2023. Fishback, who worked with the philosopher Jeff McMahan, cited elsewhere in this book, and obtained a philosophy degree after leaving the Special Forces, was to have written an essay for Andrew Bacevich and Daniel A. Sjursen, eds., *Paths of Dissent: Soldiers Speak Out against America's Misguided Wars* (New York: Metropolitan Books, 2022), 14. But his deepening struggles with mental illness interfered. He died in 2021 at the age of 42.

4. Klay, *Redeployment*, Front Matter.
5. McGurl, *Program Era*, 23.
6. Eric Bennett, *Workshops of Empire: Stegner, Engle, and American Creative Writing During the Cold War* (Iowa City: University of Iowa Press, 2015), 171.
7. The ending of Raymond Carver's short story about the death of Chekhov, "Errand," offers an especially clear example of the technique. After Chekhov dies at a hotel, his wife Olga gives a bellboy very precise instructions about how to summon a mortician. The instructions are almost surreal in their specificity, as though Olga is composing a short story based on her imagination of how the bellboy might complete his errand. The strange, dreamlike urgency and detail of the instructions constitute the story's emotional and narrative climax. But in the final paragraph, at the moment when the reader expects the bellboy to depart, he instead bends down and picks up a champagne cork on the floor that had been bothering him. The story ends. What is the significance of the bellboy's final gesture? Any number of interpretations might be offered, but it is certainly not obvious how picking up a cork provides a narrative resolution to the problem of Chekhov's death. The placement of the bellboy's gesture at the end of the story endows it with an aura of great meaning, even as the nature of the gesture does not fit any easily articulated narrative expectation. The dissonance creates a sense of depth or mystery. See Raymond Carver, "Errand," *New Yorker*, May 24, 1987, 30.
8. As Sacks notes, Bennett himself has satirized the market for workshop-quality stories of authentic veteran suffering in *A Big Enough Lie* (Evanston, IL: TriQuarterly Books, 2015). The novel contains both a plausible imitation of a military memoir of the Iraq War (a war that, of course, has been criticized for being based on lies), and the story of a floundering non-veteran creative writing workshop student who achieves popular success by writing the (fraudulent) memoir. (For a memorable illustration of the criticism that the Iraq War was based on lies, see Sam Smith, "The Revision Thing: A History of the Iraq War, Told Entirely in Lies," *Harper's*, October 2003.) It is difficult not to wonder if Bennett's novel would have received more attention in critical discussions of Iraq War fiction if it had been presented as the work of a veteran. As the novel suggests, the aura of authenticity seems to powerfully

shape readers' perceptions of fictional works, particularly in the case of war fiction.

In tension with these observations, a recent book-length work of literary analysis, David Eisler's *Writing Wars*, argues that veteran authors "came to monopolize the cultural authority over the literary representation of war in the twentieth century," but "ceded that authority" to non-veteran authors writing about the wars in Iraq and Afghanistan. Eisler, *Writing Wars: Authorship and American War Fiction, WWI to Present* (Iowa City: University of Iowa Press, 2022), 3. Eisler argues that non-veteran authors have come to play a greater role in the production of war literature not as a result of demographic trends, cultural divides between the most likely sources of military volunteers and the most likely sources of literary writers, or changing attitudes in the publishing industry, but as a result of veteran authors in the era of the all-volunteer military seeking "ways to unburden themselves from the sole responsibility to interpret these conflicts in fiction." Eisler, 4.

9. Sacks, "First-Person Shooters." U.S.-based Iraqi novelist Sinan Antoon offers a similar critique of Brian Turner's poetry in his essay "Embedded Poetry: Iraq; Through a Soldier's Binoculars," *Jadaliyya*, June 11, 2014. The most widely discussed book of poetry about U.S. military service in the Iraq War remains Turner's early, award-winning *Here, Bullet* (Farmington, ME: Alice James Books, 2005). Within the book, the most widely discussed, anthologized, and quoted poem may be "Sadiq" (Arabic for "friend"), although another poem, "The Hurt Locker," provided the title for Kathryn Bigelow's film. Turner, *Here, Bullet*, 11, 56. The present study does not address poetry about the Iraq War, but it may be worth briefly noting that "Sadiq" seems to reflect the "trauma hero" vision of wartime killing criticized by Scranton. After beginning with an epigraph on archery from a Persian poet, Sa'di, "Sadiq" concludes with the admonition that "it should break your heart to kill." In between, the speaker offers advice to a listener, "my friend," who will apparently one day be in a position to kill another human being. Instead of inviting the friend to question whether such killing is necessary, the speaker focuses on how a killer should *feel* about the act of killing. On the one hand, the speaker strongly advises against feeling good about killing. On the other hand, the speaker describes the "nightmare" that a killer should experience as an almost epic, Marvel-scale achievement of anguish. According to the speaker, a killer should not simply be traumatized, but should be heroically traumatized, in a process involving "seared" veins, "muscle" fed with "courage," perhaps with a "god shin[ing] down," and in one's "fists," the "crackling" of lightning-like

"pain and anger." If Sa'di offers a guide to heroic excellence in archery, "Sadiq" could be read as a guide to heroic excellence in trauma.

Antoon's essay notes the remarkable fact that the photograph on the cover of *Here, Bullet*, which features Turner standing, in his words, "'sort of like John Wayne'" in an otherwise empty desert, originally contained three Iraqi prisoners "'on their knees, their hands...flexcuffed behind their backs,' with 'sandbags over their heads.'" The Iraqis in Turner's photograph were airbrushed out of the cover image. Antoon concludes by suggesting that Turner's book reflects all too well what Antoon sees as the mainstream narrative of the Iraq War: "'We' tried to help those wretched Iraqis, but it was all just too messy...'Mistakes were made' along the way...The civilian victims are disappeared. The soldiers *are* the victims. Did the war wage itself?" The concluding question resonates with *The Yellow Birds*' presentation of the Iraq War and its harms as the product of impersonal forces, rather than being the responsibility of anyone in particular, as discussed in Chapter 5.

10. The Second Battle of Fallujah in November 2004 "was probably the toughest battle the U.S. military had seen since the end of the Vietnam War more than three decades earlier." Ricks, *Fiasco*, 398–406. Given the significance of Second Fallujah, especially for the Marine Corps, it is another of Klay's fitting gestures that the first, title story in his collection would be dedicated to the experiences of a marine veteran of the battle (1).
11. Apparently many other authors of Iraq War fiction and memoirs also thought a lot about shooting dogs in Iraq. For examples from fiction, see David Abrams, *Brave Deeds* (New York: Black Cat, 2017), 80; Adam Kovac, *The Surge* (Indianapolis: Engine Books, 2019), 146; Will Mackin, *Bring Out the Dog* (New York: Random House, 2018), 166; Walker, *Cherry*, 126, 140, 160–62, 168. For non-fiction, see Tyler E. Boudreau, *Packing Inferno: The Unmaking of a Marine* (Port Townsend, WA: Feral House, 2008), 82; Eric Fair, *Consequence: A Memoir* (New York: Henry Holt and Company, 2016), 134; David Finkel, *The Good Soldiers* (New York: Picador, 2009), 1, 292; Clint Van Winkle, *Soft Spots: A Marine's Memoir of Combat and Post-Traumatic Stress Disorder* (New York: St. Martin's Griffin, 2009), 74; Young, *Eat the Apple*, 160–63. In an illustration of the many intersections between contemporary debates about the U.S. military and about U.S. domestic policing, the journalist Radley Balko has noted that his stories about SWAT teams repeatedly shooting dogs during raids tend to provoke especially strong reactions from readers. Radley Balko, *Rise of the Warrior Cop: The Militarization of America's Police Forces* (New York: Public Affairs, 2014), 290.
12. Bruner, *Making Stories*, 17.

13. A more literal substitution of violence to Iraqis for violence to dogs appears in a non-fiction work about an Army unit returning from Iraq, David Finkel's *Thank You for Your Service* (New York: Farrar, Straus and Giroux, 2013). In the book, a soldier describes how his unit became friendly with two stray dogs. Then an Iraqi policeman who was bothered by the barking and growling of one of the dogs sliced its Achilles tendon. "[S]ome soldiers boasted later that they had held the Iraqi down and done the same to him." Finkel, 91.
14. Scranton, "Trauma Hero."
15. In addition, doubts might be raised about the desirability of shifting away from the standard realist MFA style and toward greater ideological critique. What is probably the least successful story in *Redeployment*, "Psychological Operations," offers a reminder of the advantages of the program-era approach. To a greater extent than any other story in the collection, "Psychological Operations" explicitly addresses the domestic political debates surrounding the Iraq War. In fact, the story consists primarily of a very lengthy representation of such a debate between the Christian Arab-American Iraq War veteran narrator and a leftist African-American student who has converted to Islam and criticizes the Iraq War (172). Although technically the story abides by the program-era injunction to "show don't tell," what it shows is a lot of telling—including, for example, the leftist student casually referring to the killing of an armed insurgent as "murder," and the veteran retorting: "'Even you don't think it's murder...You're smarter than that'" (186). One way to respond to the critical demand for fiction that addresses the larger contexts of and ideological questions raised by the Iraq War, without simply relying on the representation of political dialogue, might be to take inspiration from a work that "Psychological Operations" itself happens to refer to in passing: the HBO television series *The Wire* (171). Just as *The Wire* offers a panoramic perspective on crime in a major American city by portraying a variety of institutions that shape crime rates, so a work of fiction could approach the Iraq War through the many institutions that played a role in it, such as the Bush White House, Congress, the military, the defense industry, the news media, foreign policy analysts in think tanks and academia, and, in the deeper background, economic actors and institutions that seek a steady supply of inexpensive oil.
16. Klay, *Citizen-Soldier*.
17. The word "pacifist" appears twice, in passing (55, 64). For an account of pacifist strands in the thought of modern figures including Emerson, Tolstoy, and "Tolstoy's greatest American heir," Martin Luther King, Jr., see Moyn, *Humane*, 17–22, 180. For a pacifist work of fiction from before the program era, although one that seems to except violent revolution against a warmongering

government as an exception to the demands of pacifism, see Trumbo, *Johnny Got His Gun*, 242–43. Trumbo's novel also relies heavily on Christian imagery, as when the injured protagonist envisions himself as "a new kind of Christ... the new messiah of the battlefields saying to people as I am so shall you be." Trumbo, 240. In this and other senses, *Johnny Got His Gun* might be seen as an almost idealized embodiment of the soldier-as-victim narrative.

18. A more historically informed reading might emphasize the apocalyptic nature of Jesus' message, and thus that it was not intended as a source of values for our world. See Bart D. Ehrman, *Jesus: Apocalyptic Prophet of the New Millennium* (Oxford: Oxford University Press, 1999).
19. Within the Catholic church, to which the chaplain narrator of "Furnace" belongs (147), Pope John Paul II opposed both the Iraq War and the Gulf War before it. Frank Bruni, "Pope Voices Opposition, His Strongest, to Iraq War," *New York Times*, January 14, 2003. But as Meagher suggests, many military chaplains seem to view their primary role not as offering spiritual guidance, but as relieving the debilitating moral disturbances that soldiers sometimes feel regarding their actions. Meagher, 137–41. Especially for the more militant strands of contemporary evangelical Christianity, there may be no tension between the two. Meagher 140; Bacevich, *New American Militarism*, 122–46; Kristin Kobes Du Mez, *Jesus and John Wayne*. As part of her account of how militant evangelical Christians have worked to spread their values within the U.S. military, Du Mez notes that by 2005, "40 percent of active duty personnel identified as evangelical, and 60 percent of military chaplains did." Du Mez, 213.
20. For a list of such works, see Chapter 10.
21. In his acknowledgments, Klay includes a long list of books that he consulted while researching the stories in *Redeployment*, including memoirs about aspects of the war he presumably did not experience at first hand. To take one example, some of the details of mortuary affairs work described in "Bodies" echo observations in Goodell and Hearn, *Shade It Black*.
22. Pederson, *Sin Sick*, 151.

CHAPTER SEVEN

1. Benedict, *Lonely Soldier*, 1–2.
2. For an exceptionally well-informed if admittedly subjective chronological list of significant literary works about the post-9/11 wars, see Peter Molin, "Iraq and Afghanistan War Fiction, Poetry, and Film 2020," *Time Now* (blog), December 31, 2020. There are only a handful of novels about the Iraq War

on Molin's list before *Sand Queen*, including Nicholas Kulish, *Last One In* (New York: Ecco, 2007), a satire written by a journalist who was embedded with the marines in Iraq. Other literary novels that are not set in Iraq, but deal with the Iraq War as a theme, do not appear on the list. See, for example, Nicholson Baker, *Checkpoint* (New York: Vintage, 2005); Ian McEwan, *Saturday* (London: Jonathan Cape, 2005).

3. Consistent with my argument about the effects of rising moral cosmopolitanism on Iraq War fiction, the literary scholar Giorgio Mariani describes *Sand Queen* as a "cosmopolitan" work in which Benedict "present[s] the reader with an account of war that is not limited to showing the sufferings of 'our side' but struggles to make us aware of how war feeds on ignorance and prejudice against the Other." Giorgio Mariani, *Waging War on War: Peacefighting in American Literature* (Urbana: University of Illinois Press, 2015), xvi.
4. Jennifer Haytock has noted how *Sand Queen* draws on "the female Gothic," "a genre in which women's lives are rendered as horror tales, the familiar and domestic shown as threatening, especially in their normalcy." Jennifer Haytock, "Women's/War Stories: The Female Gothic and Women's War Trauma in Helen Benedict's *Sand Queen*," *War, Literature, and the Arts* 27, no. 1 (2015): 1, 3, 5.
5. In fairness, similar criticisms could be made of some of the other novels mentioned in this book, such as *FOBBIT*, where, for example, one of the characters refers to a checkpoint guard "ralphing his guts all over the front desk." Abrams, *FOBBIT*, 46.
6. It is unclear whether the novel intends this claim as casual hyperbole. The idea that anything close to half the students in a high school in the United States, including one in upstate New York, were enlisting in the military around March 2000 is wildly implausible. According to the Bureau of Labor Statistics, for the country as a whole, "[f]rom 1998 to 2003, four percent of recent high school graduates not enrolled in school had enlisted in the Armed Forces by the October when they were age 18." Bureau of Labor Statistics, "Enlistment of Youth in the Armed Forces," *TED: The Economics Daily*, February 27, 2006, https://www.bls.gov/opub/ted/2006/feb/wk4/art01.htm.
7. Klay has criticized the "notion of a military filled with ne'er-do-wells who are in it only for the money" both as "false," because "it's actually the middle class that's best represented in the military, and the numbers of high-income and highly educated recruits rose to levels disproportionate to their percentage of the population after the war on terror began," and also as "frustrating," because "it takes the decision to put one's life at risk for one's country and transforms it, as if by magic, into a self-interested act." Klay, *Citizen-Soldier*.

Edstrom paints a more sinister picture of military recruitment, noting, for example, that the 2002 No Child Left Behind Act included a provision requiring schools to share student information with military recruiters for use in targeted recruitment, and that "high-propensity candidates are often the most socially, economically, and developmentally vulnerable." Edstrom, *Un-American*, 23–24.

8. In fact, as Benedict has noted, at least three female soldiers died in Iraq due to dehydrating themselves in an attempt to avoid frequent visits to latrines where they might be raped. Helen Benedict, "The Private War of Women Soldiers," *Salon*, March 7, 2007.
9. This detail, like many others in the list, echoes Benedict's reportage. In *The Lonely Soldier*, Benedict quotes a female soldier's observation that "[t]here are only three things the guys let you be if you're a girl in the military—a bitch, a ho, or a dyke." Benedict, *The Lonely Soldier*, 5. Similar observations appear in Goodell and Hearn, *Shade It Black*, 85; Williams, *Love My Rifle*, 13.
10. The Obama administration gradually opened combat positions to women, with Defense Secretary Ashton Carter lifting all remaining restrictions in 2015.
11. Tom A. Peter, "Finally, a Realistic Iraq War Novel," *New Republic*, August 2, 2016.
12. For a discussion of "moral injury," and the suggestion that "holistic responsibility" might provide a better framework for arriving at a just understanding of wrongdoing, see Chapter 1 above.

CHAPTER EIGHT

1. Kyle Smith, "'American Sniper' Is the Year's Most Extraordinary Film," *New York Post*, December 23, 2014.
2. From a review of Clint Eastwood's *American Sniper* by Paul Edwards, "The Sociopath as Hero," *CounterPunch*, February 4, 2015. See also Lindy West, "The Real American Sniper Was a Hate-Filled Killer. Why Are Simplistic Patriots Treating Him as a Hero?" *Guardian*, January 6, 2015.
3. Chris Kyle, *American Sniper* (New York: HarperCollins, 2013).
4. The glorification of quantified killing through "confirmed kills" seems to echo the government use of enemy "body counts" as a metric of success in the Vietnam War. But there is a significant difference between the two. According to journalist Matthew Cole, "there is no such thing as a 'confirmed kill' in the US military...Instead, many snipers keep a private, unofficial tally of their dead." "Confirmed kills" "are self-reported, unofficial, and prone to error and

exaggeration." Matthew Cole, *Code over Country: The Tragedy and Corruption of SEAL Team Six* (New York: Bold Type Books, 2022), 222. Cole quotes a book by James Hatch, a former SEAL, who writes that "[c]onfirmed kills are a comic fallacy...I still haven't found the office in the Pentagon that's responsible for confirming kills." Cole, 222–23.

5. For Kyle's biography, see Nicholas Schmidle, "In the Crosshairs," *New Yorker*, May 27, 2013.
6. In a broader historical perspective, one of the surprising aspects of the exceptional popular success of *American Sniper* is that it was about a sniper. As the Afghanistan veteran and author Adrian Bonenberger has noted, "[f]or much of human history, a person who stayed back from combat and killed the enemy from afar was seen as unscrupulous at best. The original sniper is Paris, who dastardly kills the Greek hero Achilles from long range with a bow and arrow." Adrian Bonenberger, "There Are No War Heroes: A Veteran's Review of American Sniper," *Deadspin*, January 23, 2015. Bourke describes how in World War II "snipers were disliked intensely by other soldiers," and some snipers "admitted that their business was 'little better than murder' and 'a filthy sort of business.'" Bourke, *Intimate History*, 54–55.
7. See Kelly Lawler, "Seth Rogen, Michael Moore Ignite 'Sniper' Debate," *USA Today*, January 19, 2015; Amanda Taub, "Every Movie Rewrites History. What American Sniper Did Is Much, Much Worse," *Vox*, January 22, 2015. A footnote in Chapter 1 offers a brief discussion of the differences between Eastwood's film and Kyle's book.
8. Matthew Cole and Sheelagh McNeill, "'American Sniper' Chris Kyle Distorted His Military Record, Documents Show," *Intercept*, May 25, 2016.
9. Schmidle, "In the Crosshairs." Kyle himself admitted that earlier drafts of the book contained inaccuracies. In response to criticisms of a draft, he privately wrote that "'there is some over[-]dramatization'" and "'some flat out lies...The book has not turned out the way I intended. I was hoping that DOD would do more as far as getting rid of BS, but they just took out the name DevGru.'" Cole, *Code over Country*, 225.
10. Peter Molin, "Does Anyone Remember American Sniper?," *Time Now* (blog), July 1, 2018.
11. For a highly influential, nonfiction, contemporary right-wing American perspective on war, killing, and military service in general, see Grossman, *On Killing*, 311–12. Grossman, who retired from the Army as a lieutenant colonel in 1998, describes himself as a "killologist." He appears to be the primary source of the "sheepdog" ideology, the popular belief in right-wing military, police, and gun-rights circles "that people can be divided

into three groups—sheep, wolves, and sheepdogs—and it's the sheepdogs, 'blessed with the gift of aggression,' who are responsible for protecting the sheep from the wolves." Josh Eells, "Lt. Col. Dave Grossman, the 'Killologist' Training America's Cops," *Men's Journal*, September 9, 2019; Jasper Craven, "The Police's 'Sheepdog' Problem," *New Republic*, June 11, 2020; see also Grossman, *On Killing*, 183–85. The idea appears prominently in the film version of *American Sniper*, although not in the book. Sheepdog ideology was also present in Iraq. For example, Michael Steele, an Army colonel whose men murdered three unarmed Iraqis in 2006 after allegedly receiving permission to "kill all military-aged males," referred to his soldiers as "'sheepdogs.'" Raffi Khatchadourian, "The Kill Company," *New Yorker*, June 29, 2009. The sheepdog might seem a more benign model than the wolf, Hitler's preferred canine avatar, but in practice such distinctions may fade away, as when Steele, while inexplicably holding up a flag recovered from the World Trade Center, invited his soldiers to think of themselves not as "sheepdog" protectors but as wolf-like predators: "'Men, it is time to go hunting. You're the hunter. You're the predator. You're looking for the prey.'" Khatchadourian. For Hitler's invocation of wolves, see Ehrenreich, *Blood Rites*, 267.

In another indication of the blurring lines between war and crime, or at least between the military and policing, Grossman has become, in his post-military career, one of the leading police trainers in the United States. He is a proponent of what critics have called "warrior policing," instructing trainees with messages such as: "'We are at war. And our cops are the frontline troops in that war...It's your job to put a piece of steel in your fist and kill those sons of bitches when they come to kill our kids...Cops fight violence. What do they fight it with? Superior violence." Eells.

Surprisingly, Grossman's *On Killing*, originally published in 1995, continues to be frequently cited in reputable scholarship as a source on the psychology of killing. From a sociological perspective, the book might be seen as a kind of map of the contemporary right-wing authoritarian American mind, from the book's early, nostalgic imagining of a patriarchal rural American past; to the book's references to recurring objects of right-wing moral panic, including satanic murders, pornography, snuff films, rampant unrecognized child sexual abuse, and violent video games; to the book's concluding section, which blames violent video games for America's violent crime rate—despite the fact that violent crime began rising in the 1960s (before video games), then fell in the 1990s (despite the popularity of violent video games), and despite the fact that Europeans also consume violent video games but have far lower homicide rates. Grossman, *On Killing*, xxvii–xxix, 33, 137, 212,

303–36. Ignoring the fact that Timothy McVeigh was inspired to bomb the Oklahoma City federal building by *The Turner Diaries*, a white supremacist novel in which terrorist acts spark a race war, Grossman attributes McVeigh's bombing to a "new cult of vengeance" popularized by movies such as *Dirty Harry*. Grossman, 324–25; see Belew, *Bring the War Home*, 110, 210. Far from being a traditional work of social science, *On Killing* in many ways resembles a right-wing American jeremiad, from the introductory ode to the men who "stood shoulder to shoulder with Crockett and Travis at the Alamo," enduring "great physical and psychological trauma and horror in order to give us our freedoms," to the ominous warning toward the end that "[w]e are most assuredly on the road to ruin, and we need desperately to find the road home from this dark and fearful place to which we have traveled." Grossman, xxxiv, 328. Yet according to Grossman, students have been assigned *On Killing* at the FBI and DEA Academies, West Point, and the Air Force NCO Academy, and the book has appeared on the Marine Corps Commandant's Required Reading List. Grossman, xv.

To be fair, Grossman's book is not the only mainstay of military reading lists that might be criticized for uncritically reflecting authoritarian values or lacking scholarly foundations. Another prominent example would be the amateur history of the Korean War by T.R. Fehrenbach, *This Kind of War* (Washington, D.C.: Brassey's, 1963). Fehrenbach's work has often been praised within the military as a reminder of the importance of military preparedness. As Secretary of State and retired General Colin Powell stated in a blurb for the 50th anniversary edition, the book "has been studied by two generations of soldiers," and it has been repeatedly included in professional military reading lists. One well-informed observer has stated that Fehrenbach's book was, along with Michael Shaara's *The Killer Angels* (New York: Ballantine Books, 1974) and Anton Myrer's *Once an Eagle*, one of the three books that "virtually every Army officer read" in the first decades after the Vietnam War. Major General Robert Scales, "O! The Damage 'Once an Eagle' Has Done to the Army," *Best Defense*, December 18, 2013.

From a contemporary perspective, Fehrenbach's book appears less as a pragmatic argument in favor of military preparedness, and more as a surprisingly racist tirade on behalf of the need for authoritarian leadership within the military. Not only does Fehrenbach offer frequent references to Korean "hordes," disgust toward "the underlying filth of the Orient," and asides such as a description of "half-wild Algerians, to whom no war was complete unless a little fun could be had out of it, too." Fehrenbach, *This Kind of War*, 98, 262. He also presents as a model of military leadership those American officers who, after the Civil War, "had driven the Indians without surcease, hammering them across the snows and mountains until their women sickened and their infants died." Fehrenbach, 302. Fehrenbach's celebrated critique of the lack of military preparedness before the Korean War focuses less on the military's failure to plan for a defense of Korea, prepare logistically, or effectively train soldiers, and more on the general lack of "discipline" in the wake of the Doolittle Board's attempt "to iron out the inequities of the so-called 'caste system' of the Army.'" Fehrenbach, 23, 291–98. Fehrenbach's central warning is against "the liberal society" of the United States destroying the military by causing it to acquiesce in "the liberal view of life" and "egalitarian" values. Fehrenbach, 292–93.

As for the 1,291-page *Once an Eagle*, its didacticism, sexism, and adherence to the conventions of conservative mid-twentieth-century popular fiction recently provoked a debate over whether it is, in the words of defense analyst Andrew Exum, "one of the worst novels ever written." Matt Gallagher, "In Defense of 'Once an Eagle,'" *Time: Battleland*, August 29, 2011. In terms of the categories of narrative discussed in this book, *Once an Eagle* is, above all, a fairly traditional soldier-as-hero story detailing the courageous exploits of the hero Sam Damon, although Damon echoes the idea of the soldier-as-victim in a concluding speech on the wastefulness of war. Myrer, *Once an Eagle*, 1158–73. The novel's ideological values may not be quite as authoritarian as, for example, those of the John Wayne film *The Green Berets*, also released in 1968, but a fan of the film would find very little to object to in Myrer's book. For a perceptive critique of *Once an Eagle*'s arguments regarding military leadership specifically, see Darrell Fawley III, "It's Time to Retire Sam Damon," *Modern War Institute*, August 20, 2021.

It is also easy to imagine troubling lessons being drawn from Shaara's nostalgic, sentimental portrayal of military heroism on both sides at the Battle of Gettysburg in *The Killer Angels*. Despite occasional references to the role of slavery in the Civil War as a topic of ideological dispute, the novel's narrative structure invites the reader to focus above all on the valor shared between the two sides rather than any moral differences. Without either endorsing or entirely rejecting Lost Cause mythology, the novel suggests that individual bravery and heroism in battle were the most morally salient features of the Civil War—not the fact that one side engaged in the mass killing of Americans on behalf of, in Alexander Stephens' words, the Confederacy's "corner-stone" principle "that the negro is not equal to the white man," and "that slavery, subordination to the superior race, is his natural and normal condition." Alexander H. Stephens, "Corner Stone Speech," March 21, 1861.

12. Harari assembles the scholarly criticisms of Fussell and concludes that "[i]t was only in the 1960s, due to the influence of the Vietnam War, of the fear

of nuclear war, and of the antiauthority youth culture, that the disillusioned interpretation of war in general and World War I in particular became the standard popular view." Harari, "Martial Illusions," 45–47. Similarly, Bourke describes the persistence of traditional patriotic and heroic war-ideals after World War I. Bourke, *Intimate History*, 5.

13. The video work of Pat Dollard provides an illustration, earlier and even more extreme than Kyle's memoir, of what a right-wing, enthusiastically pro-war artistic representation of the Iraq War might look like. Dollard, previously a Hollywood talent agent, collected video footage while embedded with the Marine Corps in 2004 and assembled it into a violent, hardcore punk-backed trailer for an unmade documentary. The trailer contains, among other things, "evidence of a possible war crime…a Marine clutches the head of a dead Iraqi and raises it in front of the camera like a jack-o'-lantern." In Dollard's words, "'[t]he message of my movie is simple: If you're a young person in America, the coolest, fucking most badass and most noble thing you can be today is a combat Marine.'" Dollard received praise from Ann Coulter and other right-wing media, as well as "even more enthusiastic" support "from soldiers and their family members." Evan Wright, "Pat Dollard's War on Hollywood," *Vanity Fair*, March 20, 2008.
14. A broader critique of modern attempts to revive the values of pre-modern aristocratic warrior cultures, from nineteenth-century reactionaries, through the fascists of the early twentieth century, to white nationalists in the present day, might note that such attempts rest on a misconception similar to the one that motivates some religious fundamentalists to defend their beliefs as "scientific." Just as the fundamentalist believes she is returning to the beliefs of the pre-modern faithful, but, in fact, by insisting that those beliefs are scientifically valid, asserts something that the pre-modern believers never could have intended, so the fascist may believe that he is simply returning to the values of warriors from an ancient past, when, in fact, he takes a very different position from them, because the archaic warriors never asserted that war violence is honorable and glorious under contemporary political, economic, and cultural conditions. On fundamentalism, see generally Gregory Brazeal, "Between Description and Prescription: Law, Wittgenstein, and Constitutional Faith," *West Virginia Law Review* 120 (2017), 363, 369–77. On the anachronism of ancient warrior values under changed historical circumstances, see Constant, "The Spirit of Conquest," and the discussion of Constant in Hans Sluga, *Politics and the Search for the Common Good* (Cambridge: Cambridge University Press, 2014), 74–85. On the contemporary American Right's increasing proximity to fascist thought, see Damon Linker,

"Opinion: Get to Know the Influential Conservative Intellectuals Who Help Explain G.O.P. Extremism," *New York Times*, November 4, 2023. For example, the widely read and discussed Costin Alamariu, a former student of the Straussian philosopher and Yale professor Steven B. Smith, has declared: "'I believe in fascism...I believe in rule by a military caste of men who would be able to guide society toward a morality of eugenics.'" Linker, "Get to Know."

15. Buchanan, *Going Scapegoat*, 3–4. The continuing acceptance of derogatory "cowboys and Indians" rhetoric is particularly jarring in light of the fact that "American Indians, proportionally, provide more soldiers to America's wars than any other demographic group in the country." Junger, *Tribe*, 118. It is no coincidence that two of the foundational novels in the contemporary canon of Native American literature, N. Scott Momaday's *House Made of Dawn* (New York: HarperCollins, 1968) and Leslie Marmon Silko's *Ceremony*, deal with the experiences of Native American veterans returning from World War II. Recent research has also emphasized that the assimilationist Native American boarding school system, in which many Native children were "forcibly removed from their homes," stripped of their tribal culture, and subjected to "beatings, malnutrition, hard labor, and other forms of neglect and abuse," "molded Native children to feed into the American military." Zach Levitt, Yuliya Parshina-Kottas, Simon Romero, and Tim Wallace, "War Against the Children," *New York Times*, August 30, 2023.

    Other examples of the abuse of Native American symbols by the Navy SEALs, specifically, appear in Matthew Cole's research into alleged war crimes by SEAL Team Six. Cole reports that one team, "known as the Redmen, employed a Native American warrior as a mascot." After completing a year of service, members received custom-made hatchets "stamped with a Native American warrior in a headdress and crossed tomahawks." The hatchets were eventually used "to hack dead and dying militants." Since the creation of the team in 1980, many operators were described as having "experienced a 'metamorphosis of identity and persona' into Native American warriors." Matthew Cole, "The Crimes of SEAL Team 6," *Intercept*, January 10, 2017.

16. Two of the classic studies of Vietnam War literature dedicate lengthy sections to the centrality of John Wayne in mid-twentieth-century American war culture. Tobey C. Herzog, *Vietnam War Stories: Innocence Lost* (London: Routledge, 1992), 16–24; Kinney, *Friendly Fire*, 11–42. Allan Dwan, dir., *Sands of Iwo Jima* (Los Angeles: Republic Pictures, 1950), seems to have been particularly influential. Vietnam veteran Ron Kovic describes crying as a boy after watching John Wayne "charge up the hill and get killed just before he reached the top" in *Sands of Iwo Jima*. Kovic, *Born on the Fourth of July*,

69–70. In another of the most widely read Vietnam War memoirs, Philip Caputo similarly describes enlisting in the Marines because "I saw myself charging up some distant beachhead, like John Wayne in *Sands of Iwo Jima*." Philip Caputo, *A Rumor of War* (1977; 40th anniv. ed., New York: Picador, 1996), 6. Gustav Hasford, author of *The Short-Timers* (New York: Harper and Row, 1979), the basis for Stanley Kubrick, dir., *Full Metal Jacket* (Burbank, CA: Warner Bros. Pictures, 1987), likewise writes: "When we were kids and John Wayne charged up Suribachi, he was 40 feet high on the screen and tromping on wicked Orientals, a big white Godzilla, a hero of Homeric proportions, a *winner*." Gustav Hasford, "Vietnam Means Never Having to Say You're Sorry," *Penthouse*, June 1987, reprinted at GustavHasford.com. "In 1961, by one survey, 50 percent of Marines at Camp Pendleton had joined the Corps after watching *The Sands of Iwo Jima*." Van Creveld, *The Culture of War*, 314.

17. Howard Hawks, dir. *Rio Bravo* (Burbank, CA: Warner Bros., 1959).
18. Du Mez, *Jesus and John Wayne*, 57.
19. Bourke, *Intimate History*, 14. "If an evangelical could be defined as anyone who liked Billy Graham, by the 1970s a conservative might well be defined as anyone who loved John Wayne." Du Mez, *Jesus and John Wayne*, 54. More recently, the militant Christian films of Mel Gibson have attracted similar devotion. Du Mez, 210–11.
20. For prominent defenses of the corporal punishment of children in contemporary evangelical Christian culture, including in the writings of James Dobson, see Du Mez, *Jesus and John Wayne*, 53–54, 74–87, 97. Social scientists often use questions about childrearing values as a measure of authoritarian predisposition. See, for example, Karen Stenner, *The Authoritarian Dynamic* (Cambridge: Cambridge University Press, 2005), 23. For the possible influence of family organization and operation on ideological preferences regarding authoritarianism and hierarchy in the broader social world, see Henrich, *WEIRDest*, 282–83.
21. Schmidle, "In the Crosshairs."
22. See, for example, Shay, *Achilles in Vietnam*, 9.
23. According to a recent history, warbands "sometimes included a few women," like the pregnant Freydis from the Vinland sagas, who scares away Indigenous attackers by slapping her breast with a sword. Valerie Hansen, *The Year 1000* (New York: Penguin Books, 2020), 6, 24–25, 39.
24. Bourke, *Intimate History*, 1–31. Expressions of pleasure in killing are not difficult to find in the interdisciplinary literature on violence. Examples can even be found in non-state societies. When asked about warfare, for example, an Enga horticulturalist in the New Guinea highlands told an anthropologist: "'This

is what our forefathers said: When a man was killed, the clan of the killers sang songs of bravery and victory. They would shout Auu! ('Hurray!' or 'Well done!') to announce the death of an enemy.'" Wrangham, *Goodness Paradox*, 257. Michael Herr describes a photographer colleague's disbelief when asked to create a book that would "take the glamour out of war." "I mean, how the bloody hell can you do *that*? Go and take the glamour out of a Huey...Can *you* take the glamour out of a Cobra...?" Herr, *Dispatches* (New York: Knopf, 1977), 248. Similarly, Karl Marlantes tries to evoke "the transcendental realm one reaches through violence" by inviting the reader to imagine being a platoon commander who is "twenty-one or twenty-two" and feels "immortal," with command over dozens of "lean hard bodies" "all with automatic rifles, rockets, and grenades," as well as machine guns and "the power to call in jet aircraft that...can spew jellied fire" or to order "artillery with shells as thick as your waist." Marlantes, *What It Is Like*, 67. More recently, then-LTG James Mattis provoked controversy in 2005 when he explained during a panel discussion that "[i]t's a hell of a hoot" and "fun to shoot some people." "General: It's 'Fun to Shoot Some People'," *CNN*, February 4, 2005. The journalist Sebastian Junger has described combat as "insanely exciting." "[F]or a nineteen-year-old at the working end of a .50 cal during a firefight that everyone comes out of okay, war is life multiplied by some number that no one has ever heard of." Sebastian Junger, *War* (New York: Twelve, 2010), 144–47. For a general exploration of the "enduring attraction of war," and especially its power to "give us purpose, meaning, a reason for living," see Chris Hedges, *War Is a Force That Gives Us Meaning* (New York: PublicAffairs, 2002), 3. For an especially enthusiastic account of "the joy of combat" by a leading military historian, former instructor at various U.S. military institutions, and unabashed reactionary militarist, see Van Creveld, *The Culture of War*, 106–28.

25. Fleck, *Handbook*, 82–83.
26. Fleck, 37.
27. See, for example, Andrew Gelman, Jeffrey Fagan, and Alex Kiss, "An Analysis of the New York City Police Department's 'Stop-and-Frisk' Policy in the Context of Claims of Racial Bias," *Journal of the American Statistical Association* 102, no. 479 (2007): 813.
28. *Floyd v. City of New York*, 959 F. Supp. 2d 540 (2013). Full disclosure: I served as a clerk for Judge Shira Scheindlin in the United States District Court for the Southern District of New York in 2012–2013.
29. Across its 377 pages, *American Sniper* contains no humanizing, individual portraits of Iraqis. Not a single Iraqi person is quoted as speaking in the book, so far as I am aware. Few are even named, other than an insurgent sniper named

Mustafa (139). Even the Iraqi vice president whom Kyle briefly escorts receives no name (182–84). Instead, Iraqis appear almost entirely as a faceless enemy. They sometimes multiply like monstrous hordes from a fantasy movie: "I started killing a lot of Iraqis—we all were—but for everyone we shot, four or five seemed to materialize to take their place" (89). "As the nights went on, I realized the number of insurgents was growing" (176). They are aggressive, barely human "savages" (4, 219).

Sometimes Kyle follows the usual tropes of dehumanization and presents his enemies in Iraq as an infestation of rodents: "You push the rats from one hole and they congregate in the next" (142). "Ramadi was infested with insurgents" (270). The troops hope "to catch the insurgents before they could slide back into whatever sewer they'd emerged from" (235). At other times, enemies are represented as an almost inanimate force: "[a] flood of bad guys came at us" (264); "piles of insurgents littering the road" (268). "We were slaughtering the enemy...[O]ur kill total [was] becoming astronomical..." (297). Like emissions of fluid, insurgents who run out of the backs of buildings are "squirters" (293), a term that comes up repeatedly in combat veteran accounts of the Iraq War. At still other times, Kyle discusses insurgents in the language of game-hunting: "[W]e bagged them" (271). Kyle also describes the Iraqi men who work with the United States as effeminate and not real men. They have "high-pitched screams" (66) and wear "long man-jammies and scarves" (243).

Of Islam in general, Kyle has nothing positive to say. In a subsection titled "EVIL," he begins by observing: "I had never known that much about Islam...I knew about the Crusades, and I knew that there had been fighting and atrocities forever. But I also knew that Christianity had evolved from the Middle Ages. We don't kill people because they're a different religion" (86). Kyle, of course, tattooed his arm with a Crusader's cross in the color of blood (219), and later chose a logo for his tactical training company consisting of a Punisher skull with a Crusader cross in one eye, alongside the motto: "Despite what your mama told you...violence does solve problems" (366). After an Iraqi woman accuses Kyle of shooting her husband for carrying a Koran, the shot is investigated and Kyle admits exclaiming in a heated moment: "I don't shoot people with Korans—I'd like to, but I don't" (199). The clearest illustration of Kyle's anti-cosmopolitan, militant Christian nationalism may come in his dismissal of Iraqi elections: "I never really believed the Iraqis would turn the country into a truly functioning democracy...But I didn't risk my life to bring democracy to Iraq. I risked my life for my buddies, to protect my friends and fellow countrymen...I never once fought for the Iraqis. I could give a flying fuck about them" (194).

For a critical cultural history of contemporary white American evangelical Christianity and its ties to militarism, nationalism, and white supremacy, see Du Mez, *Jesus and John Wayne*. On the role of dehumanization in colonialism, see Said, *Orientalism*, 251–52. For social science research on dehumanization or "pseudospeciation" and its prevalence in violent conflict, see Sapolsky, *Behave*, 412, 570; Shay, *Achilles in Vietnam*, 103–19. Bourke presents the depersonalization of the enemy as one of four especially common rationalizations of killing in combat, along with obeying orders, reciprocity and revenge, and the analogy to sports and especially hunting. Bourke, *Intimate History*, 213, 219–21. As described in this chapter, Kyle's memoir draws on each of the four rationalizations.

30. Journalist David Philipps states that after investigations of Kyle's shots in Ramadi, the Army "had enough doubts" about the justifications for the shots "that it shut Kyle's whole platoon down for the rest of the deployment." David Philipps, *Alpha: Eddie Gallagher and the War for the Soul of the Navy SEALS* (New York: Crown, 2021), 85–86.
31. See, for example, Gabriel Chin and Scott Wells, "The 'Blue Wall of Silence' as Evidence of Bias and Motive to Lie: A New Approach to Police Perjury," *University of Pittsburgh Law Review* 59 (1998): 233; Joseph Goldstein, "'Testilying' by Police: A Stubborn Problem," *New York Times*, March 18, 2018; Christopher Slobogin, "Testilying: Police Perjury and What to Do About It," *University of Colorado Law Review* 67 (1996): 1037. Philipps describes the intense culture of loyalty within the SEALs. Philipps, *Alpha*, 80–85. For example, "Demo Dick" Marcinko, the founding commander of SEAL Team Six, told the unit in an introductory address that "'[t]his command...will be like a friggin' Mafia...And you never talk family business outside the family.'" Philipps, 80–81. Marcinko would later be criminally convicted and incarcerated for a kickback scheme. Philipps, 83.

    Incidentally, the figure of the whistleblower may deserve some mention in a study of contemporary war culture like the present one. The representation of whistleblowers as heroes is a relatively new and still contested cultural development. From a moral perspective that places a greater value on loyalty and obedience to authority than the avoidance of cruelty, the whistleblower may seem less like a figure of virtue and more like a traitor, someone who betrayed "us" by exposing "our" wrongdoing toward "them." But from a more morally cosmopolitan perspective that places less emphasis on the lines between in-group and out-group, the whistleblower who exposes harms against others may seem deserving of praise. For a rare, ambivalent portrayal of a minor act of whistleblowing in the Iraq War, further muddied by the whistleblower's sense that his motives were not pure, see John Crawford, *The Last True Story I'll Ever Tell: An Accidental Soldier's Account of the War in Iraq* (New York: Riverhead Books, 2005), 56–58.

Whistleblowers have appeared as heroic subjects in a number of popular films inspired by current events, including Sidney Lumet, dir., *Serpico* (Hollywood, CA: Paramount Pictures, 1973); Michael Mann, dir., *The Insider* (Burbank, CA: Touchstone Pictures, 1999); and Brian De Palma, dir., *Casualties of War* (Culver City, CA: Columbia Pictures, 1989), a fictionalized portrayal of the incident on Hill 192, which earlier served as the basis for Michael Verhoeven, dir., *o.k.* (1970); and Elia Kazan, dir., *The Visitors* (Beverly Hills, CA: United Artists, 1972). Two of the most well-known whistleblowers of the post-9/11 era have also been the subject of films: Oliver Stone, dir., *Snowden* (Beverly Hills, CA: Endgame Entertainment, 2016); Tina Satter, *Reality* (New York: Seaview Productions, 2023).

By contrast, so far as I am aware, the military has never publicly celebrated the moral righteousness of whistleblowers in the way that it routinely celebrates those who excel at inflicting violence. There are no military installations or buildings named after, for example, Hugh Thompson Jr. or Ronald Ridenhour, who interrupted and exposed, respectively, the My Lai massacre; Robert Storeby, who exposed the incident on Hill 192; Joseph Darby, who exposed the torture at Abu Ghraib; or Ian Fishback, whose protests, as noted earlier, led to legislation prohibiting detainee abuses.

32. Dave Philipps, "Navy SEALs Were Warned Against Reporting Their Chief for War Crimes," *New York Times*, April 23, 2019. For a book-length account of Gallagher's case, see Philipps, *Alpha*.

More generally, the SEALs have struggled in recent years with a series of scandals and a perception of flamboyant publicity-seeking, contrary to the restrained, quiet professionalism depicted in fictional works such as Lea Carpenter's admiring novel *Eleven Days*. For example, in an article on the rampant abuse of performance-enhancing drugs at the SEAL training course, BUD/S, one former SEAL states that an "often heard unofficial adage in the SEALs holds that, 'if you ain't cheating, you ain't trying.'" Dave Philipps, "Death in Navy SEAL Training Exposes a Culture of Brutality, Cheating and Drugs," *New York Times*, September 5, 2022. Other recent scandals included an alleged sexual assault, positive tests for cocaine use, and murder charges after an apparent hazing incident. Dan Lamothe, "Navy SEALs Kicked Out of Iraq for Drinking Alcohol after Reported Sexual Assault, Officials Say," *Washington Post*, July 25, 2019. For additional allegations of "unjustified killings, mutilations, and other atrocities," as well as an account of the public dispute between SEALs over who killed Osama bin Laden, see Cole, "Crimes of SEAL Team 6"; Matthew Cole, "SEAL Team 6 Responds to the Intercept's Investigation of Its War Crimes," *Intercept*, January 18, 2017. Cole has since developed his reporting on SEAL Team Six into a book, *Code over Country*.

Other prominent SEAL veterans who have generated negative news coverage in recent years include Eric Greitens, who was forced to resign as the governor of Missouri after allegedly blackmailing and sexually coercing a woman during an affair; Carl Higbie, a Trump appointee who resigned after recordings emerged in which he expressed his dislike for Muslims and gays, argued that African-American women believe "breeding is a form of government employment," called for the murder of undocumented immigrants, and dismissed soldiers with PTSD as lying or having "a weak mind"; Erik Prince, the founder of Blackwater, a military contractor whose employees were responsible for, among other things, the massacre of seventeen Iraqi civilians in Nisour Square in 2007; Tim Sheehy, who stated during his Senate campaign that he lied to a federal law enforcement officer about having accidentally shot himself; and Ryan Zinke, a congressional representative from Montana who, as President Trump's Secretary of the Interior, was found to have repeatedly violated ethical rules and lied to investigators. See Matt Apuzzo, "Blackwater Guards Found Guilty in 2007 Iraq Killings," *New York Times*, October 22, 2014; Liz Goodwin, "Sheehy Apologized and Asked for Leniency after Alleged 2015 Gun Incident," *Washington Post*, April 17, 2024; Blake Hounshell, "Eric Greitens's Turbulent Political Career Stands on the Brink," *New York Times*, July 28, 2022; Andrew Kaczynski, "Trump Appointee Carl Higbie Resigns," *CNN*, January 19, 2018; Lisa Rein and Anna Phillips, "Ex-Interior Secretary Zinke Lied to Investigators in Casino Case, Watchdog Finds," *Washington Post*, August 24, 2022.

In a chapter on the history of the SEALs, Philipps locates Eddie Gallagher as "part of an unsanctioned subculture in the SEALs that prized killing above nearly everything else," a culture of "pirates," in contrast to the "'boy scouts,' who saw law and order as vital both to the mission and to the brotherhood's soul." Both the pirates and the boy scouts existed within the SEALs' broader culture of "independence and unconventional thinking," including "a certain admiration for outsmarting the military bureaucracy." Philipps, *Alpha*, 68, 72, 78. Philipps describes the human and moral consequences of the pirate culture. In Vietnam, for example, the SEALs routinely carried out kidnappings and assassinations without accountability and based on intelligence that was "often suspect." Philipps, 74–75. A Vietnam veteran SEAL memoir described the theft of money, the taking of body parts as trophies, and setting booby-traps that could kill children. Philipps, 75–76. Bourke mentions a SEAL veteran who carried out illegal operations in Cambodia and later described being "frequently ordered to massacre women and children." Bourke, *Intimate Killing*, 211. In the war in Iraq, SEALs participated in the CIA torture at Abu Ghraib and "began shooting enemy fighters through the top of the head in a way that split the skull open," a practice they called "'canoeing.'" Philipps, 84–85.

33. Gidget Fuentes, "A Jekyll and Hyde Portrait Emerges of the SEAL Accused of Murdering an Islamic State Prisoner," *Navy Times*, November 15, 2018 (internal quotation marks omitted).
34. Although a panel of officers ultimately found that the botched prosecution in Gallagher's case had failed to prove beyond a reasonable doubt that Gallagher murdered the detainee, such a verdict obviously does not imply that Gallagher was in fact innocent of the crime. Among other things, "a key witness changed his story on the stand to favor Chief Gallagher." Dave Philipps, "Navy SEAL Chief Accused of War Crimes Is Found Not Guilty of Murder," *New York Times*, July 2, 2019.
35. Philipps, "Navy SEALs Were Warned."
36. Dave Philipps, "Anguish and Anger from the Navy SEALs Who Turned in Edward Gallagher," *New York Times*, December 27, 2019.
37. Philipps, "Navy SEALs Were Warned."
38. Philipps, "Not Guilty." One of Gallagher's most vocal congressional defenders was Republican Representative Duncan Hunter, who served as a marine in Iraq and later served time in federal prison for stealing campaign funds. Hunter appeared to admit to a war crime of his own by arguing Gallagher "did one bad thing that I'm guilty of, too—taking a picture with a body...A lot of my peers, a lot of them, did the same thing." Dave Philipps, "Judge Removes Prosecutor in Navy SEAL's War Crimes Court-Martial," *New York Times*, June 3, 2019.
39. Philipps, "Not Guilty"; "Mukasey: Waterboarding Is Not Torture," *CNN*, December 11, 2014. Kerik also served a brief, confident, apparently incompetent role in the Iraq War. Chandrasekaran, *Imperial Life in the Emerald City*, 95–103.
40. Dave Philipps, "Trump May Be Preparing Pardons for Servicemen Accused of War Crimes," *New York Times*, May 18, 2019.
41. Dave Philipps, "Trump Clears Three Service Members in War Crimes Cases," *New York Times*, November 22, 2019.
42. Further support for the conclusion that soldiers in Iraq were unlikely to report other soldiers for violations of the ROEs is not difficult to find. With

regard to the Navy SEALs specifically, a previous footnote already noted reporting on alleged unpunished war crimes by members of SEAL Team Six.

43. Kyle also describes committing a wide variety of crimes out of uniform, including in a series of bar fights and arrests that testify to the extraordinary lenience elite servicemembers receive in the American criminal justice system (54, 203, 327–28). As Kyle observes, "[y]ou always have team guys getting in trouble during off-time and training. Bar fights are a big problem" (218). In a subsection titled "FIGHTS AND MORE FIGHTS," Kyle proudly notes that "[f]ighting is a fact of life when you're a SEAL. I've been in a few good ones" (310). Because all the assault charges against Kyle for his bar fights and rioting are eventually dropped, the episodes are presented, without shame, as a series of harmless adventures (315).

A particularly clear illustration of the difference between Kyle's perspective on his apparent crimes and the view that might have come out in a criminal prosecution can be found in Kyle's brief reference to a drunken collision after his retirement from the Navy. Kyle notes that at the time, "drinking was all I did" (369). "[O]ne night I turned a corner too fast in my truck," and "[a]ll I know is I totaled my truck and came out without a scratch" (370). Kyle's posthumous *New Yorker* profile provides details that his own account does not:

> Just before 2 A.M. on March 5, 2010, Kyle was driving alone in central Dallas, near Love Field, when he lost control of his truck and crashed into a wooden fence, nearly ending up in someone's swimming pool. A policeman found Kyle with "bloodshot eyes, slurred speech, breath smelling of alcoholic beverage, unsteady balance and nystagmus." Kyle told him, "I'm stupid. I was drinking and driving. I missed the turn. It was my fault." The officer arrested him, on a D.W.I. charge. Kyle slept in jail until the morning, when he was released. A judge later dismissed the charges.

The criminal justice system once again imposed no penalty on Kyle, presumably because of his elite military service. By contrast, when Eddie Ray Routh was arrested for drunk driving, "no judge dismissed the charges; he was found guilty and held on a fifteen-hundred-dollar bond. Unable to pay, he served a thirty-day jail sentence." Schmidle, "In the Crosshairs."

44. "[A]s a rule movable property of private persons may not be confiscated." Fleck, *Handbook*, 293.

45. Apparently as a result of Kyle's use of the Punisher skull, it "gained increased currency among police unions, gun-loving militiamen, and neo-Nazis." Sam

Thielman, "How Do You Stop the Far-Right Using the Punisher Skull? Make It a Black Lives Matter Symbol," *Guardian*, June 11, 2020.

CHAPTER NINE

1. Roy Scranton, "Back to Baghdad: Life in the City of Doom," *Rolling Stone*, July 17, 2014. By contrast, the biographical blurb on the back cover of *War Porn* notably makes no mention of Scranton's military service, describing only the author's literary and academic credentials.
2. Roy Scranton and Jake Siegel, "In 'Fire And Forget,' Vets Turned Writers Tell Their War Stories," interview by Terry Gross, *Fresh Air*, NPR, November 11, 2013. In the interview, Siegel is presented as the co-editor of *Fire and Forget*. The 2013 paperback of *Fire and Forget*, however, lists fellow Iraq War veteran novelist Matt Gallagher as Scranton's co-editor, although it contains a story by Siegel.
3. Scranton, "Back to Baghdad." The quotations in the following paragraphs also come from this article.
4. In comparing his service in the Iraq War to participation in a criminal conspiracy, Scranton echoes a remarkable anti-war speech and book produced in the 1930s by a retired Marine Corps major general who came to believe that his service (which extended across multiple continents, from China to Mexico and Central America to Haiti and the Dominican Republic to Europe) had been a "racket" for the benefit of bankers, industrialists, and speculators. See Smedley D. Butler, *War Is a Racket* (New York: Round Table Press, 1935). Earlier, Butler had also testified that he had been approached by a conspiracy of business leaders who were attempting to set up a fascist dictatorship in the United States. Jonathan M. Katz, *Gangsters of Capitalism: Smedley Butler, the Marines, and the Making and Breaking of America's Empire* (New York: St. Martin's Griffin, 2021).
5. @RoyScranton, June 18, 2019.
6. It is often unclear which character is speaking some of the most bigoted lines (for example, 50, 86–87, 271–72). SPC Wilson also casually mocks "retards" on more than one occasion (for example, 272).
7. Aaron's linguistic tics, such as the use of the terms "groks" (303) and "aces" (301), hint at a background outside of the punk scene or the military. "Grok" is a neologism invented by the science fiction writer Robert Heinlein in *Stranger in a Strange Land* (New York: G.P. Putnam's Sons, 1961). It entered countercultural usage in the 1960s—again, suggesting an affinity with hippie rather than punk culture. "Aces" is a slang term from the 1950s that it is difficult to imagine many punks or soldiers using as Aaron does, even sarcastically.

8. The postmodernist theorist Jean Baudrillard's work looms in the background of *War Porn*. Baudrillard defined pornography in terms of its transparency, declaring that "[t]he illusion of desire has been lost in the ambient pornography," that "[i]n porn, nothing is left to desire," and that "we have moved into...the transparency of sex, with signs and images erasing all its secrets and ambiguity." Jean Baudrillard, "The Conspiracy of Art," in *The Conspiracy of Art*, trans. Ames Hodges (New York: Semiotext(e): 2005), 15. Baudrillard also infamously interpreted the Gulf War through his theories of simulation, simulacra, and the hyperreal, concluding, in a play on the title of Jean Giraudoux's *The Trojan War Will Not Take Place*, that "the Gulf War did not take place." Jean Baudrillard, *The Gulf War Did Not Take Place*, trans. Paul Patton (Bloomington: Indiana University Press, 1995). In addition, Baudrillard wrote a well-known 2004 essay titled "War Porn" on the violence of the Iraq War. Jean Baudrillard, "War Porn," *Journal of Visual Culture* 5, no. 1 (2006): 86.
9. It is typical of the cultural shifts toward moral cosmopolitanism described throughout this book that in the latest trilogy of Star Wars movies, there is, for the first time, a stormtrooper, Finn, who is given a human face, an individual story, and the capacity for heroism. J.J. Abrams, dir., *Star Wars: The Force Awakens* (San Francisco, CA: Lucasfilm Ltd., 2015). But it remains the case, obviously, that the film does not celebrate as heroes those stormtroopers who continue to serve the evil First Order.
10. Roy Scranton, "The Trauma Hero and the Lost War: World War II, American Literature, and the Politics of Trauma, 1945–1975" (PhD diss., Princeton University, 2016), 89–107. Scranton subsequently adapted the dissertation into a book. Roy Scranton, *Total Mobilization: World War II and American Literature* (Chicago: University of Chicago Press, 2019).
11. James Campbell, "Combat Gnosticism: The Ideology of First World War Poetry Criticism," *New Literary History* 30, no. 1 (Winter 1999): 203.
12. Harari, *Ultimate Experience*, 125, 145, 299.
13. Harari, 240.
14. Harari, 15.
15. Harari, 304.
16. Harari, 17.
17. Roy Scranton, "Opinion: 'Star Wars' and the Fantasy of American Violence," *New York Times*, July 2, 2016.
18. Scranton, "Fantasy."
19. Scranton, *Total Mobilization*, 222.
20. Scranton, "Fantasy."
21. Scranton, "Back to Baghdad."

22. Scranton and Siegel, "Vets Turned Writers."
23. Roy Scranton, *Learning to Die in the Anthropocene: Reflections on the End of a Civilization* (San Francisco: City Lights, 2015); Roy Scranton, *We're Doomed. Now What? Essays on War and Climate Change* (New York: Soho Press, 2018). Scranton's second novel, *I Heart Oklahoma!* (New York: Soho Press, 2019), appears to extend his earlier works' fascination with extreme violence and destruction. The back cover describes the novel as moving "from our bleeding-edge present to a furious Faulknerian retelling of the Charlie Starkweather killings in the 1950s, capturing in its fragmented, mesmerizing form the violence at the heart of the American dream."
24. Ernst Jünger, *Storm of Steel*, trans. Michael Hofmann (New York: Penguin Books, 2003); Friedrich Nietzsche, *On the Genealogy of Morals*, trans. Walter Kaufmann (New York: Vintage Books, 1967) [1887]; Schmitt, *The Concept of the Political*. For an analysis of changes in Western cultural attitudes toward violence over the course of modernity, including the illiberal "revolt against the primacy of life" in writers such as De Maistre, Nietzsche, and Bataille, see Taylor, *A Secular Age*, 319, 369–74, 635, 646–75.
25. Frantz Fanon, *The Wretched of the Earth*, trans. Richard Philcox (New York: Grove Press, 2004); Jean-Paul Sartre, "Preface," in Fanon, *Wretched*, xliii; Georges Sorel, *Reflections on Violence*, trans. T.E. Hulme (New York: Dover Publications, 2004). For a critical account of Fanon's political commitments in practice, see Kwame Anthony Appiah, "Liberation Psychology," *New York Review of Books*, February 24, 2022.
26. Hannah Arendt, *On Violence* (Orlando, FL: Harcourt, 1970), 56.
27. Elaine Scarry, *The Body in Pain: The Making and Unmaking of the World* (Oxford: Oxford University Press, 1985), 4.
28. The critic Emily Nussbaum has discussed the phenomenon of the "bad fan," who views criminal antiheroes as heroes and cheers on their criminality and violence. Emily Nussbaum, "The Great Divide," *New Yorker*, March 31, 2014. As in the disclaimer at the start of "All in the Family" noted by Nussbaum, there is a long tradition of the producers of potentially voyeuristic materials attempting to protest the purity of their intentions, from Samuel Richardson's *Pamela*, whose full title states that it is being published "in order to cultivate the principles of virtue and religion in the minds of the youth of both sexes"; to the expressions of intended moral edification appearing in seduction novels during the early American republic; to the message placed before the pre-code gangster movie *Scarface*, stating that the picture is "an indictment of gang rule in America." Howard Hawks, dir., *Scarface* (Beverly Hills,

CA: United Artists, 1932); Hunt, *Inventing Human Rights*, 53; Gordon Wood, *Empire of Liberty: A History of the Early Republic, 1789–1815* (Oxford: Oxford University Press, 2009), 566. Of course, not all creators of stories that present wrongdoers as heroes, or at least antiheroes, are "of the Devil's party without knowing it." An equally long tradition has recognized that, in the words of Jean Genet, "[t]here is no allure like that of an outlaw," or as Walter Benjamin wrote, "the figure of the 'great' criminal, however repellent his ends may have been," has often "aroused the secret admiration of the public." Jean Genet, "The Criminal Child," in *The Criminal Child: Selected Essays*, trans. Charlotte Mandell and Jeffrey Zuckerman (New York: New York Review Books, 2020), 15; Walter Benjamin, "Critique of Violence," in *Reflections: Essays, Aphorisms, Autobiographical Writings* (Boston: Mariner, 2019), 295.

29. Bourke, *Intimate History*, xvi.

CHAPTER TEN

1. Senator Bob Kerrey, who served in Vietnam as a 25-year-old lieutenant in the Navy SEALs, quoted in Gregory L. Vistica, "One Awful Night in Thanh Phong," *New York Times*, April 25, 2001. See also Amy Waldman, "Bob Kerrey Reveals His Role in Deaths of Vietnam Civilians," *New York Times*, April 25, 2001. Kerrey spoke these words during a discussion of a mission in which "around midnight on Feb. 25, 1969, Kerrey and his men killed at least 13 unarmed women and children." Vistica, "One Awful Night." According to one account, Kerrey's SEALs murdered a sleeping elderly couple and their three children with knives in order to prevent them from making noise, then murdered another group of about a dozen women and children with machine guns. Then the unit covered up their murders. Philipps, *Alpha*, 77. For an alternative account emphasizing factual and moral ambiguity, see Shay, *Odysseus in America*, 110–12.
2. Quantitative evidence of the prevalence of unreported misconduct would of course be particularly difficult to find. In a 2006 Army Surgeon General's office survey of soldiers and marines in Iraq, "about two-thirds of Marines and half the Army troops surveyed said they would not report a team member for mistreating a civilian or for destroying civilian property unnecessarily." Moreover, "[t]en percent said they had personally mistreated non-combatants. 'Less than half of soldiers and Marines believed that non-combatants should be treated with dignity and respect,' the report stated." Thomas E. Ricks, *The Gamble: General David Petraeus and the American Military Adventure in Iraq,*

2006–2008 (New York: Penguin Press, 2009), 7. In the survey, "10 percent of soldiers and marines acknowledged...that they 'modified' their ROE [rules of engagement] in order 'to accomplish the mission.'" Wood, *What Have We Done*, 85. Interestingly, the survey responses from Iraq are similar to the responses in a study of Vietnam veterans: "about 20 percent of the men admitted to having witnessed atrocities during their tour of duty in Vietnam, and another 9 percent acknowledged personally committing atrocities." Herman, *Trauma and Recovery*, 79.

3. Mayer, *Dark Side*, 238–60. Someone later took a photo of "American soldiers giddily cavorting over" Jamadi's corpse. Mayer, 259.

   Despite the Senate Intelligence Committee's extensive report on CIA torture in 2012, no CIA employees were ever prosecuted. Gina Haspel, who oversaw a secret CIA prison in Thailand where detainees were tortured and played a central role in the destruction of videotaped evidence of CIA torture in 2005, became the director of the CIA under President Trump. Adam Goldman, "Gina Haspel, Trump's Choice for C.I.A., Played Role in Torture Program," *New York Times*, March 13, 2018. The Obama administration's decision not to prosecute anyone at the CIA for torture was based on the recommendation of then-Assistant U.S. Attorney John Durham, who would later conduct a widely criticized four-year investigation that attempted, unsuccessfully, to prove President Trump's claims of political persecution by the FBI. Department of Justice, "Statement of Attorney General Eric Holder on Closure of Investigation into the Interrogation of Certain Detainees"; Charlie Savage, "After Years of Political Hype, the Durham Inquiry Failed to Deliver," *New York Times*, May 17, 2023. For a critical account of atrocities, incompetence, and subsequent cover-ups throughout the history of the CIA, see Tim Weiner, *Legacy of Ashes: The History of the CIA* (New York: Doubleday, 2007). For a heroic portrayal of the Senate torture investigation, see Scott Z. Burns, dir., *The Report* (Brooklyn, NY: Vice Studios, 2019).

   Within the military, multiple investigations of detainee abuses in Iraq eventually led to a large number of low-ranking enlisted soldiers being convicted of various crimes but generally receiving short or no sentences. The investigations were often conducted so as to exclude accountability for high-ranking officers. Only one officer was ever charged, and his sole conviction was eventually dismissed. Wood, *What Have We Done*, 67–68; Mayer, 334. Filmmakers continue to memorialize the military's detainee abuses. Notable recent examples include the portrayal of torture at Guantánamo Bay in Kevin Macdonald, dir., *The Mauritanian* (Santa Monica, CA: 30West, 2021), and the portrayal of torture at Abu Ghraib prison in Paul Schrader, dir., *The Card Counter* (Universal City, CA: Focus Features, 2021).

The civilian Bush administration officials who bore the greatest responsibility for creating the conditions for detainee abuses after 9/11, and in some cases directly authorized torture, including Vice President Dick Cheney, Defense Secretary Donald Rumsfeld, and Deputy Assistant Attorney General John Yoo, also were never prosecuted. Mayer, 306. For a concise account of Yoo's violation of professional legal norms in his 2002 memos authorizing torture, see Brooks, *How Everything Became War*, 197–203. Yoo, a former clerk to Supreme Court Justice Clarence Thomas, remains a professor at the U.C. Berkeley School of Law.

In comparison to the lack of consequences for the Bush administration officials whose decisions authorized torture, soldiers who objected to detainee abuses sometimes received punishment. For example, Alyssa Peterson, an intelligence specialist with the 101st Airborne Division who refused on principle to participate in detainee interrogations after her first two nights interrogating caged detainees in Tal Afar in 2003, was reprimanded for her "empathy" and placed on guard duty. She committed suicide later that year. Wood, 71–72.

4. Philip Zimbardo, *The Lucifer Effect: Understanding How Good People Turn Evil* (New York: Random House, 2007), 415–16.
5. To be clear, I do not mean to minimize the unintentional or mistaken killing of Iraqi civilians, or to exaggerate the constraints imposed by U.S. ROEs. The journalist David Wood, perhaps echoing the perceptions of soldiers he interviewed, states that the increasingly strict ROEs in Iraq and Afghanistan "sometimes put soldiers in the dangerous position of trying to determine if some guy down the alley at dusk was holding a weapon in a threatening manner or just carrying it home, whether his intent was 'hostile'...For an American soldier, guessing wrong could mean court-martial. Or death." Wood, *What Have We Done*, 84; see also Wood, 195–96. In fact, however, it is extremely difficult to find examples of soldiers being court-martialed for using force based on a good faith, arguably reasonable, but incorrect guess. Wood himself offers several examples of soldiers killing civilians based on mistaken judgments and facing no discipline. Wood, 85–87. His only examples of soldiers being prosecuted for killing Iraqis involve the premeditated murder of detainees whom the soldiers perceived as "insurgents," at a time when soldiers believed suspects who had attacked them were routinely being released to attack them again. Wood, 198–204. Even these cases hardly seem typical. One of the soldiers Wood describes, Mathew Golsteyn, was

later pardoned by President Trump. Wood, 199–200, 202–4; Dave Philipps, "Trump Clears Three Service Members in War Crimes Cases," *New York Times*, November 22, 2019.

On the contrary, there is a great deal of evidence that investigators often interpreted ROEs expansively and with great deference to the judgment of soldiers, similar to the deference that is routinely shown in domestic U.S. courts toward police when evaluating allegations of excessive force under the Fourth Amendment. See *Graham v. Connor*, 490 U.S. 386 (1989). In Erik Edstrom's memoir of his service in Afghanistan, he repeatedly emphasizes how the U.S. military went out of its way to avoid accepting or imposing responsibility for the unjustified killing of Afghans: "It's always a mistake, always the result of extenuating circumstances, and always excused." Edstrom, *Un-American*, 6. Edstrom describes being told in Afghanistan that he could avoid liability for the killing of a civilian by making sure to include in his sworn statement that he "'felt threatened'" and "'saw suspicious activity.'" Edstrom, 146. He also offers a concrete illustration of the military covering up the unjustified killing of civilians. One day, his unit came under attack and called in two Kiowa helicopters for support. When the Kiowas fired rockets into a nearby village, Edstrom assumed the helicopters "must have positively identified the armed fighters." Edstrom, 169. Later, he learned that the Kiowas had seen no weapons or fighters. But the battalion XO saw three dead civilians on a video feed. Rather than recategorizing the dead civilians as "enemy KIA," as one of the pilots proposed, the Army simply reported the "Battle Damage" as "UNKNOWN." Edstrom, 171. In disgust, Edstrom decided to "blow the whistle" and request an immediate transfer. Edstrom, 177.

Edstrom also describes a soldier fatally shooting an unarmed Afghan man who, during the daytime, rolled up a plastic speed bump that had been recently laid down outside of the military's compound and tried to carry it away to his tractor. Not only was the soldier not investigated, but the killing was "printed as a military case study for others to read," an illustration of "a proportionate, textbook response to 'defend protective equipment.'" The case study was "handed out as learning materials across southern Afghanistan." Edstrom, *Un-American*, 185–86.

In the words of a marine sergeant who deployed to Iraq three times between 2003 and 2006, "'the Rules of Engagement changed frequently and were contradictory. When they were restrictive, they were loosely enforced. Shootings of civilians that were known were not reported because marines did not want to send their brothers-in-arms to prison when all they were trying to do was protect themselves in a situation they'd been forced into.'" Quoted in Meagher, *Killing from the Inside Out*, 135.

The events surrounding the notorious Haditha massacre support the marine sergeant's claim. On November 19, 2005, in Haditha, Iraq, marines intentionally killed multiple households of unarmed Iraqi civilians, including women, children, and an old man in a wheelchair. A one-year-old baby was also killed. A lance corporal would later defend his shooting of children because the house as a whole was "declared hostile." Ricks, *The Gamble*, 4. A corporal concluded, "'Personally, I think I did everything perfectly that day,'" because "'they were all insurgents.'" Ricks, 5. The next day, a marine spokesman offered an incorrect statement making no mention of the massacre of twenty-four civilians. Despite the mayor and town council of Haditha requesting an investigation, the military conducted no investigation of the incident until the newly arrived Army Lieutenant General Peter Chiarelli heard weeks later that reporters were asking questions about it. Multiple officers in the marines' chain of command viewed the events in Haditha as not unusual, "'nothing out of the ordinary...including the number of civilian dead.'" Ricks, 6.

Based on the investigation's findings that the killings in Haditha were indiscriminate, but that all levels of the marines' command viewed "'civilian casualties, even in significant numbers, as routine,'" Ricks, 7, it seems entirely plausible that other incidents similar to the massacre took place earlier without resulting in investigations. The Haditha massacre is thus another illustration of a general principle already suggested by the discussion of the scandals at Abu Ghraib and Mahmudiya in the introduction: when U.S. military atrocities come to public attention, they often do so only as a result of highly contingent events. Even then, the risk of court-martial, much less of serious punishment, may be exaggerated in the minds of soldiers. In the case of the Haditha massacre, for example, only one marine was convicted of a single count of negligent dereliction of duty, and he avoided prison. Charlie Savage and Elisabeth Bumiller, "An Iraqi Massacre, a Light Sentence and a Question of Military Justice," *New York Times*, January 27, 2012.For the purposes of this chapter, however, the question is not whether U.S. forces carried out atrocities in Iraq, but whether atrocities were more common in Iraq than in Vietnam.

6. Zimbardo, *Lucifer Effect*, 373. "Only one soldier was found guilty for these crimes, Lieutenant William Calley, Jr." President Nixon intervened to prevent his transfer to prison, and Calley "returned to his community to become a paid after-dinner speaker and honored businessman." Zimbardo, 373–74.

Calley "was extremely popular in the South," and the Louisiana senator Allen Ellender stated that "'[t]he villagers got what they deserved.'" Grandin, *End of the Myth*, 210, 328.

7. Moyn, *Humane*, 182–83; Turse, *Kill Anything That Moves*, 238–39. The role of atrocities in the CIA's Phoenix Program has also been documented. Turse, *Kill Anything that Moves*, 189–91.
8. Daniel Denvir, "The Secret History of the Vietnam War," *Vice*, April 17, 2013. The journalist who uncovered the study, Nick Turse, notes that "[t]he files also contained 500 allegations" that were not substantiated, some of which have subsequently been proven, such as the massacre of civilians by the 101st Airborne Division's Tiger Force, "which would be confirmed and made public only in 2003." He also learned through interviews with veterans mentioned in the files "how incomplete" the archives were. Nick Turse, *Kill Anything That Moves*, 14–15, 17.
9. Turse, *Kill Anything That Moves*, 4, 108–9, 192, 258; Walzer, *Just and Unjust Wars*, 188–95; Tirman, *The Deaths of Others*, 237.
10. Denvir, "Secret History." On the dehumanizing effect of the "body count" in Vietnam, see Bourke, *Intimate History*, 220–21. The signs of dehumanization in writings on the Vietnam War often seem to go beyond what one finds in writings on the Iraq War, such as in references to a "'mere gook rule' which declared that killing a Vietnamese civilian did not really count." Grossman, *On Killing*, 190.
11. See Denvir, "Secret History"; Morris, "By Force of Arms," 655.
12. Frederick, *Black Hearts*, xx.

    How common was substance abuse by U.S. troops in Iraq?

    Writings about the Iraq War suggest that drinking and drug use were common in some places at some times, but rare in many others. For examples of widespread substance abuse in non-fiction about the Iraq War, see Frederick; Packer, *Assassin's Gate*, 247. In fiction, see Phil Klay, *Redeployment* (New York: Penguin, 2014), 129; Walker, *Cherry*, 155. For examples of Iraq War fiction that do not portray widespread substance abuse, see Gallagher, *Youngblood*; Pitre, *Fives and Twenty-Fives*, 23, 199; Robinson and Kovite, *War of the Encyclopaedists*; Scranton, *War Porn*; Van Reet, *Spoils*. A recent history of drug use in war claims, without support, that "[i]n general, soldiers on missions in Afghanistan and Iraq drank both excessively and frequently." Lukasz Kamienski, *Shooting Up: A Short History of Drugs and War* (Oxford: Oxford University Press, 2016), 27, 282–84. Upon reading these words, Gallagher, the author of *Youngblood*, "wondered what Iraq War I'd spent 15 months in. Did some soldiers and Marines strike up bargains for whiskey with townspeople, or have their spouses ship them tequila in empty shampoo bottles? Of course. But my Iraq, and the one of most of my peers, was as dry as a Baptist grandmother's cabinet." Matt Gallagher, "Shooting Up: How War and Drugs Go Together," *The Intercept*, March 26, 2016. Various fictional works and memoirs describe soldiers and contractors receiving small quantities of disguised liquor in the mail. See, for example, Fair, *Consequence*, 180; Kovac, *The Surge*, 89. Bryan Castner describes Special Forces troops obtaining beer and sharing it. Castner, *The Long Walk: A Story of War and the Life That Follows* (New York: Anchor Books, 2012), 216.

Setting aside alcohol, the abuse of prescription drugs by soldiers in Iraq seems to have been more serious and more common than the abuse of street drugs. Kamienski describes soldiers receiving "bags of antidepressants and sleeping meds in Iraq," and a black market for Valium and steroids emerging. Kamienski, *Shooting Up*, 283. Matt Young described receiving steroids in the mail from Japan. Young, *Eat the Apple*, 222–25. In his memoir, the Iraq War veteran John Crawford describes occasionally obtaining a bottle of Turkish whiskey, and once participating in the theft of beer from Iraqis, but also regularly taking Valium, becoming addicted, and going through withdrawal after his return. Crawford, *The Last True Story I'll Ever Tell*, 218.

Of course, there are many works of fiction that describe veterans suffering from substance abuse problems after their return from Iraq, including nearly all of the works discussed in this book. For a list of fictional works dealing with veteran substance abuse that also includes veterans from the war in Afghanistan, see David F. Eisler, *Writing Wars*, 126. Among works not addressed in this book, Eisler cites Stephen Markley, *Ohio* (New York: Simon & Schuster, 2018) and Jesse Goolsby, *I'd Walk with My Friends If I Could Find Them* (Boston: Houghton Mifflin Harcourt, 2015).

In any case, consistent with Frederick's claim, the sporadic abuse of drugs and alcohol by misbehaving soldiers or mismanaged units in Iraq is very unlike the routine, pervasive drinking, marijuana, and later opiate abuse, as well as sex with prostitutes, described throughout Vietnam War literature and documented in surveys and other research. See, for example, Larry Heinemann, *Close Quarters* (New York: Farrar, Straus and Giroux, 1977); Kamienski, *Shooting Up*, 187–217.

13. Herr, *Dispatches*, 39, 198. On the other hand, although *Dispatches* is usually categorized as non-fiction, Herr has acknowledged that "[a] lot of [the book] is fictional." Paul Ciotti, "Michael Herr: A Man of Few Words," *L.A. Times*, April 15, 1990.
14. Shay, *Achilles in Vietnam*, 31.

15. We have already seen fictional representations of the killing of civilians at checkpoints in Iraq, often with impunity, in *The Yellow Birds* and several other works noted throughout this book. The journalist George Packer suggests that such killings were common and rarely investigated, much less prosecuted. He writes: "Far too many Iraqis, sometimes families with children, went down in a hail of gunfire when they failed to understand the bewildering array of signs and hand signals and orders shouted in English." Yet "[n]o one knows how many Iraqis have died in such situations, because the American military makes a point of not keeping track of civilian deaths and conducting investigations only under extraordinary pressure." Packer, *Assassin's Gate*, 235–36. See also Tirman, *Deaths of Others*, 330.
16. On the uncounted civilian victims of U.S. airstrikes in Iraq, see Azmat Khan and Anand Gopal, "The Uncounted," *New York Times*, November 16, 2017.
17. Iraq veteran Tyler Boudreau persuasively defends a similar conclusion after describing the testimony at the Iraq War-era Winter Soldier investigation presented by the Iraq Veterans Against the War in 2008. Boudreau, *Packing Inferno*, 92–93.
18. "Vietnam War," in *Encyclopedia of American War Literature*, eds. Philip K. Jason and Mark A. Graves (Westport, CT: Greenwood Press, 2000), 350, citing John Newman, *Vietnam War Literature: Annotated Bibliography* (3rd ed. 1995).
19. Philip K. Jason, "Introduction," in *Fourteen Landing Zones: Approaches to Vietnam War Literature*, ed. Philip K. Jason (Iowa City: University of Iowa Press, 1991), ix, xv. Similarly, Haytock notes that in Vietnam War literature, "literary representations of the soldier persistently delve into criminality and trauma." Jennifer Haytock, "Representing Soldiers," in *War and American Literature*, ed. Haytock, 42, 52.
20. Mark A. Heberle, "Vietnam Fictions," in *The Edinburgh Companion to Twentieth-Century British and American War Literature*, eds. Adam Piette and Mark Rawlinson (Edinburgh: Edinburgh University Press, 2012), 205, 208.
21. Kinney, *Friendly Fire*, 4.
22. Kinney, 6.
23. Harari, *Ultimate Experience*, 189.
24. Robin Moore, *The Green Berets* (New York: Crown Publishing Group, 1965); John Wayne and Ray Kellogg, dirs., *The Green Berets* (Burbank, CA: Warner Bros., 1968); Walter Hölbling, "Literary Sense-Making: American Vietnam Fiction," in *Vietnam Images: War and Representation*, eds. Jeffrey Walsh and James Aulich (New York: Macmillan, 1989), 123; Jerome Klinkowitz, "Writing under Fire: Postmodern Fiction and the Vietnam War," in *Postmodern*

Fiction: A Bio-Bibliographical Guide, ed. Larry McCaffery (Westport, CT: Greenwood Press, 1986), 79, 81.

25. Hölbling, "Literary Sense-Making," 123.
26. For example, John Cassidy, *A Station in the Delta* (New York: Ballantine Books, 1979).
27. James Webb, *Fields of Fire* (New York: Bantam Books, 1978). In film, a comparable work would be John Irvin, dir., *Hamburger Hill* (Los Angeles, CA: RKO Pictures, 1987). Although the movie apparently intends to shock the viewer with its graphic violence, it ultimately offers a somewhat nostalgic portrait of U.S. military heroism and self-sacrifice, in part by choosing to focus on a battle where the enemy was clearly defined. The only notable killing of a Vietnamese civilian in the film results early on from an indiscriminate Communist attack, and is followed by a lingering shot of the dead Vietnamese woman's child cradling her.
28. Webb, *Fields of Fire*, 447–48.
29. Although Webb would eventually become a Democratic senator from Virginia, in the later 1970s he was seen as a bombastic conservative among veteran writers. In that period, he published an essay called "Why Women Can't Fight" and told an interviewer that he "'wouldn't go across the street to watch [Jane Fonda] slit her own wrist.'" Matt Gallagher, "The Forever War over War Literature," *New Republic*, July 17, 2020.
30. Heinemann, *Close Quarters*.
31. Even *Apocalypse Now*, a relatively early Vietnam War film that explicitly addresses themes of U.S. criminality, adopts a highly ambiguous perspective on that criminality. Francis Ford Coppola, dir., *Apocalypse Now* (Beverly Hills, CA: United Artists, 1979). On the one hand, the film portrays the war as a senseless, extravagantly wasteful spectacle, and it depicts an American soldier, CPT Willard, murdering an injured Vietnamese woman.

    On the other hand, CPT Willard is one of the protagonists of the film, not its villain. If anything, the film seems to promote the idea that ordinary morality must be suspended in war. The plot suggests that Marlon Brando's rogue COL Kurtz has grasped a secret, dark truth that the narrow-minded military and political establishment refuses to accept: namely, that the United States could win in Vietnam if only it were willing to commit more atrocities. The first time we hear Kurtz's voice, during an intercepted radio broadcast, he argues as much, praising enemy soldiers who hacked off children's polio-inoculated arms: "These men...were filled with love...but they had the strength...to do that. If I had ten divisions of those men, our troubles here would be over very quickly." The rest of the film, far from showing that Kurtz is "insane" as his establishment accusers claim, suggests that Kurtz is correct and that it is the establishment that has failed to understand the dark truth of war. In further support of COL Kurtz's insights, Martin Sheen's CPT Willard later discovers that Kurtz's illegal assassinations of three Vietnamese men and one woman were effective. As CPT Willard states in voiceover, "[e]nemy activity in his old sector dropped off to nothing. Guess he must have hit the right four people." The movie presents a more critical view of those who accuse Kurtz of murder than of Kurtz for having engaged in murder. Ultimately, CPT Willard kills COL Kurtz, purging his forbidden wisdom through an act of sacrificial violence.

In other words, *Apocalypse Now*, despite its anti-war reputation, is effectively a narrative defense of the apparently perennial idea that Dick Cheney expressed on September 16, 2001 when he stated that the United States would have to work on "the dark side" in order to defeat its enemies. The idea that a lawless enemy can only be defeated by "taking the gloves off" and lifting legal or moral constraints on violence recurs frequently in counterinsurgency, no matter how often theorists argue that atrocities may, perversely, strengthen insurgents by increasing their support. A movie that reflects the insights of mainstream counterinsurgency theory is not *Apocalypse Now* but Gillo Pontecorvo, dir., *The Battle of Algiers* (Los Angeles: Allied Artists, 1966), in which French paratroopers win the battle but lose the war by engaging in torture and other tactics that alienate the Algerian population.

The aesthetic choices in *Apocalypse Now*, including the diagetic use of Wagner's "Ride of the Valkyries" in the helicopter attack scene, also have the obvious effect of glamorizing war. At the start of his Gulf War memoir, marine veteran Anthony Swofford describes his platoon gearing up for deployment by watching *Apocalypse Now* and other Vietnam War films, which are "all pro-war, no matter what the supposed message," because "[f]ilmic images of death and carnage are pornography for the military man." Anthony Swofford, *Jarhead: A Marine's Chronicle of the Gulf War and Other Battles* (New York: Scribner, 2003), 2–3. The defense of atrocity in *Apocalypse Now* may be less surprising when one considers that the original script was written by John Milius, who would go on to write and direct the nationalist-militarist fantasy *Red Dawn* (Beverly Hills, CA: United Artists, 1984), as well as *Conan the Barbarian* (Universal City, CA: Universal Pictures, 1982), a celebration of violence in which Arnold Schwarzenegger, in his first line, echoes words sometimes ascribed to Genghis Khan, declaring that what is best in life is to "crush your enemies, see them driven before you, and to hear the lamentations of their women."

32. See, for example, Helen Benedict's *Sand Queen* and Roy Scranton's *War Porn*, discussed in Chapters 7 and 9 above, as well as Benjamin Buchholz's *One Hundred and One Nights* (New York: Little, Brown, 2011), Pitre's *Fives and Twenty-Fives*, Whitney Terrell's *The Good Lieutenant* (New York: Farrar, Straus and Giroux, 2016), and Van Reet's *Spoils*. There are also several stories written from Iraqi or Afghan points of view in Katey Schultz, *Flashes of War* (Baltimore: Apprentice House, 2013), 3, 17, 23, 25, 27, 87, 91, 121, 141. For an analysis of the juxtaposition of Iraqi and Afghan voices with American voices in *Sand Queen*, *Fives and Twenty-Fives*, and Joydeep Roy-Bhattachary's *The Watch* (London: Hogarth, 2012), see Jennifer Haytock, "Reframing War Stories: Multivoiced Novels of the Wars in Iraq and Afghanistan," *Modern Fiction Studies* 63 (2017), 336, 337–38. Like *The Watch*, Elliot Ackerman's *Green on Blue* (New York: Scribner, 2015) is another early novel by an American author about the war in Afghanistan featuring an Afghan narrator. But while *The Watch* features both Afghan and American narration, the sole narrator of Ackerman's novel is an Afghan boy.
33. Robert Olen Butler offers particularly detailed representations of Vietnamese culture in *The Alleys of Eden* (New York: Henry Holt and Company, 1981), although he does not attempt to write from a first-person Vietnamese perspective in that work. As Jennifer Haytock notes in her introduction to Vietnam War literature, "much American literature ignores the experience of the Vietnamese, not only the enemy but also civilians and South Vietnamese soldiers fighting alongside Americans." Haytock, *Routledge Introduction*, 124–25.
34. Heberle, "Vietnam Fictions," 210. Heberle adds: "Fiction focused on Vietnamese figures...is often stereotypically sexist and racist, treating even friendly Vietnamese with indifference, bewilderment, condescension, contempt or hatred." Heberle, 211.
35. For a particularly celebrated example of a Vietnam War novel addressing the traumas of homecoming, see Larry Heinemann, *Paco's Story* (Farrar, Straus and Giroux, 1986), which notoriously won the 1987 National Book Award instead of Toni Morrison's *Beloved*.
36. For the distinction between generational cohort effects, life-cycle effects, and period effects in the analysis of changes in public opinion, see Inglehart, *Cultural Evolution*, 23, 27.
37. "One of the most pervasive concepts in social science is that one's basic personality structure crystallizes by the time one reaches adulthood. Considerable evidence indicates that people's basic values are largely fixed when they reach adulthood, and change relatively little thereafter." Inglehart, 15.

38. Pynchon, *Gravity's Rainbow*. See James Dawes, "The American War Novel," in *The Cambridge Companion to the Literature of World War II*, ed. Marina MacKay (Cambridge: Cambridge University Press, 2009), 56, 62, 64.
39. Viet Thanh Nguyen, *The Sympathizer* (New York: Grove Press, 2015).
40. Nguyen, born in 1971, belongs to the outer edge of the generational "cohort" that produced the American literature of the Iraq War.
41. Viet Thanh Nguyen, "Opinion: Bob Kerrey and the 'American Tragedy' of Vietnam," *New York Times*, June 20, 2016.
42. In a recent work dedicated entirely to the analysis of works written during the earliest years of the life-cycle of World War II literature, between 1939 and 1941, James Heffernan argues for the distinctive qualities of what he calls "punctual literature." James A.W. Heffernan, *Politics and Literature at the Dawn of World War II* (London: Bloomsbury Academic, 2023), 8.
43. Jones describes how the men of C-for-Charlie company "boisterously desecrated" Japanese corpses. Jones, *The Thin Red Line*, 73.
44. James Jones, *From Here to Eternity* (New York: Charles Scribner's Sons, 1951).
45. Oliver Stone, dir., *Platoon* (Los Angeles: Orion Pictures, 1986); Oliver Stone, dir., *Heaven & Earth* (Burbank, CA: Warner Bros., 1993); Le Ly Hayslip, *When Heaven and Earth Changed Places: A Vietnamese Woman's Journey from War to Peace* (New York: Doubleday, 1989).
46. O'Brien depicts, among other things, the gratuitous killing of water buffalo and dogs, and the burning of a village. Tim O'Brien, *Going After Cacciato* (New York: Broadway Books, 1978), 50–52, 77–79, 177, 253–54, 260–65, 270–71, 276–77.
47. Tim O'Brien, *In the Lake of the Woods* (Boston: Houghton Mifflin, 1994). Of course, it is possible to find counterexamples to the life-cycle trend described here. For example, it has already been noted that the 1990s witnessed a resurgence of celebrations of heroic U.S. military service in World War II, such as Brokaw's *The Greatest Generation*, and Steven Spielberg, dir., *Saving Private Ryan* (Universal City, CA: DreamWorks Pictures, 1998). It might be noted, however, that these works were in some ways less crudely heroic than World War II films from earlier decades such as *Sands of Iwo Jima*, noted above. The popularity of these works in the 1990s might also be attributed to a period effect that outweighed the ongoing life-cycle effect, with the period being defined by celebratory nationalist enthusiasm in the wake of the fall of the Berlin Wall, the disintegration of the Soviet Union, the U.S. victory in the Gulf War, and a booming domestic economy.
48. Robert Altman, dir., *M*A*S*H* (Los Angeles: 20th Century Fox, 1970). Something similar might be argued about Kurt Vonnegut's *Slaughterhouse-Five*.

Vonnegut was born in 1922, in the same generational cohort as Altman, and it would be difficult to argue that by 1969, when the novel was published, American culture had experienced a dramatic shift toward concern for the German victims of Allied bombing in World War II (a "life-cycle" effect). But it is very plausible to view the novel as shaped by the "period" effect of anti-war culture during the Vietnam era—an influence driven home by the novel's inclusion of numerous references to the Vietnam War and the late 1960s. See Vonnegut, *Slaughterhouse-Five*, 31, 76, 151, 242, 268. If American war literature is to be periodized, it probably makes more sense to group *Slaughterhouse-Five* with other war literature of the Vietnam era than it does to place the novel alongside, for example, *The Naked and the Dead* or *The Thin Red Line*.

Clint Eastwood's release of *Letters from Iwo Jima* (Burbank, CA: Warner Bros., 2006), a Japanese-language portrayal of the Battle of Iwo Jima from Japanese points of view, alongside *Flags of Our Fathers* (Burbank, CA: Warner Bros., 2006), which focuses on American perspectives, could also be seen as an illustration of a "period effect." *Letters* arguably reflects the growing contemporary tendency to incorporate non-American perspectives into representations of wars that decades earlier tended to be represented only from the American side. Similarly, and in anecdotal support of this book's argument that the recent cultural shift toward a criminalized view of war resulted more from underlying changes in values than from any specific features of the post-9/11 wars, at least two Hollywood comedies released in the period just before 9/11 already featured plots that portrayed U.S. soldiers as literally criminals: Gregor Jordan, dir., *Buffalo Soldiers* (London: FilmFour, 2001), and David O. Russell, dir., *Three Kings* (Los Angeles, CA: Village Roadshow Pictures, 1999).

49. William March, *Company K* (Tuscaloosa: University of Alabama Press, 1989).
50. See, for example, March's presentation of an ordinary sergeant's account of pounding the face of a wounded German soldier "with the butt of my rifle until it was like jelly." March, 173. In another story, a veteran on death row for murdering a police officer describes being ordered during the war to murder several prisoners. March, 210.
51. James C. Scott, *Seeing Like a State: How Certain Schemes to Improve the Human Condition Have Failed* (New Haven, CT: Yale University Press, 1998), 355. Similarly, Sanford Levinson writes that one reason the Vietnam Memorial can be "so immensely moving," even to those who find the war itself indefensible, may be that the memorial "does not include any writing specifying the 'correct' political message." Sanford Levinson, *Written in Stone: Public Monuments in Changing Societies* (Durham, NC: Duke University Press, 1998), 106. Shay powerfully describes the experiences of veterans visiting

the wall. Shay, *Odysseus in America*, 164–79. To the extent that there is a cultural expectation that war memorials should celebrate soldiers as heroes, however, the lack of celebration in the Vietnam Memorial might itself be seen as conveying a message. Robert Harrison describes the memorial's "silent refusal to honor those who died in the Vietnam War...[proclaiming] its thousands of names (morally) unaccounted for, even as it accounts for every last one of them." Robert Pogue Harrison, *The Dominion of the Dead* (Chicago: University of Chicago Press, 2003), 140–41. Grossman, characteristically, expresses the traditional nationalist-militarist reaction to Maya Lin's memorial wall, describing it as a "'black gash of shame.'" Grossman, *On Killing*, 277.

52. Van Creveld, *The Culture of War*, 229–45.
53. Levinson, *Written in Stone*, 53. Levinson also notes, however, the existence of a German cemetery in Bitburg containing memorial tombstones of SS war criminals. President Reagan honored the cemetery with a visit in 1985.
54. Levinson, 56, quoting Robin W. Winks, "A Place for Liberty Monument," *New Orleans Times Picayune*, August 17, 1992, B7.
55. Again, I leave aside the planned Global War on Terrorism memorial, for the reasons stated in Chapter 1. I also reiterate that my goal in this work is not to evaluate whether the narratives of soldier criminality in Iraq War fiction are just. For the reasons stated in Chapter 1, in the footnote discussing moral injury, I suspect that justice might demand a more holistic assessment of responsibility than an individualistic, decontextualized, retributivist understanding of "criminality" can provide.

APPENDIX

1. Buchholz, *One Hundred and One Nights*. Peter Molin notes that "[a]s far as I can tell," Buchholz's novel is "the first novel about war in Iraq written by a US military veteran." Peter Molin, "War Fiction: Benjamin Buchholz's One Hundred and One Nights," *Time Now* (blog), November 3, 2019. In a "Reading Group Guide" after the end of his novel, Buchholz explicitly invokes "empathy" as his justification for writing from an Iraqi perspective. Buchholz, *One Hundred and One Nights*, appendix 5.
2. Ackerman, *Green on Blue*. In Molin's 2020 list, Ackerman's novel is the first about the war in Afghanistan that is identified as having been written by a veteran. Molin, "Iraq and Afghanistan War Fiction, Poetry, and Film 2020." Ackerman later wrote a shorter and more traditional war novel, *Waiting for Eden*. Echoing the soldier-as-victim plot of *Johnny Got His Gun*, *Eden* features

a brain-damaged Iraq War veteran, Eden, who has suffered such serious wounds that he weighs only 70 pounds—"they've cut all of him off up to the torso"—and cannot move or speak. Ackerman, *Waiting for Eden*, 4, 16, 86–87. But *Eden*, unlike *Johnny*, conveys no outraged condemnation of the political decisions that resulted in the veteran's injuries. On the contrary, the novel is written from the unearthly perspective of a friendly ghost who celebrates Eden's toughness, for example in a scene depicting his training at SERE school, and focuses on themes of love rather than any observations that might provoke political discomfort. Ackerman, *Waiting for Eden*, 3–4, 73–78. In general, Ackerman's voluminous writings might be criticized for being ideologically sanitized, despite the fact that Ackerman himself seems to have participated in the kinds of morally difficult situations that play a central role in so many other authors' writings about the post-9/11 wars. For example, Ackerman has been identified as the assault force commander in a 2008 raid in Azizabad, Afghanistan, that resulted in the deaths of dozens of Afghan children. Brett Murphy, "Inside the U.S. Military's Raid against Its Own Security Guards That Left Dozens of Afghan Children Dead," *USA Today*, August 17, 2021.

3. Elliot Ackerman and James Stavridis, *2034: A Novel of the Next World War* (New York: Penguin Press, 2021); Elliot Ackerman and James Stavridis, *2054: A Novel* (New York: Penguin Press, 2024).
4. Brian Van Reet, *Spoils*, 51–52, 119–28, 201–2, 323.
5. For another work of fiction portraying the conflict between an authoritarian NCO and a more empathetic lieutenant, see Roman Skaskiw, "Television," in Scranton and Gallagher, *Fire and Forget*, 105–25. Skaskiw's story, which focuses on the lieutenant's efforts to speak to the family of a child who was shot by American soldiers, suggests a relatively underexplored narrative possibility in Iraq War fiction: the persuasive representation of American soldiers attempting to mitigate their harms to Iraqis.
6. Gallagher, *Youngblood*, 13, 90, 99, 323. The novel also describes the gory consequences of another platoon following the ROEs and shooting a car that fails to stop at a checkpoint. The occupants of the car turn out to be Iraqi civilians. Gallagher, 45–49. Outside of literature, the use of drop weapons by a group of Army soldiers who murdered Afghan civilians in 2010 and kept their body parts as trophies is described in Mark Boal, "The Kill Team: How U.S. Soldiers in Afghanistan Murdered Innocent Civilians," *Rolling Stone*, March 28, 2011. See also Edstrom, *Un-American*, 145. For a statement by a marine who deployed to Iraq three times and was encouraged to use drop weapons, and later drop shovels, see Meagher, *Killing from the Inside Out*, 135.

7. Abrams, *FOBBIT*, 111–14.
8. Abrams, 224–25.
9. Abrams, *Brave Deeds*, 37–38, 42–44, 101, 142, 182–83, 246.
10. Abrams, 99. Kevin Powers, the author of *The Yellow Birds*, also published another novel featuring Iraq War veterans, a thriller in which "an alleged videotape of a war crime" plays a central role. Stephen Amidon, "A Veteran's Latest Thriller Offers a Nuanced Look at the Toll of War," *Washington Post*, May 21, 2023, reviewing Kevin Powers, *A Line in the Sand* (New York: Little, Brown and Company, 2023).
11. Kovac, *The Surge*, 158–67, 170.
12. Kovac, 154.
13. Pitre, *Fives and Twenty-Fives*, 22–23, 206, 265.
14. Brandon Caro, *Old Silk Road* (New York: Post Hill Press, 2015). Caro, who served as a Navy corpsman in Afghanistan, has written about his own struggles with addiction. Brandon Caro, "The Specter of Addiction and Suicide among Veterans," *At War: Notes from the Front Lines*, October 23, 2015.
15. Caro, *Old Silk Road*, 260–73.
16. Young, *Eat the Apple*, 93–95.
17. Young, 95.
18. Young, 98.
19. Young, 99.
20. Young, 240. Although not a memoir, the journalist David Finkel's *The Good Soldiers* is a work of narrative non-fiction that follows a group of infantry soldiers deployed to Iraq as part of the 2007 "surge." The book primarily presents the soldiers as victims trapped in a futile, often brutal occupation. But it begins by emphasizing the traumatized guilt some soldiers experienced as a result of their violence toward Iraqis. One has "started dreaming about the people he had killed and wondering if God was going to ask him about the two who had been climbing a ladder." Another "started seeing himself shooting a man in the head, and then seeing the little girl who had just watched him shoot the man in the head, every time he shut his eyes." Finkel, *The Good Soldiers*, 1. Later, Finkel describes the mistaken American killing of several civilians, including two Reuters journalists, as captured in a video that would eventually attract international attention after being leaked to WikiLeaks by Chelsea Manning. Finkel, 105–14.
21. Edstrom, *Un-American*, 2.
22. Edstrom, 106–9.
23. Edstrom, 129 (italics removed). This is the same series of incidents mentioned above as an example of the use of "drop weapons."

24. Edstrom, 11. Edstrom also offers a particularly grisly example of a crime committed by a soldier after returning home. "One of my soldiers is serving life in prison after murdering and dismembering the body of someone whom he never knew, in a bathtub in Oregon." Edstrom, 4, 220.
25. Fair, *Consequence: A Memoir*, 5. For another example of an Iraq War memoir in which murky allegations of complicity in torture lead to a degree of moral anguish that seems greater than what similar allegations would likely have produced in the past, see Bill Russell Edmonds, *God Is Not Here: A Soldier's Struggle with Torture, Trauma, and the Moral Injuries of War* (New York: Pegasus Books, 2015).
26. Fair, *Consequence*, 122. Fair's self-condemnation also provides an occasion to note the diversity of ideological views that exist in the U.S. military. In contrast to Fair's perspective, a survey of soldiers and marines in Iraq conducted by the Army Surgeon General's office in 2006 found, according to a journalist's summary, that "one-third of its 1,767 respondents believed torture should be allowed if it helped gather important information about insurgents, and even more said they approved of such illegal abuse if they believed it would help save the life of a comrade." Ricks, *The Gamble*, 7.
27. For Caputo's less forceful articulation of a "need to atone…for the deaths I had caused," see Caputo, *A Rumor of War*, 330, 334. In addition to the killings that Caputo refers to in these pages, for which he received murder charges that were later dismissed, he describes his platoon rampaging through a village, burning huts and exploding buildings like "an incendiary mob"; a corporal murdering a wounded, unarmed Viet Cong; and another soldier murdering an old woman who accidentally spit betel-nut in his face. Caputo, *A Rumor of War*, 302, 311–12, 315–19. What may be the other most widely read memoir of U.S. military service in Vietnam, Kovic's *Born on the Fourth of July*, includes a detailed description of the accidental killing of an even larger number of Vietnamese civilians, all "[c]hildren and old men." Kovic, 210–17. Kovic's memoir is primarily about the victimization of U.S. servicemembers in the war—such as Kovic himself, who was paralyzed in combat—rather than being about U.S. wrongdoing toward the Vietnamese.
28. Crawford, *Last True Story*, 47–48.
29. Crawford, 95.
30. Crawford, 213.
31. Goodell and Hearn, *Shade It Black*, 21.
32. In an example of conduct that might be prosecuted in the military but that does not qualify as "criminal" in the sense relevant to this book, Castner is charged with disobeying orders and relieved of command one month into

his first deployment. But the disobedience was based on his well-meaning attempt to circumvent bureaucratic obstacles in a logistics matter involving the transport of broken EOD robots. Castner, *The Long Walk*, 36–37, 47–49.

33. Castner, *The Long Walk*, 148. By contrast, Brian Turner's essay-memoir *My Life as a Foreign Country*, rather than fixating on the morality of the Iraq War or his participation in it, is mostly dedicated to lyrical meditations on various personal experiences, such as how, when Turner visited a Dutch sex show on his way back to Iraq, he realized "that I carried a desire within me that was equal in measure to the floor show's gestures toward the infinite." Brian Turner, *My Life as a Foreign Country* (New York: W.W. Norton & Company, 2014), 126. But even Turner's book contains glimpses of moral disquiet, such as when an officer declares over the radio, "'You are authorized to shoot children,'" and another soldier confides to Turner, "'Dude. I don't think I can shoot children.'" Turner, *My Life*, 129.
34. Bellavia, *House to House*, 43. Toward the end of the memoir, however, Bellavia states that "God and I have had our heart-to-heart," and that he is "unapologetic" and "forever proud" of his war. Bellavia, 307–8.
35. Roxana Robinson, *Sparta* (New York: Picador, 2013), 80–82, 177, 234, 239, 318, 368, 375.
36. Robinson, *Sparta*, 380.
37. Whitney Terrell, *The Good Lieutenant*, 3–23, 48, 275.
38. Terrell, *Good Lieutenant*, 258–60.
39. Terrell, 275.
40. Atticus Lish, *Preparation for the Next Life* (New York: Tyrant Books, 2015), 56.
41. Lish, *Preparation*, 69. The preceding is only a selective catalogue of the novels and short stories about the Iraq War or with the Iraq War in the background that contain glimpses of murder, war crimes, fatal negligence, and innocent but needless killings. To close by noting a few final examples, Joyce Carol Oates' *Carthage* (New York: Ecco, 2014), 133–34, describes soldiers in Iraq committing various war crimes, such as taking body parts as trophies, including "[e]ntire faces sliced off though rarely in one piece." Hilary Plum's experimental *Strawberry Fields* (Albany: Fence Books, 2018), 217–20, contains within its collage of textual fragments references to atrocities such as the torture of detainees in Iraq. As noted earlier, many of the stories in Mogelson's *Heroic, Happy Dead* feature veterans who commit crimes after returning from their deployments. But there are also allusions to harms to Iraqis, such as an unspecified "debacle at the mosque" that made national news, and later the mistaken killing of an Iraqi child. George Saunders' mildly surreal short story "Home" describes the troubled homecoming of a disturbed veteran

who apparently participated in an atrocity in the mildly Iraqi-sounding city of "Al-Raz." George Saunders, "Home," *New Yorker*, June 6, 2011. Katey Schultz describes the accidental shooting of an Iraqi family at a checkpoint in "Checkpoint," in her *Flashes of War*, 83–86. In an indication of the prevalence of representations of civilian checkpoint shootings in Iraq War literature, a near-miss even appears in the most well-known graphic novel of the U.S. military experience in Iraq, Maximilian Uriarte's *The White Donkey: Terminal Lance* (New York: Hachette Book Group, 2016), 124. After deploying to Iraq as an infantry marine and then as a combat artist and combat photographer, Uriarte created a popular comic strip, *Terminal Lance*, which was published in the *Marine Corps Times* and thus, not surprisingly, did not generally focus on U.S. military criminality.

42. Lish, *Preparation*, 330.

Acknowledgments

One of my hopes when I began working on this book was to retroactively rationalize my working life up to that point, from literature to law to the military. Whether or not the project succeeded in that sense, it offers me an opportunity to thank some of the many people who helped along the way.

Above all, I thank the members of my PhD special committee—Dan Schwarz, Jason Frank, and Liz Anker—for welcoming me back to Ithaca after so much time away. I also thank Doug Mao and Jonathan Culler, who, along with Dan, were the members of my committee before I left Cornell the first time around.

For establishing the Cornell Prison Education Program, which offered me my first exposure to American mass incarceration and helped inspire my turn toward law school, thank you to Pete Wetherbee. Thank you to John Fitzpatrick of the Harvard Prison Legal Assistance Project for guidance as I first began representing incarcerated clients. For their support in my time as a public defender in Seattle, thank you to Marcus Naylor, Dillon Johnson, and the entire team at the Northwest Defenders Division. Above all, thank you to my students at Auburn Correctional Facility and my clients in Seattle.

Thank you to the many soldiers in the 6th LOD, 364th ESC, 377th TSC, 89th SB, and 22nd LOD who provided models of often unheralded service during my time in the Army Reserve JAG Corps. I am also deeply grateful to Bud Carpeneti, Shira Scheindlin, Daryl Levinson, and Martha

Minow for the advice and support that made it possible for me to find my dream job. Thank you to my students and colleagues at the University of South Dakota Law School. It is deeply rewarding to have the opportunity to introduce the next generation of South Dakota lawyers to the criminal law.

For feedback on earlier drafts and advice about academic publication, thank you to Eric Bennett, Jennifer Haytock, Peter Molin, and the two anonymous readers at Lever Press. Thank you to Sean Guynes and Lever Press for showing the world what an academic press should be.

I wish I could express my gratitude to several professors who influenced me and offered encouragement when I crossed paths with them: Gordon Baker, Michael Gearin-Tosh, Joel Porte, and Richard Rorty. Thank you also to the late John L'Heureux for his tolerance and wisdom. For exposing me as an undergraduate to ideas that continue to influence my thought, thank you to Joshua Landy and Thomas Sheehan. To my undergraduate advisor, Tobias Wolff, my gratitude is mixed with regret for not having asked more questions.

My greatest thanks go to my parents and to Taly, Dvora, and Tova, limitless sources of sunshine even in dark times.

Bibliography

Abrams, David. *Brave Deeds*. New York: Black Cat, 2017.

Abrams, David. *FOBBIT*. New York: Black Cat, 2012.

Ackerman, Elliot. *Green on Blue*. New York: Scribner, 2015.

Ackerman, Elliot. *Waiting for Eden*. New York: Vintage Books, 2018.

Ackerman, Elliot, and James Stavridis. *2034: A Novel of the Next World War*. New York: Penguin Press, 2021.

Ackerman, Elliot, and James Stavridis. *2054: A Novel*. New York: Penguin Press, 2024.

Adichie, Chimamanda Ngozi. *Half of a Yellow Sun*. New York: Knopf, 2006.

Aeschylus. *The Oresteia*. Translated by Hugh Lloyd-Jones. Oakland: University of California Press, 1979.

Ambrose, Stephen. *Band of Brothers*. New York: Touchstone, 1992.

Antoon, Sinan. *The Corpse Washer*. Translated by Sinan Antoon. New Haven, CT: Yale University Press, 2013.

Antoon, Sinan. "Embedded Poetry: Iraq; Through a Soldier's Binoculars." *Jadaliyya*, June 11, 2014.

Antoon, Sinan. "Opinion: Fifteen Years Ago, America Destroyed My Country." *New York Times*, March 18, 2018.

Arendt, Hannah. *On Violence*. Orlando, FL: Harcourt, 1970.

Aristophanes. *Lysistrata*. In Aristophanes, *Lysistrata and Other Plays*. Translated by Alan H. Sommerstein. New York: Penguin Books, 2003.

Arquilla, John. "The Big Kill." *Foreign Policy* (online), December 3, 2012.

Auden, W.H. "The Shield of Achilles." In W.H. Auden, *Collected Poems*. New York: Vintage International, 1991.

Avant, Deborah, and Renée de Nevers. "Military Contractors and the American Way of War." In The Modern American Military, edited by David M. Kennedy, 135–52. Oxford: Oxford University Press, 2013.

Bacevich, Andrew J. *America's War for the Greater Middle East: A Military History*. New York: Random House, 2016.

Bacevich, Andrew J. "I Lost My Son to a War I Oppose. We Were Both Doing Our Duty." *Washington Post*, May 27, 2007.

Bacevich, Andrew J. *The New American Militarism*, updated ed. Oxford: Oxford University Press, 2013.

Bacevich, Andrew, and Daniel A. Sjursen, eds. *Paths of Dissent: Soldiers Speak Out against America's Misguided Wars*. New York: Metropolitan Books, 2022.

Baker, Nicholson. *Checkpoint*. New York: Vintage, 2005.

Balko, Radley. *Rise of the Warrior Cop: The Militarization of America's Police Forces*. New York: Public Affairs, 2014.

Baudrillard, Jean. "The Conspiracy of Art." In *The Conspiracy of Art*, translated by Ames Hodges. New York: Semiotext(e), 2005.

Baudrillard, Jean. *The Gulf War Did Not Take Place*. Translated by Paul Patton. Bloomington: Indiana University Press, 1995.

Baudrillard, Jean. "War Porn." *Journal of Visual Culture* 5, no. 1 (2006): 86–88.

Belew, Kathleen. *Bring the War Home: The White Power Movement and Paramilitary America*. Cambridge, MA: Harvard University Press, 2018.

Bellavia, David. *House to House: A Soldier's Memoir*. New York: Free Press, 2007.

Benedict, Helen. *The Lonely Soldier: The Private War of Women Serving in Iraq*. Boston, MA: Beacon Press, 2009.

Benedict, Helen. "The Private War of Women Soldiers." *Salon*, March 7, 2007.

Benedict, Helen. *Sand Queen*. New York: Soho Press, 2011.

Benjamin, Walter. "Critique of Violence." In *Reflections: Essays, Aphorisms, Autobiographical Writings*. Boston: Mariner, 2019.

Bennett, Eric. *A Big Enough Lie*. Evanston, IL: TriQuarterly Books, 2015.

Bennett, Eric. *Workshops of Empire: Stegner, Engle, and American Creative Writing during the Cold War*. Iowa City: University of Iowa Press, 2015.

Beowulf: A New Verse Translation. Translated by Seamus Heaney. New York: Farrar, Straus, and Giroux, 1999.

Bierce, Ambrose. *Civil War Stories*. New York: Dover Publications, 1994.

Bird, Sheila M., and Clive B. Fairweather. "Military Fatality Rates (By Cause) in Afghanistan and Iraq: A Measure of Hostilities." *International Journal of Epidemiology* 36, no. 4 (2007): 841–46.

Blasim, Hassan. *The Corpse Exhibition and Other Stories of Iraq*. Translated by Jonathan Wright. New York: Penguin Books, 2014.

Boudreau, Tyler E. *Packing Inferno: The Unmaking of a Marine*. Port Townsend, WA: Feral House, 2008.

Bourke, Joanna. *An Intimate History of Killing: Face-to-face Killing in Twentieth-Century Warfare*. London: Granta, 1999.

Bourne, Randolph. *Untimely Papers*. New York: B.W. Huebsch, 1919.

Brant, George. *Grounded*. London: Oberon Books, 2013.

Brazeal, Gregory. "Between Description and Prescription: Law, Wittgenstein, and Constitutional Faith." *West Virginia Law Review* 120, no. 2 (2017): 363–426.

Brazeal, Gregory. "Bureaucracy and the U.S. Response to Mass Atrocity." *National Security and Armed Conflict Law Review* 1, no. 1 (2011): 57–71.

Brazeal, Gregory. "Justice Theater in the Criminal Law Curriculum." *Cardozo Law Review* (forthcoming).

Brazeal, Gregory. "Law, War, and Four Modes of Conflict." *Oregon Review of International Law* 20, no. 2 (2019): 531–81.

Brazeal, Gregory. "Markets as Legal Constructions." *University of Cincinnati Law Review* 91, no. 3 (2023): 595–679.

Brecht, Bertolt. *Mother Courage*. Translated by Eric Bentley. New York: Grove, 1991. First published in 1939.

Brokaw, Tom. *The Greatest Generation*. New York: Random House, 1998.

Brooks, Rosa. *How Everything Became War and the Military Became Everything*. New York: Simon & Schuster, 2016.

Brown University. Costs of War. https://watson.brown.edu/costsofwar/.

Brown, Wendy. *Undoing the Demos: Neoliberalism's Stealth Revolution*. Brooklyn, New York: Zone Books, 2015.

Brundage, W. Fitzhugh. *Civilizing Torture: An American Tradition*. Cambridge, MA: Harvard University Press, 2018.

Bruner, Jerome. *Acts of Meaning: Four Lectures on Mind and Culture*. Cambridge, MA: Harvard University Press, 1990.

Bruner, Jerome. *Actual Minds, Possible Worlds*. Cambridge, MA: Harvard University Press, 1987.

Bruner, Jerome. *Making Stories: Law, Literature, Life*. Cambridge, MA: Harvard University Press, 2002.

Buchanan, David A. *Going Scapegoat: Post-9/11 War Literature, Language and Culture*. Jefferson, NC: McFarland, Inc., 2016.

Buchholz, Benjamin. *One Hundred and One Nights*. New York: Little, Brown, 2011.

Büchner, Georg. *Woyzeck*. In Georg Büchner, *Complete Plays,* Lenz, *and Other Writings*. Translated by John Reddick. New York: Penguin Books, 1993.

Bull, Hedley. *The Anarchical Society: A Study of Order in World Politics*. 4th ed. New York: Columbia University Press, 2012.

Busch, Benjamin. *Dust to Dust: A Memoir*. New York: Ecco, 2012.
Butler, Judith. *The Force of Non-Violence: An Ethico-Political Bind*. London: Verso, 2020.
Butler, Judith. *Frames of War: When Is Life Grievable?* London: Verso, 2009.
Butler, Robert Olen. *The Alleys of Eden*. New York: Henry Holt and Company, 1981.
Butler, Smedley D. *War Is a Racket*. New York: Round Table Press, 1935.
Buzzell, Colby. *My War: Killing Time in Iraq*. New York: G.P. Putnam's Sons, 2005.
Cage, Caleb S. *War Narratives: Shaping Beliefs, Blurring Truths in the Middle East*. College Station: Texas A&M University Press, 2019.
Campbell, James. "Combat Gnosticism: The Ideology of First World War Poetry Criticism." *New Literary History* 30, no. 1 (Winter 1999): 203–15.
Caputo, Philip. *A Rumor of War*. 1977. 40th anniv. ed. New York: Picador, 1996.
Caro, Brandon. *Old Silk Road*. New York: Post Hill Press, 2015.
Carpenter, Lea. *Eleven Days*. New York: Vintage Contemporaries, 2013.
Carver, Raymond. "Errand." *New Yorker*, May 24, 1987.
Cassidy, John. *A Station in the Delta*. New York: Ballantine Books, 1979.
Castner, Brian. *The Long Walk: A Story of War and the Life That Follows*. New York: Anchor Books, 2012.
Chandrasekaran, Rajiv. *Imperial Life in the Emerald City: Inside Iraq's Green Zone*. New York: Vintage Books, 2007.
Cole, Matthew. *Code over Country: The Tragedy and Corruption of SEAL Team Six*. New York: Bold Type Books, 2022.
Cole, Matthew. "With Medal of Honor, SEAL Team 6 Rewards a Culture of War Crimes." *Intercept*, May 22, 2018.
Cole, Matthew, and Sheelagh McNeill. "'American Sniper' Chris Kyle Distorted His Military Record, Documents Show." *Intercept*, May 25, 2016.
Constant, Benjamin. "The Spirit of Conquest and Usurpation and Their Relation to European Civilization." In *Constant: Political Writings*, edited by Biancamaria Fontana, 44–169. Cambridge: Cambridge University Press, 2010.
Cowley, Malcolm. *The Literary Situation*. New York: Penguin Books, 1947.
Cozzens, James Gould. *Guard of Honor*. New York: Harcourt, Brace and Company, 1948.
Crane, Stephen. *The Red Badge of Courage*. New York: D. Appleton and Company, 1895.
Crawford, John. *The Last True Story I'll Ever Tell: An Accidental Soldier's Account of the War in Iraq*. New York: Riverhead Books, 2005.
Culler, Jonathan. *Structuralist Poetics: Structuralism, Linguistics and the Study of Literature*. London: Routledge, 2002.

Darda, Joseph. *Empire of Defense: Race and the Cultural Politics of Permanent War*. Chicago: University of Chicago Press, 2019.

Davis, David Brion. *The Problem of Slavery in the Age of Emancipation*. New York: Vintage, 2014.

Dawes, James. "The American War Novel." In *The Cambridge Companion to the Literature of World War II*, edited by Marina MacKay, 56–66. Cambridge: Cambridge University Press, 2009.

Deer, Patrick. "Beyond Recovery: Representing History and Memory in Iraq War Writing." *Modern Fiction Studies* 63, no. 2 (2017): 312–35.

Deer, Patrick. "Crime Fiction and War." In *The Routledge Companion to Crime Fiction*, edited by Janice Allan et al., 343–52. New York: Routledge, 2020.

Deer, Patrick. "The Iraq War." In *The Routledge Companion to Literature and Trauma*, edited by Colin Davis, 418–27. New York: Routledge, 2020.

Deer, Patrick. "Mapping Contemporary American War Culture." *College Literature* 43, no. 1 (Winter 2016): 48–90.

Denvir, Daniel. "The Secret History of the Vietnam War." *Vice*, April 17, 2013.

Department of the Army. *FM 3–24: Counterinsurgency*. December 2006.

Dos Passos, John. *Three Soldiers*. New York: George H. Doran Co., 1921.

Dower, John W. *War without Mercy: Race and Power in the Pacific War*. New York: W.W. Norton, 1986.

Draper, Robert. *To Start a War: How the Bush Administration Took America into Iraq*. New York: Penguin Press, 2020.

Dubik, James. "Foreword." In Sherman, *Afterwar*, xi–xvii.

Dudziak, Mary L. *War Time: An Idea, Its History, Its Consequences*. New York: Oxford University Press, 2012.

Du Mez, Kristin Kobes. *Jesus and John Wayne: How White Evangelicals Corrupted a Faith and Fractured a Nation*. New York: Liveright, 2020.

Dunant, Henry J. *A Memory of Solferino*. Translated from the French [translator unknown]. Geneva: ICRC, 1959. First published 1862.

Dwyer, Philip, and Mark Micale, eds. *The Darker Angels of Our Nature: Refuting the Pinker Theory of History and Violence*. London: Bloomsbury Academic, 2022.

Edmonds, Bill Russell. *God Is Not Here: A Soldier's Struggle with Torture, Trauma, and the Moral Injuries of War*. New York: Pegasus Books, 2015.

Edstrom, Erik. *Un-American: A Soldier's Reckoning of Our Longest War*. New York: Bloomsbury Publishing, 2020.

Ehrenreich, Barbara. *Blood Rites: Origins and History of the Passions of War*. New York: Henry Holt and Co., 1997.

Ehrman, Bart D. *Jesus: Apocalyptic Prophet of the New Millennium*. Oxford: Oxford University Press, 1999.

Eisler, David F. *Writing Wars: Authorship and American War Fiction, WWI to Present.* Iowa City: University of Iowa Press, 2022.

Elford, George Robert. *Devil's Guard.* New York: Dell Publishing, 1971.

Elias, Norbert. *The Civilizing Process: Sociogenetic and Psychogenetic Investigations.* Translated by Edmund Jephcott. Hoboken, NJ: Blackwell Publishing, 2000.

The Epic of Gilgamesh. Translated by N.K. Sandars. New York: Penguin Books, 1972.

Euripides. *The Trojan Women.* In Euripides, *The Trojan Women and Other Plays.* Translated by James Morwood. Oxford: Oxford University Press, 2009.

Fair, Eric. *Consequence: A Memoir.* New York: Henry Holt and Company, 2016.

Fallon, Siobhan. *You Know When the Men Are Gone.* New York: New American Library, 2011.

Fanon, Frantz. *The Wretched of the Earth.* Translated by Richard Philcox. New York: Grove Press, 2004.

Farria, Dewaine. *Revolutions of All Colors.* Syracuse, NY: Syracuse University Press, 2020.

Fazal, Tanisha M. "Dead Wrong?: Battle Deaths, Military Medicine, and Exaggerated Reports of War's Demise." *International Security* 39, no. 1 (Summer 2014): 95–125.

Fehrenbach, T.R. *This Kind of War.* Washington, D.C.: Brassey's, 1963.

Feldman, Noah. "Choices of Law, Choices of War." *Harvard Journal of Law and Public Policy* 25, no. 2 (2001): 457–85.

Fick, Nathaniel. *One Bullet Away: The Making of a Marine Officer.* Boston: Houghton Mifflin Company, 2005.

Filkins, Dexter. *The Forever War.* New York: Vintage Books, 2008.

Finkel, David. *The Good Soldiers.* New York: Picador, 2009.

Finkel, David. *Thank You for Your Service.* New York: Farrar, Straus and Giroux, 2013.

Finnemore, Martha. *The Purpose of Intervention: Changing Beliefs about the Use of Force.* Ithaca, NY: Cornell University Press, 2003.

Firmani, Mark. "At War with Monsters in Postwar Iraqi Literature." *Los Angeles Review of Books*, February 24, 2018.

Fleck, Dieter, ed. *The Handbook of the International Law of Military Operations.* Oxford: Oxford University Press, 2008.

Fountain, Ben. *Billy Lynn's Halftime Walk.* New York: Harper-Collins, 2012.

Frederick, Jim. *Black Hearts: One Platoon's Descent into Madness in Iraq's Triangle of Death.* New York: Crown, 2010.

Freedman, Lawrence. *Strategy: A History.* Oxford: Oxford University Press, 2013.

Fussell, Paul. *The Great War and Modern Memory.* Oxford: Oxford University Press, 1975.

Gallagher, Matt. "Where's the Great Novel about the War on Terror?" *Atlantic*, June 14, 2011.

Gallagher, Matt. *Youngblood*. New York: Atria, 2016.

Gat, Azar. *War in Human Civilization*. Oxford: Oxford University Press, 2006.

Gebhardt, Miriam. *Crimes Unspoken: The Rape of German Women at the End of the Second World War*. Cambridge: Polity, 2020.

Gelman, Andrew, Jeffrey Fagan, and Alex Kiss. "An Analysis of the New York City Police Department's 'Stop-and-Frisk' Policy in the Context of Claims of Racial Bias." *Journal of the American Statistical Association* 102, no. 479 (2007): 813–23.

Genet, Jean. "The Criminal Child." In *The Criminal Child: Selected Essays.* Translated by Charlotte Mandell and Jeffrey Zuckerman. New York: New York Review Books, 2020.

Gilman, Owen W., Jr. *The Hell of War Comes Home: Imaginative Texts from the Conflicts in Afghanistan and Iraq.* Jackson: University Press of Mississippi, 2018.

Goldstein, Joshua S. *War and Gender: How Gender Shapes the War System and Vice Versa*. Cambridge: Cambridge University Press, 2001.

Goodell, Jess, and John Hearn. *Shade It Black: Death and After in Iraq*. Philadelphia: Casemate, 2011.

Goolsby, Jesse. *I'd Walk with My Friends If I Could Find Them*. Boston: Houghton Mifflin Harcourt, 2015.

Grandin, Greg. *The End of the Myth: From the Frontier to the Border Wall in the Mind of America*. New York: Metropolitan Books, 2019.

Grenier, John. *The First Way of War: American War Making on the Frontier.* Cambridge: Cambridge University Press, 2005.

Griffin, Stephen M. *Long Wars and the Constitution*. Cambridge, MA: Harvard University Press, 2013.

Grossman, Dave. *On Killing: The Psychological Cost of Learning to Kill in War and Society*, rev. ed. New York: Back Bay Books, 2009.

Gupta, Suman. *Imagining Iraq: Literature in English and the Iraq Invasion*. New York: Palgrave Macmillan, 2011.

Habermas, Jürgen. *The Divided West*. Translated and edited by Ciaran Cronin. Malden, MA: Polity, 2006.

Hansen, Valerie. *The Year 1000*. New York: Penguin Books, 2020.

Hanson, Victor Davis. "Genesis of the Infantry." In *The Cambridge History of Warfare*, 2nd ed., edited by Geoffrey Parker, 15–30. Cambridge: Cambridge University Press, 2005.

Harari, Yuval Noah. "Martial Illusions: War and Disillusionment in Twentieth-Century and Renaissance Military Memoirs." *The Journal of Military History* 69, no. 1 (January 2005): 43–72.

Harari, Yuval Noah. *The Ultimate Experience: Battlefield Revelations and the Making of Modern War Culture, 1450–2000*. Basingstoke: Palgrave Macmillan, 2008.

Harrison, Robert Pogue. *The Dominion of the Dead*. Chicago: University of Chicago Press, 2003.

Hathaway, Oona A., and Scott J. Shapiro. *The Internationalists: How a Radical Plan to Outlaw War Remade the World*. New York: Simon & Schuster, 2017.

Hathaway, Oona A., Paul K. Strauch, Beatrice A. Walton, and Zoe A.Y. Weinberg. "What Is a War Crime?" *Yale Journal of International Law* 44, no. 53 (2019): 54–113.

Hayslip, Le Ly. *When Heaven and Earth Changed Places: A Vietnamese Woman's Journey from War to Peace*. New York: Doubleday, 1989.

Haytock, Jennifer. "Reframing War Stories: Multivoiced Novels of the Wars in Iraq and Afghanistan." *Modern Fiction Studies* 63, no. 2 (2017): 336–54.

Haytock, Jennifer. "Representing Soldiers." In *War and American Literature*, edited by Jennifer Haytock, 42–56. Cambridge: Cambridge University Press, 2021.

Haytock, Jennifer. *The Routledge Introduction to American War Literature*. London: Routledge, 2018.

Haytock, Jennifer. "Women's/War Stories: The Female Gothic and Women's War Trauma in Helen Benedict's *Sand Queen*." *War, Literature, and the Arts* 27, no. 1 (2015): 143–50.

Hedges, Chris. *War Is a Force That Gives Us Meaning*. New York: PublicAffairs, 2002.

Heinemann, Larry. *Close Quarters*. New York: Farrar, Straus and Giroux, 1974.

Heinemann, Larry. *Paco's Story*. Farrar, Straus and Giroux, 1986.

Heinlein, Robert. *Stranger in a Strange Land*. New York: G.P. Putnam's Sons, 1961.

Heller, Joseph. *Catch-22*. New York: Simon & Schuster, 1961.

Hemingway, Ernest. *A Farewell to Arms*. New York: Scribner, 1929.

Henrich, Joseph. *The WEIRDest People in the World: How the West Became Psychologically Peculiar and Particularly Prosperous*. New York: Picador, 2020.

Herman, Judith L. *Trauma and Recovery*. New York: Basic Books, 1992.

Herr, Michael. *Dispatches*. New York: Knopf, 1977.

Hersey, John. *A Bell for Adano*. New York: Knopf, 1944.

Herzog, Tobey C. *Vietnam War Stories: Innocence Lost*. London: Routledge, 1992.

Hirschman, Albert O. *The Passions and the Interests: Political Arguments for Capitalism before Its Triumph*. Princeton, NJ: Princeton University Press, 1977.

Hirschman, Albert O. *The Rhetoric of Reaction: Perversity, Futility, Jeopardy*. Cambridge, MA: Belknap Press, 1991.

Hobbes, Thomas. *Leviathan*, edited by Richard Tuck. Cambridge: Cambridge University Press, 2004.

Hölbling, Walter. "Literary Sense-Making: American Vietnam Fiction." In *Vietnam Images: War and Representation*, edited by Jeffrey Walsh and James Aulich, 123–41. New York: Macmillan, 1989.

Hölbling, Walter. "The Second World War: American Writing." In *The Cambridge Companion to War Writing*, edited by Kate McLoughlin, 212–25. Cambridge: Cambridge University Press, 2009.

Holmstedt, Kirsten. *Band of Sisters: American Women at War in Iraq*. Mechanicsburg, PA: Stackpole Books, 2007.

Homer. *The Iliad*. Translated by Robert Fagles. New York: Penguin Books, 1990.

Horton, Alex. "Small Kill Team." In *The Road Ahead: Fiction from the Forever War*, edited by Adrian Bonenberger and Brian Castner, 29–44. New York: Pegasus Books, 2017.

Hunt, Lynn. *Inventing Human Rights: A History*. New York: W.W. Norton, 2007.

Hynes, Samuel. *The Soldiers' Tale: Bearing Witness to Modern War*. New York: Penguin Books, 1997.

Inglehart, Ronald F. *Cultural Evolution: People's Motivations Are Changing, and Reshaping the World*. Cambridge: Cambridge University Press, 2018.

Iraq Veterans Against the War and Aaron Glantz. *Winter Soldier: Iraq and Afghanistan: Eyewitness Accounts of the Occupations*. Chicago: Haymarket Books, 2008.

Isenberg, Nancy. *White Trash: The 400-Year Untold History of Class in America*. New York: Penguin Books, 2016.

Jason, Philip K. "Introduction." In *Fourteen Landing Zones: Approaches to Vietnam War Literature*, edited by Philip K. Jason, ix. Iowa City: University of Iowa Press, 1991.

Jones, James. *From Here to Eternity*. New York: Charles Scribner's Sons, 1951.

Jones, James. *The Thin Red Line*. New York: Charles Scribner's Sons, 1962.

Junger, Sebastian. *Tribe: On Homecoming and Belonging*. New York: Twelve, 2016.

Jünger, Ernst. *Storm of Steel*. Translated by Michael Hofmann. New York: Penguin Books, 2003. First published in 1961.

Kakutani, Michiko. "Human Costs of the Forever Wars, Enough to Fill a Bookshelf." *New York Times*, December 25, 2014.

Kamienski, Lukasz. *Shooting Up: A Short History of Drugs and War*. Oxford: Oxford University Press, 2016.

Katz, Jonathan M. *Gangsters of Capitalism: Smedley Butler, the Marines, and the Making and Breaking of America's Empire*. New York: St. Martin's Griffin, 2021.

Keegan, John. *The Face of Battle*. New York: Viking Press, 1976.

Kennedy, David. "Speech: Modern War and Modern Law." *University of Baltimore Law Review* 36, no. 2 (2007): 171–94.

Kennedy, David M. "Introduction." In *The Modern American Military*, edited by David M. Kennedy, 1–11. Oxford: Oxford University Press, 2013.

Kinder, John M. "The Good War's 'Raw Chunks': Norman Mailer's The Naked and the Dead and James Gould Cozzens's Guard of Honor." *Midwest Quarterly* 46, no. 2 (Winter 2005): 187–202.

Kinney, Katherine. *Friendly Fire: American Images of the Vietnam War*. Oxford: Oxford University Press, 2000.

Klay, Phil. *The Citizen-Soldier: Moral Risk and the Modern Military*. Washington, D.C.: Brookings Institution Press, 2016.

Klay, Phil. *Redeployment*. New York: Penguin, 2014.

Klein, Ezra. *Why We're Polarized*. New York: Avid Reader Press, 2020.

Klinkowitz, Jerome. "Writing Under Fire: Postmodern Fiction and the Vietnam War." In *Postmodern Fiction: A Bio-Bibliographical Guide*, edited by Larry McCaffery, 79–92. Westport, CT: Greenwood, 1986.

Kovac, Adam. *The Surge*. Indianapolis: Engine Books, 2019.

Kovic, Ron. *Born on the Fourth of July*. New York: McGraw-Hill Book Company, 1976.

Kovite, Gavin Ford. "When Engaging Targets, Remember." In *Fire and Forget: Short Stories from the Long War*, edited by Roy Scranton and Matt Gallagher, 157–72. Boston, MA: Da Capo Press, 2013.

Kulish, Nicholas. *Last One In*. New York: Ecco, 2007.

Kurtz, J. Roger, ed. *Trauma and Literature*. Cambridge: Cambridge University Press, 2018.

Kyle, Chris. *American Sniper*. New York: HarperCollins, 2013.

Leffler, Melvyn P. *Confronting Saddam Hussein: George W. Bush and the Invasion of Iraq*. Oxford: Oxford University Press, 2023.

Leitch, Vincent B., ed. *The Norton Anthology of Theory and Criticism*. New York: W.W. Norton and Company, 2001.

Levinson, Sanford. *Written in Stone: Public Monuments in Changing Societies*. Durham, NC: Duke University Press, 1998.

Lilly, J. Robert. *Taken by Force: Rape and American GIs in Europe during World War II*. London: Palgrave Macmillan, 2007.

Lish, Atticus. *Preparation for the Next Life*. New York: Tyrant Books, 2015.

Litz, Brett, Nathan Stein, Eileen Delaney, Leslie Lebowitz, William P. Nash, Caroline Silva, and Shira Maguen. "Moral Injury and Moral Repair in War Veterans: A Preliminary Model and Intervention Strategy." *Clinical Psychology Review* 29, no. 8 (2009): 695–706.

Luckhurst, Roger. "In War Times: Fictionalizing Iraq." *Contemporary Literature* 53, no. 4 (2012): 713–37.

Luckhurst, Roger. "Iraq War Body Counts: Reportage, Photography, and Fiction." *Modern Fiction Studies* 63, no. 2 (Summer 2017): 355–72.

Luckhurst, Roger. "Not Now, Not Yet: Polytemporality and Fictions of the Iraq War." In *Trauma and Contemporary Literature*, edited by Marita Nadal and Mónica Calvo, 51–72. New York: Routledge, 2014.

Luckhurst, Roger. "War and Whiteness." In *War and American Literature*, edited by Jennifer Haytock, 315–29. Cambridge: Cambridge University Press, 2021.

Lukas, Michael David. "Workshopping the Next Generation of American War Literature." *VQR* 86, no. 2 (Spring 2010): 208–12.

Lynn, John A. *Battle: A History of Combat and Culture*. New York: Basic Books, 2003.

Mackin, Will. *Bring Out the Dog*. New York: Random House, 2018.

Mailer, Norman. *The Naked and the Dead*. New York: Rinehart & Company, 1948.

Makiya, Kanan. *The Rope*. New York: Pantheon Books, 2016.

Mannheim, Hermann. *War and Crime*. London: Watts & Co., 1941.

March, William. *Company K*. Tuscaloosa: University of Alabama Press, 1989.

Mariani, Giorgio. *Waging War on War: Peacefighting in American Literature*. Urbana: University of Illinois Press, 2015.

Markley, Stephen. *Ohio*. New York: Simon & Schuster, 2018.

Marlantes, Karl. *What It Is Like to Go to War*. London: Corvus, 2011.

Masmoudi, Ikram. *War and Occupation in Iraqi Fiction*. Edinburgh: Edinburgh University Press, 2015.

Mayer, Jane. *The Dark Side: The Inside Story of How the War on Terror Turned into a War on American Ideals*. New York: Doubleday, 2008.

Mazower, Mark. *Governing the World: The History of an Idea, 1815 to the Present*. London: Penguin Books, 2012.

McCann, Colum. "Foreword." In *Fire and Forget: Short Stories from the Long War*, edited by Roy Scranton and Matt Gallagher, vii–xii. Boston, MA: Da Capo Press, 2013.

McEwan, Ian. *Saturday*. London: Jonathan Cape, 2005.

McGurl, Mark. *The Program Era: Postwar Fiction and the Rise of Creative Writing*. Cambridge, MA: Harvard University Press, 2009.

McLoughlin, Kate. *Authoring War: The Literary Representation of War from the Iliad to Iraq*. Cambridge: Cambridge University Press, 2011.

McMahan, Jeff. *Killing in War*. Oxford: Oxford University Press, 2009.

Meagher, Robert Emmet. *Killing from the Inside Out: Moral Injury and Just War*. Eugene, OR: Cascade Books, 2014.

Meagher, Robert Emmet, and Douglas A. Pryer, eds. *War and Moral Injury: A Reader*. Eugene, OR: Cascade Books, 2018.

Meyers, Diana Tietjens. *Victims' Stories and the Advancement of Human Rights*. New York: Oxford University Press, 2016.

Michener, James A. *Tales of the South Pacific*. New York: Macmillan, 1947.

Mogelson, Luke. *These Heroic, Happy Dead*. New York: Tim Duggan Books, 2016.

Molin, Peter. "Iraq and Afghanistan War Fiction, Poetry, and Film 2020." *Time Now* (blog), December 31, 2020.

Molin, Peter. "Time Now: The Iraq and Afghanistan Wars in Art, Film, and Literature." *Time Now* (blog), https://acolytesofwar.com.

Momaday, N. Scott. *House Made of Dawn*. New York: HarperCollins, 1968.

Moore, Robin. *The Green Berets*. New York: Crown Publishing Group, 1965.

Morris, Madeline. "By Force of Arms: Rape, War, and Military Culture." *Duke Law Journal* 45 (1996): 651–781.

Moyn, Samuel. *Humane: How the United States Abandoned Peace and Reinvented War*. New York: Farrar, Straus and Giroux, 2021.

Myrer, Anton. *Once an Eagle*. New York: HarperPerennial, 1968.

Nguyen, Viet Thanh. "Opinion: Bob Kerrey and the 'American Tragedy' of Vietnam." *New York Times*, June 20, 2016.

Nguyen, Viet Thanh. *The Sympathizer*. New York: Grove Press, 2015.

Nietzsche, Friedrich. *On the Genealogy of Morals*. Translated by Walter Kaufmann. New York: Vintage Books, 1967. First published in 1887.

Nussbaum, Emily. "The Great Divide." *New Yorker*, March 31, 2014.

Nussbaum, Martha. *The Cosmopolitan Tradition: A Noble but Flawed Ideal*. Cambridge: Belknap Press, 2019.

Oates, Joyce Carol. *Carthage*. New York: Ecco, 2014.

O'Brien, Tim. *Going After Cacciato*. New York: Broadway Books, 1978.

O'Brien, Tim. *In the Lake of the Woods*. Boston: Houghton Mifflin, 1994.

O'Brien, Tim. *The Things They Carried*. Boston: Houghton Mifflin, 1990.

Packer, George. "Home Fires." *New Yorker*, March 31, 2014.

Pederson, Joshua. *Sin Sick: Moral Injury in War and Literature*. Ithaca, NY: Cornell University Press, 2021.

Peebles, Stacey. "Blood, Force, Influence: Studying the Representation of Violence." In *Critical Insights: Violence in Literature*, edited by Stacey Peebles, 23–37. Ipswich, MA: Salem Press, 2014.

Peebles, Stacey. "The Forever Wars." In *War and American Literature*, edited by Jennifer Haytock, 254–68. Cambridge: Cambridge University Press, 2021.

Peebles, Stacey. *Welcome to the Suck: Narrating the American Soldier's Experience in Iraq*. Ithaca, NY: Cornell University Press, 2011.

Peter, Tom A. "Finally, a Realistic Iraq War Novel." *New Republic*, August 2, 2016.

Philipps, David. *Alpha: Eddie Gallagher and the War for the Soul of the Navy SEALS*. New York: Crown, 2021.

Pinker, Steven. *The Better Angels of Our Nature: Why Violence Has Declined*. New York: Viking, 2011.

Pitre, Michael. *Fives and Twenty-Fives*. New York: Bloomsbury, 2014.

Pivar, Ilona L., and Nigel P. Field. "Unresolved Grief in Combat Veterans with PTSD." *Journal of Anxiety Disorders* 18, no. 6 (2004): 745–55.

Plato. "Republic." In *Plato: Complete Works*, edited by John M. Cooper, 971–1223. Indianapolis, IN: Hackett Publishing Co., 1997.

Plum, Hilary. *Strawberry Fields*. Albany: Fence Books, 2018.

Powers, Kevin. "Opinion: What Kept Me from Killing Myself." *New York Times*, June 16, 2018.

Powers, Kevin. *The Yellow Birds*. New York: Little, Brown, 2012.

Prescott, Orville. "Books of the Times." Review of *The Thin Red Line*, by James Jones. *New York Times*, September 17, 1962, L29.

Pynchon, Thomas. *Gravity's Rainbow*. New York: Viking Press, 1973.

Rayburn, Joel D., and Frank K. Sobchak, eds. *The U.S. Army in the Iraq War, Volume 2: Surge and Withdrawal, 2007–2011*. Carlisle Barracks, PA: United States Army War College Press, 2019.

Remarque, Erich Maria. *All Quiet on the Western Front*. Translated by A.W. Wheen. New York: Ballantine Books, 1982. First published in 1928.

Ricks, Thomas. *Fiasco: The American Military Adventure in Iraq*. New York: Penguin Press, 2006.

Ricks, Thomas E. *The Gamble: General David Petraeus and the American Military Adventure in Iraq, 2006–2008*. New York: Penguin Press, 2009.

Ricks, Thomas. *Making the Corps*. New York: Scribner, 1997.

Robinson, Christopher, and Gavin Kovite. *War of the Encyclopaedists*. New York: Scribner, 2016.

Robinson, Roxana. *Sparta*. New York: Picador, 2013.

Rorty, Richard. *Contingency, Irony, Solidarity*. Cambridge: Cambridge University Press, 1989.

Rousseau, Jean-Jacques. *The Basic Political Writings*. Indianapolis: Hackett Publishing Company, 1987.

Roy-Bhattachary, Joydeep. *The Watch*. London: Hogarth, 2012.

Rubin, Lyle Jeremy. *Pain Is Weakness Leaving the Body: A Marine's Unbecoming*. New York: Bold Type Books, 2022.

Saadawi, Ahmed. *Frankenstein in Baghdad*. Translated by Jonathan Wright. New York: Penguin Books, 2018.

Sacks, Sam. "First-Person Shooters: What's Missing in Contemporary War Fiction." *Harper's*, August 2015.

Said, Edward W. *Orientalism*. New York: Vintage Books, 1978.

Samet, Elizabeth D. *Looking for the Good War: American Amnesia and the Violent Pursuit of Happiness*. New York: Farrar, Straus and Giroux, 2021.

Samet, Elizabeth D. *No Man's Land: Preparing for War and Peace in Post-9/11 America*. New York: Farrar, Straus and Giroux, 2014.

Sapolsky, Robert M. *Behave: The Biology of Humans at Our Best and Worst*. New York: Penguin Press, 2017.

Sartre, Jean-Paul. "Preface." In Fanon, *The Wretched of the Earth*.

Scarry, Elaine. *The Body in Pain: The Making and Unmaking of the World*. Oxford: Oxford University Press, 1985.

Schambelan, Elizabeth. "Special Journey to Our Bottom Line: On Hazing and Counterinsurgency." *n+1*, no. 34 (Spring 2019).

Schmidle, Nicholas. "In the Crosshairs." *New Yorker*, May 27, 2013.

Schmitt, Carl. *The Concept of the Political*. Translated by George Schwab. Chicago: University of Chicago Press, 1996. First published in 1932.

Schultz, Katey. *Flashes of War*. Baltimore: Apprentice House, 2013.

Scott, James C. *Against the Grain: A Deep History of the Earliest States*. New Haven, CT: Yale University Press, 2017.

Scott, James C. *Seeing Like a State: How Certain Schemes to Improve the Human Condition Have Failed*. New Haven, CT: Yale University Press, 1998.

Scott, Tony, dir. *Top Gun*. Hollywood, CA: Paramount Pictures, 1986.

Scranton, Roy. "Back to Baghdad: Life in the City of Doom." *Rolling Stone*, July 17, 2014.

Scranton, Roy. *I Heart Oklahoma!* New York: Soho Press, 2019.

Scranton, Roy. *Learning to Die in the Anthropocene: Reflections on the End of a Civilization*. San Francisco: City Lights, 2015.

Scranton, Roy. "Opinion: 'Star Wars' and the Fantasy of American Violence." *New York Times*, July 2, 2016.

Scranton, Roy. *Total Mobilization: World War II and American Literature*. Chicago: University of Chicago Press, 2019.

Scranton, Roy. "The Trauma Hero and the Lost War: World War II, American Literature, and the Politics of Trauma, 1945–1975." PhD diss., Princeton University, 2016.

Scranton, Roy. "The Trauma Hero: From Wilfred Owen to 'Redeployment' and 'American Sniper.'" *Los Angeles Review of Books*, January 25, 2015.

Scranton, Roy. *War Porn*. New York: Soho Press, 2016.

Scranton, Roy. *We're Doomed. Now What? Essays on War and Climate Change*. New York: Soho Press, 2018.

Scranton, Roy, and Jake Siegel, "In 'Fire And Forget,' Vets Turned Writers Tell Their War Stories." Interview by Terry Gross. *Fresh Air*, NPR, November 11, 2013.

Senate Select Committee on Intelligence. *The Senate Intelligence Committee Report on Torture: Committee Study of the Central Intelligence Agency's Detention and Interrogation Program*. Brooklyn, NY: Melville House, 2014.

Shaara, Michael. *The Killer Angels*. New York: Ballantine Books, 1974.

Shay, Jonathan. *Achilles in Vietnam: Combat Trauma and the Undoing of Character*. New York: Atheneum, 1994.

Shay, Jonathan. *Odysseus in America: Combat Trauma and the Trials of Homecoming*. New York: Scribner, 2002.

Sheehan, James J. *The Monopoly of Violence: Why Europeans Hate Going to War*. Boston, MA: Houghton Mifflin, 2007.

Sherman, Nancy. *Afterwar: Healing the Moral Wounds of Our Soldiers*. Oxford: Oxford University Press, 2015.

Sherman, Nancy. *The Untold War: Inside the Hearts, Minds, and Souls of Our Soldiers*. New York: W.W. Norton & Company, 2010.

Shiller, Robert J. *Narrative Economics: How Stories Go Viral and Drive Major Economic Events*. Princeton, NJ: Princeton University Press, 2020.

Shiller, Robert J. "Narrative Economics." *American Economic Review* 107, no. 4 (2017): 967–1004.

Silko, Leslie Marmon. *Ceremony*. New York: Penguin, 1977.

Singer, Peter. *The Expanding Circle: Ethics, Evolution, and Moral Progress*. Princeton: Princeton University Press, 1981.

Singer, Peter. *One World Now: The Ethics of Globalization*, 3rd ed. New Haven, CT: Yale University Press, 2016.

Skaskiw, Roman. "Television." In *Fire and Forget: Short Stories from the Long War*, edited by Roy Scranton and Matt Gallagher, 105–25. Boston, MA: Da Capo Press, 2013.

Slahi, Mohamedou Ould. *Guantánamo Diary: Restored Edition*. New York: Back Bay Books, 2017.

Sledge, E.B. *With the Old Breed at Peleliu and Okinawa*. New York: Ballantine Books, 1981.

Slobogin, Christopher. "Testilying: Police Perjury and What to Do about It." *University of Colorado Law Review* 67 (1996): 1037–60.

Slotkin, Richard. *Regeneration through Violence: The Mythology of the American Frontier*. Norman: University of Oklahoma Press, 2020.

Sluga, Hans. *Politics and the Search for the Common Good*. Cambridge: Cambridge University Press, 2014.

Smith, Sam. "The Revision Thing: A History of the Iraq War, Told Entirely in Lies." *Harper's*, October 2003.

The Song of Roland. Translated by Frederick Goldin. New York: W.W. Norton & Company, 1978.

Sorel, Georges. *Reflections on Violence*. Translated by T.E. Hulme. New York: Dover Publications, 2004.

Stendhal. *The Charterhouse of Parma*. Translated by Margaret Mauldon. Oxford: Oxford University Press, 1997. First published 1839.

Stenner, Karen. *The Authoritarian Dynamic*. Cambridge: Cambridge University Press, 2005.

Stiglitz, Joseph E., and Linda J. Bilmes. *The Three Trillion Dollar War*. London: W.W. Norton, 2008.

Swofford, Anthony. *Jarhead: A Marine's Chronicle of the Gulf War and Other Battles*. New York: Scribner, 2003.

Tait, Theo. "The Hemingway Crush." *London Review of Books*, January 3, 2013.

Taub, Amanda. "Every Movie Rewrites History. What American Sniper Did Is Much, Much Worse." *Vox*, January 22, 2015.

Taylor, Charles. *A Secular Age*. Cambridge, MA: Harvard University Press, 2007.

Teitel, Ruti G. *Humanity's Law*. Oxford: Oxford University Press, 2011.

Terrell, Whitney. *The Good Lieutenant*. New York: Farrar, Straus and Giroux, 2016.

Thorpe, Helen. *Soldier Girls: The Battles of Three Women at Home and at War*. New York: Scribner, 2014.

Tilly, Charles. *The Politics of Collective Violence*. Cambridge: Cambridge University Press, 2003.

Tilly, Charles. "Reflections on the History of European State-Making." In *The Formation of National States in Western Europe*. Princeton: Princeton University Press, 1975.

Tirman, John. *The Deaths of Others: The Fate of Civilians in America's Wars*. Oxford: Oxford University Press, 2011.

Tolstoy, Leo, *The Sebastopol Sketches*. Translated by David McDuff. New York: Penguin Books, 1986. First published in 1855.

Tolstoy, Leo. *War and Peace*. Translated by Constance Garnett. New York: Barnes & Noble Classics, 2005. First published 1869.

Traverso, Enzo. *Fire and Blood: The European Civil War 1914–1945*. Brooklyn, NY: Verso, 2016.

Trumbo, Dalton. *Johnny Got His Gun*. Philadelphia: J.B. Lippincott & Co., 1939.

Turner, Brian. *Here, Bullet*. Farmington, ME: Alice James Books, 2005.

Turner, Brian. *My Life as a Foreign Country*. New York: W.W. Norton & Company, 2014.

Turse, Nick. *Kill Anything That Moves: The Real American War in Vietnam.* London: Picador, 2013.

Uriarte, Maximilian. *The White Donkey: Terminal Lance*. New York: Hachette Book Group, 2016.

Van Creveld, Martin. *The Culture of War*. New York: Ballantine Books, 2008.

Van Reet, Brian. "A New Kind of Desert: A Reading of Nico Walker's *Cherry*." *Brian Van Reet* (blog), August 22, 2018.

Van Reet, Brian. "Big Two-Hearted Hunting Creek." In *Fire and Forget: Short Stories from the Long War*, edited by Roy Scranton and Matt Gallagher, 173–90. Boston, MA: Da Capo Press, 2013.

Van Reet, Brian. *Spoils*. New York: Back Bay Books, 2017.

Van Winkle, Clint. *Soft Spots: A Marine's Memoir of Combat and Post-Traumatic Stress Disorder*. New York: St. Martin's Griffin, 2009.

"Vietnam War." In *Encyclopedia of American War Literature*, edited by Philip K. Jason and Mark A. Graves, 350. Westport, CT: Greenwood Press, 2000.

Voltaire. *Candide ou l'Optimisme*. Paris: Éditions Gallimard 1992. First published in 1759.

Vonnegut, Kurt. *Slaughterhouse-Five*. New York: Delacorte, 1969.

Walker, Niko. *Cherry*. New York: Vintage Books, 2018.

Walzer, Michael. *Just and Unjust Wars*. New York: Basic Books, 2015.

Webb, James. *Fields of Fire*. New York: Bantam Books, 1978.

Weber, Max. *From Max Weber: Essays in Sociology*. Translated by H.H. Gerth and C. Wright Mills. Oxford: Oxford University Press, 1946.

Weber, Max. "The Profession and Vocation of Politics." In *Weber: Political Writings*, edited by Peter Lassman and Ronald Speirs, 309–69. Cambridge: Cambridge University Press, 1994.

Weil, Simone. "The Iliad, or the Poem of Force." *Chicago Law Review* 18 (1965): 5–30.

Weiner, Tim. *Legacy of Ashes: The History of the CIA*. New York: Doubleday, 2007.

Whitman, James Q. *Hitler's American Model: The United States and the Making of Nazi Race Law*. Princeton, NJ: Princeton University Press, 2017.

Williams, Kayla. *Love My Rifle More Than You: Young and Female in the U.S. Army*. New York: W.W. Norton and Company, 2005.

Winter, Jay. "Introduction." In Fussell, *The Great War and Modern Memory*, ix–xiv.

Witt, John Fabian. *Lincoln's Code: The Laws of War in American History*. New York: Free Press, 2012.

Wittgenstein, Ludwig. *Philosophical Investigations*. Translated by G.E.M. Anscombe. Oxford: Blackwell Publishing, 1953.

Wolfe, Christopher Paul. "Another Brother's Conviction." In *The Road Ahead: Fiction from the Forever War*, edited by Adrian Bonenberger and Brian Castner, 85–90. New York: Pegasus Books, 2017.

Wood, David. *What Have We Done: The Moral Injury of Our Longest Wars*. New York: Little, Brown and Company, 2016.

Wood, Gordon. *Empire of Liberty: A History of the Early Republic, 1789–1815*. Oxford: Oxford University Press, 2009.

Woolf, Virginia. *Mrs. Dalloway*. London: Hogarth Press, 1925.

Wrangham, Richard. *The Goodness Paradox: The Strange Relationship between Virtue and Violence in Human Evolution*. New York: Vintage Books, 2019.

Wrangham, Richard, and Dale Peterson. *Demonic Males: Apes and the Origins of Human Violence*. Boston: Houghton Mifflin Company, 1996.

Wright, Evan. *Generation Kill: Devil Dogs, Ice Man, Captain America, and the New Face of American War*. New York: G.P. Putnam's Sons, 2004.

Wright, Geoffrey A. "The Anatomy of Shame: Combat Trauma and the Undoing of the Self in Iraq War Memoirs." *PsyArt* 21 (2017): 159–78.

Young, Matt. *Eat the Apple*. New York: Bloomsbury Publishing, 2018.

Zimbardo, Philip. *The Lucifer Effect: Understanding How Good People Turn Evil*. New York: Random House, 2007.

Zipp, Samuel. *The Idealist: Wendell Willkie's Wartime Quest to Build One World*. Cambridge, MA: Harvard University Press, 2020.